AF378339

Hg2|Art

Edited by Laura K. Jones

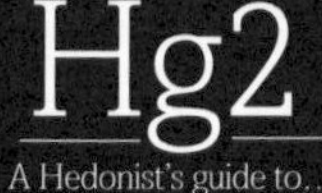

A Hedonist's guide to...

in association with

artica.

A Hedonist's guide to Art
Edited by Laura K. Jones

MANAGING DIRECTOR – Tremayne Carew Pole
MARKETING DIRECTOR – Sara Townsend
DESIGN – Nick Randall
REPRO – Advantage Digital Print
PRINTER – Leo Paper
PUBLISHER – Filmer Ltd

Email – info@hg2.com
Website – www.hg2.com
Published in the United Kingdom in October 2010 by
Filmer Ltd
10th Floor, Newcombe House,
45 Notting Hill Gate, London W11 3LQ

ISBN – 978-1-905428-50-2

This book is dedicated to Cliff, Jeanie & Stephen Jones, and to Andy Collishaw

Contents

CHAPTER 2:
LIFESTYLES OF THE ARTISTS – HOMAGE TO VASARI

FOREWORD
by Charles Saatchi

Dear Ms Jones,

Can't think of anything interesting to contribute.
Sorry to be a dud.

Kind regards,

Charles Saatchi

PREFACE

Three people involved in the art world who were about to write something for this collection, within the space of two months of me pulling it all together, no longer could. Two died relatively young, and the third was put in jail for a very long time, for a rather minor offence. From that perspective, I suppose, the art world is dangerously hedonistic. Lost weekends, railing against the world as you flail through Soho in the early hours, the explosion of pressure after a month of solitary in the studio. It all takes its toll. Famous or obscure, the ones who have been there will know what I'm talking about.

Artists have extreme natures. But extremity in the art world is really about the way the work is produced. It's about what it takes to bring your vision to fruition – and to do it without interference from anyone else. That can mean abusing your body and your mind, yes, but it's not really just *about* the party. Artists are, I suggest, incapable of the 9 to 5. They move in a world that doesn't tend to bring them up against pension provisions, contracts, or a mocha cappuccino on the way to the office.

So what has art got to do with hedonism? Not that much, in a sense: the average artist's life is a lonely one: it probably involves considerable self-sacrifice, and maybe life-long poverty. If you prefer, in a phrase, starvation and madness. Even successful artists are walking on the edge of the abyss of failure. That's partly the point.

Fashions change, the new guard supplants the old, there is not room in the galleries or in the pages of the art-press for everyone. Yet somehow this heart-stopping existence goes hand-in-hand with - and demands - a kind of lust for life that would make the most impervious man blush.

Art is its own boss, artists are their own bosses. Maybe it's fair to say they are self-indulgent, childlike even at times, yet the work gets done: the attention to detail is key: and the unfettered relationship to the world is I believe a necessary condition for the making of it.

There is a history of art still waiting to be written, and that is the history not of works and styles and movements, but the history of charisma. All the successful artists have it, or by dint of their commitment, evolve it.

Herewith - the artists, the gallerists, the hangers-on, the writers, the critics, the curators, the supporters and the detractors. All offering up a take on the naturally occurring extremities within their world. The solitude, the gambling, the drinking and the drugging, the tears and the madness – but also the delight in isolation, the successes, the audacious paths well trodden, the development of movements, the chance encounters, and the precise approaches and conditions needed to make that thing called art.

Laura K Jones

CHAPTER 1:
PHILOSOPHY/
IDEOLOGY/IDEAS

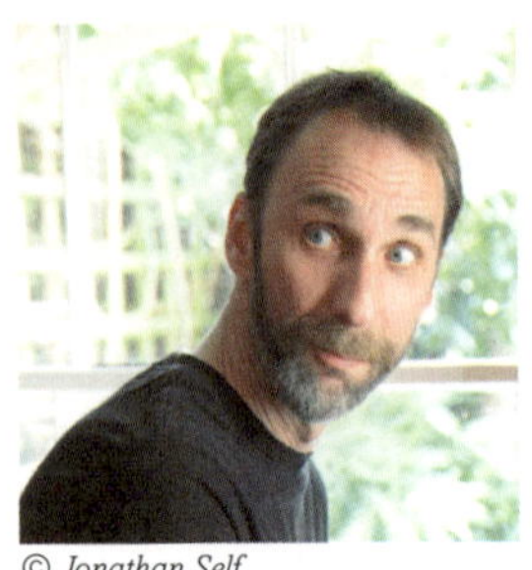

© Jonathan Self

I Know What I Hate (an excursus)

by Will Self

Will Self is a novelist and journalist. He lives in London.

MOST CONTEMPORARY FINE ART is moribund crap and wouldn't last five minutes out there in the cultural open air, where it would soon be winnowed out by those great howling tsunamis of I-Know-What-I-Like; it desperately requires an entire support-system in order to keep it alive, and it's as well that all concerned with the art world get a clear picture of what's involved. In this very brief excursus I aim to identify how to indefinitely extend the lives of these aesthetic stillbirths, to the greater advantage of gallerists, investors, curators, critics – and, of course, the artists themselves.

First let us consider the coefficient of authenticity and originality. It's a common assumption of the callow and the self-seeking that neither is required in the contemporary art world. Not so. A modicum of either one or the other is a necessity, and for a true sufficiency both must be present. It's axiomatic that most of the people who buy most of the art are mostly devoid of either authenticity or originality – which is why they're attracted to collecting contemporary art in the first place; therefore the artists *must* be able – at least initially - to make good the deficiency.

In former ages, artists also needed to be able to make good the cultural deficiency of their buyers – but fortunately postmodernism has obviated the need for this, reducing all hierarchies of aesthetics to a typology of the decorative. So, now, all the stupid and crass rich need to be able to pronounce are certain buzz words – the names of artists, methodologies, schools – in order to be considered as justifying their own place among the elite of the zeitgeist.

It is quite possible for an artist to continue to produce highly financially viable work long after he has been sucked dry of his integrity by these vampiric creatures, but it's better for all concerned if he does retain a secret chamber – or garret – within which he continues to suffer. The psychological state of the artist who sells for high prices in the contemporary market can be likened to that of a Soviet citizen during the Terror: inside his psychic garret he continues manfully to suffer existential crises – and even to go hungry; but on the outside he is drinking Cristal, chatting amiably and accepting yet another canapé.

The second factor to note is the role of the critic (under which heading I subsume everyone from newspaper reviewers to academic art historians and prancing TV pundits) in the contemporary art world. If John Ruskin was alive today and could see quite how irrelevant the critic has become to the transaction of the business of contemporary art, he would probably tear his own penis off, varnish it liberally, and put it on sale in a provincial craft gallery. Because contemporary art is bought by stupid people, they cannot read contemporary art criticism – which anyway has become exponentially more gnomic. Indeed, it's arguable that there is some kind of inverse correlation between stupid buyers and recondite critics.

As with artistic integrity, this state of affairs is often taken to imply that the tyro artist can do without discursive – let alone formal - commentary at all. Not so. The critic may write toxic eye-bleeding-inducing prose read by no one, but she is still an essential participant in the triage that takes place on the cultural battlefield: laying down a heavy covering barrage of jargon so that the casualty (artwork) can be stretchered into the operating space of the gallery. It's true that as it is with the figurative, so it is with the conceptual: only a small proportion of 'artworks' will actually 'make it', but then none at all would survive were it not for an expeditiously applied newsprint tourniquet.

Which brings us, logically enough, to the operating theatre itself: it is not without accident that the signature private galleries of the last thirty years – the Saatchi and the White Cube – should have unconsciously aped the pictorial space of surgical rendering. If you want to keep terminal artworks alive you must have an antiseptic environment with ready access to large transfusions of financial liquidity. The key significance of investment in the construction and mediation of 'value' in the contemporary art world has been much anatomised, and I don't propose to hack away at the cadaver myself, except to note that we haven't witnessed quite such willingness - on the part of the gallerist as much as the artist - to kiss rich arse, since the time of the Medici.

Does it matter? After all *plus ça change…* and yet, there is a jarring dissonance contained in the notion of conceptual art as interior decoration for Modernist people-barns. Bill Gates has got it about right when he 'hangs' VDU displays around his walls, each one beaming out an image of an Old Master. And, arguably, Damien Hirst has got it right as well with his cabinets full of pill pots, and his vitrines coiled with the ganglia of medical technology. Hirst's works only make explicit what is implicit in the whole socialised medicine of the contemporary art world – and isn't it amazing that there's still a waiting list for admission?

Imaginary Value

by Sam Leith

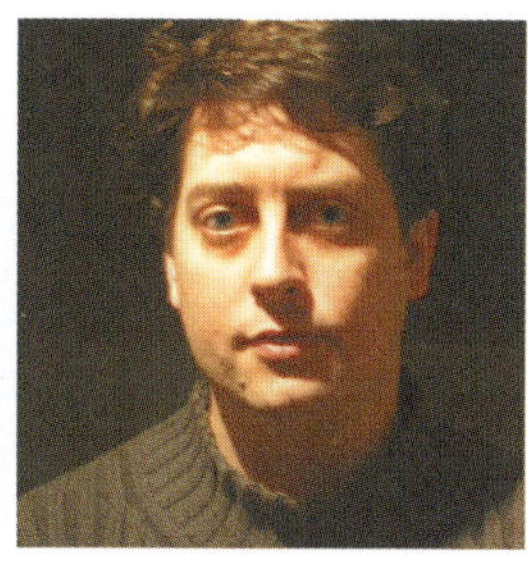

Sam Leith is a 36-year-old living sculpture yet to be taken up by a gallerist. He recently put all the gold he owns into a tin can and pegged it to the price of Manzoni's Merda D'Artista. *Nobody's buying. His last book was* Sod's Law *(Atlantic). Nobody was buying that, either.*

ART AND HEDONISM? THEY are, surely, so close to being the same thing as makes no difference. By hedonism we understand excess - and by excess, surplus. And art - grab a passing Marxist; he'll tell you - is all about surplus. It's all about added value, see? It is froth and bubble: the spindrift of late capitalism.

I remember being introduced to the artist Keith Coventry in the Academy Club by his then dealer, my old friend Mark Inglefield. Coventry's eyes were alight, his nostrils flaring, and his pocket filled with fifty-pound notes. He'd sold a painting and taken the proceeds in cash. The look on his face as he fanned these great big pink notes out, works of art themselves. "Blushers, I call them," he said, giggling. "Blushers!" He wasn't a bread-head or anything. He just loved fifty-pound notes. Loved them! Who wouldn't?

There was old Coventry, happy as a clam, having swapped something material and visually attractive and unique and of entirely imaginary value for something material and visually attractive and massively reproducible and of entirely imaginary value. Everything that is solid melts into air, as the great man said.

I love it when artists pay for their meals with a doodle, or put a scream in a jam-jar. Or when art appears *ex nihilo* somewhere it wasn't supposed to be. The old Academy Club, back when it was downstairs on the corner of Beak and Marshall streets, had a table on which a drunken Ralph Steadman had drawn a glorious big cartoon of a fish riding a bicycle in biro. Art!

Even better, think of that man who painstakingly, agonisingly, drew dollar bills and exchanged them for real goods and services to the face value of the bills. J S G Boggs, he was called. It's a funny sort of hedonism, I know, that has you cross-eyed with concentration for hours and hours over a fake $100 bill, which you then exchange for a measly $100 dollars of groceries. But you then sell the change and the receipt to a collector for a fortune. Perhaps you even throw in the groceries. Boggs got busted in Florida for possession of methamphetamines a few years back. Hedonism!

What a brilliant joke it was of Piero Manzoni's to can his own poo and insist that it retail at the exact price, gramme for gramme, as gold. It's worth far more now, obviously. And likewise, Michael Landy's much more recent work Art Bin, a giant skip into which he encouraged others to throw their "failed" works of art. Damien, Tracey, Gillian and co all queued up to dump some stuff. One creates value; one destroys it. Or, rather, transforms it: what fails as a Tracey Emin piece succeeds as part of a Landy piece. But in both cases, here is value -- ever imaginary -- being juggled like mercury. You're having a laff, intcha? Hopefully, yes.

Remember when the Momart warehouse fire in 2004 destroyed scores of works by contemporary British artists? There was wailing and moaning: from bereaved collectors, grief-stricken gallerists, artists whose favourite children had perished in the blaze. There was also sneering and mocking from the trash newspaper peanut gallery: exultation at the destruction of something that arty-farty types had cared about and spent their blushers on.

But amid all of this it was one of the Chapman brothers – their piece *Hell* was regarded as the most important work destroyed in the fire -- who ventured what still seems to me not only one of the most brave and graceful, but one of the most profound remarks about art to have been uttered in years.

"It's only art," Dinos said. "We'll make it again."

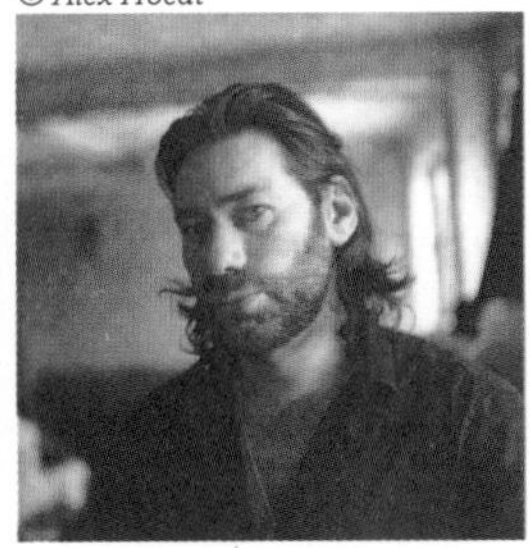

The Ten Commandments of Art

by Mat Collishaw

Mat Collishaw is an artist living in London. He came out of Goldsmiths College in the late eighties and formed part of the group of Brit artists that came to be known as the YBAs. Gaining notoriety overnight for his close-up image of a bullet wound in a dead man's head – first shown at the now legendary Freeze exhibition - he has since become known for sounding like he is being gently garroted when he talks.

COMMANDMENT NUMBER ONE
Remain dignified while drinking cheap wine from a plastic cup.

This is largely a problem of the past although one will find areas of the Eastend art world where this practice still operates.

Hoxton's Trolley Gallery, for example, excels in an unusual array of drinking receptacles and the owner can often be seen supping from the bowl of a toilet brush. Follow his lead if you must; but there are slightly less life threatening ways to imbibe your evening's alcohol. Straight from the bottle is my tip.

COMMANDMENT NUMBER TWO
Have sympathy for the Devil.

When discussing your visits to Nazi prison camps with fellow Brit artists, take care not to offend their sensibilities by undermining their sincerity of feeling, or questioning their empathic core.

Such blunders can lead to a bruising around the eye, and a visual meal on a plate for the waiting paparazzi.

COMMANDMENT NUMBER THREE
Never be defeated.

To avoid the humiliation of ejection from a favourite drinking hole, if all else fails, simply evacuate your bowels in the foyer.

(If this gesture is not executed correctly the action can backfire and result in a life-time ban from the establishment and the spread of E. coli.)

COMMANDMENT NUMBER FOUR
Reputation, Reputation, Reputation.
(For gentlemen)

It is not wise to arrive at an evening's event with a pair of ladies' knickers projecting from the top pocket of your blazer. Aside from severely impairing your chances with other women this practice can occasionally lead to misunderstandings with museum curators and serious collectors.

Writing a tell-all book about the escapades of your fellow artists and attempting to exorcise yourself from the indulgence and debauchery will be no antidote to this indiscretion.

COMMANDMENT NUMBER FIVE
Beware false profits. And prophets.

When making sales of artworks to collectors it is considered wise to check their pedigree before money changes hands. Some unscrupulous acquisitors may suddenly decide that your particular brand of neo-conceptual bathroom furniture is no longer in vogue. This generally results in them shifting a job lot of your works to an auction house where the sudden surplus of your oeuvre will guarantee a humiliating downfall.

Some collectors may circumnavigate this route by simply staging an arson attack at their storage facility, thereby assuring full whack from their insurance company.

Steer well clear of these men and women. If you happen to come up against them in a dark alleyway, or at a dinner party, I suggest clamping a phone to your ear and not breaking your pace.

COMMANDMENT NUMBER SIX

You shall not make wrongful use of your trade.

It is wise not to fall into the trap of making your life imitate your art to the extent of becoming inert and losing the capacity to breathe properly. Fashioning a crack pipe from discarded plastic may appear amusing to you and your friends when presented as an artwork in genteel restaurants and upscale art galleries, however, such rakish behaviour can prove harebrained or even fatal should the art work suddenly become apparatus for consuming certain substances.

This rule was wisely applied by a veteran of the London art scene Danny Daschund. After spending several years hunting Great White sharks for financial gain, Daschund discovered that that self same mammal then felt inclined to make hideous attacks on the locals living around the beach that he owns in Porto Rico. Many lives were lost to these vengeful creatures and Daschund was obliged to limit bathing to his gold and marble pool. There's a lesson in there somewhere.

NB. A top hat holds no defence against ignoring this commandment.

COMMANDMENT NUMBER SEVEN

Do not bear false witness.

The celebration of beauty is a noble art and should be respected without prejudice. Some art world figures have, in a headstrong scramble to establish their bellicose nature, perverted this ideal to an unacceptable degree.

Art is not the place for the fully fit and physically able to celebrate the gross deformities of others. As a joke, such posturing is potentially acceptable but when proposed as a serious elucidation on the notion of beauty, this position is offensive and grotesque.

NB. If your interests are to confuse the liberal minded fraternity to the point where they exalt your pseudo-fascism then it may, after all, be acceptable to stick with this idea.

COMMANDMENT NUMBER EIGHT

Never apologise.

If you are going to use difficult and sensitive issues in your work, do it with gusto. Rip off that image of the evil paedophile, use that film of the woman, erm, eloping with the Alsatian hound. In short, throw caution to the wind.

If you receive complaints from anyone walk quickly in the other direction blocking out the noise by singing "…" to yourself.

COMMANDMENT NUMBER NINE
Avoid the creative crossover.

It's sometimes tempting to enhance your image by wearing the mantle of another discipline. However, making sculptures out of chicken wire and painting bits of canvas do not automatically qualify you to expand your horizons. If it's the case that your work is rubbish anyway it might be wise to make that shift. But, the world is already inundated by monstrously self-regarding troubadours and 'mad for it' DJs. Do everyone a favour and stick to your i-pod.

COMMANDMENT NUMBER TEN
Never eulogise the damned.

Many unbalanced creatures of the night fall under the excessive consumption of drugs and alcohol. Their inevitable deaths then become monuments to the weak minded, their legend preserved like a pickled liver, held up to be cherished and toasted as an example of hard-core heroism. Jack Kerouac was a twat. Talking shit while dribbling is no way to set an example to the next generation.

Critics Should Cultivate No Friends

by Brian Sewell

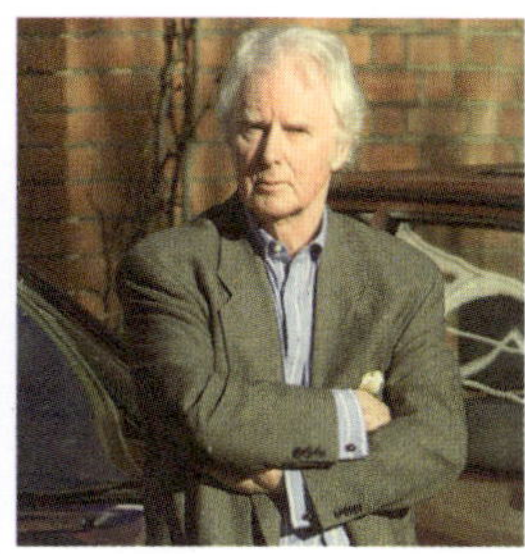

Brian Sewell has been the art critic of the London Evening Standard for 30 years. He has been Critic of the Year five times and has won the Hawthornden and Orwell Prizes.

THIRTY YEARS AGO, WHEN my life as an art critic began, it was made clear that more was expected of me than a column of objective criticism in a daily newspaper. Museums, galleries, the Arts Council and the Royal Academy expected abject compliance with their press releases, art dealers expected back-scratching reviews for which there were obvious rewards, and all artists – other than those already climbing the lower slopes of Mount Olympus – expected studio visits of which the consequences were to be their immediate fame and fortune. To the institutions I could offer only a flea in the ear. To the dealers I could reasonably say that there were so many of them that I had resolved to offend none by reviewing none – a rule to which I still adhere unless they are showing the latest work of an artist of international interest (Freud, Auerbach, Hirst and Emin, perhaps), or a retrospective of someone undeservedly neglected, or a glimpse into some overlooked aspect of Picasso or another giant of the 20th century. The pleadings of artists, from anxious to unctuous, however, I felt that I should not ignore and was, for a while, diligent in dancing attendance on them.

I was swiftly to learn that in this I was in grave error. Artists work in studios that are half a day's journey from any sane man's home, a mile from deserted Underground stations at which no taxi ever lurks, on wilder shores where threatening bodies strut and in areas of urban dereliction more arid than any inflicted by the bombs and rockets of an almost forgotten war. Artists work alone in rooms above mean streets where the trashing of cars is the evening entertainment. Artists work in groups in buildings, waiting for redevelopment, that were designed for some prosperous commercial or industrial purpose; in these the common staircases and passages are ill-lit and un-cared for, and the lavatories – if any – recall those of eastern Turkey in a long summer water shortage. In such settings as these can the critic really expect to be rewarded with the discovery of masterpieces?

To this the short answer is "No". There are two broad categories of aspiring artists: those who have money enough from background or family to buy the best canvas, the best brushes and best paints, whose self-confidence is boundless, but in whose work there is not the slightest evidence of talent, and those who support themselves as best they can with other jobs, as hopeful as resting actors, but who can never afford materials and tools of any quality, who have little obvious self-confidence yet are driven by some wholly unjustified conviction that Rembrandt or Rosa Bonheur is within them, struggling to be reborn. Between these there are a few, a very few, who produce what might be described as honest paintings not dependent on the Newspeak of the art world, the cod-philosophies and jabberwocky justifications that we know as artists' statements and curatorial interpretations, but instead are honestly conceived, properly crafted, decently presented and of some intellectual and aesthetic appeal to the informed collector – but to discover one of these working in a block of studios, the critic must walk the wasteland of a hundred others occupied, half by the pretentious, boastful and vain, and half by those undone by their hapless insecurity.

To trawl the studios within reach of the Whitechapel Gallery when, in the 1980s, it annually mounted the Whitechapel Open, was a penitential experience worse by far than any of Dante's Circles of Hell or the tribulations of the Pilgrim's Progress, but at least the critic was safe from temptation into moral turpitude. To trek to the single studio in Ealing, or Croydon, or Beckton, was in all three cases to be bribed with the body of its occupant – a powerful woman in the prime of middle age, a trembling boy, and another more accustomed to such bargaining. When much the same happened to me on tours of studios in New York and Berlin I began to wonder whether such reciprocation might be universal.

On a related but less threatening note, I have always felt, as a critic, disabled by even simple hospitality. How could I, having accepted a painter's glass of wine, chocolate biscuit or sticky bun, then tell the world how contemptible I thought the paintings? How could I – if spontaneous friendship flowered – as sometimes it did – trust myself to be dispassionate about the work? For decades I knew Patrick Procktor as a friend, but always refused to write about his paintings (though I have a self portrait) because I could not bear to tell the whole truth and hurt his feelings. I think of Charles Saatchi as a friend, but to review his exhibitions – as I must – and express opinions that are wounding, induces in me a condition of acute anguish. No. Critics should be distant and cultivate no friends. Only that way can they trust themselves to tell the truth.

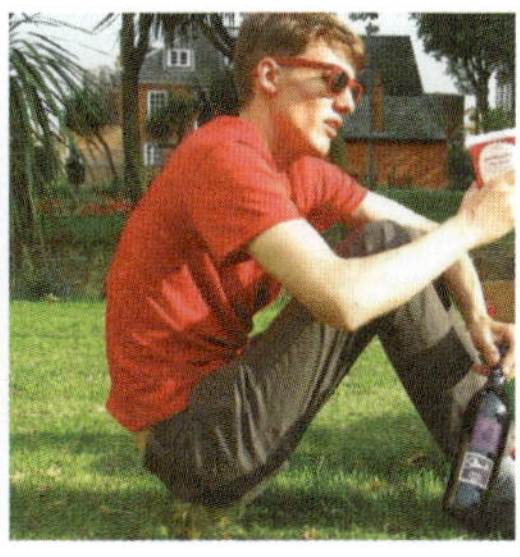

Plastic Pellets

by Edward Fornieles

Ed Fornieles is an artist playing with culture. Here are his thoughts.

I FIND THE ABILITY to sublimate my sexual energy back into my art harder and harder with the rise in Internet pornography. This is why I don't have wireless in my studio.

It's interesting that no one has made a good piece of art with the Internet yet.

If you want to remain contemporary, just go shopping. It's a great way to know what's going on, and my advice is to buy successful products because a bit of that success is bound to rub off on you.

The Vatican seems a less and less moral place yet they still seem stylish. Soon they will have none of the moral stuff left, but will remain a strong force because they've got all that style.

Before, people would walk outside and see trees and nature and think 'god isn't this beautiful', and that had something to do with how complex it is and it all sort of worked. But now I think we can have a similar feeling when we look down a street, or pick up a magazine or browse the Internet. Its all so complex and it all sort of works.

The life of a King of old used to be considered a luxurious one, but I think there was a turning point around the invention of the sofa.

Leisure time is a distinct type of time, its not exactly killing time but it is somewhere near it. It's the slight strangulation of time.

I think that the spa is something that art can learn from, those places can really change your mood, put you into another headspace: they can up lift and make you feel better about the day. And that's part of what art can do at its best.

I like the idea of making art for the majority, it's better to touch a lot of people a little than to give a few people deep tissue massages.

It's sad that the 1950s image of the future has been given up on. It was going to be a world where humans were serviced by robots. And giving up on it feels like we've given up on the dream of human equality.

It sometimes seems like the electric toothbrush is all that remains of that 1950s future.

I've always dreamed of a world where pleasure was serviced by robots, the i-player seems the nearest thing to it.

It's hard for art to escape a sense of Luxury. Gilbert and George for instance I think of as austere artists, making work about pain and shit and struggle. But if I had one of their works in my living room, I got to tell you it would be something to nestle in front of after a hard day's work.

The Casino is also a great place where humans can demonstrate some of their best virtues such as bravery, honesty, hope and a willingness to fight against the odds.

I like Botticelli's The Birth Of Venus: pure stage show.

I remember being successful on a chocolate egg hunt when I was a kid. It taught me the lesson that there is such a thing as too much of a good thing and that success comes at a price. I think these were important lessons to learn.

Cigarettes seem like adult sweets, there is something about unwrapping the pack that is like the unwrapping of a chocolate bar. The feeling of excitement and expectation is also very similar.

I have begun to see myself not as the judge of products but of their advertising. I'm willing to invest now into a good campaign - that's where a lot of modern creativity is channelled and sometimes I just want to get a bit of that. I think it's only natural.

Television is a great way to monitor tastes, because it dictates and informs at the same time. And when something is successful you can tell because suddenly there are two or three of the same type of shows all at once. This is why I think I'm going to begin using vampires in my art work. Vampires must be speaking to a lot of people at the moment.

Death sometimes seems like the only way to get attention.

Death is a sure fire way to get attention. It's like everyone has one chance to say to people 'hey, look over here'.

And it tends to be the more famous the death the bigger the bang. It's almost as if when a famous person dies, it's not just the person who dies it's all the images that have been printed of them dying as well. I think that's sometimes a good reason to want to be famous, to have a big death.

There was something very sculptural about Michael Jackson. I think near the end he was more sculpture than singer.

There is something odd about looking at an image of a recently dead celebrity, because you're not going to be able to grow with them anymore, they've stopped. It's sad. I think I would loved to have seen an old Michael Jackson.

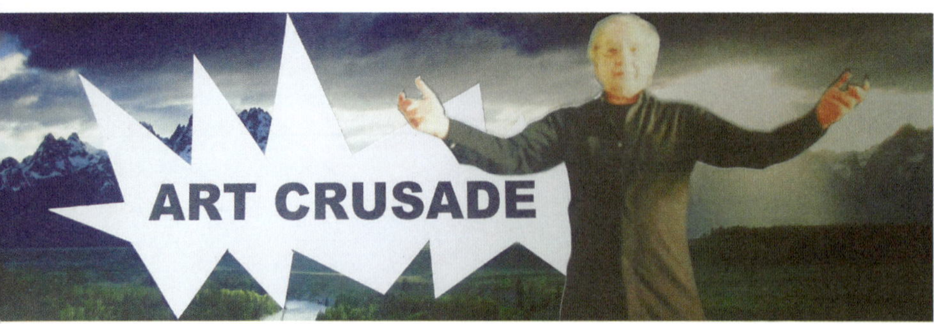

The Transfiguration

by Alex Melamid

Alexander Melamid is God. This was confirmed to him by a floating figure with a bandage over one ear, who appeared to him in his kitchen on the 11th December 2008. On that day Melamid was assigned the task of spreading the word that art – and especially his own artworks, many of which are oil paintings of hip-hop icons – is humanity's salvation. Melamid, a 65-year-old Russian artist, rocketed to fame in the West as one half of émigré art duo Komar and Melamid who bought and sold Andy Warhol's soul for $0.00 and sold it for 30 rubles.

I KNOW THAT WHAT I am going to tell you will sound improbable at best, deranged at worst. At the very beginning I was planning to keep it to myself like people do when they have something embarrassing to hide. In a situation like this, most would not share something as significant even with a shrink, a priest, a rabbi, God's angels, a pollster or a census worker. It's that embarrassing!

If not for a certain editor called Laura who insisted I contribute to this very publication, my story would have stayed buried forever, but her charm proved irresistible; she convinced me that the unsaid should be brought to light.

Although this case is of such crushing importance to me as a human being, it is probably more consequential to mankind and humanity itself. To give you some backstory, I want to tell you that my sleeping pattern has deteriorated with age, alcohol abuse and the bad thoughts that have become progressively worse. Besides, I am an artist and artists of a certain age generally don't sleep well. We can never be sure if we are the messengers of God or the beneficiaries of Mammon. My artistic biography is even more complicated because I am burdened by a Russian Communist past that tugs on my inner strings making gnawing pain an integral part of my existence.

I awoke on the morning of 11 December 2008 suspended in the luminescence of the dusty air of my bedroom flooded by the Manhattan sunlight. Strangely I couldn't feel my body's presence even though my mind was clear. I could, I figured, focus my eyes on the blond-wood Ikea shelf and the right- side lower quarter of the open Mac laptop sticking out and throwing a queer shadow on the wall. But the creaks and squeaks of my body didn't send any neurological signals to my brain. I simply didn't feel anything physically. When I sent some commands from my mind to the body – I tried first to move my worn-out feet then the tips of my fingers then my wayward penis - but I got no response. As I remember the fear of a paralysis or atrophy didn't cross my mind. I was in a state of bewilderment and glee.

"Now what?" I thought. I decided to try to redirect my thought signals outwards. An unusual shadow on the wall in front of me was shaped into a self-portrait of Andy Warhol - the one with his fingers at his lips. Lo and behold! My attempt to dissect it lengthwise in two, separate it by a couple of inches and turn the right part 180 degrees worked flawlessly. I realised right away the magnitude of what I had done. To change the shape of a shadow one must move the sun! A grandiose feat for a Russian-American artist! My position in the art world and in the history of art had changed in a New York moment. How many artists in history could claim to have moved the sun? I believe none.

But I didn't stop there. My next move was of lesser significance but was more labour intensive and delicate. My open laptop showed only a quarter of the screen and a quarter of the keyboard - the rest was obstructed by a free standing shelf. The computer was precariously positioned on a flimsy folding table but I managed to drag it safely into the open air with a lot of mental effort.

The screen blazed on and I saw, naturally, the face of Jeffrey Deitch, a quite famous New York Soho dealer, in his extravagantly trendy round frame glasses. And I thought "Poor Jeffrey, to jerk around in freezing New York, sweating away in an overheated gallery breathing rank air thickened with the cleansing, odourising, moisturising chemicals, pressing harder and harder for money, money, money… I'd like you to calm down, Jeffrey, I see you in the dry warm caressing air of California…" (Having such a power as I do, one needs to be nice to the environment). And you know what? A year to the day after that, Jeffrey was appointed director of the Los Angeles Museum of Contemporary Art!

I am glad I made the right transfer. Jeffrey's appointment was met enthusiastically by such people as the CEO of LACMA Michael Govan, director of MOMA Glenn Lowry, the collector Eli Broad, and many more.

Anyway, suspended in the luminescence of the dusty air of my bedroom flooded by the Manhattan sunlight I understood with razor sharp clarity that what had happened to me is not a mere metamorphosis but rather a transfiguration or indeed even *the* transubstantiation.

Almost two years have passed since the events described. A lot of truly amazing and I would say miraculous things have happened in the meantime. Thankfully I don't have space to go into it (my essay shouldn't exceed 800 words by much, she says). But having taken all that has transpired into consideration, I have come to the conclusion that I am not just a very advanced artist or a man of a genius but someone much more powerful and let me say singular, on top of everything and everyone.

That all means that I am God now!

And it feels good. Very good.

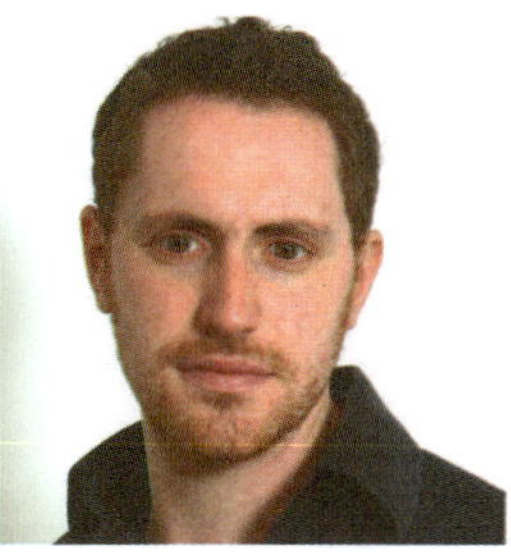

I'm a People Person

by Hugo Rifkind

Hugo Rifkind is a writer for The Times. He has no idea why they started sending him to interview artists, but he has always been glad that they did.

WHENEVER I INTERVIEW AN ARTIST, there always comes a point where they realise I'm not terribly interested in their art. Sometimes it just baffles them; more usually it annoys them. But they're invariably right. I'm not that interested in art. I'm much more interested in artists.

Take Damien Hirst. Oh, come on, let's get it over with, you knew we were going to eventually. The most interesting thing about Damien Hirst isn't the stuff he saws in half. It's the fact that *he* saws them in half; it's the effect that sawing them in half has on him. Or take Leonardo Da Vinci. If you met him, would you really want to talk about the Mona Lisa? It would be like meeting a tiger, but only caring about its kill. No, you want Da Vinci on witchcraft and sodomy. You want him bitching about the Medicis. You want him slagging off Dan Brown.

It's a journalistic approach, this. It's philistine in its focus, for reasons of populism, and because of that it tends to make artists sniffy, or panicked, or both. I once met Gavin Turk just after he'd been interviewed by somebody else, and he was fuming. All she'd seemed to want, he said, was to make out that he was some wacky, crazy, abnormal artist type. It was simplistic, he reckoned, and tired.

"Gavin, mate," I wanted to say, although I didn't, because I'm obsequious. "Gavin, mate, what do you expect? You chopped Sid Vicious's head off a statue and put yours on, instead. God knows you had your reasons, but face it, it's just not a normal thing to do."

You can see, though, why artists mind this sort of thing. It takes away the excuse of "art", and just asks "what the hell are you *doing* with your life?" The journalist Carole Cadwalladr conducted a near legendary interview of this sort in 2006, with the brothers Jake and Dinos Chapman. To paraphrase, after three minutes in their presence, during which Cadwalladr tried to get them talking about their collaborative process, she asked whether they ever felt artistic language to be "poncy". To which Jake, or maybe Dinos (who cares?) replied "Get out now. Just get the fuck out of here. What right do you have to come in here and talk to me like that? Go on, just go."

Cadwalladr's offence, I think, had been to reduce the role of "artists" to that of "human being who does art". Artists hate that, because it stops them from feeling so different and special. But journalists have to do it, because it's our job to explain things to people who *don't* already know them, not to people who do. And again, on any sort of level, what's more interesting? Clown heads scribbled on top of Goya? Or the people who thought it might be a good idea?

This doesn't need to be bitchy. It's just, there's a place for personality in art, and it needn't be lowbrow and Heat-esque, or Emin-esque and self-conscious either. It can be very basic, and very human. Indeed, the more basic and human, the better. And I say that, I hope, speaking as somebody who is not a total idiot. I did the best part of a degree in Philosophy of Art once, and, with the wind in my sails, I can bullshit with the best of them. But sent to interview an artist, the last thing I want to do is talk about their art. Artists have a habit of confusing themselves with their art. To reiterate, they often don't realise that the most interesting thing about them is not what they have made, but why it was *them* who made it.

For me, this question has real value. I interviewed Sir Peter Blake once, and the moment he clicked for me was the moment I realised that he considered himself to have been a 1960s hanger-on. To me, he was the creator of the very template of Swinging London. To himself he was just someone who was there, watching, still genuinely thrilled to have the odd anecdote stacked away about the strange conversations he had with Paul McCartney when he'd stopped by on acid.

I interviewed the sculptor Richard Wilson, and I now understand why he sometimes seems as much engineer as artist; how he picked up his love of oil and concrete and dirt as a 1970s proto-punk in a quasi-commune-come-squat on the South Bank, hoisting motorbikes up three floors with a crane, and pulling them apart. Before I interviewed Conrad Shawcross, I wanted to know just how confident a well-bred 25-year-old had to be in order to eschew thoughts of proper careers and, instead build a vast, clockwork, animated knitting machine and flog it to Charles Saatchi. He turned up two hours late and didn't understand the question and, as a result, sort of answered it.

I could go on, and on, and on, but you probably get the idea. My point is that you can be interested in the art world without understanding much about art. Despite what some may wish to tell you, there's no shame in that. People are more interesting than stuff, almost always.

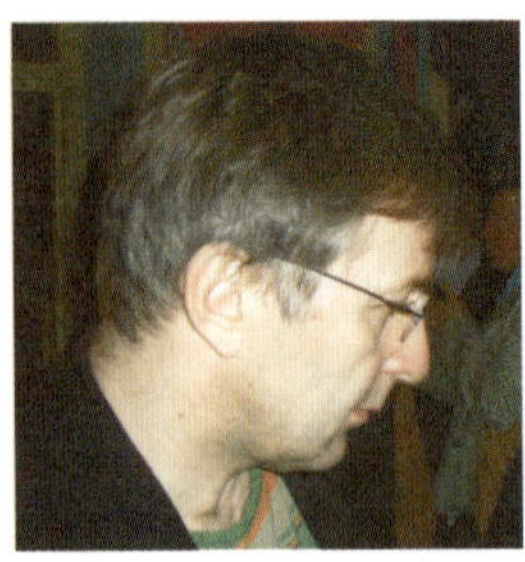

The Umpteen Commandments of Uncool

by Matthew Bown

Occasionally Matthew Bown's gallery manager checks the bank account and tells him he should "do a more commercial show". But that sounds like running a white-goods emporium. He's overjoyed when people share his likes and he regards every sale as a little miracle, a magical conjunction of collector, artist and exhibition, rather like some rare alignment of planets. But he's a little depressed when they share his dislikes, because he wants to feel he's ahead of the crowd. In any case, the longer he deals with art, the less sure he becomes of his taste.

EVER SINCE BANKSY, ART is Uncool.

Ever since the curators began dressing like priests, art is Uncool.

Ever since art was called upon to 'enhance inter-cultural dialogue', art is Uncool.

Ever since the daughters of the oligarchs, *circumornitae ut similitudo templi,* became the crown-princesses of the art-world, art is Uncool.

Ever since the fashion houses took over the auction houses, Art is Uncool.

Ever since the Turner Prize put art on TV, art is Uncool.

Ever since art that looks like it came straight off the walls of some crummy Lebanese restaurant in the Bayswater Road began selling for fortunes in Middle Eastern sales, art is Uncool.

Ever since Jeff Koons sculptures – collisions of bubbles in a glass of gallery Prosecco - became 'the cornerstone' of the world's top private collections, art is Uncool.

Ever since Northern worthies clubbed together to buy t' Angel of t' North, art is Uncool.

Ever since identikit paintings made by studio assistants and resembling brightly-coloured share-certificates became the galleries' cash-cow, art is Uncool.

Ever since the anodyne art made under the world's most repressive regimes was hailed as 'edgy', art is Uncool.

Ever since the first thing you see on entering TATE is the shop, art is Uncool.

Ever since Our Lady of Margate, Tracey Emin, began doing charity work, art is Uncool.

Ever since José and Alberto Mughrabi bought 600 Warhols, art is Uncool.

Ever since the face-off between nation-states at the Venice Biennale became the most important show on earth, art is Uncool.

Ever since posh kids with no discernible psychological problems started becoming artists, art is Uncool.

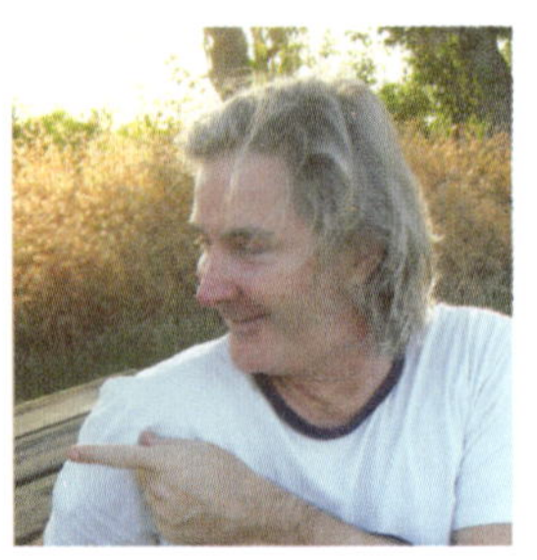

I Only Pretend to Like Art

by Guy Kennaway

Guy Kennaway is a novelist living in Pilton, Somerset. He wrote this piece during Frieze week, after seeing six American women covered in plastic surgery and mink emerge from a pair of limousines in a litter-strewn street in the East End. A young gallerist walked backwards and unctuously down the street in front of them. The whole group stopped to heap praise on some mediocre graffiti before continuing on a studio tour. Kennaway sometimes writes to entertain, sometimes to annoy, and sometimes to do both.

FOR SOME TIME NOW, I have only pretended to like contemporary art; I was just too scared to say when it did nothing for me. I don't mind people making art per se - it is a perfectly harmless activity - but I don't see why we all have to revere it. Art has become ridiculously self-important. I couldn't go anywhere without having to give an apparently intelligent and sensitive opinion about some show or some artist or other. I found myself judging a person by how fashionable the art was on their walls. I have even - more fool me - bought work because I thought other people would think me cool if I owned it. Sad, but true.

Curators and gallerists are the new clergy, and it's a corrupt and suffocating religion they peddle. They are like medieval pardoners selling promises to send the buyer to heaven, or weasely priests flogging counterfeit relics to frightened, gullible fools who think their possession will save the souls.

There are certain assumptions in this orthodoxy that it is forbidden to challenge. For instance - that the use of fabricators never devalues art. If a writer doesn't pen his own words, it's called passing off, and is actionable in law. Another assumption is that irony can excuse crap. If the Queen came out for the Trooping the Colour on a horse that limped, people wouldn't say "Oh isn't that mare ironic?", they would say "That mare looks lame"- an adjective that should properly be used for the vast majority of art produced today.

I don't blame the artists, who are in many cases well intentioned simpletons drawn to the cash. The ones in the dock are the gallerists, the curators and the stupid billionaires who clutch their worthless splinters of old pine because they've been told it's actually part of Jesus' cross. Global economics have created a huge number of very rich people, many who had nothing to do with the creation of their own wealth, who wander around easily manipulated by the clever bishops of the galleries being promised fast track entry into the heaven of the art cognoscenti. How do the clergy do it? By attributing magical powers to essentially meaningless objects.

The artists all go along with it - and who can blame them? If a billionaire told my plumber he was a genius and would pay him two hundred grand for fitting a radiator on a wall in his mansion, I doubt my plumber would argue.

I really believe there's considerably more skill required to fit a central heating system than to create most contemporary sculptures.

If art, as someone clever said, is a conspiracy by rich people and clever people to make poor people think they're stupid, the most culpable conspirators are the art critics, men and women whose only job is to obfuscate - the opposite of what a writer should be doing - and to hint that the reasons you cannot understand their garbled propositions are A, you are not intelligent enough, and B, you are not rich enough.

A man in my local town had a large Banksy stencilled on the wall of his garden shed. It quickly became a site of pilgrimage. The local population - me included - went on about how great it was, and soon it was valued at £100,000 if it were ever to be levered off the building and auctioned.

The man who owned the shed disliked the adoring crowds, and one night took a bucket of whitewash and obliterated the image. I thought he was mad - now I realise he's the only sane one of us left.

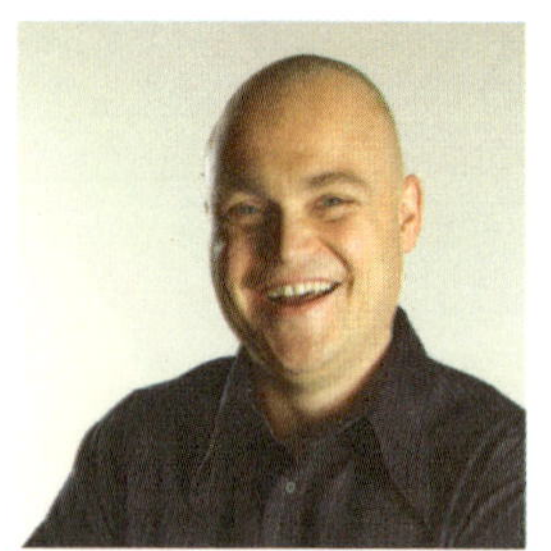

Art: I Know What I Like; It's Just the Words That Bother Me

by Al Murray

Al Murray's day job sees him apeing the manners of a boorish pub landlord in a polyester sports jacket. Wherever he goes, people try to engage him with catchphrases uttered from that character's mouth. The line "A glass of white wine for the lady!" crops up a lot. If must grate on his nerves. Al's vocation is a million miles away from the contemporary art world as we know it, but that doesn't mean he's got nothing to say about it.

I AM ONE OF THE UNARTED. Like a lost tourist at Tate Modern looking for The Globe, I've blundered in here. Like one of them I'll find the exit soon enough, don't panic.

Why am I UnArted? I cannot draw, so as a callow youth - as if there's any other kind in a book about art – others' efforts interested me little. My mother would drag me round galleries, or – like when we went to the Louvre – try to get me to slow down and look at the paintings. (Ah there, you see – I am UnArted – I only remember the paintings. The UnArted really do need things on canvas painted with brushes or they start to gulp for breath). I think we got round the place in half an hour. Result: much more fun was had dropping metro tickets off the Eiffel Tower and squinting hard at them 'til they disappeared from view.

Unless it was a picture "of" something (and, all too often, the UnArted need to know what a painting is "of" - and often the more like a photograph it is the better, though paradoxically the UnArted don't think photographs are art at all), I wasn't all that interested. As a teenager I snuck into London, coming down from Milton Keynes through Euston station, and liked to walk into town. Never once did I give the Henry Moore that's installed outside Euston a second look. It didn't look like art to me, it didn't look like anything. Growing up in the Athena poster era, we had earnest art teachers who you could see steeling themselves for maximum puerile reaction when talking about nudes. We'd be marched down to the local gallery and try to think of something erudite to say and fail.

But these feelings can dim. They can be superseded. Every now and again I'd see something and gawp. I'd go – wow. A friend of mine on his foundation year at The Slade suggested we meet in London and go to a gallery: I remember some Rothkos (and forgive my ignorance as to which ones they were, these were my toddler steps – I can picture you now, you're sniggering at a child learning to walk) and thinking – holy crap. Huge slabs of maroon, or purple (don't laugh). These weren't po-faced Madonnas, or funny shaped Picasso people, but huge great slabs of colour – art-brain-Lego for the untrained.

But! The trouble is, even as I have just begun to remember not to drag my knuckles like an early primate in an unprecedented age of art literacy, there's one thing that niggles. And it's all the stuff that surrounds art – especially the stuff that gets said. The pronouncements, the things that artists and their advocates end up saying about their art. In fact, it's about now that the word art requires a capital A. I'm going to start capitalising it, just because I can.

Because Art is quite different to art. When it's Art it "should" do things, it "demands" things, it "holds up a mirror" to things. "Asks questions". As one of the UnArted this can all be a bit worrying and confusing. Now I'm not so bone-headed as to say I want art to be pretty, look nice, or even be "of" something any more. Because now I am a man, I have given up childish things. But when I read a pronouncement, or a theory, or a manifesto for Art, I usually end up thinking –"Oh yeah? Maybe that says more about you than it does about Art, my dear".

As a for instance (and you're right, I've chosen it because it makes my point well), Wagner came up with a concept called Gesamtkunstwerk – lots of compound German words that are not entirely translatable, but it comes out near enough as TotalArtWork. Wagner believed that music (the toppermost of the Arts) should be harnessed to create an unprecedented hybrid of opera/musical theatre/*son et lumiere*/drama that was completely conceived by the one Artist. Now he either thought this because he believed it was the right next step for Art, or because he was a complete and utter control freak - character references bear this out - and more pertinently, because he knew it was something that *he* could actually do.

Artists after all – even the ones with capital As – are only human. Their options are often penury, bankruptcy or failure. So you'd better find something you can actually do. But no one wants to admit that – craftsmen do; artisans too – but capital A Artists need to be above all that. So while Picasso said "I paint objects as I think them, not as I see them," (and I see what he means and it sounds great), maybe it was that he found in Cubism a way to not be like the other guy, something he knew he could do well and express himself through.

"Çeci n'est pas une pipe" declares The Treachery of Images. And of course, Magritte's right, it's not a pipe. (Actually, it's "of" a pipe, phew). But it's an incredibly striking image. After all, The Son of Man is a bloke with an apple in front of his face – well, yes René, a *picture* of a bloke with an apple in front of his face. And whatever Magritte may have said about it, what he could do was paint images that really made you think.

And while Salvador Dali may have said that "Surrealism will at least have served to give experimental proof that total sterility and attempts at automatisations have gone too far and have led to a totalitarian system", he still happened to be just great at painting melting clocks. And boy did he know it. Frida Kahlo liked painting her own image. Again and again and again. And again. She found a hook and she ran with it.

So Artists' pronouncements on Art are surely sincere, but may also, possibly, be a way of saying anything other than "This is what I'm good at, so…er…please buy my new painting/ installation/sculpture". Moulds get broken yes, but that's what is expected of capital A Artists now. In lots of ways the need to come up with something new is as conservative as the UnArted only making a beeline for paintings "of" things. If everyone's radical, then is *anyone* radical anymore?

So when I go to an Art gallery now, I no longer rush up to the roof to drop pennies or metro tickets, I don't mutter "what's it supposed to be of?", but I also don't read the explanation that tells me what I ought to know in order to appreciate the thing I'm looking at.

It's like having a joke explained to you – you either get it, or you don't.

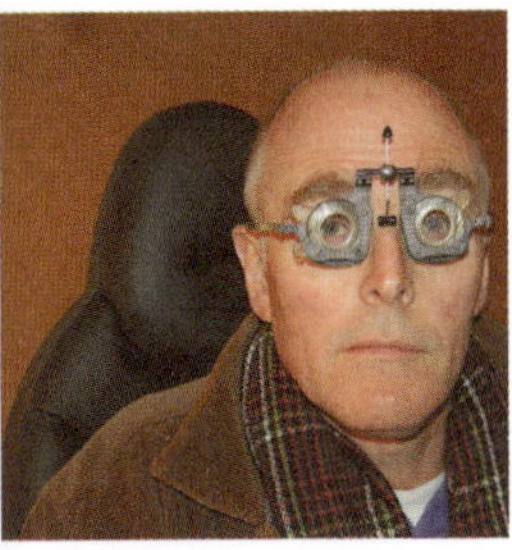 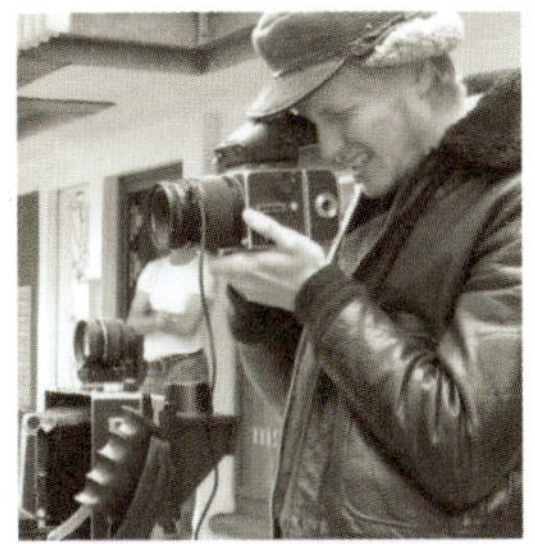

Richard Wentworth – left
Ross McNicol – right

The Accident of Encounter:

*Letters between Richard Wentworth
and Ross McNicol*

*Since the 1970s the artist Richard Wentworth has played a leading role in New British
Sculpture. He worked for Henry Moore on leaving art school and has taught art episodi-
cally throughout his life - at Goldsmiths in the 1980s, at the Architectural Association, and as
Master of the Ruskin School. He is now head of sculpture at the Royal College of Art.*

*Born in 1979, artist Ross McNicol graduated in Philosophy from King's College London,
apprenticed with photographers and studied art informally with Anselm Kiefer. In 2007, he
co-founded The Wallis Gallery. He lives and works in London.*

D EAR RICHARD,

The boy with electrostatic hair holding a balloon in one hand and the yellow rail of the bus
in the other, that you recently described, stuck to me over my lunch of left-over chicken
and noodles, as did our discussion about what it means to impart something. The verb
'impart' is somewhere described as 'to bestow something, especially an abstract quality'.

You don't seem to teach art and I've never been to art school. You say you're an artist
who likes young ones, and not a teacher. But perhaps you are an imparter. I don't
remember ever hearing you pass judgment on an artwork as you might expect an art
teacher to. I think one of the Latin roots, impertire, i.e. "to share in", might be closer to
what we're talking about and what you do; maybe you're an impertirer. Everyone is an
impertirer as well as a receiver; but we are able to choose to some extent what to share
out and what to share in, and those choices are quite important aren't they?

Dear Ross,

What humans give and take from each other is very odd. We call it culture.

My childhood was in a German refugee part of London, but I was too young (ring fenced?) to understand/ get 'it'. I was sent to an achieving school next to a building site. My brother said they were building a Cinemagogue.

I can trace all sorts of curiosity, desire and unease to these days. The last totally opaque London fogs and the whimpering of empire. Unlike Marina Warner, I cannot remember Suez in a haptic way. Khrushchev in London and Sputnik, yes.

***

Dear Richard,

Some famous couples between whom important cultural mimes were probably transmitted or imparted: Seamus Heaney and Paul Muldoon, Johann Christian Bach and Wolfgang Amadeus Mozart, Woody Guthrie and Bob Dylan, Ralph Waldo Emerson and Henry David Thoreau, Ezra Pound and T S Eliot, Camille Pissarro and many others, including Paul Gauguin, Georges Seurat and Paul Cezanne. More gratifying for me are the stories of an inverted relationship between mentor and protégé; when the latter blows the former out of the water, like Wittgenstein and Russell.

What did you teach Henry Moore?

***

Dear Ross,

My parents moved to near Henry Moore's place in 1961, following the death of my grandfather. Now I see Moore's gentlemanly solidity as intriguing in the context of the dissolution of deference. Profumo Affair versus Cuba crisis, domestic politics haunted by immense housing crises and immigration/racist debates, Stones/Beatles, Trans-Atlanticism, Vietnam/Prague, Robert Fraser/Kasmin. And then there was genial, benign, assured Henry. It was effectively a holiday job for me, poorly paid but interesting to witness the professional space of running a 'family firm' and to recognise the humdrum procedures of making little things bigger. Processes are always great metaphors so long as you don't have to adopt them and become a fellow tradesman. People say I was often outspoken, which I find embarrassing. Did I say childish stupid things? Probably. Anyway, you always seem to ask a well pitched question, Ross.

***

Dear Richard,

I like that kind of outspokenness.

I listened to a podcast about Vasari's 'Lives of Artists' in a studio in Paris, whilst solarising giant prints of Anselm Kiefer doing the Hitlergruß; so the bits about artists apprenticing with older ones stuck out at that time. Michelangelo was not happy with his bio in the first edition, because Vasari suggested he had been 'taught', i.e. he wasn't born with it, like maybe Giotto. Vasari had presented Michelangelo as the greatest thing before sliced bread but he also tried to drill home the importance in his success, of training. Anyway MikeA got around it by commissioning his own separate biography of his divine life and talents. So many superstars receive some signposts from their forbears along the way, whether thanks to hard work and luck or birth or both. But it looks like the relationship of mentor and mentee imparts the most, most successfully. I don't know what that means for art schools, but you probably manage quite close relationships with RCA students don't you? What happens to most people that graduate with an art degree?

***

Dear Ross,

I became a London art student in 1965. Zoë Wanamaker was a student with me on Foundation. It was a busy 'Bauhaus' course, committed young teachers/artists. A then Constructivist-minded Stuart Brisley set a serious minded example amongst others.

The accident of encounter drives so much, and we certainly discussed the Nouvelles Realités crowd. Even knowing who Camargo and de Soto were helped inoculate a young English artist against the climate of humanist bronze vs. coloured steel ping pong binary debate. I used to go from the RCA to Caro's events at St Martin's, but it takes a while to see what all these 'positions' really mean. Perhaps Bridget Riley who I know a little is the real 'stayer' through all this. There is no accounting for kinds of persistence!

Dear Richard,

Persistence is essential for lasting satisfaction. And persistence fosters welcome synchronicities.

There is a beautiful synchronicity recounted in the composer Ligeti's biography that led to his apprenticeship. His parents were sent to Auschwitz and he fled Hungary in a post train. He got ill on the way to Cologne and when he arrived, the authorities found the address of his idol, Stockhausen, (whom he had had no contact with) scribbled on a piece of paper in his pocket. They assumed it was the address of a relative or friend so they delivered him to Stockhausen, who ended up taking him in and went on to impart a fair amount to him. (The most famous result, Lux Aeternae making it to a starring role in Kubrick's 2001.) I tried to verify my memory of Ligeti's story and can't find evidence for it so I may have made some of it up, but you know the point about circumstances and people.

***

Dear Ross,

I think we are really talking about encounter and risk. I remember BonMot Hockney saying 'there is only love and fear'. Getting the contact without being tactless is a great puzzle to me. How did my children learn to make friends? How did you be-friend Ed Fornieles, and what made you rock up in Lyon in 'o3?

***

Dear Richard,

Optimism, curiousness and perhaps in some respects passivity are what's behind it. So when you asked me out of the blue, whether - after just meeting you - I wanted to jump on a plane that moment to Lyon to do an exhibition with some students, you had a sense I would be the kind of person to say yes, without thinking. I can relate nearly all my greatest experiences past and present to spontaneous yes-saying and whimsical departures.

I asked Anselm Kiefer about his relationship with Joseph Beuys. I think I read on White Cube's website or Wikipedia that he had "studied informally" with Beuys. So I asked him what he took away from the 'studies'. Turns out he went to visit Beuys (didn't go to his classes) and showed his degree show work. Beuys was the only one that 'got' the Hitler salutes, and told Kiefer to make more. Hence he continues that series to this day. But that seems to be the extent of his 'informal studies' with Beuys. I don't mean to underplay the importance of such an encounter but perhaps for Jay Jopling and the art historians that 'lineage' is very important and worth exaggerating to simplify the explanation of his provenance. So, "studied informally with" enters his biography in a very Beuysian way.

Anselm did apprentice with an artist and apparently blossomed under him. But he was not a well known figure and so it's Beuys' name that sits next to Kiefer's in the bios. And isn't that somewhat similar to your history?

***

Dear Ross,

The accident of my glimpsing John Berger's world in the summer of Pet Sounds has long-term meaning - meeting a kindly young Peter de Francia. Things bounce in surprising ways and the consequence is not always immediately apparent. London was porous and villagey at this time. People like David Medalla were prominent agencies. I was sent out to get macrobiotic food for a fluey Yoko Ono and her filmmaker hub. I hung shows for Indica for a while, and remain unsure if I hung YO's when John Lennon turned up.

There's nothing special in all this, but it was an art 'teacher' who gave me some of these permissions and models. An able potter who thought like an artist and questioned things. From a modest sensible background, this probably grounded him and held him back a touch? He had done National Service, which was a major cultural release agent. I am from the next privileged space after that: sexual freedoms, some colour magazines and being taught by Continental Europeans.

The potter is Gordon Baldwin. His wife Nancy worked on scenes and costumes at Covent Garden, so they knew lots about resourcefulness and dead-lining.

He took me and some others to the Whitechapel Rauschenberg show.. Imagine what that meant in the same year as Churchill's state funeral in black and white.

***

Dear Richard,

Making artwork and watching others do it, I often think we/they are tapping into elements of a collective consciousness. And to be successful at it requires a lot of movement and interaction with other minds and other places. I think there's a stench and stigma attached to meeting people if you're an artist, and living outside the studio, because of the advent of the careerist artist.

For our life cogs to keep moving most of us use whatever is at hand in our age – in my space and time, a wheelie suit case, a computer, a power point, free wifi in Folkstone service station- to telescope us closer to friends, strangers and alien culture.

***

Dear Ross,

At the German Embassy last evening I met an American who looked like a small taut Claus Oldenburg. He was a space communications engineer who had just won the equivalent co-lab award for his Inmarsat work. This smaller Oldenburg had left Stanford, encountering immediately the Sputnik story… Fold time back and you can find the Wright boys on their beach. Big impressions have unaccountable consequences over fifty years on.

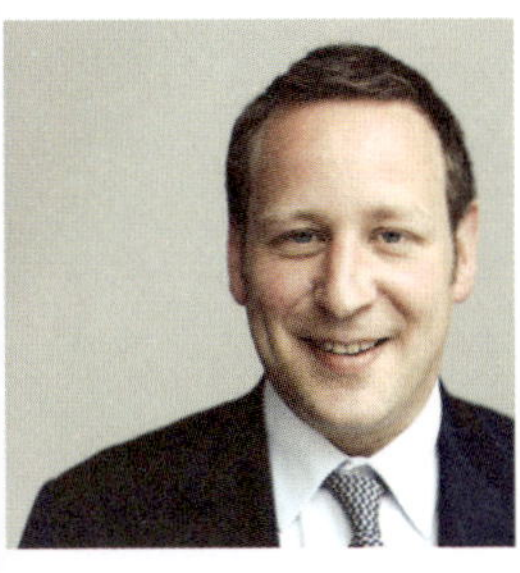

My New Job

by Ed Vaizey

Our new Minister for Culture Ed Vaizey MP was elected as the Member of Parliament for Wantage and Didcot in May 2005, and was Shadow Culture and Creative Industries Minister 2006-2010. Born in 1968, he attended Merton College, Oxford, before spending two years working as a political researcher. After practising as a barrister he became director of a public relations company and then a political speech writer. Nurturing the health of the arts - it's a pretty big job he's got ahead of him.

I WAS LUCKY ENOUGH TO grow up around the arts, being taken to art galleries, exhibitions and theatre from a young age. So I am one of those people who assume the arts are – or should be – part of everybody's life.

So as the new Minister for Culture, I want school children to be exposed to the joy of creativity, immersed in music and reaping the undisputed benefits of a cultural education. I want them to grow up with their eyes open to the wonders that exist in our museums, theatres and libraries, to be given the confidence and vocabulary that will lead them to seek out the brilliance on offer right across the country and – in this digital age – across the world.

In Britain, we are unbelievably good at developing world class talent and our cultural sectors are thriving. Nowhere rivals Britain for world class museums and galleries. Being British, we just tend not to shout about it enough.

While I believe in the importance of art for art's sake, there is an economic interest in nurturing the health of this sector, with our creative industries employing around two million people and growing faster than the rest of the economy in recent years. Given the Government's priority to restore the nation's finances, it makes complete sense that we focus our efforts on areas where we have real potential and natural advantage. But even without this powerful, pragmatic incentive, culture brings undisputed value to our lives.

That is why we politicians need to challenge our own creativity and find new ways to protect the arts from a crisis in future funding. It is no secret that our fiscal deficit means tough decisions ahead and reductions in public spending - culture will not be seen as a soft touch for easy cuts but nor can it escape completely from a share of the pain. Restoring the National Lottery to its original purpose to support good causes will help, when the arts will again receive twenty per cent of the funding - bringing in an extra £50 million a year.

But in the longer term we want to bring about a societal shift that will see our cultural bodies benefit from the generosity of those people who take social responsibility seriously. Philanthropy was the foundation of many of our most important institutions - the British Museum, the Royal Shakespeare Company, hundreds of public libraries all exist because of exceptional altruism and the commitment of private donors to share and inspire.

We want to encourage a growth in cultural philanthropy. Only a tiny fraction of the billions given by individuals to charity goes to arts and culture. But the squeeze on public spending means that we need a healthy mixed economy to emerge, a mix of astute commercial activity, public investment and private giving.

There are things Government can do to help encourage individuals and businesses to give to the arts. We want to reform Gift Aid, making it simpler, easier and more attractive to give. And we want to look at changes to the Acceptance-in-lieu Scheme, which has seen countless precious works saved for the nation in the hundred years since its inception. If we could extend this scheme to make it possible for donors to give works of art to the nation during their lifetimes, there could be huge benefits.

And lastly, we want to reward high performing arts organisations with longer term funding deals, giving them the confidence to approach sponsors and donors and plan for the future.

So as 2012 gets ever closer, when Britain will be in the spotlight as never before, I want to make the case for the role of culture and philanthropy in a civilised nation. To reaffirm Government's commitment to nurturing and supporting the arts, placing them at the centre of the responsible society we are building and to helping build a secure future for those cultural institutions who do so much to enhance Britain's standing around the world.

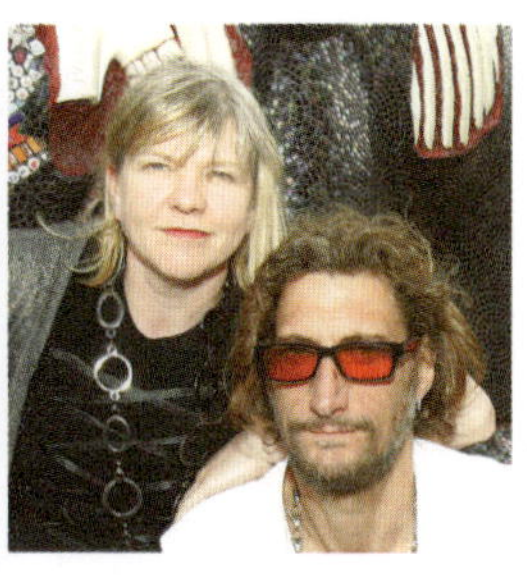

Art and Death

*By Nick Reynolds and
Baroness Carrie Reichardt*

*Nick Reynolds' life has been a life of contrasts – he went
from spending five years on the run with his father Bruce who
"masterminded" the Great Train Robbery to serving in the Falklands War. These days he
plays harmonica with the band Alabama3 (responsible for the Sopranos theme tune) and
specialises in reinstituting the popularity of death masks. Recent commissions include the late
great Situationist Malcolm McLaren, the legendary helmsman of the Colony Room, Michael
Wojas and the artist and dandy of the underworld Sebastian Horsley.*

*Carrie Reichardt - aka The Baroness - has been a leader in the area of subversive ceramics for
many years and can surely be labelled as one of England's true anarchist potters. She works
from her amazing mosaic covered home The Treatment Rooms in west London - one of the
country's most complete and important mosaic displays on public view.*

I F YOU FOUND YOURSELF paranoid in a Texan woodland cabin, on a hell-hot
afternoon, with the dead body of an executed man that had spent half of his life
banged up on Death Row - you might put it down to being trapped in an appalling
nightmare. But for us it was real.

Two months previously, after an Alabama 3 gig in London, a familiar character wearing
a bra made of pigs' heads sat next to me. It was Baroness Carrie Von Reichardt, an
eccentric ceramicist and craftivist. The previous year, she had dedicated a mosaic mural
to a pen pal of hers that had been executed on America's Death Row. Now, time had
run out for another pen pal, John "Ash" Amador. Carrie said she was going to Texas to
witness his execution, and to film the experience. Believing him to be the victim of a
gross miscarriage of justice, she was mosaic-ing a truck in his memory as a form of
protest, and entering it into the UK's first art car parade. Her story compelled me to do
something, so I offered to journey with her and create his death mask. A copy for his
family, one for the truck or 'mobile mausoleum', and another for the central piece in an

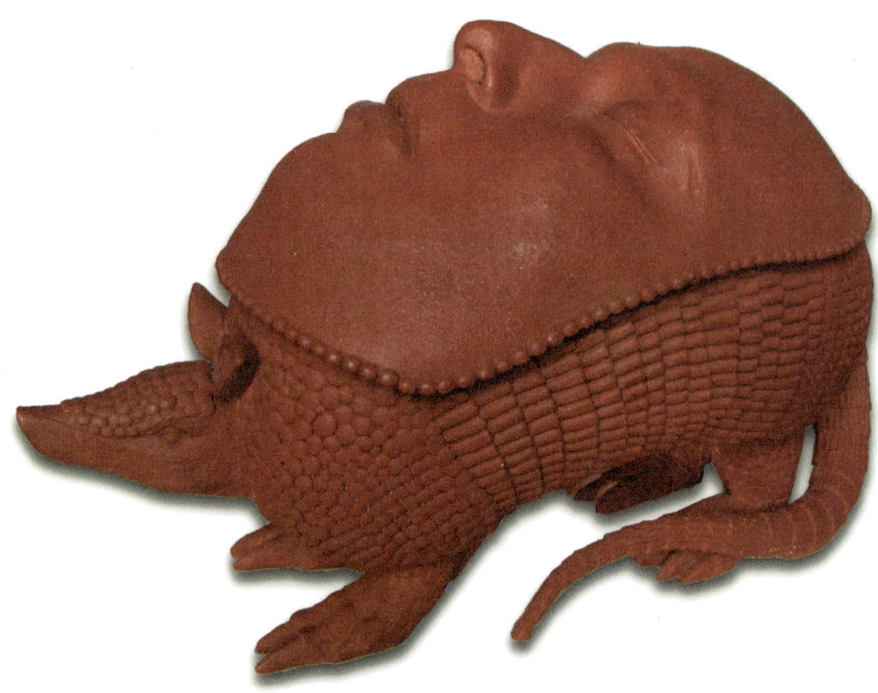

John Amador's Death Mask Mounted on Texas State Symbol, The Armadillo, by Nick Reynolds

exhibition called 402 - Amador's execution number. We'd give him some sort of a life after death, that couldn't be taken away by the state.

Death masks are the only true, three-dimensional representations available of the subject in death. Unlike paintings or photographs, they are created by taking a mould, directly from the subject's actual features. During the casting process some of the mystery of death seems to pass into the cast, giving it an almost totemic quality – as if their last breath had frozen into a form, mimicking the deceased, minus the soul.

My initiation into this neglected practice began in 1995 whilst observing the filmic rise of gangster chic. I was working on a project entitled Cons to Icons, an exhibition comprising of life casts of the UK's most notorious living criminals. The aim was to explore the paradox in how some people vilified by the media one minute, are feted on the celebrity circuit the next.

I was keen to add George "Taters" Chatham, aka 'Attila the Hun of the Pillaging Game' to my collection. Accredited with stealing £100m in his lifetime only to gamble it away, his heists included Wellington's swords from the Victoria and Albert Museum (in 1948) and the Eastcastle Street mail van raid in 1952, (then England's largest cash haul). When I finally got a contact for him, I found that the man was dead. I asked his sister if I could cast his head anyway. She wasn't keen at first, then, when she saw her brother had died with a smile on his face, she took it to be a sign he'd made peace with God, and allowed me. I didn't tell her that it was in fact the weight of his jowls and gravity, which had produced the effect.

Ned Kelly, Himmler, Napoleon (whose mask was altered by Magritte and Dali), JMW Turner, Mary Queen of Scots, Beethoven and Stalin have all been immortalised in this way, but the art of the death mask has all but disappeared, its function replaced by photography, X-ray and video. I wanted to try to restore the tradition, and with John Schoonraad (one of the worlds top life casters) formed Memorial Casts, the UK's only company specialising in this field. The ancient tradition of making death masks had become my visual métier.

John "Ash" Amador, a Hispanic American, was executed for the 1994 murder of a San Antonio taxi driver. He went to his death, still protesting his innocence, with an armful of lethal sodium pentothal. Once certified dead, his body was taken to the local Texan undertakers. We went to explain our mission, but they were adamant the death mask was not to be made on their premises. They thought we were freaks, so we just put him on the back seat of the hire car, opened the body bag and took his arm out so that his wife could hold his hand. We drove to some woods where Amador's widow had a tiny cabin. In surroundings resembling a Friday The Thirteenth film, we cast his head and the arm into which the fatal injection was delivered.

We worked fast because we were paranoid the police would arrive. What should have been a traumatic and tragic moment became a strangely cathartic and spiritual experience. Now, all that was left was a grueling four-hour journey to the next morgue, in a two-car convoy.

Carrie Reichardt: "In the film taken of the day, we look so wan. The waiting and waiting for a reprieve, the jeers of hatred and racism from locals who live near the prison, the acceptance that a killing has taken place, making the mask, and bringing to light the brutality of Death Row, then - perhaps the most arduous of all - the sneaking of a body around Texas. It was beyond exhausting."

"God forgive them for they know not what they do," were Amador's last words. Typically every Texan newspaper had changed this statement to, "God forgive me," inferring Amador had admitted to the killing – something he never did. Speaking on a mobile phone to him not long before he died, he told us, "It's called capital punishment because it's for people with no capital - there are no rich people on Death Row", and added that having a death mask made was an honour, normally reserved for the likes of kings. He said he used to feel that he was nobody and now he felt like someone.

I naively told him that his mask, we hoped, would become a thorn in the conscience of the American establishment. We later thought perhaps we'd made some difference when the UN General Assembly imposed a moratorium on US state-sponsored killing "with a view to abolish the death penalty," two executions after Amador's, but the moratorium was overturned and the Texas killing machine rolls on.

Still, through press, the exhibition (which his family flew from Texas to London for), and the truck winning first prize in the best-decorated category, Amador's legacy lives on. In fact his mobile mausoleum has been featured in several exhibitions and has become a regular on the festival circuit.

Most Death Row prisoners have accepted they're going to die a long time before it happens. What some are desperate for is to leave something positive and everlasting behind. We hope we've achieved that for one person and his family.

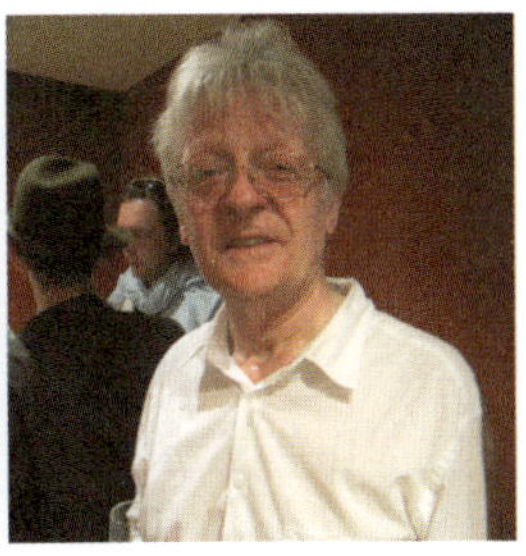

It Looked Like a Load of Rubbish to Me

by Barry Miles

Yoko Ono met John Lennon in Barry Miles and John Dunbar's Indica bookshop and Gallery, a veritable hub of burgeoning counterculture in the 60s. Miles later went on to write books on Allen Ginsberg, Jack Kerouac, William Burroughs, Charles Bukowski, and Frank Zappa. His Hippie *and the official McCartney biography* Paul McCartney: Many Years From Now *were both New York Times best sellers. His most recent book is* London Calling: a counter-cultural history of London since 1945 *(Atlantic Books).*

THE INDICA GALLERY IS best known for being where Yoko Ono first met John Lennon, which was on November 7, 1966 when we were still hanging the show in preparation for the opening of Yoko at Indica, the next day. The gallery was at 6 Mason's Yard off Duke Street Saint James's; the yard is now home to the White Cube Gallery. Originally the bookshop was on the ground floor, but by this time it had moved to new premises at 102 Southampton Road. John Lennon often dropped by to visit with John Dunbar, the director of the gallery, and it was accidental that John and Yoko met on this occasion rather than at the opening.

Lennon particularly liked Yoko's Ceiling Painting. The work appeared to be a blank canvas flat on the ceiling with just one word written on it in tiny letters. Lennon climbed a step-ladder, and balancing at the top, peered through his little round glasses, and through a larger round magnifying glass that was hanging on a chain next to the canvas, to look at the word. John said, "I went up the ladder and I got the spyglass and there was tiny writing there … and you look through and it just says 'YES'."

The most popular piece in the show was Yoko's all white chess set: all the pieces and all the squares were white and the board sat on a white table with two white chairs. Sharon Tate and Roman Polanski visited the show several times late at night, spending hours playing with the chess set until they could no longer keep all the pieces in their minds and had to abandon their game. They never bought the piece.

In the mid-sixties, Optical Art was very popular: it went well with Vidal Sassoon Mary Quant haircuts, André Courrèges dresses and the dotty Heals shower curtains that Damien Hirst so clearly grew up with.

At first the only gallery to feature Op Art work in London was Signals but when the Indica Gallery started up in the autumn of 1965, it also featured the work of kinetic artists. When Signals closed in October 1966, Indica Gallery took up many of their artists. Indica's first proper show, opening 4 June 1966, was the Groupe de Recherche de l'Art Visuel, (GRAV) a loose collective of kinetic artists. John Dunbar drove to Italy to represent the gallery at the XXXIII Venice Biennial. He was on his way back to London when the news came through on the car radio that the Argentinean Julio Le Parc, the co-founder of GRAV, had been awarded the International Painting Grand Prix. Julio was reported to have fainted when he heard the news. Indica was showing the winner of the most prestigious art prize in the world in its first show.

The Americans had wanted Robert Rauschenberg to win, but were quite prepared to buy the work of whoever won. At that time the bookshop, which I ran, was still on the ground floor. On John's first day back we were standing in the bookshop when a large man in an eye-catching tartan jacket burst in the door. Identifying us the proprietors he announced, "I'm a big American collector! Lemme see your Le Parcs!"

John polished his granny glasses, "I'm a little English art dealer," he said. "And the Le Parcs are all downstairs." The American bought the biggest that we had. It was only later that we found out that the price list given us by Le Parc was a joke. He had not expected us to sell anything – to him it was just a friendly, sympathetic bohemian estab-lishment - and had put random prices down, ranging from ten pounds to thousands. John quickly contacted Le Parc's Parisian gallerist Denise René for a more accurate list and renegotiated with the Big American Collector.

The GRAV show was very popular and received a lot of press: it was more like a fair-ground sideshow than a conventional art show.

One of Julio's pieces was Passage Accidenté, a set of eight square black wooden boxes, about ten inches deep, arranged like large stepping stones outside the gallery. Each had a projecting piece of wood on the bottom, like the keel of a boat, to make it unstable so that they tipped and moved as you walked over them. Children loved them, and quite a few adults enjoyed playing on them too. One lunchtime we set off for the café to find that they had disappeared - the dustmen had assumed they were rubbish and thrown them on the back of their cart. John ran to the phone but by the time we located them they were on a refuse barge heading down the Thames.

The London evening papers had a wonderful time reporting how works by that year's Biennial winner had been mistaken for rubbish. Fortunately Julio found it amusing.

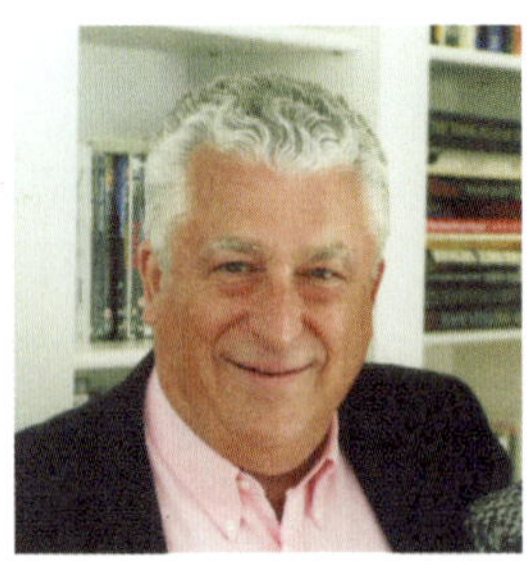

The Urge to Hedonism is a Good Urge

by Alex Wengraf

Alex Wengraf has retired from life as an art dealer specialising in Old Master Paintings. He believes that when you destroy young people's ability to take pleasure in beauty, you are a pervert. He is a sceptic who cannot believe, even though he has seen. He does look at Contemporary Art, pointing out that to state one argument is not necessarily to be deaf to another; that because a man has written a book about Montenegro, is no reason why he should not go to Richmond.

PURITANISM IS DEFINED AS the nasty feeling that someone somewhere is having a good time. The vice of Puritanism is hypocrisy and its artistic expression is minimalism: "Less is More". Puritanism may be understood as mental anorexia, or as conceptual art (all art is conceptual first), and the more fundamentalist the practitioner, the more vacuous it gets. Puritanism likes to parade as purity.

Hedonism is its opposite – hedonism is fat, and full, fun, nutritious and deeply sensual. Think of tactile values, being enveloped in the velvet of rich Venetian colours. Think of a Bach Chorale, or a Beethoven Symphony, of fresh ground coffee and new mown grass. Think of eating foie gras to the sound of trumpets, of oysters with Guinness, Champagne and Madonna.

The urge to Puritanism, which I would call the flight from the senses, seems to exist as a minority (sometimes a large minority) in all cultures from Hindu ascetism, to Islamic and Southern Baptist fundamentalism. There are indeed fine Calvinist Dutch landscapes consisting only of grey sky with flat landscape and not so much as a tree, and there are still lifes of a single empty water jug or of one wild strawberry; and there are portraits of people with grave faces, dressed in black. There are paintings of a single featureless, textureless colour, which are all highly regarded as fine works.

But sticking to Old Master paintings the opposite is more common, and speaks more to my heart. The colours of gold and lapis lazuli in a Simone Martini altarpiece, and the sweet faces in Fra Angelico in Florence and Stefan Lochner in Cologne, the richness of Titian, swirling flesh and fruit and vegetation in Rubens, embroidered velvet cloth in Largillière, and great swathes in Van Dyck, and the touchy-feely bloom on the peaches of a Chardin, these speak of the pleasures of material existence, juice and sweetness of life, wealth of spirit and self confidence in the body. The landscapes of trees and houses, palaces and cottages, flowers in gardens, flowers whose scientific names end in grandiflora, globulosa, magnificans; flowers in elaborate silver vases on groaning sideboards. Peasants and soldiers carousing, aristocrats in fine clothes, the glory of God, if you will, and the delight of mankind.

The vice of hedonism is idolatry, where the object, sculpture or painting comes to be admired more than what is represented. In our secular times this is called aesthetics. But some very minimalist art can fall into that trap too – they shush you up in museums where you are now required to worship, to go round with a silent admiring reverence. And this is very odd because at the same time in churches they sing and clap and dance.

Better, surely, to have concerts in the museum and dance and shout and laugh and live the art: enjoy it and mock it too if necessary. If it is good enough, it can take it. Admire the nude lady for her sexy body and the nude man for his virile strength. Whatever turns you on, Baby. Art, not for art's sake, but for your own sake; for pleasure and understanding and consuming human emotions. Nothing wrong with admiring the way it's made as well, the painterly technique – but if you do not enjoy it first you won't put in the work needed to understand the culture and artisan skill and facture that produced it.

In his memoirs, the former director of the National Gallery Kenneth Clarke says that paintings and women have given him most pleasure in life. It is not by chance that most connoisseurs are fond of great wines, smoke (fewer these days) Havana cigars, dress well, go to the opera and surround themselves with fine things and go to fine restaurants. Wine, women and song. This is not just a question of money, as it is equally true of poorer people. Everyone can enjoy a feast, and have a party. I would advise not to trust an art 'expert', rich or poor, who does not like his food; and the word 'good taste' is not an accident of the language. It all goes together. It is the ancient antagonism of Apollo and Dionysus. Puritanism and minimalism are all in the mind, in the clear light of the sun god Apollo. Leave that to science. Hedonism is the joy of the body, the dance, the rapture of Bacchus/Dionysus. Fill the golden chalice with ruby wine, roll the drum, and surround me with rich colours, tapestries, with human warmth and joy.

Yes, there is also evil out there in the world. But these rich paintings can represent that too, the flesh suffering and the mind in anguish. Look at Grünewald's Isenheim Altarpiece in Colmar. So there can be a hedonism of grief too, but those minimalist paintings are in denial, suffering silently. I would rather have joy and suffering out in the open than internalised and introverted.

If you want to keep it to yourself, remain silent (to paraphrase Wittgenstein).

The painted picture of your silence is still silent.

Please pass the port.

ECONOMICS AND EXHIBITIONISM

By Susanne Oberbeck

Susanne Oberbeck is a musician and vocalist in the band
No Bra.

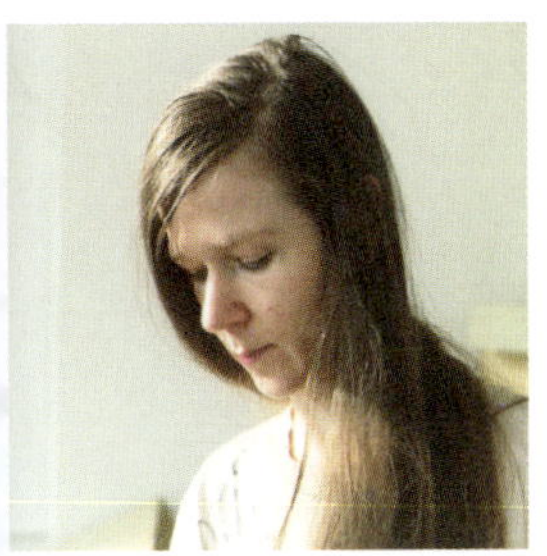

© Wolfgang Tillmans,
Susanne, No Bra 2006

EVERY TIME YOU SEE A PAIR OF TITS, SOMEONE IS MAKING MONEY, BE IT A FRACTION OF A PENNY OFF THE SALE OF A TITS MAGAZINE. WHICH IS NOT TO BE SNIFFED AT BECAUSE THOSE PENNIES ADD UP.

EXCEPT FOR THOSE CRAZY OVERSEXED FEMALE FLASHERS YOU SEE EVERYWERE NOWADAYS, SHAMELESSLY THROWING THEIR CHEAP, SLEAZY SEXUALITY AT YOU.

YOU CAN'T OWN SOUND NOR CAN YOU OWN AN EXPERIENCE, LOVE, LUST OR ANY OTHER EMOTION, AT LEAST NOT IN ANY PHYSICALLY MANIFEST WAY. THESE ARE INTANGIBLE AND THEY DON'T HOLD YOU DOWN.

IT'S EASY TO SEE HOW PRIESTS WERE ELEMENTAL IN ESTABLISHING THE IDEA OF AN INFLATED VALUE, SO TYPICAL OF THE ART MARKET TODAY. TO MAKE SOMETHING UNAVAILABLE, OR SEEM UNAVAILABLE INCREASES ITS DESIRABILITY AND VALUE. MORALITY OR AN UNDERLYING IDEA OF IT IS ESSENTIAL FOR CAPITALISM TO FUNCTION.

NEW YORK IS ONE OF THE FEW U.S. STATES WHERE IT'S LEGAL FOR A FEMALE TO WALK DOWN THE STREET TOPLESS, THOUGH IT'S RARELY DONE. PEOPLE ARE TOO JADED TO GIVE A FUCK, THERE'S ENOUGH/NOT ENOUGH SEX AROUND AND ENOUGH DRUGS TO CURB/NOT CURB YOUR INTEREST IN SEX. THAT'S THE IDEA ANYWAY.

IN SUCH AN AREA OF EXTREME HYPER-CAPITALISM, SOME FORM OF FREEDOM OF EXPRESSION OR OTHERWISE SEEMS POSSIBLE THAT FALLS OUTSIDE OF THE GENERAL CULTURAL AND SOCIETAL NORMS. HISTORIC EXAMPLES LIKE THE SUBVERSIVE CAMP OF FILMS PRODUCED BY THE FACTORY AND PAUL MORRISSEY, EVEN YOUR AVERAGE QUEEN MINCING DOWN THE STREET, OR EARLY HIP HOP AND GRAFFITI CULTURE AND ITS SUBVERSION OF LANGUAGE, INDICATED A COLLAPSE OF LAWS, EVEN THOUGH PEOPLE SEEMED MORE INTERESTED IN MAINTAINING A HEDONISTIC LIFESTYLE AND ACQUIRING THE SAME PRIVILEGES THE ESTABLISHMENT HAD, BY CREATING A KIND OF SUBVERSIVE, YET CLEARLY VISIBLE PARALLEL UNIVERSE.

YOU CAN'T ARGUE WITH POWER AND IT WOULD GET BORING ANYWAY.

BOTH MOVEMENTS ALSO MADE A MOCKERY OF THE PERSONALITY CULT TYPICAL OF 20TH CENTURY AMERICAN CULTURE, VIA THE IDEA THAT ANYONE FABULOUS ENOUGH COULD BE FAMOUS FOR DOING NOT VERY MUCH, OR ANYONE WITH A SPRAY CAN, BALLS AND SOME STYLE COULD MAKE THEIR MARK AROUND TOWN, YET REMAIN ANONYMOUS.

VARIATIONS OF BOTH MOVEMENTS HAVE SINCE BEEN WATERED DOWN INTO MAINSTREAM CULTURE, REDUCED TO THE SENSIBILITY OF THE SAME KIND OF HOUSEWIFE THAT INITIALLY INSPIRED IT, OR USED TO HAMMER HOME NON-THREATENING MESSAGES ABOUT EQUALITY ETC, OR SIMPLY AS DECORUM. BEING FAMOUS FOR DOING NOTHING HAS NOW BECOME A MAINSTREAM OBSESSION THAT DIDN'T GET THE JOKE.

WHAT WAS A RESPONSE TO AN OPPRESSIVE OR BORING SOCIETY, HAS BEEN REDUCED TO LIFE STYLE REFERENCES THAT ARE LACKING THE CORE OF THE INITIAL IDEA: TO BE FREE AND BE ABLE TO EXPRESS ONESELF. A REHASH CULTURE MERELY REPRESENTS THE IDEA OF SELF EXPRESSION, AND SEEMS TO BE CATERING TO PEOPLE'S NARCISSISSM RATHER THAN SOME SENSE OF INVENTION, FREEDOM OR COMMUNITY.

ONLY WHEN YOU HAVE YOUR PICTURE TAKEN DO YOU REALLY LIVE. YET THE NEED TO BE DOCUMENTED SUCKS THE LIFE OUT OF ANY PARTY.

IT'S THIS KIND OF VOLUNTARY OBJECTIFICATION, CHARACTERISTIC OF CAPITALISM, THAT IS NOW APPARENTLY BEING SOLD AS COUNTER CULTURAL FREEDOM OF EXPRESSION.

WE LIVE IN AN OPPRESSIVE SOCIETY BUT IT'S NOT THE SAME KIND OF OPPRESSION PEOPLE WERE RESPONDING TO IN THE 80S OR 60S, HENCE IT'S NOT SUBVERSIVE TO COPY WHAT PEOPLE WERE DOING THEN. MAYBE THIS TYPE OF NEED FOR SELF EXPRESSION HAS IMPOVERISHED PEOPLE'S LIVES THROUGH IMAGE OBSESSION, NARCISISSM AND PERSONALITY CULT.

PRESUMING A LOT OF ARTISTS MAKE ART BECAUSE THEY FIND THEIR OWN SITUATION BORING OR UNLIVABLE, OR FIND IT IMPOSSIBLE TO EXPRESS THEMSELVES ADEQUATELY IN REAL LIFE, AND WANT TO SOMEHOW CREATE A WAY OUT, OR A VISION FOR SOMETHING BETTER.

IT'S NOW THE IDEA OF FREEDOM, PHANTASY OF THE REBEL OUTLAW, SEX ICON, DRUG ADDICT ETC. THAT PEOPLE CAN MARVEL AT OR ANALYZE, COLLECTORS CAN BUY. LIKE ANY FORM OF CONSUMPTION, THIS CONTRIBUTES TO PEOPLE'S ACCEPTANCE OF LIVING IN A NORMATIVE, REPRESSIVE SOCIETY. ORDINARY LIFE HAS BECOME SO BORING THAT EVERYONE IS LOOKING TOWARDS CELEBRITIES.

ANY ART THAT DEALS WITH SEXUALITY COULD BE HUGELY SUBVERSIVE OF A NORMATIVE HETEROSEXUAL SOCIETY, AND THAT INCLUDES A LOT OF ROCK'N'ROLL, YET THE MINUTE IT IS BEING MARKETED OR EVEN PLACED IN ANY KIND OF RIGHTEOUS POLITICAL CONTEXT, A LOT OF ITS SUBVERSIVE POWER IS TAKEN AWAY. EVEN TO REVIEW OR ANALYZE ART OR MUSIC ULTIMATELY TAKES AWAY THE MAGIC AND PUTS IT IN SOME KIND OF SAFE RELATION TO WHAT IS CONSIDERED NORMAL.

ART SHOULD TALK ABOUT WHAT IT WANTS RATHER THAN WHAT IT IS. TO WANT SOMETHING DOESN'T TELL YOU ANYTHING ABOUT WHO OR WHAT YOU ARE, EVEN THOUGH PEOPLE LIKE TO THINK IT DOES.

THE IDEA OF SUBVERSIVENESS IS BEING SOLD, BUT IT'S NOT ACTUALLY SUBVERSIVE. THEREFORE ART SHOULD NOT BE A REPRESENATION OF AN IDEA BUT THE REAL THING.

"REAL ART HAS THE CAPACITY TO MAKE US NERVOUS. BY REDUCING THE WORK OF ART TO ITS CONTENT AND THEN INTERPRETING THAT, ONE TAMES THE WORK OF ART. INTERPRETATION MAKES ART MANAGEABLE, COMFORTABLE." – SUSAN SONTAG

ART SHOULD WIN PEOPLE OVER BY BEING POETIC AND NOT POLITICAL IT SHOULD NOT BE ABOUT JUDGEMENT, INTERPRETATION OR VALUE BUT ABOUT EXPERIENCE, AND PEOPLE SHOULD NOT BE ABLE TO PUT THEIR FINGER ON IT THAT EASILY. ARTISTS SHOULD SUBVERT THE CODES WITH WHICH ART IS BEING READ RATHER THAN USING THEM TO FIT INTO SOME KIND OF LIFESTYLE COMMERCIAL MODEL OR IDENTITY POLITICS, WHICH ESSENTIALLY KEEPS EVERYTHING IN PLACE.

ART SHOULD MAKE PEOPLE NERVOUS, NOT BECAUSE IT IS TRYING TO MAKE A POINT ABOUT SOMETHING BUT BECAUSE WE LIVE FOR THRILLS.

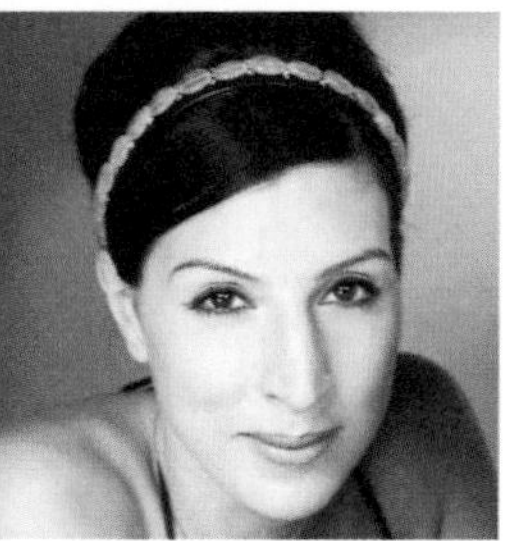

The Emperor's New Clothes: The Karma of Insincere Buying, or Why Crap Floats

by Medeia Cohan-Petrolino

Medeia Cohan-Petrolino is the Head Curator for the University of the Arts London where she runs the unique Emerging Artist Programme, which supports over 200 alumni artists per year. She curates a variety of exhibitions for the University Arts Gallery, manages the University's 600 piece collection, advises some of the UK's top collectors through the Artist and Collectors Exchange, and runs the annual best of degree show exhibition, Future Map.

AT ANY LEVEL IN THE ART WORLD, from emerging artist to established artist, the balance of genius versus drivel weighs heavily in favour of the latter, but rarely does this dictate which artists will be fought over by gallerists and which works will end up in the homes of top collectors. How come the crap wins out?

There are a number of reasons: 1. The art world is subjective and unpredictable. 2. Good PR can facilitate the success of even the most prosaic artist and, 3. Just about everyone is after the next hot young thing (rather than the thing they love) and therefore prone to cover all bases by spread- or copy buying.

A top collector will see a lot of work, and is in a good position to make decisions about what works to buy, sometimes based on personal taste (which is completely subjective) and other times as an investment (which is about numbers rather than taste). In his or her slipstream will come copy buyers and amateur collectors who create a certain amount of hype or even a frenzy around an artist who may have done very little to warrant such attention.

The old adage of the Emperor's New Clothes (or in this instance the Collector's New Painting) is surely apposite here. If you remember the Hans Christian Andersen tale, the Emperor (Collector) hires two tailors (we'll call them art consultants or gallerists) to create new robes for him - (replace robes with painting and our analogy is underway).

These consultants convince the Collector that they will commission the most unbelievable painting ever painted, made from rare materials, and speaking of artistic depths that will appear invisible to those who are unworthy or ignorant. Our blustering Collector himself is banned from seeing a preview of the painting but in an effort to appear superior and erudite, goes along with the sham and invites all of his art world peers to an unveiling of the work. When the work is presented it appears to be a blank wall, but the Collector, in an effort to prove his intelligence pretends he sees a masterpiece. A child in the crowd acknowledges the complete absence of the painting and everyone laughs at the Collector, who is completely mortified.

While this is a fantastical scenario the point rings true. Gallerists in conjunction with PR wizards often spin a conceptual story that is so dizzying, that buyers often feel compelled to purchase the work, if only to save face. While they may not understand or enjoy the work, they have been convinced of its value, and their own arrogance or insecurity won't allow them to walk away from this 'once in a lifetime' opportunity.

In 2008 I discovered a painter whose talent was immediately apparent. I contacted several of the collectors whom I advise and suggested that they view her work and consider adding her to their collections. I had a very strong feeling about her, but no one acted upon my recommendation at the time.

Taking my own advice, I commissioned her to make a new work for me for a steal. Soon after that, Charles Saatchi bought a series of three large works, and at the end of that same year I showed her work in a group exhibition where another well-known collector purchased a piece, thus sparking an almighty buzz around the artist.

Those same collectors who initially passed on the opportunity to buy were now begging to put their name on a waiting list, happy to pay ten times what I had paid just a year before.

The lesson here is that the endorsement of major collectors leading to a massive rise in prices are often the determining factors around which artists succeed, and conversely, around which bright new prodigies are deemed obsolete.

There are of course still people out there who buy work purely for the love of the piece, who are not influenced by the hype around an artist or the status associated with owning the work. Alas, the unparalleled increase of new art collectors over the past decade means that these mavericks are few and far between.

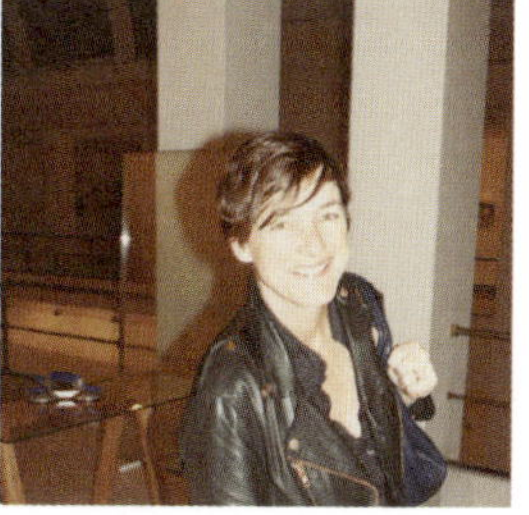
© Juergen Teller

Awesome Creatures
by Sadie Coles

Sadie Coles opened Sadie Coles HQ in 1997, after six years at Anthony d'Offay where she presented a new programme of younger artists. Early exhibitions at SCHQ included John Currin, Sarah Lucas, Gregor Schneider, Elizabeth Peyton, and Richard Prince. The gallery has continued to exhibit in temporary spaces across London to suit specific projects.

I'VE BEEN IN THIS for twenty years now. An innocent from Arnolfini joining the mighty d'Offay Gallery in 1990 completely unaware that crossing from public to commercial was so loaded.

The world opened up by such huge degrees for me, d'Offay gave me and others an inspiring education, and he always responded to contemporary art as a Holy Grail: elusive, vital, magic, above ordinary value. ·

I don't feel different about what excites me - it is the artists. They are awesome creatures to hold in high regard. I am star-struck by their ideas and their ability to communicate and invent. How do they do it and why is it so stimulating, fascinating, engaging, courageous?

Even the failures are beautiful.

I used to have a reputation for partying late into the night but actually I was mostly listening, trying to understand new ideas, desires, developments and working out ways to collaborate, assist, adapt. It was a time when an extraordinary bunch of characters with big ideas and ambitions collided and the whole world seemed receptive to the energy of youth.

I still love the late night rant of ambitious ideas and possibilities and this is the same now as it was then. These people are making our culture for God's sake. They are heroes.

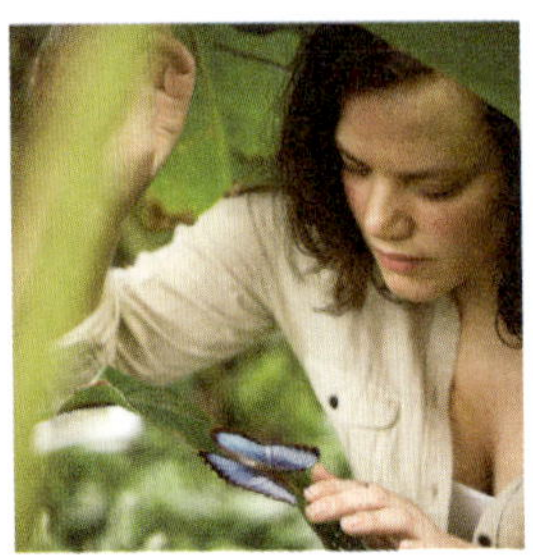

Be Careful How You Pronounce it: When Etymology & Entomology Collide

by Bridget Nicholls

Bridget Nicholls is the founder/director of Pestival, a festival dedicated to 'Insects in the arts and the art of being an insect'. She recently won the Observer Ethical Awards 2010 in the conservation category and was also awarded the first Zoo Art Fellowship of the Zoological Society of London. Brought up on an animal rescue sanctuary in Sussex, activities such as feeding Bengal eagle owls, finding peacocks in the bed and untangling frog-mating pile-ups were just part of a normal day.

I WAS AT THE Venice Biennale, ostensibly to meet one of the Pestival artists Noboru Tsubaki (more of him later) but also to promote Pestival to the art world and make a radio show for Resonance FM with the artist Bob and Roberta Smith.

One night after an opening for Jan Fabre (Belgian insect artist and great grandson of Henri Fabre - the godfather of modern entomology), I met an intense but knowledgeable Spanish artist. We really clicked and she seemed to love the whole Pestival concept.

We talked for what seemed like hours locking minds on this crazy idea to make a whole festival of insects in art. Just as we were reaching for our pens to exchange contact details she said…."I'm just so proud you took this bold step to see *incest* as something to celebrate rather than squash and shun and see as dirty". This is when I realised that art and science can be interesting bedfellows, even if the crossover is sometimes a bit disturbing.

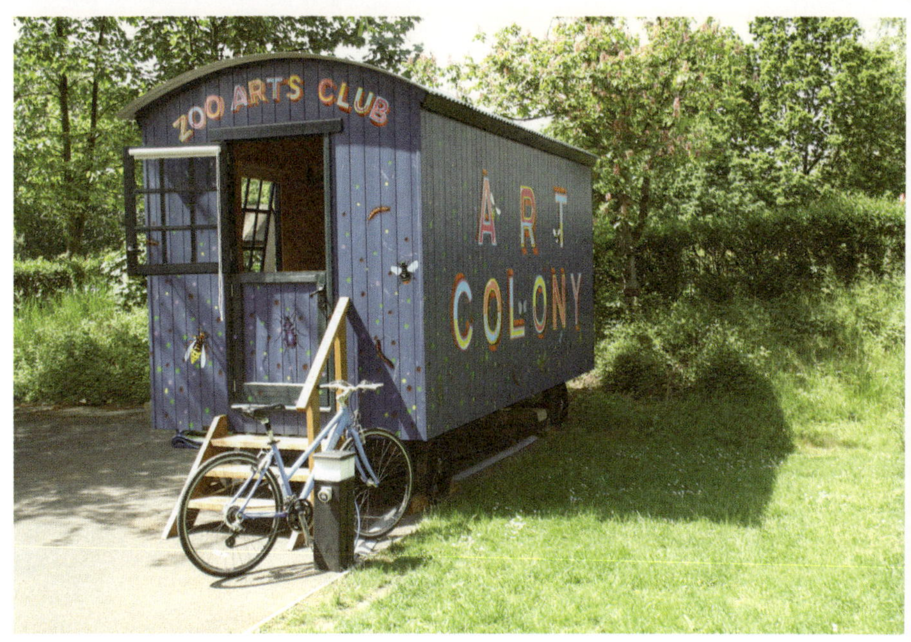

The Bob and Roberta Smith painted Art Colony new office at London Zoo. Bridget Nicholls

But, to the real work in hand: as long as you are singing from the same hymn sheet, artists can make expressive comments out of hard scientific data. They can create a different emotive understanding of the world around them than science can present. With this and the key point - that we wouldn't be here without insects – in mind, Pestival took over my life. (I also hoped to help create a cultural shift in the way people perceive their place in the ecosystem through understanding their relationship with insects.)

I would never have thought, in 300 million years - the same amount of time that insects have been around - that I would end up dedicating six years of my life to putting on an international art festival about insects. But then I caught the bug. (Sorry, couldn't help that one.)

It started in 2004 when I went to a rustic insect film festival in the Pyrenees. The whole village turned up in the local square dressed as insects – it was magical and spellbinding, utterly shabby and totally surreal, like a David Lynch movie. Everyone present seemed to think their behaviour was normal. Pestival was hatched then and there in the mountains, and when I finally came back to sea level, I knew that London needed one of these experiences too.

The first Pestival happened at the London Wetland Centre with Tessa Farmer, Paul Fryer and John Keane involved as artists. That was also the year Pestival nearly got me arrested. The American musician David Rothenberg was booked to perform a duet with a rash of south-west Australian crickets, on the bill with the musician Robyn Hitchcock and the comedian Stewart Lee. I said to David that – because I didn't have the money to put him up for the first day – he could stay in the flat beneath me to give him time to sort out his accommodation. The flat had been empty for six months…. but the owners just so happened to come home that night to a selection of insect-loving musician squatters throwing an impromptu party. On the first day of Pestival #1, while saving Tessa Farmer's entire dead-insect piece from being eaten by a Hawaiian goose on the loose, I also had to sweet-talk the police who were there to interview me about the squatters. "Wait, so insects have *what* exactly to do with the break-in madam?" Charges were dropped.

That brings us to the second Pestival at Southbank Centre. How did we turn it into a 21-acre insect utopia? And how did we persuade people to fund such an idea?

Our first vote of confidence came from the Bioscience Foundation The Wellcome Trust. We got through to the second round for their Large Arts Award and then had to pitch our idea. Despite the fact that I had a serious disagreement with our scientist during the pitch ...he said that insects were categorically not biomedical or artistic (the funding remit) and I of course had to point out how Sniffer bees and bioleaching were both directly biomedical *and* artistic. We still got the award. With the Wellcome behind us, other funders quickly followed.

We also had to get the metaphor of our Japanese artist-in-residence Noboru Tsubaki's piece - Michael Jackson as a Vegetable Wasp - across to the audience whilst grappling with the Japanese to English translation of the piece ourselves.

We decided to bring book art to the festival. One piece was a collaboration between Mark Cockram's Studio 5, the Forensic Entomology department at the Natural History Museum and the Hide Bugs that clean the new bones of the Natural History Museum collection. Instead of making books to be savoured, Mark turned his hand to books to be devoured. He went about dipping each page in Marmite in preparation for the sacrifice. The only problem was that the Hide Bugs didn't like Marmite…and with a week to go the books had to be remade and dipped in Bovril…Who would have known that Hide Bugs prefer Bovril?

Insects. You never know what they're really thinking.

Trying to do health and safety risk assessments for insects is also interesting. How do you get around the fact that flies are allowed on the premises but maggots are not so welcome? Well you get out a life cycle chart and show that maggots *become* flies, so must surely be allowed in too.

And now here I am at the Zoo…the first Zoo Arts Fellow and I'm working out of Bob and Roberta Smith's especially painted shepherd's hut. Doesn't get much better. As artists in residence for the next three years, we will be building a laboratory of art and conservation using cutting edge research and technology.

I'm right next to the Snowdon Aviary and over the canal from the hunting dogs, so the background noise of *my* particular workplace is the sound of the dogs ripping the flesh of their carrion dinner apart, lightened a jot by the lyrical song of the somewhat luckier exotic birds.

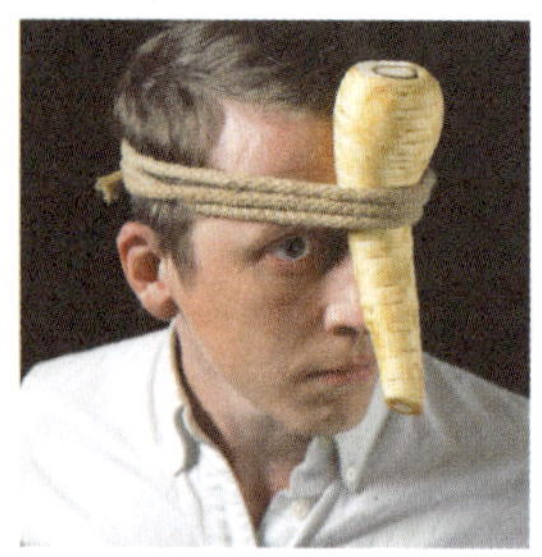

The Crazies? – The Wilder Shores of Performance Art

by Racky - aka Richard La Rue

© Adam Laycock

Racky is a performance artist living and working in London. Wolfgang Tillmans recently called him one of the 'heroes of the underground'. His main inspiration is the work of William S Burroughs and the work of his own friends and associates. He has collaborated with artists such as Richard Torry, Genesis P Orridge, No Bra, Mathew Glammore and Selfish Cunt whilst maintaining his own strong artistic vision of transforming the mundane.

IT IS BETTER TO LIVE your life by aesthetic reasoning than moral opinion.

Aesthetic reasoning proves that culture and society are banal, restrictive, un-ambitious, hypocritical, stifling, self-loathing and repetitious. Most morality, laws, and psychological techniques are pointless, arbitrary, self-serving and designed to provoke the precise lawbreaking that they are pretending to restrain, punish, correct and/or cure.

There is no point being simply an artist. Art must be viewed as merely the medium through which aesthetic change in society and culture can be affected.

Decorative art or that which is only beautiful must be destroyed or abandoned.

So must irony.

How does this relate to you and I and Performance/Art?

At the height of his fame Jim Morrison, mocked his tame audience's idolatry by pulling out his penis at a concert in Miami, U.S.A. Or did he? Nobody is sure, but the mere idea that he may have, effectively destroyed The Doors' live career.

This is worth considering, perhaps celebrating.

Was it too high a price to pay?

Not for a genuine rebel leader.

To understand society you must separate yourself from it. Be in it but not of it. This can be done in the same way that transcendent states of mind can be achieved. For instance, like Aleister Crowley, you could eat excrement. Very few people admit to eating excrement. If you were to do this and admit to it you would have instantly separated yourself from mainstream culture/society. You could in fact be said to have transcended it.

By performing an unusual act you have achieved an unusual state of mind, thus attaining an unusual perspective.

Once separate from society you are able to study reactions to yourself and your behaviour. From this observation you can understand the formulas that keep culture/society/the world recreating the same prosaic behaviours over again like a trained monkey or robot dog.

In the mainstream it is only the sciences that treat the excreta, essences and orifices of the body with any respect. In the family home and at work, piss and shit are flushed quickly away. Referred to only in jest unless they are pertaining to an illness like an upset stomach or some such.

A bloody wound is washed and covered with a plaster. To stare at a wound is considered morbid.

Visions of assholes, urethras, tumescence and labia are kept between the covers of magazines hidden under beds, bookmarked on search engines or depicted with cold detachment between dull paragraphs of medical text. Thus their study is reduced to furtive fumbling or intellectual infantilism.

The body becomes a plain mental cue by its repeated use as an exclamation mark to emphasise the effectiveness of yet another unnecessary 'health' or 'beauty' product.

This is tedious and yet it does expose the fact that the body is the first unit of consumerism.

Thus whatever your politics, it is clear and urgent that the body and its secretions should be placed on slides, lifted onto pedestals and exposed on alters to proper scrutiny by the masses of all ages without the shields and weapons of comedy and commerce.

Morality of course must be mocked, like a naughty but loved child.

Coum Transmissions, Taffy (Female Trouble), Franko B, Ron Athey, Marina Abramovic, GG Allin, Minty, No Bra and Selfish Cunt are just some of the main artists who have, in recent history, effulgently investigated the body and the symptoms of existence which it effuses.

Shitting, stripping, cutting, fucking, Sufism, Tantra and or personalised abstriction performed in broad daylight in the everyday world (which IS the proper home for art) will result in the restraining of that behaviour by either imprisonment or sectioning. So, in a culture/society where the body etc is effectively imprisoned or outlawed, the real artist *must* recognise that he/she is part criminal. (The people on the list above, for the most part understand this.)

But to operate effectively you need your freedom or most of it (unless you seek martyrdom, which can be effective for you and your aim of transforming society as long as it is as inspired or well thought out as a bank heist). Therefore you must accept the imperfect art world with all its insane invisible codes and rules of acceptable behaviour.

Oh what a bore!

Perhaps learn that grimmest of the assassins' arts, subtlety?

Due to its provocative nature it is unlikely that you will make a lot of money from your Performance/Art until you are very well known.

But you must survive!

Thus you must work (sexy dancer, drug dealer, prostitute), screw the system (claim sickness benefit whilst being entirely able to work?) or sell!

Sell artefacts from your performance, bloody tissues or stained toilet paper, or recordings of said show.

Sell your thoughts.

Sell lies.

Sell your smile.

Sell everything you own which has served its purpose; books, records, clothes etc. If you find yourself selling your body, have no qualms, for this is what everybody is doing in one way or another every minute of every day and, in the words of Lady Jaye (Genesis P-Orridge's dear departed wife and collaborator), 'The body is just a suitcase.' And like all baggage that we accumulate through life, purely a means to an end.

That end is, simply, a new, artless, Atlantis.

"There must be great golden copulations in the street."- Jim Morrison.

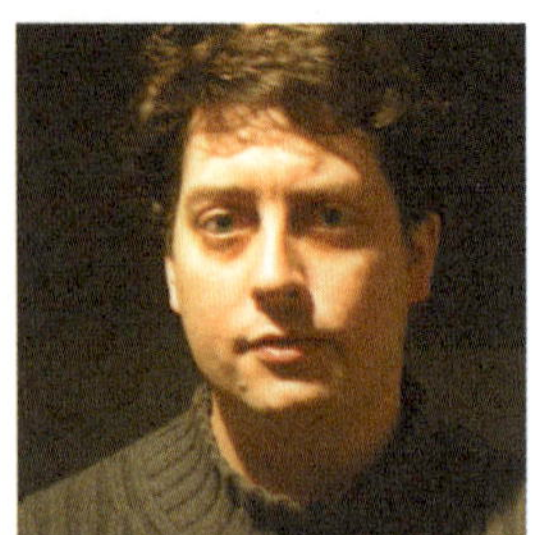

I Don't Know What I Like

by Sam Leith

Sam Leith is a freelance writer living in North London. His columns appear fortnightly in the Guardian, and weekly in the Evening Standard. His first novel, The Coincidence Engine, comes out from Bloomsbury in Spring 2011. His first child, Marlene, came out from Alice in Summer 2009. He is currently working on a book about rhetoric for Profile. The rest of it is none of our business.

"I DON'T KNOW MUCH ABOUT ART, but I know what I like." That's the cliché, isn't it? That's the sort of thing that you expect a closed-minded, uncultured numpty – what my younger brother used to refer to as "a complete Palestine" – to say when confronted with a Rothko chapel, or a Duchamp urinal, or a close-up photograph of La Cicciolina's foo-foo from Jeff Koons's back catalogue.

That's even what the Pope says in the Monty Python sketch when demanding that Michelangelo paint him "a last supper with one Christ, twelve disciples, no kangaroos, no trampoline acts, by Thursday lunch, or you don't get paid".

But hang on. That's not necessarily such a philistine thing to say. Knowing a lot about art – and tethering that to your appreciation – is one thing; but ever since the arrival of conceptual art, an informed admiration of technique has rather taken a back seat among the appreciative skills. Knowing much about art can easily put you in the position not of having a better-informed taste; but of being better informed about what you're supposed to like.

I have the exact opposite problem, and one that I suspect of actually being far more widespread: that of knowing a bit about art but having no idea what I like. This, I say with no small measure of dismay, is the position of the true philistine.

For the art geek seeking philistines to sneer at, the safest bet is someone who "doesn't know much about art" – because that's a measurable quantity. And the *cognoscenti* have persuaded each other to lap up a good deal of bilge over the years, in the interests of having something to agree on. If you're terrified of being found out, "knowing much about art" is your comfort blanket.

But many great artists don't think that way. Look at Andy Warhol, who before taking up Basquiat, declared: "I like the druggy downtown kids who spray-paint walls and trains. I like their lack of training, their primitive technique." Actually, he didn't technically say that. But Lou Reed and John Cale have him saying it on Songs for Drella, and they were there at the time so he clearly said something a bit like it.

So away with the cliché.

Coming back to me, I do know a bit about art. Not a lot. Actually, not a lot at all. Practically bugger all, in fact. But I can tell an Impressionist from a Vorticist, given a few minutes and a crib sheet. (The Impressionist drinks more and the Vorticist *sieg heils* every now and again. Plus Vorticist paintings are pointy rather than dotty.) I've had every opportunity to learn about art, and I've spent plenty of time wandering around galleries going, hum..., over here, and hem! over there, and sucking in my lips thoughtfully at the works of minor Flemish masters.

Like any fool, I can be taught to admire the artistry in Vermeer's use of light, and recognise that brushwork wasn't Magritte's strong point. I can admire the wit of a conceptual piece. But develop strong feelings towards one painting rather than another one? Feh. It happens, but pretty seldom. My chief concern in buying art would be that the colours would clash with the carpet or that Tilda Swinton would wake up at an inconvenient time and disrupt my dinner party.

I have much the same problem choosing ties. As more than one person has told me, I have no visual sense whatever. I am tone-blind. This was brought home to me years ago. Wandering around my then-girlfriend's parents' sitting room with her art-dealer younger brother, I was challenged to say which of the paintings on the walls I liked best. I looked about a bit. They all seemed nice enough. So I lit on what seemed to me rather an elegant piece of work.

"That one." This young lad nearly killed himself laughing. Apparently I'd passed over several pieces worth thousands of pounds, and gone straight to a daub that my girlfriend had made when she was in her teens. Well, I liked it. But shee: it's all just stuff to look at, isn't it?

So here's my theory. There is an epidemic of people like me. But they're all keeping schtum... because most of them are in the art world and, thanks to "knowing a lot about art", they are able to get away with it.

CHAPTER 2:
LIFESTYLES OF
THE ARTISTS –
HOMAGE TO VASARI

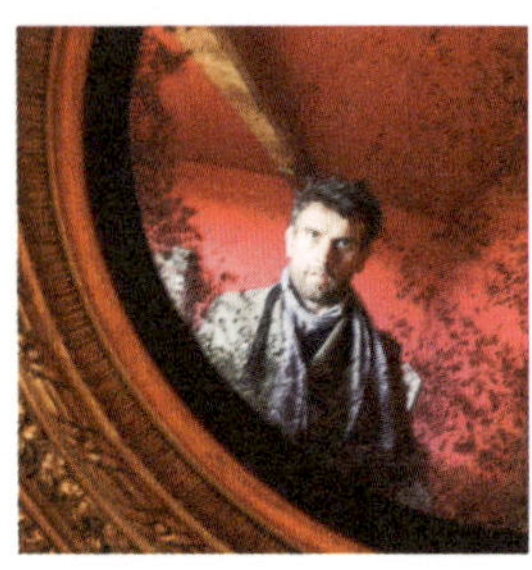

Missing Pole

by Paul Fryer

Paul Fryer remembers a particularly intense artists' holiday in Mexico, after which three of them made the journey back to London in wheelchairs.

I HAD NEVER BEEN to that part of the world before; we drove over the Sierra Madre from the sprawl of Mexico City down to the coast and the paradise of Zihuatanejo. We even stopped for lunch. It was 1998. We were told it was a miracle we weren't kidnapped.

To Troncones, a tiny dusty fishing village with a few trendy bars and a lot of gringos.

We were dropped off at Damien's place - a beautiful villa with its own pool, but not flashy. And it could easily have been so, because Damien could afford it. But it's not his style, or the style of that part of the world. We settled in, as did Damien's German friend Werner. He had run a popular restaurant in Berlin back in the really wild times in the early 90s. We decamped to a local bar and started drinking in earnest. It was early afternoon.

By the time we got to the ultimate bar in the village we were all very drunk. The German had just lost his business partner and friend and was grieving in a low-key, stiff upper lip kind of way. I couldn't resist his pain and attempted to help him abreact. He did, but badly. We ended up shouting, and crying and railing at each other. Damien observed for a while and then bellowed at us both in a terrifyingly loud voice "YOU'RE NOT THE ONLY ONES WHO CAN CRY!" and we all ended up wailing. A family moved out of the bar looking disturbed.

The waitress brought the bottle of Rum we had been drinking to the table without a word.

The next part is a little kaleidoscopic but I remember running down the beach with Damien and the German, screaming, tearing my clothes off. Mexican families looked on as the three crazy naked gringos ran into the sea, leaving a trail of garments behind them. The sea does have a healing capacity, and a sobering one. Suddenly we were restored, (relatively) sober and naked in the sea. In a Catholic country. And it wasn't a

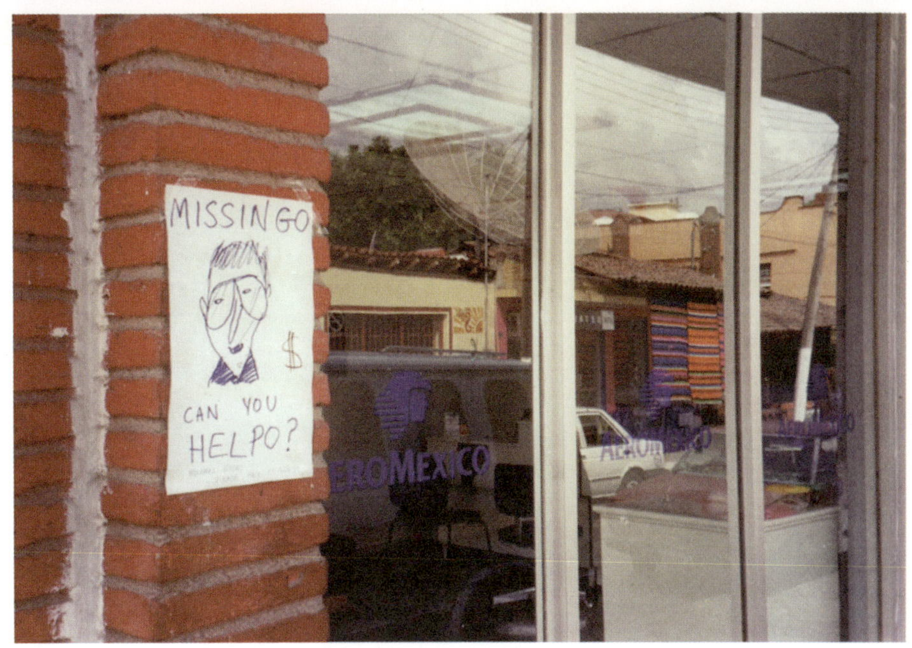

nudist beach. We paraded back up the shore in shame. It was obvious we'd outstayed our welcome at the bar. That was OK. We now had other destinations in mind. Night fell and so did we.

The Arrival of The Pole

The next morning we remembered that the Pole was arriving imminently but he didn't have a mobile phone. Or it wasn't switched on. Me and Damien gave our friend Aaron a squirt from the special Vicks Sinex bottle, a copy of the telephone directory and the instructions: "Find the Pole". He snurfed and asked what was in the bottle. We told him and showed him the source bag, purchased for $500 in the barrio the night before, where we had sat in the van in the dark listening to the murmuring of humans and cicadas in the slums around us, scared and excited to death. "$500 worth. Howd'ya think we did?"

"Well, considering three bullets cost 3 pesos, you did OK."

Aaron hit the phone and pretty soon he was a telecommunicative roboman, calling every hotel in town, looking for The Pole. There were about a hundred of them. Hotels that is, not Poles. There was only ever one of him.

"What we need is posters. An ad campaign." Damien and I got to it: We knocked out pictures of The Pole, faithful in every way to our memory of him. Fly-eye glasses, hair

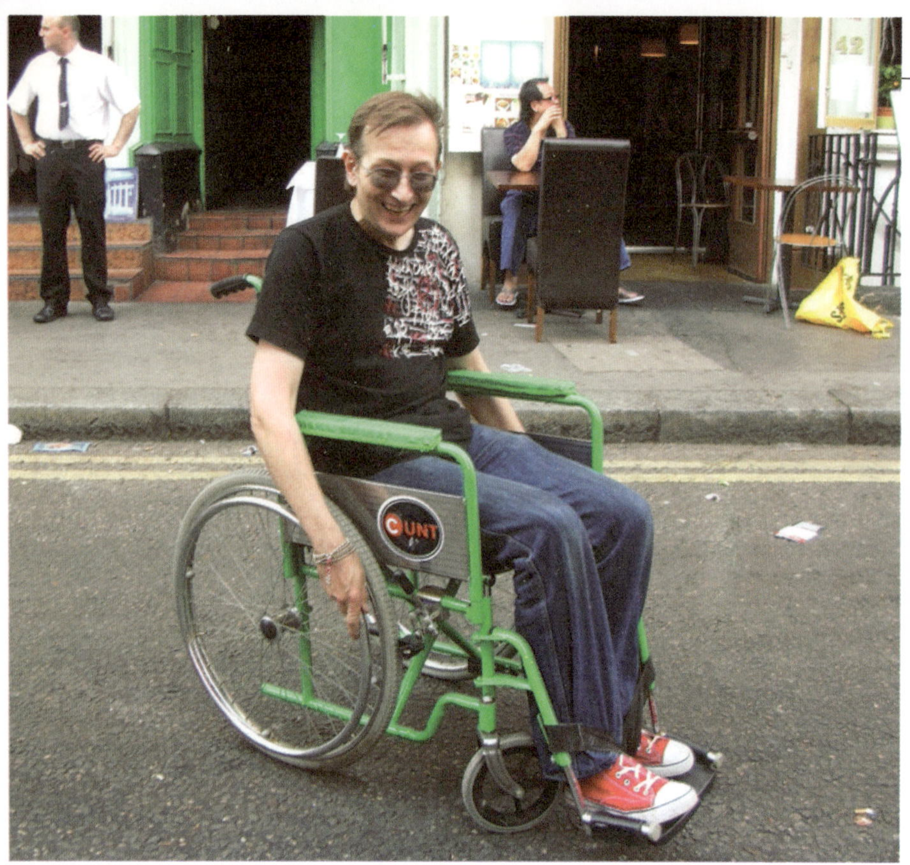

Missing Pole When Back in London. Vanessa Fristedt

in wisps as fine as spider webs, the Soho underground pallor, the crooked scar running down to the thin sardonic lips. Looking left. Looking right. Face on. And the captions "MISSING POLE", "MISSINGO" and "HAVE YOU SEEN THIS MAN?" and finally, just the boiled down headline "POLE".

I imagined the whole town searching their outhouses, standing in ponchos pointing at the posters fastened to every available lamp post and bus shelter and telegraph pole, pole POLE.

Aaron was now on the phone to the local radio station; children ran around the town putting up the mugshots. We waited.

When he finally arrived at the villa there was an excitement which could only manifest itself in more heavy drinking and hell-raising. We danced and sang and railed until the morning and then carried on. Now *el barrio* came to us like a slightly disconcerting pizza delivery service, and we all revelled in the convenient optimism of it all. And on it went. Forever.

Death Disco

Night came and went again, and a kind of determined, stoic perseverance replaced the mania of the previous evening. We went out on the town en masse and came back revitalised. Guitars were played. The madness returned and we started through the labyrinth again.   By the following morning the survivors looked shell shocked. The Pole was a keen card player and was attempting to get a game going. No one could keep up. Everybody went to bed. Everybody, that is, except me and Damien.

Night came and went.

Did I mention it was Christmas? Well, it was, the day before Christmas Eve. "We have to hang the *piñata* for the kids", Damien said, gesturing to a Batman figure made of crepe paper and card. We both looked up at the palm tree rafters, slanting up from a wall about 9 ft high. "I can get up there" I said optimistically. I began to climb. Up the wall from the back of a plastic chair, my fingers gingerly closing on the top of the parapet, grasping the wooden support of the rush matting roof with one hand and balancing backwards, transferring the weight to my arms… and smack. Suddenly I was on my arse on the tiles, 12 feet below.

Even through the anaesthetic haze of the last 48 hours I felt the shock travel through my pelvis and up my spine, a jolting, teeth-rattling impact.

"I'll get a ladder", said Damien.

To this day I don't know what possessed me to go back up. I could see a cross member, about 16 feet up, which, I was sure I could reach…by then I don't think I remembered what it was I was going up there for. I had certainly forgotten that twenty seconds previously I had grabbed a similar beam and been completely unable to keep a hold on it. After some careful balancing my hand clasped the wooden bar in question, and my grip was good. But I was almost upside down now, at an angle greater than 45 degrees, and had not allowed for the merciless pull of gravity. I fell absolutely straight back, my body almost stretched in repose, parallel to the ground. It's amazing how long it takes to drop even a short distance when it's you doing the falling. I knew I would break my back. Resigned, I wondered whether or not I would still be able to walk, or whether I would survive at all. A perplexed sadness washed over me.

There was an explosion. I had impacted a white plastic patio table, so quotidian it had been invisible. Shards of plastic fired in all directions. I lay still on my back on the cold tiles, unable to breathe, the wind completely knocked out of me.

My eyes were closed. I became aware of someone. I opened them to see Damien's eldest looking down at me. I managed what I thought was a friendly smile. It must have looked bad, because the boy turned and ran. I heard him shouting "Mummy, uncle Paul's wearing blood sunglasses…" and I closed them again and waited for the pain which I knew was rushing towards me from a hell nearby. Somebody was telling me not to move.

A few hours later I came round in a wheelchair in the tiny emergency room in Zihuat. My breathing was bad, and every time my lungs inflated two broken ribs clicked audibly on the right side of my body.

Well that was me out of the fray for the remainder of the festive season. I heard that Damien had gone looking for milk up in the village later that morning, wrapped only in a towel. The sun had baked him for half an hour, and the towel had fallen away, leaving him wandering naked and sunstruck around the dusty streets. He had forgotten why he was there by then, but luckily the local doctor had been driving past and recognised the naked loony standing in the middle of the road, picked him up and returned him to the villa.

And on it went. In a haze of powerful pain killers, I was dimly aware of the sounds of New Year's Eve celebrations around me. Suddenly all the lights went out. Someone had fired a pistol into the air and inadvertently shot through a power cable which fell onto the pavement. Another poor sod picked it up and was killed. That was the end of the party, the end of the year and the end of him. Damien gave pretty much everything up after that holiday. And really, who could blame him? Three of us came home in wheelchairs.

I haven't been back to that part of the world for some time. Drug wars and the threat of kidnapping have made it more unsafe than usual to frequent that particular district of paradise. Damien said he'd also decided not to go anymore after some bad men came to the local disco and emptied a bin liner of human heads onto the dance floor. A worrying trend in any holiday destination.

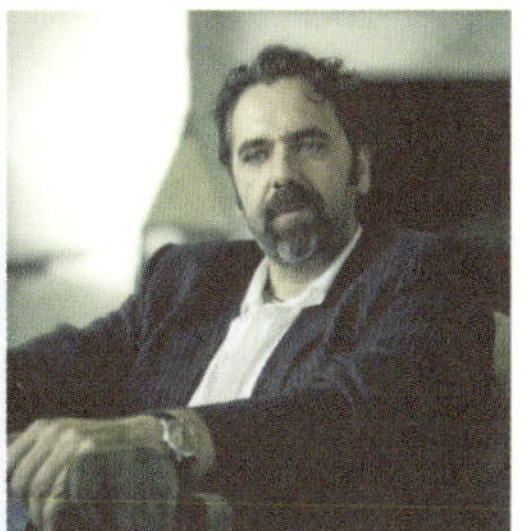

Wynn Casino Invitational

by Keith Tyson

Turner Prize winning artist Keith Tyson is influenced as much by astrophysics and mathematics, as by observation of and reflection on nature. His work presents a unique combination of scientific data with poetic expression. He doesn't mind a bit of a gamble.

IT'S 1.30 A.M IN THE EXCLUSIVE 63rd floor Sky Casino of the Wynn Hotel Las Vegas. I still have a hangover from the evening before and I'm playing in a high-roller poker tournament. Millionaire financiers and poker pros have been getting eliminated one at a time for the last five hours or so.

Johnny Chan (the former World Series of Poker champion) had been at my table earlier, but had gone out to a pair of Aces. The only other pro still in is Tony G who is dominating the other table with a hail of bets and raises…. I had been told by the casino before setting off from England that there were only going to be high stakes table game players (i.e. non-professional poker players) in this free buy-in, million dollar prize tournament. I had thought it was worth the gamble to take the trip. Anyway, I had things to do in Los Angeles so it all had fitted together nicely. So when I see that four pros are in the field I am annoyed with myself for trusting … of all things… a casino's sales pitch.

The lights of Vegas flash and pulsate seductively far below as I pause briefly to assess the situation. I'm short stacked, (meaning I have less than average chips per player), but there are only twelve of the original 86 players still left in the tournament. My "M ratio" (the ratio poker players sometimes use to assess the size of their stack against the cost of paying the blinds and antes on each orbit at the table) is only about six, and the hands are being played at speed. If I make the final table I will need a bigger stack than this if I am to make any money (even more so as Tony G is only barely visible behind *his* fortress of chips).

On my table I'm third to act after the blinds, the first two people fold and I look down at my cards..... The Jack and the Ten of Diamonds. A little weak but a hand with potential. I see the player behind me move his cards to the side as he has throughout the entire evening when he dislikes his hand, so I'm sure he's out. There's only now the small and big blinds to survive and steal. The big blind player is an aggressive Mexican dude with three times my chips and a serious moustache, so my only realistic play here is all-in or fold. Suddenly from some internal Central Processing Unit comes the command - Fuck it....

"I'm all in," I say, and place all 86,000 dollars into the pot without any facial expression, then turn to watch the lights flash below me, knowing that my fate, the cards to come and the Mexican's play are all now beyond my control....

A week later I'm back in Shoreham-by-Sea in my studio looking at a blank canvas, trying to decide where to begin, and thinking back to that Jack-Ten of Diamonds and my strange trip. Being a gambler has cost me considerable time and money over my life so far, I've had some big wins for sure, including a couple of really big casino-hurting wins, but I've also lost too, and if the bottom line was just the bottom line then I guess I would be a loser in strictly financial terms. But one learns many skills dancing with risk every day that have considerable fringe benefits as an artist. The first and most important of which is dealing with one's fear, the fear of making a mistake with an aggressive brush-stroke over your hard won photorealistic painting, of ruining your reputation with some experimental show, or putting all your production bankroll into that insane idea you had in the bath. In short, one's fear of risk.

Gamblers are not fearless despite how they are portrayed. If they were they wouldn't do it. In our antiseptic, anti-bacterial, re-insured society we desperately and ineffectively attempt to reduce risk. But gamblers crave it, they "Dare to decide," as Dostoevsky said.

Taking artistic risks is so much simpler for me because I can clearly define the artistic gamble's added value. This is art's "house-edge" as it were. When you've staked scary money on the chance of a ball falling in to a slot for twenty seconds (an action of limited entertainment value other than a rush of adrenaline), for nothing more than the potential to increase or decrease your "action," then the experience gained and the artistic merit of your artistic wagers becomes much clearer.

They look like bets of incredible value. Casinos will strive to divorce your cash from its utility and turn it into "action". In many ways this is much more honest than our every day capitalist view of cash. Money is symbolic, it's a deferred payment on human value. It doesn't do anything until it moves from one person or institution to another so the question becomes, which action brings the greatest benefits? Benefits either to one's self, to art or to society. The perspective becomes wider. To be happy with risk taking within my art is a benefit that far outweighs any pecuniary costs I have incurred to acquire the attitude.

Now back to that poker tournament… Well, the guy with the tell – (any personal mannerism that reveals the quality of one's hand) - folds as I expected, as does the small blind. The Mexican dude thinks, counts out 86,000 dollars, thinks again for a long time, then shouts "call" with his Queen - Seven off-suit. He pairs his Queen on the flop (which is all Clubs), the turn and river (the last two community cards) don't help me and so I go out of the tournament on a coin flip.

Tony G eventually wins it.

Game over…. Good decision, bad decision? Well it all depends on where you place the frame.

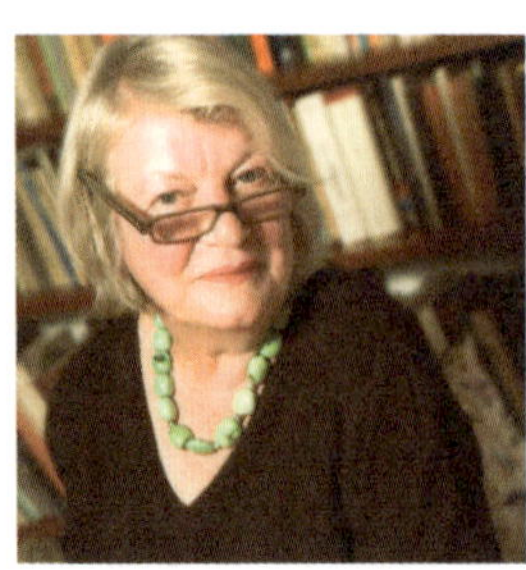

A Field Guide to Art – Art in the Countryside

A conversation between Sarah Lucas and Lynn Barber

Sarah Lucas is an artist who emerged in the late eighties as one of the key Young British Artists. Exhibiting in the famous Freeze show in 1988, she has since shown all over the world. In 1996 she was the subject of a BBC documentary, Two Melons and a Stinking Fish. She now lives in Suffolk.

Lynn Barber is one of Britain's most revered journalists. Her autobiography, An Education, was the basis of an Oscar nominated and BAFTA winning film of the same name. In 2006, Barber was one of the judges for the Turner Prize. Her friendship with Sarah Lucas seemed like a good starting point for a conversation.

LYNN BARBER:
Sarah Lucas has always struck me as the ultimate hedonist-artist because she never seems to work at her art, everything she does seems like play. I remember going to the Cologne Art Fair with her and her gallerist, Sadie Coles, years ago and me panicking because they didn't seem to have any art to sell, but they trotted off to the supermarket, came back with lots of bratwurst, beer, kippers, and pumpkins, and art started miraculously to appear. My job was drinking the beer so that Sarah could make the beercans into penis-and-balls sculptures – the punters were queueing up to buy them at 300 euros a throw. I thought: Gosh, art is so easy! I've since learned that Sarah's unique talent is that she makes it seem so.

The other thing I remember about Cologne is that I was pissed all the time. In fact any time I've seen Sarah I've been pissed and I think she has too. I do associate her with drinking. Is that fair, I asked her, and is drinking somehow integral to her art?

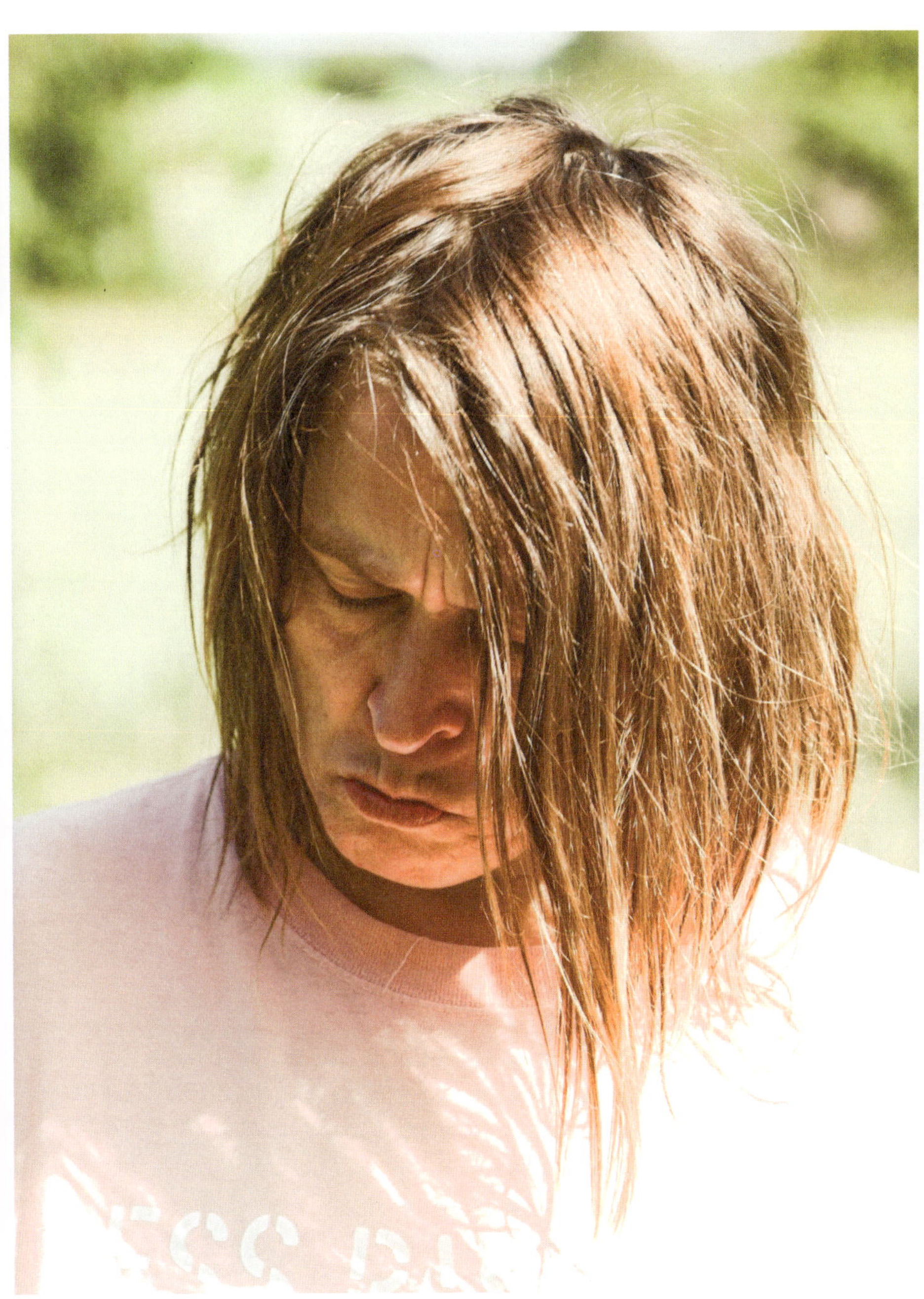

Sarah Lucas by Sarah Lucas

Sarah Lucas:

I always liked drinking and altered states in general. To begin with it was curiosity. Then I liked the release from inhibitions, which I suffered from. A friend, much later on, remarked that I like all the smiley faces. There could be some truth in that. It was a long while before I ever drank privately. It was mostly a social thing though that would still have affected the flow of ideas. I think making 'art', something I've always done without calling it art, was to keep myself company. I was a lonely child. Anyway we're all lonely at moments.

Drinking helped my confidence with others. Later, when I'd learnt to drink, I started to enjoy it sometimes on my own and found that, at a certain moment, it did get the mind racing and having fun. Anyway it kept me company at the same time as making things was keeping me company. As if we – me and the drink - were a crowd at a very particular party. On occasion I've woken up on the floor at home and thought, where's everybody gone?

I don't believe it's essential to the flow of ideas or even the best way to inspiration. Better perhaps than any other way that seemed obvious to me. It starts to take up a lot of time, like all habits. I'm sure there's much more to the world.

LB:

Has that changed, since you've moved to the country? You do seem to be leading a quieter life – has that made a difference to your art?

SL:

Yes circumstances make an absolute difference. A shop is not the same as a studio. The products are different and so are the interactions. We all sort of know through experience (we may still try to believe in them) that diets don't work. To make a real change there has to be something we'd rather do.

Coming to Suffolk was a surprise and I didn't know what to expect from it. My life at the time had become a travelling circus. I didn't get fed up with it, it was always amusing, but I was getting pretty frazzled. It was a gradual thing. At first I was more in London than here and when I was here I brought the circus with me. Then I was more here, now mostly here.

All differences are manifest always. The difference is what the difference is. The colour here, especially this time of year [June], is almost shocking. Super-real. I don't see that reflected yet in anything I'm making. But there has been a definite change. I'm not unrecognisable and the roots are still in the previous work, but something of here has crept in. I'd like to be unrecognisable, to go that far. I am unrecognisable to that child I was.

LB:
Why do you want to be unrecognisable? Do you mean you want the work to change so much we won't even know it's Sarah Lucas?

SL:
I suppose I'm thinking of myself as a raw material. Not in the sense of submitting to the surgeon's knife or anything mechanical like that. More like 'you are what you eat'. And everything's food; even ideas. Over a period of time I might find I'm composed of completely different stuff.

LB:
Please don't change too much! I love you as you are.

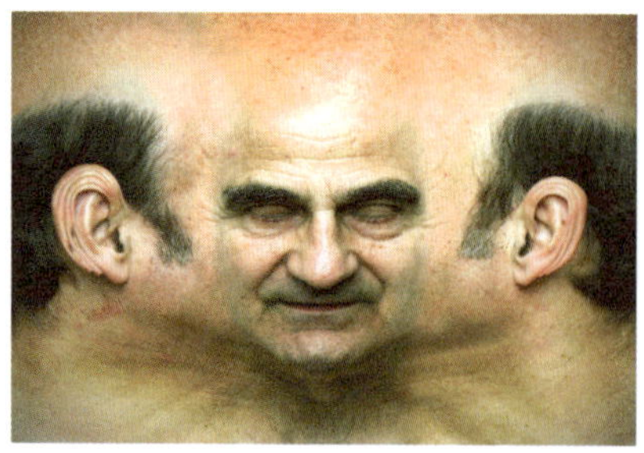

Stelarc's performances and projects – which include him surgically constructing and stem-cell growing an extra ear on his forearm - explore alternate anatomical architectures. He is Chair in Performance Art, Brunel University West London and Senior Research Fellow, MARCS Auditory Labs, University of Western Sydney. His artwork is represented by Scott Livesey Galleries, Melbourne. In 2010 he was awarded the Hybrid Arts Prize at Ars Electronica.

THE CADAVER, THE COMATOSE
AND THE CHIMERA

STELARC

1. INDIFFERENCE, EXCESS AND EXTRUSION-

We are living in an age of excess and indifference. Of prosthetic proliferation. A prosthesis not as a sign of lack but rather as a symptom of excess. The body with a THIRD HAND, EXOSKELETON locomotion and a PROTHETIC HEAD. The body now experiences parts of itself as automated, involuntary and absent to its own agency. It is profoundly obsolete and empty. Its awareness can be extruded, its physicality withdraws. The body is now remotely propelled. It becomes an extended operational system. We no longer function "all-here" in this body nor "all-there" in that body but "partly-here" sometimes and "partly-there" other times. Awareness slips and slides between spaces and situations. Imagine the consequences and advantages of being a SPLIT BODY with voltage-in, manifesting the behaviour of a remote agent and voltage-out actuating peripheral devices. This would be a more complex and interesting body- not simply a single entity with one agency but one that would be a construct of multiple and remote agents. Subjectively, the body experiences itself as more an extruded system, rather than an enclosed structure. The self becomes situated beyond the skin, and the body is emptied. But this emptiness is not an emptiness of lack but rather a radical emptiness and absence through excess. An emptiness and absence from the extrusion and extension of its capabilities, its augmented sensory antennae and its increasingly remote functioning. What becomes important is not merely the body's identity, but its connectivity- not its mobility or location, but its interface. The body acts with indifference. Indifference as opposed to expectation. An indifference that allows something other to occur, that allows an unfolding- in its own time and with its own rhythm. An indifference that allows the body to be suspended with hooks into its skin, that allows the insertion of a sculpture into its stomach and that allows an ear to be surgically constructed and a stem-cell grown on its arm.

2. ZOMBIES AND CYBORGS-

The body is an evolutionary architecture that operates and becomes aware in the world. To alter its architecture is to adjust its awareness. The body has always been a prosthetic body, one augmented, amplified and exposed by its instruments and machines. There has always been a danger of the body behaving involuntarily and of being conditioned to act automatically. A Zombie is a body that performs involuntarily, that does not have a mind of it's own. A Cyborg is a human-machine system that becomes increasingly automated. There has always been a fear of the involuntary and an anxiety of the automated. Of the Zombie and the Cyborg. But we fear what we have always been and what we have already become.

3. CIRCULATING FLESH AND THIRD LIFE-

Organs are extracted and exchanged. Organs are engineered and inserted. Blood flowing in my body today might be circulating in your body tomorrow. Ova are fertilized by sperm that was once frozen. The skin cells from an impotent male can now become sperm cells. And there is the possibility that the skin cells from female bodies can be re-engineered into sperm cells. The face of a donor body becomes a third face on the recipient. Limbs can be amputated from a dead body and reanimated on a living body. Cadavers can be preserved forever with plastination whilst comatose bodies can be sustained indefinitely on life-support systems. Cryogenically suspended bodies await reanimation at some imagined future. The dead, the near-dead, the un-dead and the yet to be born now exist simultaneously. This is the age of the Cadaver, the Comatose and the Chimera. The chimera is the body that performs with mixed realities. A biological body, augmented with technology and telematically performing with virtual systems. Second Life is a second skin, an alternate embodiment and operation in online virtual spaces. Avatars can be prompted by bodies and actuated by their code. Perhaps what we need now is not a Second Life but a THIRD LIFE. A means by which avatars can access and interface with surrogate bodies and perform with them in the physical world. This would be an inverse motion-capture system where an artificial entity, imbued with an artificial intelligence would be able to generate its presence in the physical world with multiple bodies, in diverse situations and in remote locations. Embodied agents can be actualised as Prosthetic Heads, Partial Heads, Walking Heads, Articulated Heads and Swarming Heads. Liminal spaces proliferate, blurring what it means to be a body and whether it is any longer meaningful to remain human. Perhaps what it means to be human is not to remain human at all.

4. FRACTAL FLESH, PHANTOM FLESH AND LIQUID FLESH-
By Fractal Flesh, I mean bodies and bits of bodies, spatially separated but electronically connected, generating recurring patterns of interactivity at varying scales. FRACTAL FLESH was a performance where people in other places choreographed the movements of the body. The host body is a split body and one that performs involuntarily. The body becomes simultaneously a possessed and performing body. The problem would no longer be possessing a split personality, but rather a split physicality. By Phantom Flesh, I am not only referring to on-line avatars but also, with the increasing proliferation of haptic devices on the internet, we will be able to construct more potent physical presences of remote bodies. BLENDER, a more recent project exhibited in 2006 and in collaboration with another artist, Nina Sellars, involved undergoing surgical procedures to extract biomaterial from each artist's body. The idea was that a machine installation would host and blend the biomaterials for the duration of the exhibition. A machine installation hosting a liquid body composed of biomaterial from 2 artist's bodies. It was the inverse of the STOMACH SCULPTURE where a soft and wet internal body space was the host of a machine choreography. Instead of an artwork inserted into the body, phantom flesh is sustained and animated by a machine installation. Flesh is circulating, flesh is fragmenting, flesh becomes liquid.

5. ALTERNATE ANATOMICAL ARCHITECTURES AND EXTRA EARS-

An extra ear is presently being constructed on my forearm: A left ear on a left arm. An ear that not only hears but also transmits. A facial feature has been replicated, relocated and will now be rewired for alternate capabilities. Excess skin was created with an implanted expander in the forearm. By injecting saline solution into a subcutaneous port, the kidney shaped silicon implant stretched the skin, forming a pocket of excess skin that could be used in surgically constructing the ear. A second surgery inserted a Medpor scaffold with the skin being suctioned over it. Tissue cells grow into the porous scaffold fusing it to the skin and fixing it in place. At present it is only a relief of an ear. The third surgical procedure will lift the helix of the ear, construct a soft ear lobe and inject stem cells to grow even better definition. The final procedure will implant a miniature microphone that, connected with a wireless transmitter, will internet enable the ear in any wifi hotspot, making the ear a remote listening device for people in other places. This additional and enabled EAR ON ARM effectively becomes an Internet organ for the body, an alternate anatomical architecture. A publicly accessible, mobile acoustical organ. And with stem cell growing of organs, with Organ Printing there will be an abundance of organs. It will no longer be a time of Bodies Without Organs but rather of Organs Awaiting Bodies, of Organs Without Bodies…

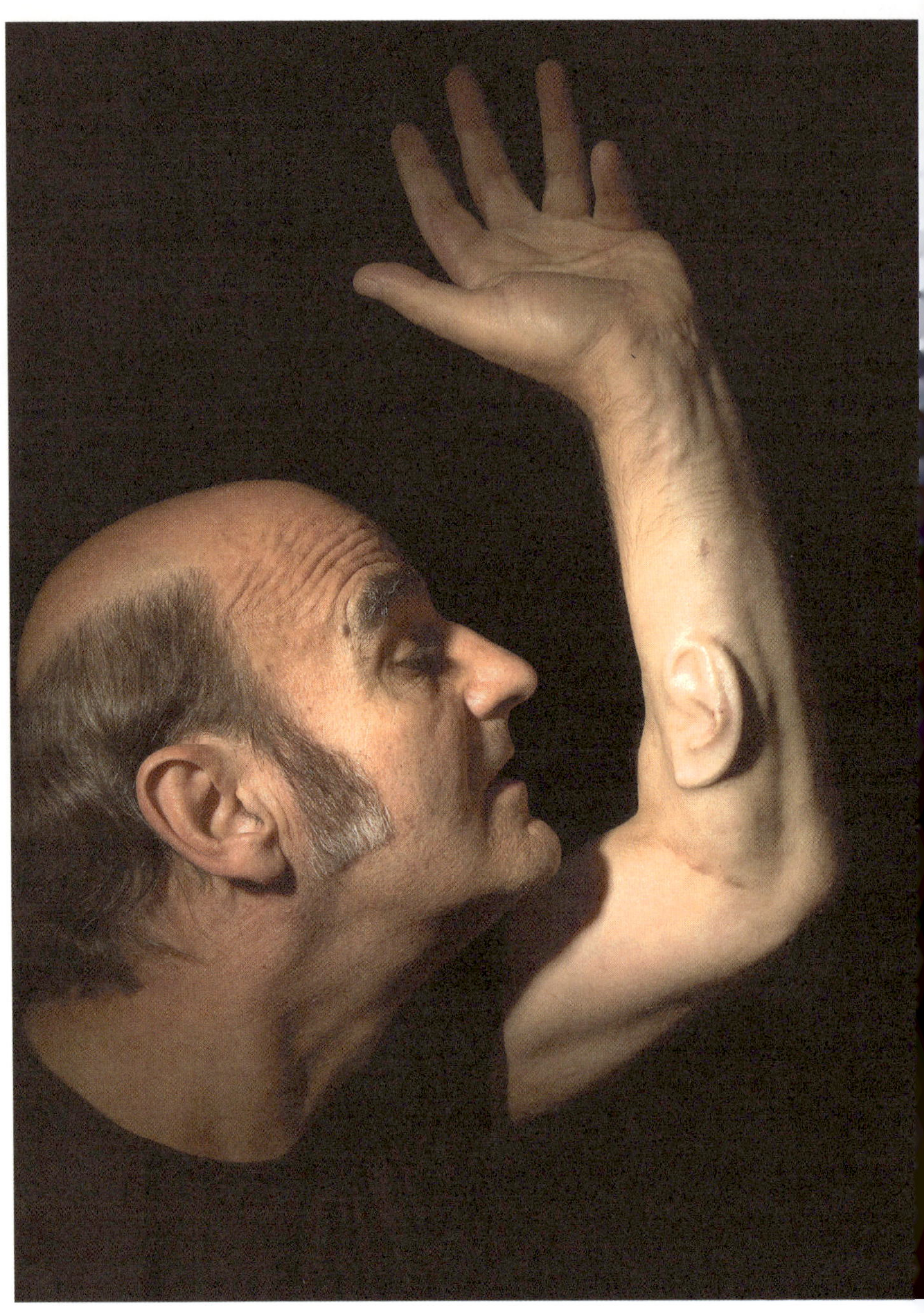

EAR ON ARM
London, Los Angeles, Melbourne 2006
Photographer- Nina Sellars
STELARC

THIRD HAND *(opposite)*
Tokyo, Yokohama, Nagoya 1980
Photographer- Simon Hunter
STELARC

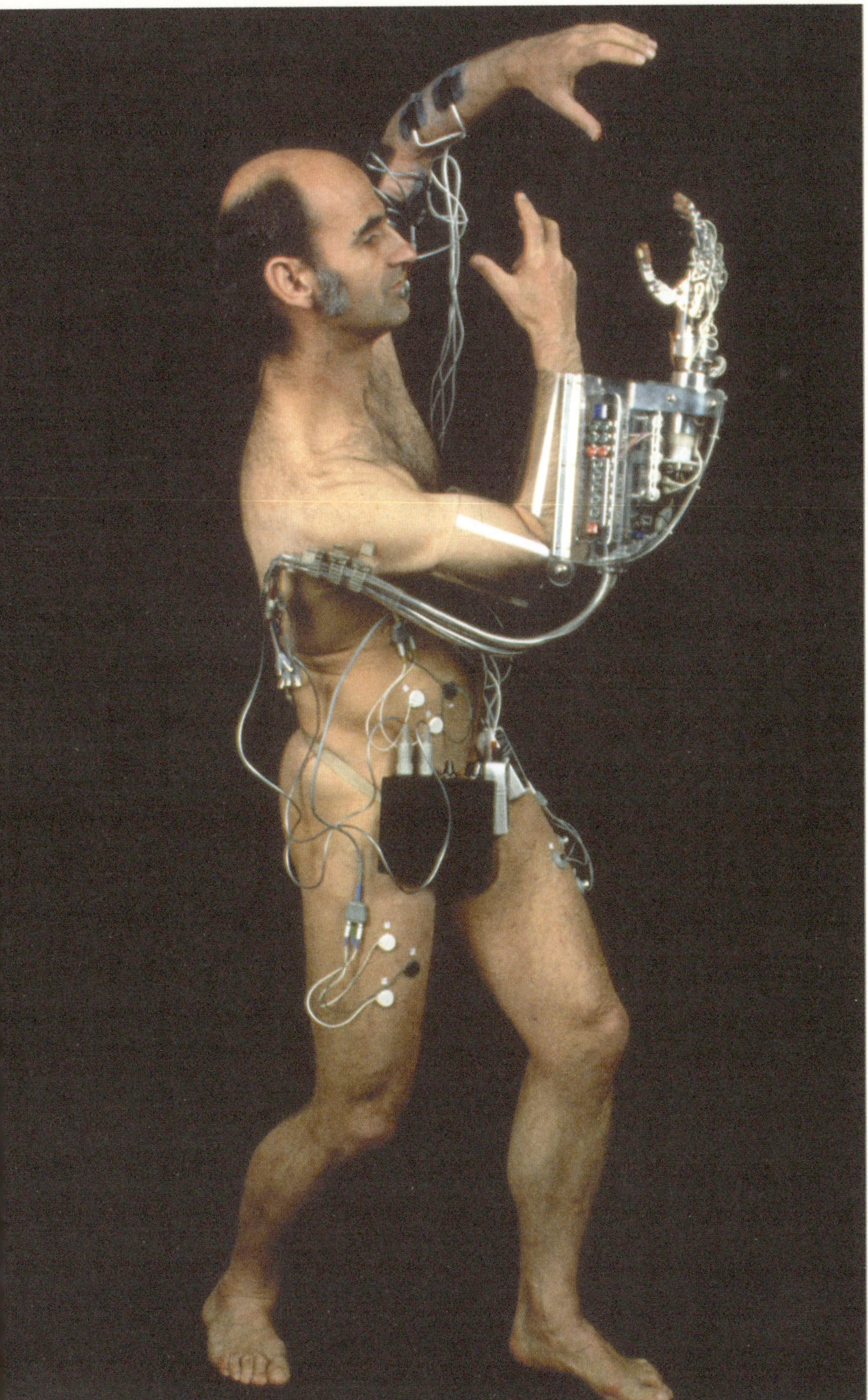

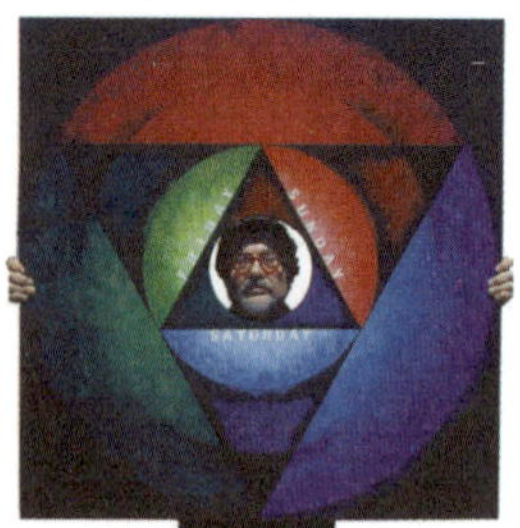
Three Day Weekend, Vitaly Komar

The Three Day Weekend - A Russian Émigré in New York

by Vitaly Komar

Vitaly Komar was born in Moscow in 1943, graduated from the Stroganov School of Art and Design in 1967, and has been living as an émigré in New York since 1978. He was one of the founders of the Sots Art movement (soviet Pop/Conceptual art). He worked in collaboration with Alex Melamid as Komar and Melamid from 1973 to 2003. In 1974, he was arrested during a performance of Art Belongs to the People and later, on September 15th, his and Melamid's work along with the works of other non-conformist artists was destroyed by Soviet Authorities at the now infamous open-air Bulldozer Exhibition.

WHEN AMERICANS SAY, "DON'T mix business with pleasure," does it mean that one's hobby can't also be one's business? As I get older, I get more and more pleasure from the process of working than from its results. Meditating while contemplating the unfinished work is now a goal in itself.

Unlike in America, in Soviet Russia people tried to rest (and drink) at work, and work on the weekends. My friends and I - underground, unofficial artists-nonconformists - were "Sunday artists." We worked on the weekends not for money, but for pleasure. Everyone was happy when, after Stalin's death, the government made Saturday the second free day of the week. My grandfather even saw in this a symbol of peaceful coexistence between Christianity and Judaism.

I believe that, due to growing unemployment, economic, political and spiritual utopias will sooner or later merge, and Muslim Fridays will become part of a three-day weekend. As Oscar Wilde said, "cultivated leisure is the aim of man." Like a caterpillar turning into a butterfly, every person will be able to go from being a "Sunday artist" to a "three-day artist." This is the goal of the "visual propaganda of happiness" in my project, "The Three-Day Weekend."

When I worked on the diptych Heaven and Earth. Forest as a Temple, I kept altering the stained-glass-like ecumenical symbol that appears between the trees. In it, a menorah is joined to a cross and a crescent moon. (Buddhists, who never divided the week into seven days, can enjoy all three days.) This landscape connects the "Three-Day Weekend" and "People's Choice" projects. For me, "People's Choice" was a collaboration not only with Alex, but with the masses, with the thousands of people that we (with the help of a professional firm) polled in various countries. We discovered that when it comes to painting, the majority of people in these countries, regardless of income, education, gender or race, wanted a blue landscape and didn't want geometric abstraction. The dream of the Soviet leadership has come true! Now every artist knows what kind of art appeals not to the rich snob, but to the people.

At one point I asked myself—what kind of landscape do I want? I realized that it's much easier to ask questions of others than to answer them myself. After I polled myself, I understood that I wanted to combine the symbolic landscape with geometric abstraction. This is how I began work on Heaven and Earth. Forest as a Temple.

As an artist who's had the experience of living in two worlds, I view the opposition between East and West as both a myth and reality.

In school, teachers taught (and I believed) that the West was a soulless evil, and that we were a force of light and good. In the archetypical language of mythology, this meant that the West was a hell, a land of the dead where, amid the bloody inferno of dusk, the evil dragon of darkness devours the sun.

A new mythology began to appear after Stalin's death. Many of us began to believe that hell was now in the East, in our Siberian Gulag, and that the glossy photos in Western magazines depicted paradise, a place that the dark forces of Soviet bureaucracy prevented us from going to. Interestingly, the protagonists of the most recent Sex and the City film frolic not in their native New York, but in Abu Dhabi. Unlike them, only a handful of Soviet artists had the opportunity to visit the foreign paradise.

When I was permitted to leave for the West, it was a supernatural opportunity to cross the boundary between heaven and hell. Soon after, I discovered a new pastime - the bars and nightlife of Manhattan. There weren't bars in Moscow. Back then we met in the dirty basements of "underground" artists, where over a bottle of vodka or port we could philosophize, engage in dangerous debates about history and art, read poems aloud, kiss each other, and so forth. Of course kissing is allowed in New York's bars, too, but smoking is now banned. I quit smoking in New York, but I can't forget how, as a schoolboy, I smoked the finest Cuban cigars. In Moscow they had cost next to nothing. This was around the time that Khrushchev kissed Castro. Totalitarian youth, dangerous and ephemeral as the smoke of a banned Cuban cigar, left me with an indelible taste of alcoholic nonconformism. Self-destructive behavior was a remnant of pre-revolutionary notions about unwashed, provincial "bohemians," a continuation of the old-fashioned, willfully eccentric, and oppositional lifestyle of the early avant-gardists. We recalled lines from Pushkin: "all that threatens us with destruction promises our mortal hearts ineffable pleasure." Russian nihilists, the forebears of the avant-gardists, dreamed of fame accorded to heroes who suffer to benefit humanity. "Benefit" was a key term in the morality of "utilitarian hedonism." Today I see the hedonism of the Russian protago-nists in Sacher-Masoch's novels as a sublimated altruism.

At the 'Bulldozer Show', when professional representatives of the state knocked me down into the autumn mud and began to pull Alex Melamid's and mine Double Self-Portrait as Lenin & Stalin from my hands, I was so scared that I didn't resist. I saw that the agents were beating those who fought back. By the beginning of the show they had already mutilated several of our Sots Art works, but I felt particularly attached to the Double Self-Portrait. When one of the agents stepped on the masonite and was about to break the painting, my fear vanished; at that moment I saw myself not as a Soviet leader but rather as Tolstoy or Ghandi. I looked up at him and quietly said: "What are you doing? This is a masterpiece." Our eyes met and for a moment we established some alternate form of contact. Maybe the word "masterpiece" reminded him of something important. Because instead of breaking it, he tossed the painting into the bed of a dump truck. A moment later, still lying on the ground and following the trash-laden truck with my eyes, I smiled. This was my shining hour. Dear God, I thought, my art doesn't leave people indifferent! I was enjoying the unique compliment… Maybe every artist secretly wishes that viewers would destroy his or her work. Gogol's "laughter through tears"— the self-irony of Narcissus glancing into a funhouse mirror—this is the hedonism of my totalitarian youth.

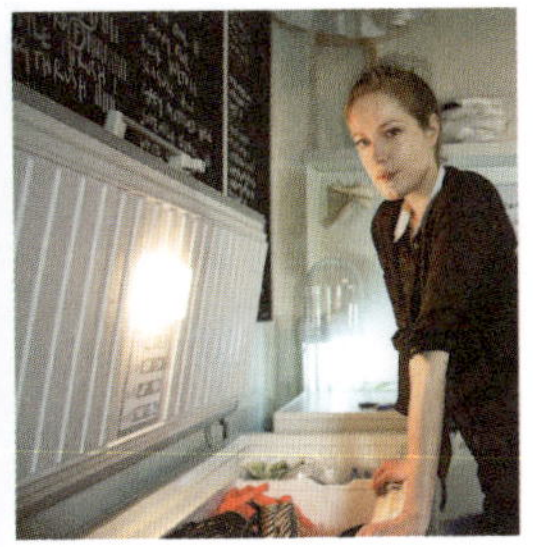

Carrion Call

by Polly Morgan

Polly Morgan is an artist who lives in London. She learned taxidermy under the tutelage of George Jamieson in Edinburgh and now spends her days gathering and peeling corpses. Banksy once called her Britain's Hottest Bird Stuffer, but she's getting on a bit now and that may no longer be the case.

I USED TO WAITRESS In a restaurant and one night the chef and I altered a menu designated for his friend, who was bringing along a date for dinner. Instead of the standard lamb shank and calves' liver, his menu listed skewered kittens and deep fried dogs' tails. When I came to take his order, he was staring at the menu, stricken, while his date, clutching the real menu, licked her lips and said "it all looks so good, I just can't choose!" Funny to think that ten years later I'm chalking Dog, Kitten, Fox, Stoat, Rat and so forth up on the blackboard above my chest freezer, and this time it really is no joke. A taxidermy studio isn't far from a restaurant kitchen. There are knives, aprons, freezers, and fresh meat in abundance.

One of the criticisms levelled at me is that I am disrespecting the animal by taking and using its corpse for my own ends. I say what tosh, this sort of attitude belongs to people who talk in baby voices to their spouses and say 'Hewwo Mr. Fox' when confronted by a scavenging baby-noshing brute. It is to foist human sentimentality onto creatures that frequently eat their own dead.

You don't see foxes gathered at gravesides mourning their parents. You do however see them lying dead on the side of the road from time to time, and what possible harm could you be doing by taking the remains home with you to make something pretty with? Depriving a few crows of a meal? I can think of worse crimes.

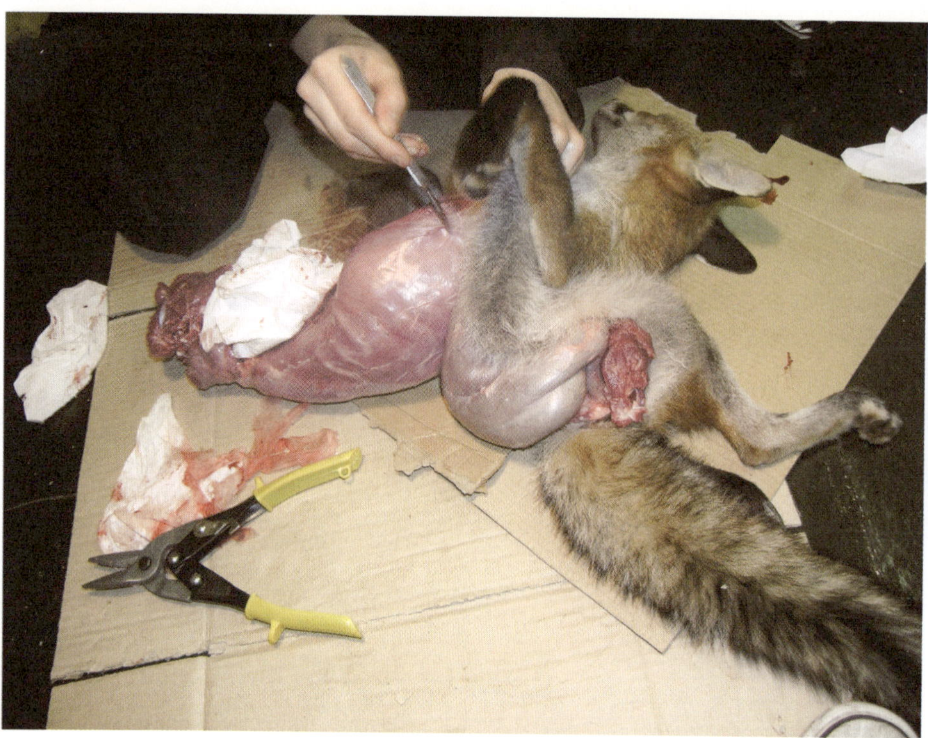

Polly Morgan Skining A Fox. © Fabio Paleari

It had never been my intention to actually eat these fallen friends, but curiosity got the better of me one night, and after a few glasses of wine I found it impossible to resist the lure of fresh glistening flesh. Anyway, am I not too a part of the cycle of life? Aren't my nourishment needs as important as an old crow's?

I can't abide eco-warriors and hippies, but one - and I like to think the only - thing we agree on is our distaste for waste. This quality was passed on to me by my dear old dad, Arden, who could often be found foraging in the dustbin, muttering 'bloody woman,' as he rescued a selection of green meat, black fruit and pink cheese that my mother had had the audacity to throw away. (On the subject of cheese, he would cultivate his own with out of date bottles of milk - woe betide anyone who mistook his miniature dairy for a legion of curdled milk!)

Back to the menu, on being donated my very own Mrs. Fox (a recent East London road casualty) the thought of finding uses for both the skin AND body was too good an opportunity to pass up and the leg was hacked off and after a festive few hours skinning her over a bottle of wine with artists Paul Fryer and Fabio Paleari, her leg was hacked off and fried up with a little garlic. It all felt terribly bohemian and primitive. Sadly the taste didn't live up to the theatre of the event. With the first bite you could just about believe you were eating steak, but a note of greasy old bin soon kicked in and you were brought back to Hackney pretty sharpish. I've had worse in McDonald's so I won't be giving up just yet.

I've discovered that chicks grow around the yolk of the egg - this is why they come out of the shell with such round bellies - presumably this nourishes them in the early stages of life. It makes skinning them a gooey, sticky affair but it hasn't escaped my attention that this would make a special kind of snack; (those culinary explorers the Vietnamese eat fully formed black chicks in the egg shell) a morsel of meat with an egg thrown in for good measure. An unsettling combination, granted, but coupled with the soft, chewable bones of a newborn I can see a skewered row of quail chicks forming an alternative kebab sometime soon.

I'm currently training my dog to eat my taxidermy waste after hearing that fresh uncooked meat is the ideal food for him. He's not much of a canine disposal unit yet as he's pickier than me, but we're getting there. If you're now dreaming up a brand new country-lane-sourced menu, I might just point out one caveat. I recently read about a man who died after eating what appeared to be the freshest road-kill deer. It turned out, post investigation, that the deer had initially been only badly injured. The driver responsible had contacted a vet to suggest he euthanise the poor creature, which he duly did. On giving the corpse back to the driver who wanted to lay her to rest near the scene of the accident, the vet probably didn't think to attach a note saying, "My body is swimming with Sodium pentobarbital. Don't eat me." But then, who would?

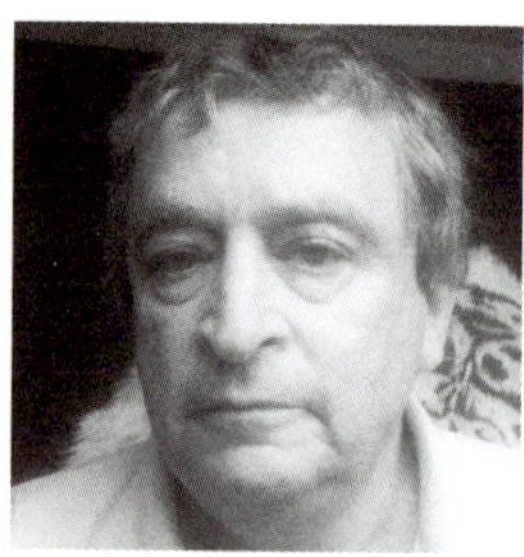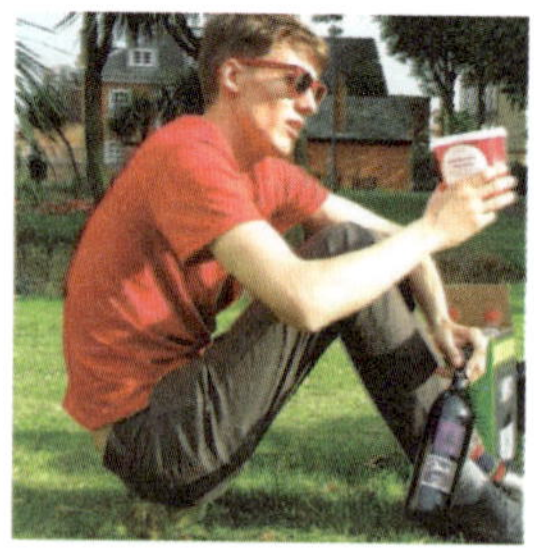

Norman Rosenthal – left
Ed Fornieles – right

Truth in Excess

by Norman Rosenthal and Ed Fornieles

Norman Rosenthal is the erstwhile Exhibitions Secretary of the Royal Academy and a key figure in the life of the YBAs and other British artists. He curated a cycle of survey exhibitions of 20th Century work that promoted the Academy as never before. In staging the seminal 1997 show Sensation he drew protests from some Academicians and much frenzied commentary from the media.

Edward Fornieles is an artist living in London. As well as being a sculptor, he also performs live art pieces in which he strips off peoples' clothes in a violent manner. He is currently studying for his M.A. at the Royal College of Art.

NORMAN: EXCESS AND HEDONISM are very different things, because hedonism implies a certain amount of self-indulgence. In a certain way it can be a way of life that is conscious – in a certain way it is fine, because everyone needs to live the life that they want to live. You only live on this planet once, but I would say that all artists of substance that I can think of in one way or another, practice their life to excess, a specific excess that they invent for themselves. It is the individuality of excess that is interesting. All artists that I have known, and all the artists that I know about in past ages, have practiced excess. Michelangelo, Van Gogh, or whoever: they are all so wrapped up in themselves and their art that they cannot fail but to act with excess. A true artist is someone who confronts the world, and confronts the truth about the world as he sees it, in a completely rigorous and excessive way.

Edward: The way you talk about it makes me think of Nietzsche's idea of a 'master drive', the idea that someone having a single obsession that dictates all actions, both consciously and unconsciously. You could describe it as a guiding principle that gives an artist's life direction and shape.

There is no right way. Each artist does it for him or herself, sort of figuring it out, and once the penny has dropped they realise, "I've got it, this is it". You can imagine them all in a room, shouting out their different things. Warhol is saying fab and pop, and Hockney is doing his bigger splash and so on.

Norman: From Andy Warhol to Jeff Koons in America, from David Hockney to Damien Hirst in England, they are all artists who have lived or continue to live a life of excess. What each does is totally extreme in its way, and none of them really gives a care about the opinions of the rest of the world. And that is part of the reason such interest in what they do is generated. And that is why we, as consumers, are so fascinated with these guys who have cut out a place in the world they have created for themselves in which they can practice their excess. As it happens all four of these artists we have mentioned come from very modest, lower middle backgrounds.

Edward: It's funny we all make thousands of decisions in our lives that have got us to where we are now. And for some people you have to take a moment to comprehend how they got there. Like the world's fastest man or a professional chess player, I just think 'wow, some really interesting decision must have been made here'.

Norman: Most people are not driven, but these people are all exceptional, perhaps with a little bit of luck thrown in. Everyone needs a lucky break as well. I perhaps deserve some of my so-called small success in the world. But I also owe a huge amount to a few lucky breaks, with meetings with certain individuals – sometimes a word of recommendation, or a chance meeting in the world can change your path for the better. Additionally I put it down to sudden insights which have given me the lifestyle that I lead, which in some ways, even though I'm not an artist, has a certain amount of excess in it.

Edward: I think that what this excess leads to, in the end, is a creating of worlds. A successful artist seems in some way to construct a cohesive world, with its own logic and set of rules. And if you're looking into this world you have to believe it; its like a successful film, your concerns have to become the concerns of the characters. I want the protagonist to win. I don't want to be thinking about their acting technique, or the lighting… Who do you think has manipulated their lives to feed back in some way into their art?

Norman: David Hockney as a young man said something like "Blondes have all the best fun" and decided to dye his hair blond for many years. He became part of the image that he created for himself: in that sense he lived his life to excess.

Edward: And that statement begins to impact on the way you look at all his paintings. It's like a shockwave that passes through all the stuff he makes. No work stands alone, the artist is always there somewhere in the back making an impression whether he likes it or not.

Norman: Being a great artist is about living your life without compromise. I have an artist friend who goes and spends a fortune on flowers. He might spend £30,000 on flowers for one evening. He lives in some ways a completely ascetic life. He even tells me "I haven't had sex for 10 years". He completely concentrates on his art to the exclusion of everything else. But he has constructed for himself an environment that, for those who have been fortunate to know him, is totally bizarre, exotic, and I suppose excessive.

Edward: And then the flipside of that, is an artist whose extremes manifest themselves in extreme austerity.

Norman: There is for example, the case of Frank Auerbach. His prices are not as high as the market would allow him to charge. But I am told he likes the idea that he can still reach his old middle class collector base. And he doesn't feel that he needs that much money and he lives an extremely austere life, which in itself is a form of excess. He still occupies the tiny studio that he has had for decades and the paint is thick on the floor. To the best of my knowledge he walks everyday from his small house across Primrose Hill, and for the last forty or fifty years he has not been abroad. He hardly wants to leave the borough of Camden, which is where he lives. He will just about get on the Tube and go to the National Gallery or maybe the Royal Academy to see one or two shows, but for him to even go south of the River Thames is a kind of problem.

He is 80 and he has been living like this for fifty years. I mean that is a form of excess as well. It is hardly normal to be like that in a world where we can go to Heathrow and for £50 go anywhere in the world on Easyjet.

There are of course those people who regularly dance all night etc but it's not real excess, it's at best conventional excess. Drugs, sex and getting drunk are not really excess in themselves. Genuine excess is about work and the way in which it is achieved and the construction of something which is really unique. And very few people achieve that or get there. People for the most part live conventional lives.

Edward: Yep, I think those other forms of excess are only really interesting when they feed back into the artists' world. When it's irrevocably part of who they are. Like Jackson Pollock, Francis Bacon or for that matter Tracey Emin with their drinking and their art, where it all seems bound up.

Norman: To play the game of excess is hard, because it involves sacrifice, which most pretend (and there are a lot of those pretenders!), or are not prepared, or even able to make. It can damage relationships, it can disrupt your life, it can bankrupt you and ultimately it's about not caring about anything except the art and its moral implications. Frank Auerbach's truth is not the same as Jeff Koons'. They have different truths. But what you can say is that their separate truths are both totally uncompromised and at the service of the art. That art is about developing a language, and the way of describing that is a special vision. First it has to be dreamt and then turned into reality. It is one thing to have a dream and it is another thing to realise it. It is not about yourself. It is much more than that.

Edward: I get very excited about the idea of developing a way of speaking because it can illuminate and adds to a vision as well as helping you make sense of the world. Talking can be a very creative act. It has the potential to add another dimension of experience into the art. But it's also not necessarily what you say. Anything can expand the work. It could be dying your hair blond, or wearing a certain pair of glasses. Which is why the details can be so exciting, they feed back into the bigger language which is the art and everything else. Are there any artists who you don't believe in?

Norman: I'm not going to tell you that. You announce your preferences through actions and friendships. But I can tell you that art is more than fashion, or for that matter self indulgence. When my artist friend spends £30,000 on flowers it doesn't seem like an indulgence. I know it to be a necessity.

Edward: I think you have hit the right word there. The word necessity seems to tie every-thing up. A convincing artist is an artist who is motivated by necessity. Where decisions don't feel like they were choices but necessary actions.

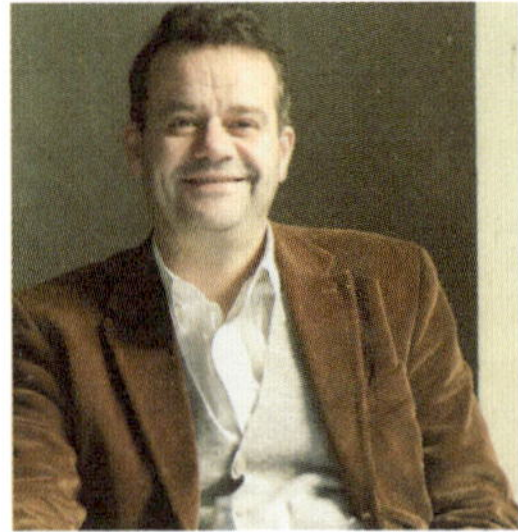

Jelly and Sharks

by Mark Hix

Mark Hix is a food writer, chef and Tatler's Restaurateur of the Year 2009. After 17 years at Caprice Holdings, he started his own ventures, opening three joints in London and Hix Oyster & Fish House in Dorset. He has written nine cookbooks. By exhibiting artists' work on his restaurants' walls in return for a food tab, he has essentially allowed the art world to eat for free for many years. That's not the only reason he's loved, but it's one of them.

MY CONNECTION WITH THE world of art was born in a bit of an arse-about-tit kind of way I suppose. Living and partying in Shoreditch, it's kind of difficult not to rub shoulders with a good proportion of today's young and great artists.

Having a restaurant in the area made it even better, and food and art became a kind of a currency and a way to collect a bit of art.

The art tab happened in Paris a lot - I vividly remember visiting Lionel Poilâne's bakery, whose walls were covered in paintings and drawings. He had adopted his father's practice of accepting work in lieu of cash, when poor artists couldn't afford to pay their monthly bread bills.

It's often quite an attractive proposition for artists - especially the less well-known ones - to have a tab in restaurants they may well not be able to frequent that often.

As you may know, I'm a bit of a jelly freak - I will suspend almost any seasonal ingredient I can get my hands on in a sweet liquid for the sake of making a visually decadent dessert. Of course in winter time it's not so easy to suspend anything in jelly as we just ain't got no fruit in the cold months in the UK.

About eight or so years ago I thought I would knock up some absinthe jellies for a dinner party I was cooking at the artist duo Tim Noble and Sue Webster's house. It was about the time I converted Tim from vegetarianism – to my chagrin, I've never yet managed to convert Sue, but I'm still trying. Anyway, after a mushroom feast of puffball and porcini I pulled out the jellies which were glowing a psychedelic green and loaded with 60% of

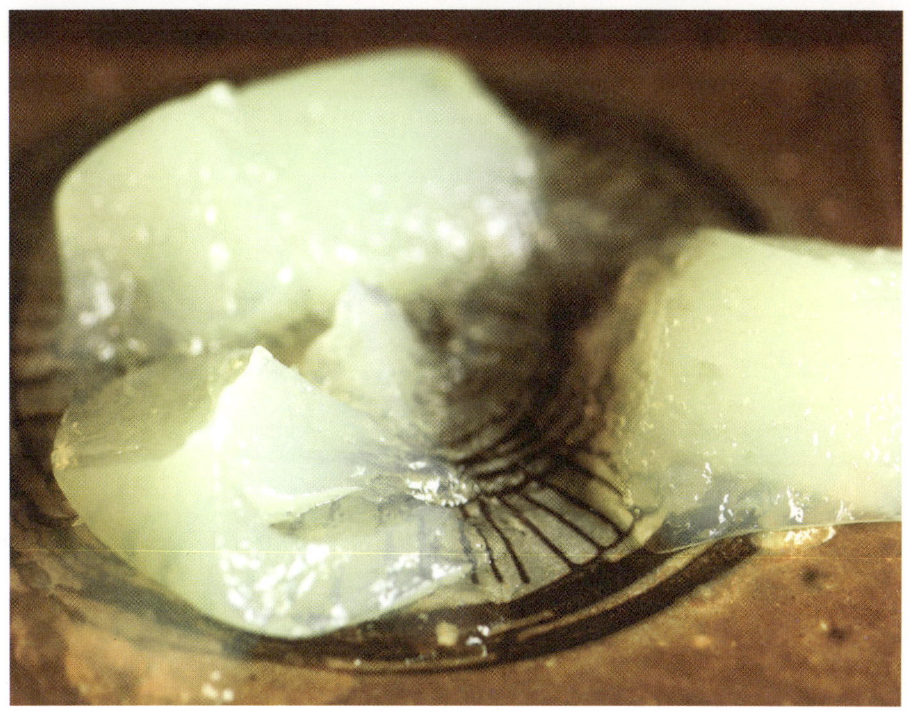

Mark Hix Absinthe Jelly. Jason Lowe

the fatal green stuff. It didn't really need the jelly to get everyone going but it certainly finished them off.

In fact it was such a success that word got around and I ended up serving it for the luminaries at a Whitechapel Gallery dinner for a hundred.

For my latest restaurant venture, HIX on Brewer Street in Soho, I asked artists to make mobiles for the ceiling space. This got mixed reactions initially but after a bit of persuasion they were all up for it and most of them actually became competitive about it.

The ceiling changed from week to week and even now the mobiles are still turning up, and it's great to have lesser known artists like Miranda Donovan hanging above the bar between a Damien Hirst and a Sarah Lucas. Even jewellery designer Stephen Webster got into it and produced jewel crusted sharks' jaws with fish swimming into them.

So it works both ways. I get the joy of having peoples' creations decorating my restaurants – (this also pulls in customers who are both art and food lovers): the artists get a plate of my food for free whenever they fancy some rock oysters, a bit of smoked salmon or a Barnsley chop.

Memories of the Nineties

By Danny Chadwick

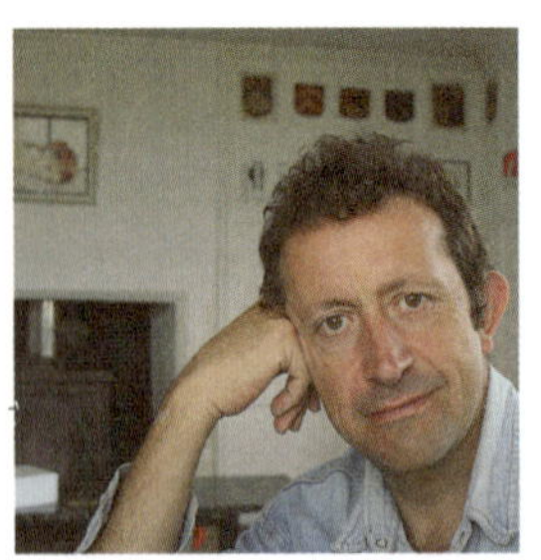

Danny Chadwick is an artist living in Gloucestershire. In London he shows with the Eleven Gallery and also with Lefevre Fine Art. He remembers the days of hedonism well. Well, sort of blurrily, actually. These are just a few of the publishable stories that spring to mind.

S TROUD, GLOUCESTERSHIRE

There was the time when Damien and I had a sort of extended play-fight in Stroud which got progressively worse and worse rolling around in the street trying to punch each other. We went back to my house separately and resumed it. I went to the bog at some point and Damien tried to lock me in. It was at this point that I went nuts and put my foot through the door and then pushed the whole door out and on top of Damien, leaving a head shaped hole in it. He spent the remainder of the night in the corner of the room clutching a hammer to defend himself from me.

Hirst show at Bruno Bischofberger Gallery in Zurich. 1997

I am not good at class A drugs but they gave me some in my sleep, and the effect was a strange homosexual episode where Damien and Keith Allen and myself tried to prove we were not gay by sucking each others' cocks. Keith says it was his idea but I think it was mine, anyway Jan Kennedy walked in in the middle of it all and was very shocked. I put my cock on the shoe polishing machine at some point.

Bisley, Gloucestershire

Damien and I were on the tail end of a bender and were in the Indian restaurant in Stroud. Decided to visit a girlfriend in Bisley and gathered the numerous bags of over-ordered curry and to Bisley we went: (a very quaint Cotswolds village). It was freezing and no response on Alice's door so Damien climbed the porch and smashed a window and nearly fell off. I said I was leaving and walked down towards the phonebox to try to get a taxi. Damien then ran amok in the tiny village shouting and throwing curry up the street.

I was connected to the taxi service when he reached me and emptied the remainder of a particularly red curry all over me and the phonebox. I was wearing white clothes. Three police cars arrived and the police were in a state of high excitement shouting at us. I heard one say "Sarge they are covered in blood". (Poor Alice had called the police having woken up to a bloodied hand reaching through her window). We kept saying "Its curry!" The sergeant asked the officer to have a sniff and he duly reported "It's curry sir." We got arrested but they were very nice in the end.

Girls and Jeep

Jay Jopling, Damien Hirst, me with six girls from Westonbirt Girls School. After a long session in the pub we let one of the girls Julia drive the Jeep home; she went too fast and, on seeing an approaching headlight, swerved in panic - the Jeep skidded then rolled over and came to a stop with me and Damien at the bottom of the heap. Damien went mad and fought to the top to get out first only to meet the wrath of the the other driver who was screaming at him and shouting and swearing, as each person popped out of the top until I finally got out.

He said "Oh its you Daniel, here, take this rope I will pull you back upright." That's the countryside for you.

Painswick Hotel, Stroud

A dinner to celebrate Marc Quinn having finally sold his Blood Head to Saatchi. Sixteen of us including Jay, Damien, Maia Norman and Georgie (Byng, Chadwick, Quinn whatever). There was not one person with any clothes on by the time the first course was served, (and there was a minor orgy going on under the table). The nudity went down almost unnoticed by the hotel staff more used to serving cream teas to old ladies.

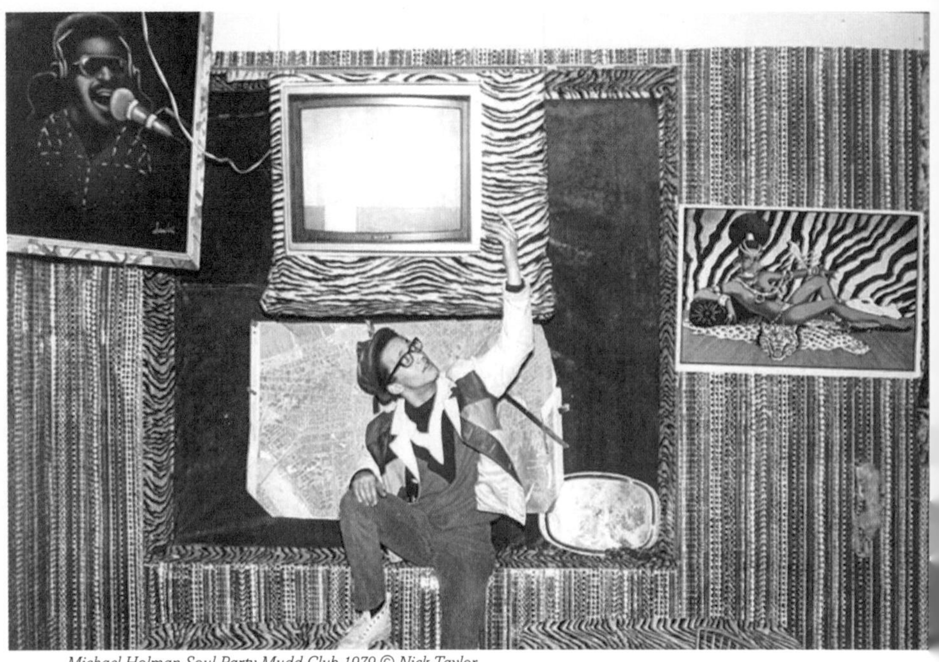

Michael Holman Soul Party Mudd Club 1979 © Nick Taylor

How to Make an Art Epoch

By Michael Holman

Michael Holman is an artist, filmmaker, subculturalist, musician, inventor of fabric sunglasses and women's neckties, writer of the film Basquiat, founder (with Jean-Michel Basquiat) of the band Gray, and an impresario who helped put Hip Hop Culture and the 80s New York Downtown art scene on the map.

NEW YORK CITY, APRIL 29th, 1979: Fab 5 Freddy - a young Brooklyn-based graffiti artist and soon to be Hip Hop icon, Stan Peskett – a Royal College of Art ex-pat British painter, and myself - recent émigré from a theatrical, art-rock scene in California, all threw a multi-media event, The Canal Zone, in a loft on Canal Street in lower Manhattan. It's said to have changed art history.

It was the first social function that brought together New York's graffiti art world with the Downtown fine art movement, and it proved to be a game changer, a tipping point. We had no idea then that it would play a pivotal role in the formation of New York's early 1980s art scene - an epoch that would rival Paris in the 1920s, San Francisco's 'Summer of Love', 1970s Punk rock London and even the 14th century Italian Renaissance, in terms of global influence.

This international community of painters, musicians, writers, filmmakers, gallerists, critics, graffiti artists and sub-cultural impresarios, along with various underground nightclubs, publications and art institutions, took advantage of the Arab oil embargo and the ensuing global recession that nearly ruined New York City in the 1970s. That recession turned out to have lain the groundwork for a ripe, Petri-dish of an environment, perfect for the cultivation of a full-blown art epoch.

Clearly the right people in the right place at the right time is crucial to the genesis of an important art scene, but what other myriad variables are needed?

Recipe for an art epoch

***

1. Start a World War.

World wars and the recovery periods that follow can be instrumental in generating major art scenes. If a decent war isn't handy, an embarrassing little "conflict," like Vietnam will do.

Pro-war and anti-war passions run high. And then there's the aftermath. Destruction, chaos and humiliation, even for the so called victors, as their economy goes into freefall. This is a time when artists and art communities sprout up like fungi, exploiting the momentary lack of provincial norms and controls - the artists' once-in-a-lifetime opportunity to sneak in some good art while the 'theys' are too distracted to notice.

***

2. Induce economic and social upheaval.

This sort of links in with point one. Big city recessions can sometimes work in favour of artists and art communities, but only when the cost of living is drastically reduced, diverting important resources away from basic survival and re-directing these same resources towards the making of art. Recessions also have a habit of freeing up space in less than desirable neighborhoods, where artists and art-oriented enterprises can flourish.

3. Feed the machine.

A. Sex: All artists seek the love and acceptance of their peers, and few artists engage in sex and companionship outside of the creative community (maybe a quickie with a banker for the rent, but that's a whole other thing). It is the intimacy and approval of fellow artists that is most important, no one else can truly understand us. Love and sex serve to strengthen the overall artist community, even as AIDS can threaten to decimate it, which just about happened in New York during the early 1980s.

B. Drugs: Where would the Impressionists be without absinthe? Early jazz pioneers without pot and cocaine? The 1960s without psychedelics? Major art movements will probably never exist, free of mind-altering substances. The art of understanding art is, in itself, a leap of faith, a suspension of certainty. Sometimes you need all doors opened, wide.

C. Rock & Roll: Obviously music has always played an inspirational, background role to the creation of fine art, from Be Bop for the Abstract Expressionists, to Warhol's Factory being a jam spot for the Velvet Underground. Music doesn't need fine art to exist, but can fine art survive without the warm embrace of music?

***

4. Add supportive venues, clubs and institutions. Shake well.

At the Mudd Club, I'd dance with my Gray band mates to Iggy Pop's Lust For Life as Johnny Lydon and David Bowie watched on. Our attitude was, "Yeah? What are you lookin' at?" We were that cool. Without these bastions of spiritual, creative and sybaritic solidarity and liberation, I am certain our scene would have never happened.

The Downtown nightlife of New York today can't begin to compare with 30 years ago where the scene was on a smaller scale, more amenable to intimacy, networking and fun. There are too many clubs today. Too many people. Too many choices. It's the age of the Internet. Back in the day, everyone was where you were…

***

5. Sprinkle on a dash of cross-disciplinary inspiration.

Fine art in 1980s New York City embraced the confidence and arrogance of graffiti art, as graffiti art incorporated 'proper' art world sensibilities. Cross-pollination of differing aesthetical styles and inspirations are inevitable in art communities, large enough to support practitioners of varying disciplines simultaneously.

***

6. Finally, acquire mega-institutional support via state, church, corporations or the monarchy…then turn up the heat…

An artist's place in the greater society is not unlike the role of a four year old in the nuclear family. The child thrives in an emotionally healthy and supportive environment, just as an artist survives and prospers in an open, supportive society. For example, the CIA has never denied supporting and promoting American Abstract Expressionism in the early 1950s, giving America - as it emerged from the wreckage of World War II - a bit of polish and shine befitting a brand-spanking-new Superpower.

The governmental support we received in NYC in the early 1980s was for the most part a bit like benign neglect. But for the kind of art we were making, that was all we needed. When Reagan was voted into office, then re-elected four years later, we just troweled on more makeup, and shoveled in more drugs.

Artists need to have the freedom to explore, make mistakes, even do serious damage, all in the name of advancing the creative process, while at the same time not suffering harsh censorship, punishment or worse - irrelevance. Of course some artists can be productive in repressive societies, but as a whole, they don't thrive, certainly not enough to help build an art epoch.

****

What major international cities are potential sites for the next great art epoch? As a future collector, gallerist or art historian, that kind of foresight would be invaluable.

Accuse me of Anglo-American bias here, but I can't imagine the next major movement happening anywhere else but New York (again) or London (again), anytime soon.

Both cities have proven track records for generating splendid, world changing art epochs. Both cities have powerful 'art worlds' that dictate global exhibition trends, consumption and criticism. Both cities are edgy yet reside in large, incredibly stable democracies. Both have super-strong music scenes and street cultures. Both are world financial capitals, multi-ethnic and open to everyone. It's difficult to create an epoch when your main capitals don't support and encourage people from completely diverse backgrounds to shine.

For all our shared and individual arrogances and cruelties towards other countries and cultures (and even our own), and for all our shared and individual shortcomings in national taste and aesthetics, U.S. and U.K. reputations for artistic output and creative genius is unmatched. For 'the city that produces the next art epoch, I'm putting my money on New York or London - or both. But I look forward to being proved wrong.

On the Avoidance of Pain

by ORLAN

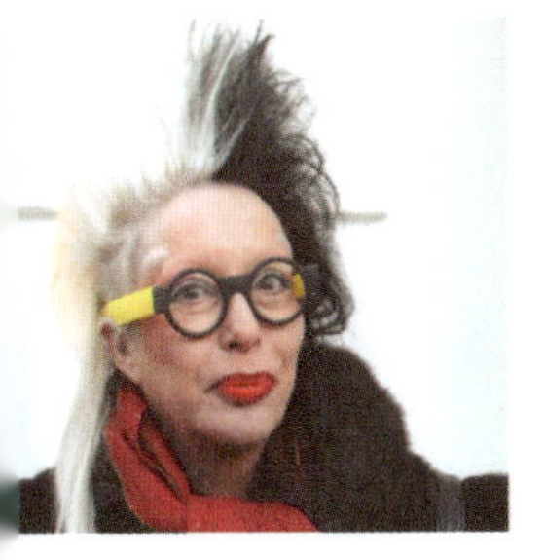

ORLAN is a transdisciplinary artist and professor at the Ecole Nationale Supérieure des Beaux-Arts of Cergy, who questions the status of the body in the society. Between 1990 and 1993, her Reincarnation of Saint-ORLAN - Nouvelles Images - an ongoing series of performances - involved a large amount of plastic surgery to her own body. During these, she started to morph herself in to simulacrums of well known paintings and sculptures. Her body or the image of her body is used as an artistic medium in itself, that is evolving permanently. Her Self-Hybridizations photographs, have her face merging with past facial representations of non-western civilizations, and The Harlequin's Coat bio-art is an installation realised in collaboration with the Symbiotica Laboratory in Australia.

BODIES HAVE SUFFERED FOR thousands of years: for headaches, toothaches and kidney-pain there was no aspirin, for childbirth there were no epidurals, before laughing-gas, amputations and operations were carried out without an anaesthetic.

Now we have almost put an end to pain, it has become highly anachronistic.

In my life and my work I have opted for the body as pleasure, for humour, for critical distance.

I have chosen the body as subject, and as object. I have moved from invention of the self to sculpture of the self, from thinking within the body to thinking of the body as a locus of pleasure.

My series of surgical operations/performances was made in the years 1990-93. The first request to the surgeon was for the avoidance of pain during and after the operations.

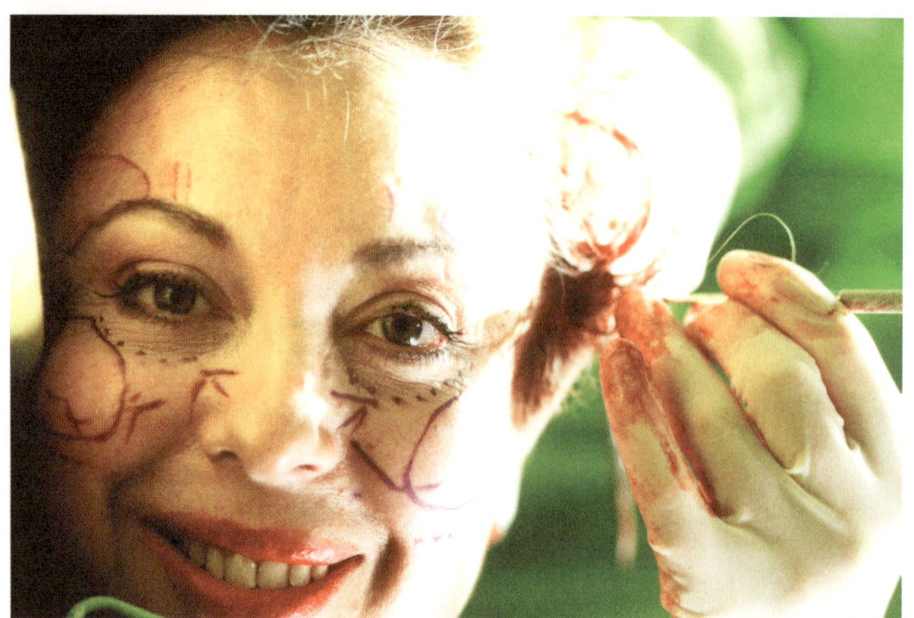

Seventh Surgery-Performance, titled Omniprésence, New York - Close-up of Laughter during the Operation cibachrome in Dia, photo – Vladimir Sichov for Sipa Press

If I had suffered during the operations I couldn't have read, couldn't have directed the photo- and video-shoots in the surgery, (the operations were shown as pieces of art in various galleries and museums around the world), I couldn't have answered questions put to me by satellite link from the Pompidou Centre, the McLuhan Centre in Toronto and my gallery, Sandra Gering, in New York.

Pain and endurance seem to me an old-fashioned way of considering one's body and its relationship to the world, like Christianity, which emphasises redemption and purification by pain and sacrifice... giving birth in pain.

Pain functions there like an alarm, it is a good thing, but I see no reason to choose to entertain it, God is not part of my working hypothesis, nor of my life. I am close to a philosophy of hedonism.

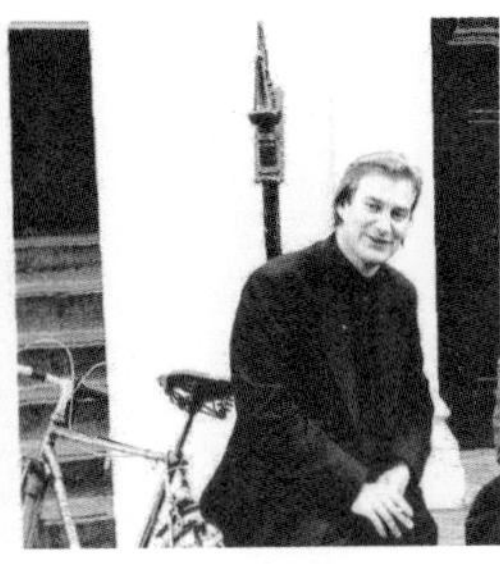

A Slice of Bacon

by James Birch

James Birch is a curator and collector who lives in London. In 1983, he opened the James Birch Gallery on the King's Road where he showed Grayson Perry, Jennifer Binnie, and Eileen Agar. In 1987 he opened Birch and Conran on Dean Street. Now he curates one-off international shows in far flung corners of the globe. He was an early member of the now defunct Colony Room – the art world's apple-green front room.

I FIRST WENT TO the Colony Room in 1977, taken there by the art patron Michael Wishart and by John Maybury, the now well-known filmmaker. I was first of all struck by how small the bar was and was surprised to run into Vicky de Lambray, a transvestite male prostitute, who had just been released from prison for blackmailing the Royal family, claiming he had given a blow job to every single one of them!

I initially heard of the Colony Room through the artist Denis Wirth-Miller and his boyfriend Dicky Chopping (the illustrator of the James Bond hard-back novels). For years they had told me about the place and were extremely good friends with Francis Bacon for whom the Colony was a favourite haunt…

Dicky and Denis were friends of my parents and when I was a child the two of them would look after me, even to the extent that my parents renamed Denis 'Nanny Worth Millions'. I became a member of the Colony Room Club in the early 80s.

In 1988, while I was organising Francis Bacon's retrospective which was to be in the Central House of Artists in Moscow, I ran into Denis and Francis on Dean Street. They said "come and have a drink with us upstairs in the Colony". But as Francis leapt up the stairs, Denis held me back saying "James, what ever you do, verbally abuse me in front of Francis - he's got it into his head that I'm your godfather and is somewhat jealous…"

As we walked in, Francis was already on his stool at the end of the bar. Denis and I sat on the worn velveteen banquette, but Francis remained with his back to us. Denis nudged me, my cue, and I said "Denis you're a fucking cunt." Whereupon Francis spun round and said "He's always been a fucking cunt and still is!" This broke the ice and we all started chatting happily.

I must say that despite this abusive language Francis was the politest man I've ever met. After Denis left that evening, I ended up having dinner with him and William Burroughs. We talked about Tangiers. Things like that happened a lot more in those days.

The year before Francis Bacon died I took Damien Hirst to the Colony Room for the first time. This had a transforming effect on the very small room that was the club, as Damien introduced all his various colourful friends from Goldsmiths College. The bar was suddenly wild and busy again like it must have been in the 50s when Bacon and co. started to frequent it.

One night, after an evening at the Colony, I brought the poet Jock Scott and the artist Abigail Fallis back to my place. The house, in the Chancery Lane/Clerkenwell borders, has always seemed to be the place for the 'nightcap', perhaps because it is over a number of floors, that people seem to like running up and down. We were having a drink when Jock turned to Abigail and said "you're a fat cow," whereupon, quite rightly, she kicked him off his chair and started pummelling into him. Then she left and I put the dazed Jock to bed in the spare room. When I woke the next morning he seemed to have gone, so I went out to lunch. It transpired that he had got himself stuck in my gallery next door and had fallen asleep.

He woke and started to panic and the only numbers he could remember was his mother in Glasgow, who was no help, and the number for the Colony – this he rang and was told by someone that I had gone away for three months!

Jock went into shock and started calling through the letter box trying to get the builders next door to kick the door in which they wouldn't do, but instead they brought him a slice of pizza, a small bottle of whisky and a bottle of water. As it wouldn't fit through the letter box, they put a straw in it, and he drank it through that.

I came home at about 6 o 'clock to hear banging on the gallery door and was just as surprised to see Jock as he was to see me.

The Colony Room saw the end of many eras but now with the loss of its original home and the sad death of its last proprietor, the Pole - Michael Wojas - much of its history lies only in the memory (hazy).

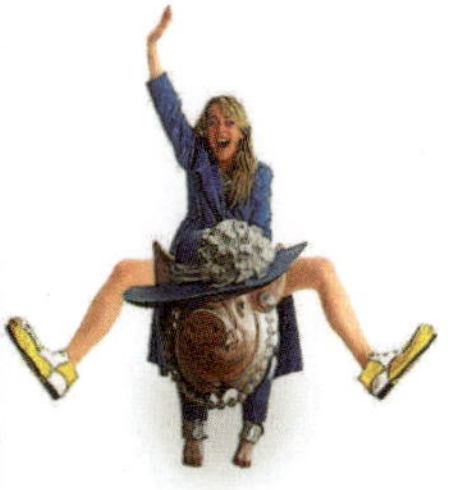

© *Oli Max*

"I'm Ashamed to Say I'm British Too"

By Vanessa Fristedt

Vanessa Fristedt - aka Swedish Blonde - is a fixture in the London art world. Her day-to-day occupation is designing brands and graphics but to many she is actually an honorary YBA. She featured in Ellen Cantor's movie Club Vanessa in 1996, and in Sam Taylor-Wood's Knackered (also 1996) where she appeared naked and miming to a singing castrato. She has been an integral part of the Art Car Boot Fair since its inception. A few years ago she bought a mahogany taxi boat from Venice during the Biennale and shipped it all the way to the Swedish Archipelago, where she now seems to have become a luxury taxi driver during the summer period.

IT WAS 1997, THE height of the party boom for London artists – especially the group that had come to be known by the press as the YBAs. Let's say it was a very vivid time for all of us.

Jake and Dinos Chapman, Mat Collishaw, Abigail Lane and a few others were part of a group show at The City Gallery in Prague. The title of the show was Close Echoes, Public Body & Artificial Space. I was invited by Abigail for pure pleasure. Little did I know I was to become her bollock-crushing bodyguard.

The city of Prague was beautiful and seemed untouched, but somewhere deep, I could sense the coldness from the Communist era creeping in the background.

Mat Collishaw had made a series of lenticular prints of young boys and flowers. Abigail showed prints of stuffed animals in household surroundings. Jake & Dinos' 'Fuck Face' sculptures of penis noses and Swastika emblems seemed to be highly cherished by the gallery attendants of the old guard. I asked one of them which art piece he preferred and he pointed at Jake & Dinos' sculpture and said "Favoriiit" with a wide smile. Having

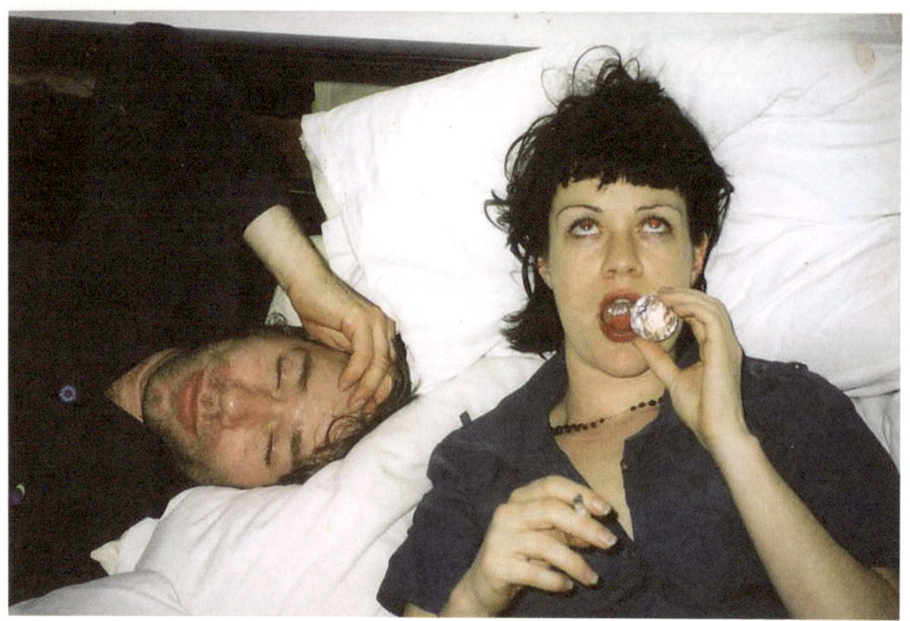

Prague bed – Mat Collishaw and Abigail Lane © Vanessa Fristedt

been used to a lot of laid-on drinks at openings, we were surprised there was nothing on offer whatsoever, so Mat took the situation into his own hands and set up his very own bar in the courtyard. A table with Absinthe and spirits miraculously appeared, all thanks to the one and only Mat. True Family Collishaw style!

Later, we went for dinner in the basement of a traditional Czech restaurant. Suddenly Abigail realised she was being poked in the back. We looked behind us to a table inhabited by an old Czech geezer, eating dumplings along with his two pals. Nothing was said: we continued to eat. A second poke arrived and Abigail got really frustrated. What on earth did this old man have against her, the smallest and cutest of us all? I turned around and told the old poof to stop hurting her: "If you touch her one more time, I promise I will crush your balls!" Believe it or not, the old man did it again. Third time unlucky! Since I had to stand by my word, I jumped up from the table, and so did the dumpling-eater.

Within a second, my hand went for his crotch and I squeezed his Czech bollocks as hard as I could. No crushing noise, just the feeling of a warm humid sac of balls wrapped in synthetic nylon fabric. (Like squeezed dumplings I suppose.) The tall Czech slowly fell over me, and with his weight, pushed me into a tight corner. Our table became worried that he was attacking me, but, no, he'd only passed out with the strength of the ball squeeze. I was surprised by my own actions. This was my first bollock crushing. I went back to our table. The man left the restaurant in silence.

Wherever we went, we kept bumping into a lost-looking English journalist in a wheelchair. I can't remember his name. Let's call him Superman. The cobbled streets were a nightmare for him and it must have been hard for him to do his job, so we took charge of wheeling him around all night long. We walked the streets looking for a late night drink and stumbled across a club in yet another basement. God knows how we managed to carry Superman in his wheelie down the narrow steep stairs. Tons of Absinthe was somehow snorted with spoons and sugar until we felt totally numb. Afterwards, we went back to Mat and Tracey Emin's hotel room (They were a couple then). The room was small, so we all laid down on the bed and started throwing cushions at each other. It escalated into a massive cushion fight. The ornaments flew, chandeliers swung and Superman flew out of his wheelchair and bounced into the bed too. Finally, we'd set him free!

The following day, a handwritten note was found under Mat and Tracey's door. The note read: "Do not repeat last night. I am ashamed to say I'm British too." There was no name, just a scribble, as if it was written by Zorro. Who was this anti-party patriot? We took the scribbled note to the nearest printers and made several t-shirts emblazoned with the scanned words. It became our mantra. We wore it for a few days to see if we could find out who the ashamed person was but the guilty one was never to be found.

In those days, it was possible to get out of bed the following day, after a night like this. These were the days when every other week would throw up a story like this.

Nothing has changed that much now actually, apart from me giving up squeezing strange mens' balls. But I could always go back to it, if pushed.

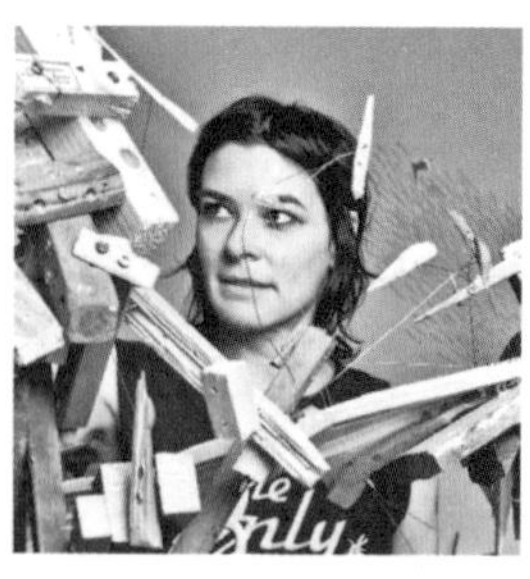

The Keys to The City

by Sue Webster

Sue Webster is an artist best known for her collaborative works using lights and shadows made under the auspices of 'Tim Noble and Sue Webster': In 2009 Sue was made Doctor of Art (Dart) at Nottingham Trent University. In the London art world and beyond, the three little words 'Tim and Sue' have now become synonymous with a certain kind of party that's certainly not to be sniffed at. If you want hedonism, here's hedonism for you.

MADAME M CHECKS INTO the not quite-officially-open yet-exclusive-members-only club house in Berlin with a handful of other invited guests, some time on Thursday afternoon accompanied by Mr D after a short flight from London's Terminal 5, with a recently married Jackie Longlegs travelling on the back seat of the same airplane.

No credit card details have as yet been requested.

A handful of guests agree to meet later for pre-something or other drinks in the penthouse inhabited by whatsisname. Said penthouse just happens to overlook the exhibition space where Madame M and Mr D are showing later that same evening a chocolate-y looking sculpture made from direct rubber casts of Mr D's penis. The penis casts make for the highlight of tonight's group exhibition somewhere on Auguststraße......

After listening to all four sides of DEUTSCHE ELEKTRONISCHE MUSIK from 1972-1983 on the portable PYE mini record player specific to room 24, Madame M and Mr D elevate themselves from floors five to eight in the stainless steel lift that somebody has already offensively graffitied by scratching a swastika with their dirty finger nails into its fawn-coloured padded leather walls.

The doors open on to the rooftop pool area. Tucked in the corner under the parasols is a small group they recognise from London; it includes the mother of a famous Young British Artist, his Mafioso type accountant, his wife, and others who run his operation. A shoeless and casually dressed man with wet hair who they recognise as being the owner of this establishment, beckons them over and offers drinks from the tray of a passing waitress, which he thrusts into their hard-working hands. Excited words are exchanged and pink bubbles spill effortlessly down dry and grateful throats. Many glasses later Madame M and Mr D leave in order to attend the opening of their show: no drinks bill ever arrives and so off they scurry into one of a long line of waiting limousines in the street below.

Once at the opening, they pour more pink bubbles down their throats. Later, at the same event, a man known only as The Gimp arrives driving a big black BMW. He steals the two heroes of the hour and drops them at Berlin's famous Grill Royale for the pre-show dinner of the aforementioned famous artist, where Madame M announces that she won't be able to survive the weekend without a package. Mr D dutifully disappears with The Gimp under strict instructions not to return without said package.

Much later Mr D arrives with The Gimp and a rather large package; he whispers to Madame M that no money was requested for said package, as it was meant as a gift in return for some earlier favour given back in London.

Mr D sits in famous artist's seat whilst famous artist visits the lavatory. Mr D is promptly and mistakenly served famous artist's pasta which he insanely gobbles up while waiters look on disturbed. The Gimp announces that he is leaving for another venue, and deposits on the table a detailed map and a secret password for entry.

Madame M and Mr D leave Grill Royale for the next venue and exchange passwords with bouncer who protects the door. The Gimp waves from across a crowded bar in which he seems to be DJing. A litre of vodka and a pair of lead crystal glasses appear.

No money has yet changed hands.

A well-known gallery owner and wife appear at the entrance but don't have correct password and are denied entry. Madame M waves them in. More lead crystal glasses are produced and vodka flows, so encouraging much crazy dancing to music coming out of speakers that blow fuses several times during the night.

Another well-known art dealer arrives: Madame M snorts vodka from the palm of his soft white hand.

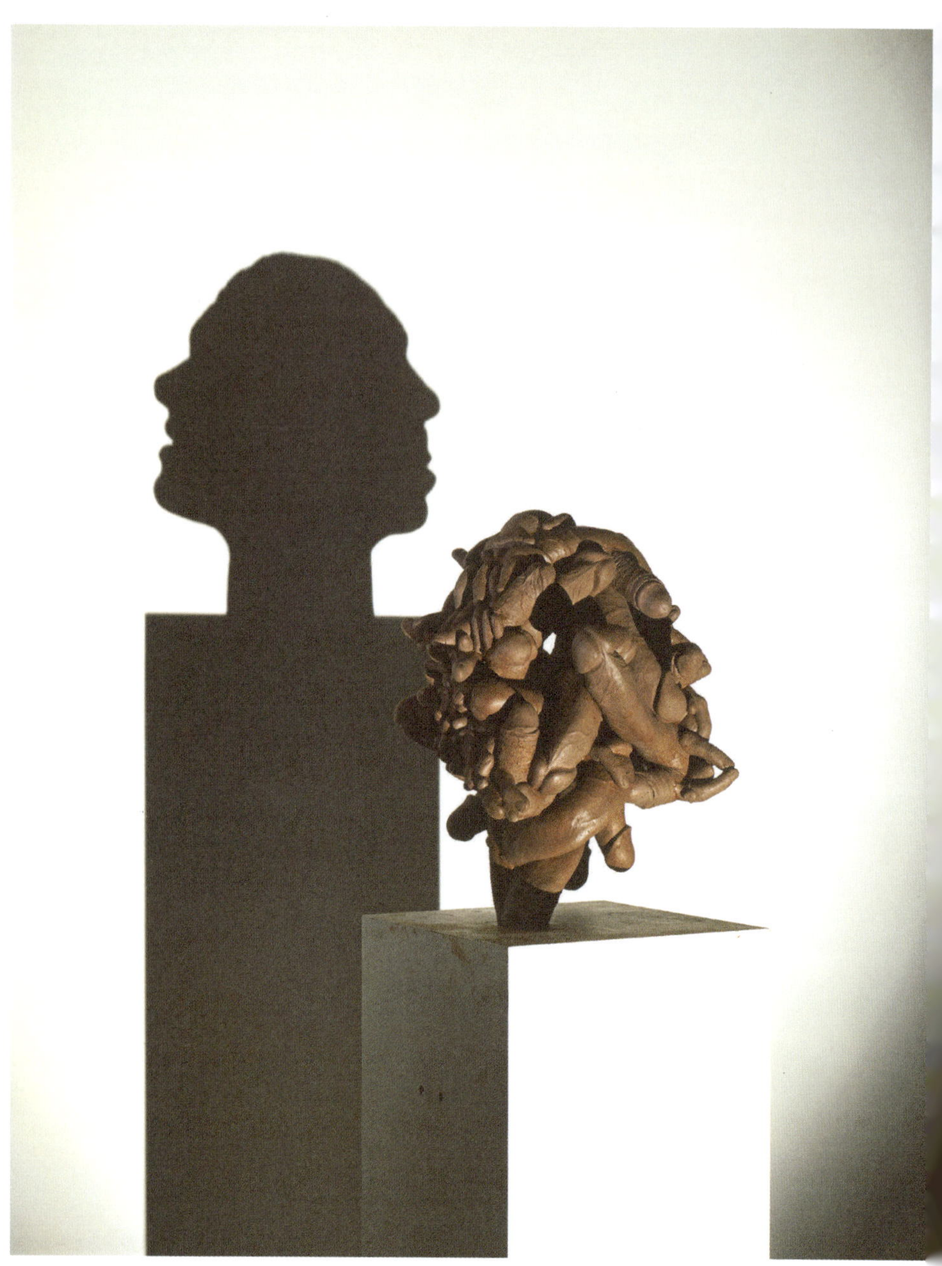

Tim Noble and Sue Webster Chocolate Narcissus 2008

Madame M and Mr D walk back to club house at Torstraße 1 where they began the night. They have a little sleep.

Downstairs the next day, where floors are being swept and windows washed in preparation for tonight's grand party for the famous artist, they are handed a tin of spray paint each and ordered by the casually dressed owner of the club to spray a sign of the club haus in pretty texts and colours on wooden hoardings that protect the special club from the outside world. Madame M and Mr D do as asked and club owner rewards them with complimentary head massage and a foot pedicure at the club house spa.

Madame M and Mr D venture outside the safety of the compound to ascend the spiky TV Tower situated on Panoramastrasse. They try to see if they can spot the rooftop pool of the exclusive club through rented binoculars. They can, and to their horror they vaguely recognise small ant-like creatures milling about the pool area, so rush back in order to meet fellow artists for cocktails and mutual insults before the night's events.

Still no money has been accepted. By now, everyone has given up offering.

Madame M and Mr D take a waiting limousine with fellow artists to see famous artist's show. Once there they notice an unattended office houses several bottles of Krug on ice so spend the entire private view proffering glasses to passing strangers.

Upon leaving, they are ushered into another waiting limousine with the well known gallery owner and wife and head back to exclusive club for the after-show party. The padded leather elevator is taken up to the seventh floor, where Champagne on ice awaits and the rock star Peaches is DJing.

Madame M loses Mr D and spends the next hour having dinner on lower floor with an ex-wife of recently deceased Malcolm McLaren. Then later, Madame M finds well-known gallery dealer and wife at other end of poolside bar and offers gallery dealer's wife some of the package. Much to Madame M's amazement, wife of gallery owner agrees and both disappear into nearby small room to share.

Well-known gallery dealer's wife reappears seconds later with two bored best friends who have come along for weekend to stop well-known gallery dealer's wife from feeling neglected. Dealer's wife shares information about package with two best friends, Madame M takes best friends Miss M and Mrs A into nearby cubicle to see package.

Madame M wanders off into other pockets of party regularly dipping into package and passing it to other best friends and fellow artists. Later, she bumps into Mrs A again who is grinning inanely and wearing dilated pupils the size of two saucepans. Mrs A clings onto Madame M's arm and announces that she "just wants to be free, like a butterfly," and is thinking of leaving her husband, whilst hurling Champagne bottles and glasses into rooftop infinity pool. She takes off her clothes and jumps in.

The rest of the party looks on.

Madame M spots the young son of a friend wandering aimlessly amongst the party and invites him back to her hotel room to view her latest etchings. Whilst doing so they listen to both sides of Lungs by Florence and the Machine on the PYE mini portable record player specific to room 24.

Madame M emerges the next day for rooftop swim. Even the roof looks hung-over and the pool is drained due to broken glass.

The third night is a repeat of the first night and of the second night. Sunday afternoon arrives and Madame M and Mr D check out of exclusive club house in Berlin. Madame M still has some of her package left and deliberates what to do. She decides to Sellotape what's left into lid of her toothpaste.

Madame M, and Mr D bump into Miss M and Mrs. A at Tegel airport where their collective hearts pound loudly as they pass through the X-Ray machine. They share a plane aisle then a cab back to London.

No money ever did change hands.

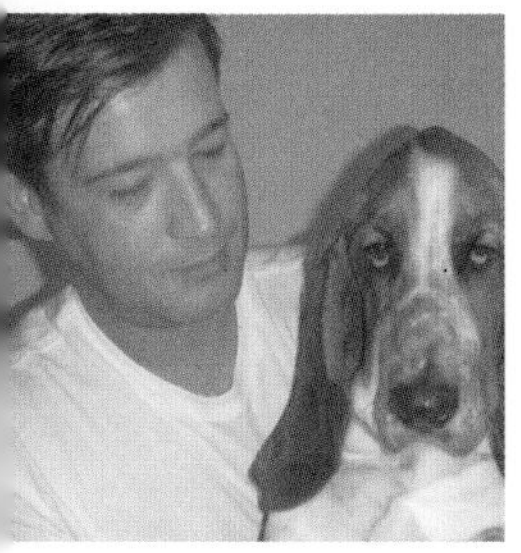

I Thought You Had To Be Dead To Make Art

by Gary Webb

Gary Webb is a sculptor who looks a bit like a wide-boy from Miami. His sculptures do too. Here are some of his thoughts on art.

BEFORE LEAVING SCHOOL, A teacher said to me, "You can only really go down the farming route." Maybe this spurred me on to be an artist. I wanted to do art but I thought you had to be dead to make it. Either that, or I thought that art was made in the after-world.

When I first went to Goldsmiths, our house in Peckham was surrounded by snipers, despite us being protected by the Swiss flag that I had hung out of my bedroom window. A girl had moved in downstairs and had got involved with the man next door, who'd been one of the Great Train Robbers - the only one to get grassed up by the others and to go to jail for a long time. When his girlfriend – our flatmate - got herself a younger boyfriend, the great big Cockney went mad and put two 'watchers' on the house. I found them on the street in their car. The beefcakes wouldn't talk to us, or even bat an eyelid.

I enjoy total complication, and misunderstandings like this in peoples' lives.

I've stopped worrying about putting things together, about letting the materials 'kiss' each other. They just do.

Experimentation always seems a bit childish. Just go ahead and make the work as it comes out of your head.

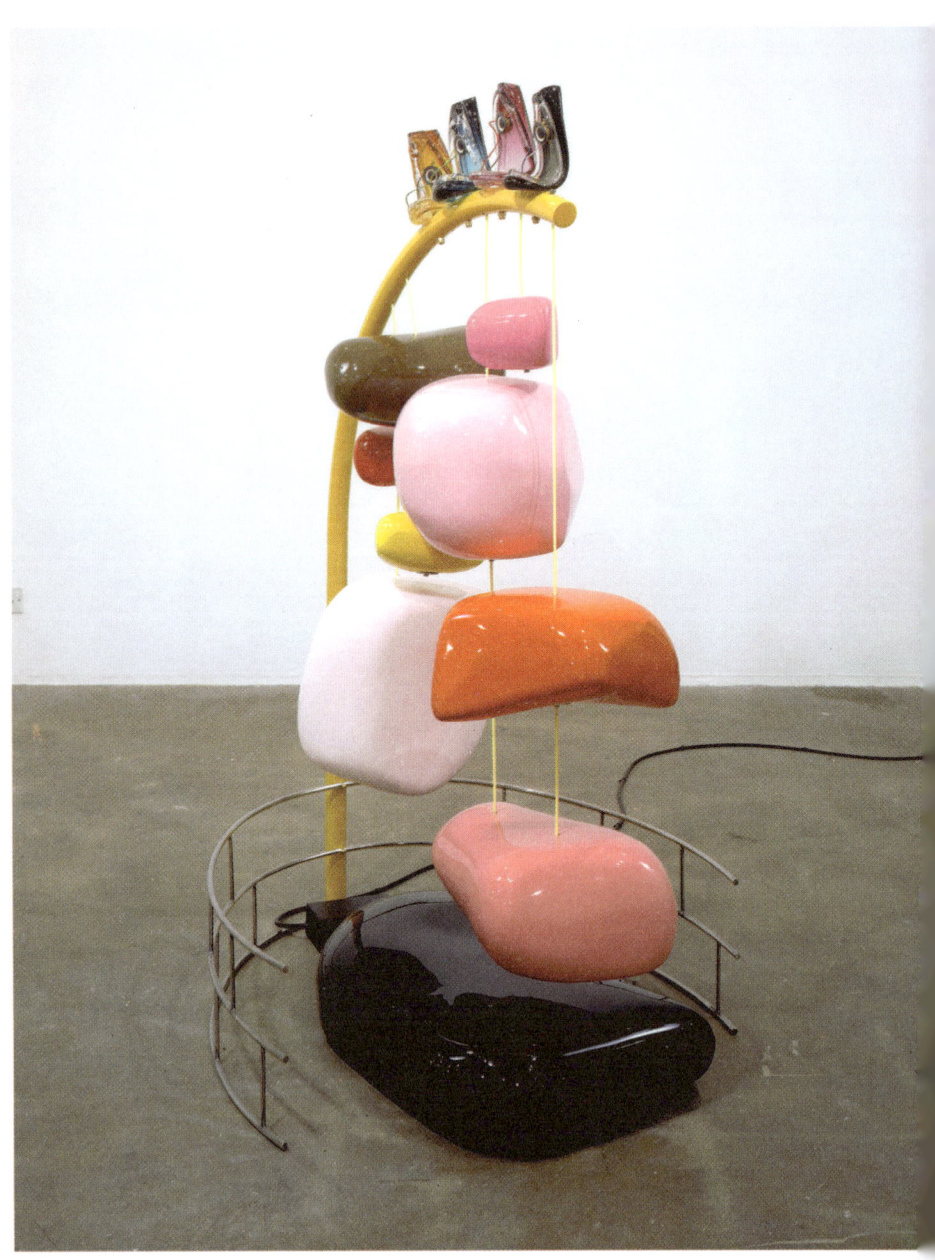

Mr Miami, Gary Webb. Courtesy of The Approach

Once, another artist "put a curse on me" because I was probably going a bit overboard, so I left and went to my friend Laura's house at four in the morning. I managed to climb over her railings and lower myself down to the outside basement part of her house. I found a twig to scratch on her window.

She finally opened the street level door, and I tried to climb back up. I lost my footing and fell so heavily on my ankle that my leg bone was sticking out of the skin. Apparently I said, "I have done something really very stupid," before passing out.

After three months in UCL, where I got MRSA (twice), I came out of hospital, went through the Rotherhithe Tunnel on my scooter, bashed into the pavement and smashed the knee of my other leg on the dashboard. Back in hospital for three months. It was difficult to work but I managed to keep in phone contact with my studio assistants and we got a fair bit done. It's good to have reliable studio assistants. And a very understanding gallerist, like mine – Jake Miller.

I'd also recommend finding a partner who looks like your art. My wife Gity looks like my sculptures. Apparently I do too.

If I go out late, (most art dinners or parties tend to go on quite late), I just wake up at exactly the same time I normally would – 7.30am – go the studio and work through any pain. You just have to pretend you don't have a hangover. Or you'd not get much done.

You have to be like a machine.

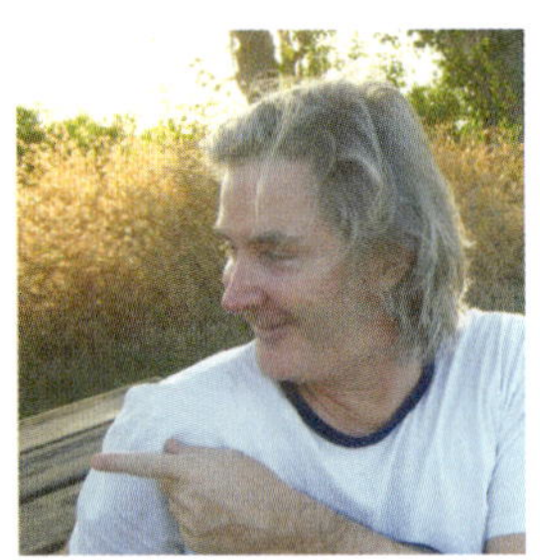

Hotel Suite Hotel Room: The Hotel Suite and the Hidden Ballroom

by Guy Kennaway

Guy Kennaway is a writer who prefers art that entertains rather than enlightens. He knows far too much about the art party in the hotel suite.

THE MANAGEMENT OF CAPRICE Holdings - the people that own The Ivy, J. Sheekey's and Scott's restaurants - made a deal with some artists to provide them with free meals in return for work to hang on the walls. It seemed to work well; Scott's and The Ivy got both the pictures and the artists, a double set of decorations for their dining room, and the artists got a few meals a month.

That evening in Scott's, there was excitement in the air; both the restaurant and oyster bar were full to standing. It was the night before the Damien Hirst extravaganza at Sotheby's, and it had been an excuse for everyone to gather in town to celebrate its success or gloat over its failure.

After Scott's I went on to the drunken kindergarten of the Groucho Club with some friends, and then up and down the noisy tube of Dean Street bars with their howling conversation and recurring people, (some from years ago, some from minutes ago), before exploding back onto the pavement. The party then split - the maniacs to Jerry's bar, and the rest of us into a sepulchral apartment near Charlotte Street to look at some art that was packed in to a room like Tutankhamun's tomb.

More people turned up, more peeled off and finally we were spun through the revolving glass door of Claridges Hotel onto the black and white marble squares which were being mopped by a man with a yellow plastic sign who we engaged in intense and apparently meaningful conversation.

With a nod from the security man we took the side lift up to the first floor and padded its thickly carpeted corridor to suite 108, the one with the flags on its balcony.

Flopped down, caught our breath, dialled 44 and ordered room service, answered the door to some more people and hit 44 to double the order. I looked around to see who we had lost and who we had accrued over the evening.

Reports came in of other parties in rooms and suites, below, around and above our own in the honeycomb of Claridges. The big hitters, the art tourists, foreign dealers, camp followers, entourages and Damien himself were all somewhere in the house.

No music, no TV, no distraction from the thing that we all loved above all other, and which was the addiction that kept us up all night, and bound us together, whether artists, lovers, wives, husbands, ex-enemies, newly found best friends or about-to-be ex-husbands: conversation.A chime of the bell brought the trolley, its sweating ice-buckets, cigarettes and glasses cushioned on starched napery, gliding over the carpet on its big rubber wheels. The waiter asked if we wanted the bottles opened, as if our lives were so sheltered we may not know how to do it ourselves.

Someone was telling a story about having her garbage stolen and various things from it turning up on the Internet. As the black sacks were only outside her house for a few hours before collection, she figured it might be possible to catch the thief red handed, so her boyfriend hung around on the opposite pavement, keeping an eye on the bag on the day the refuse was picked up. At the same time a woman happened to be walking down the street unwrapping a Starburst sweet and looking for somewhere to bin the wrapper. She saw the black sack and decided to tuck it into the top. As she did this perfectly reasonable thing the boyfriend flew across the street shouting "You little fucking bastard."

My attention was on the waiter, carefully keeping his eyes on the trolley and bottle, trained not to look around our little bubble, nor to give away what he thought of our self important world with all these noughts on the end if it.

The waiter departed, off to another suite on his party crawl with a trolley of bottles. Someone said they'd found a dead friend's 35mm camera and developed his last roll of pictures. There was a pause, as we all thought of it. "Were they any good?" a girl asked. "Quite a nice one of a beach, otherwise a bit blurred. You could tell he was dying of drink, they were mostly out of focus."

Talk turned happily to suicides. I said I had heard of a Welsh farmer who drank so much paraquat that nothing grew on his grave for three years.

Someone said that when they were at the Liverpool Biennial staying at the Adelphi, they had found behind a blanked off doorway in their hotel room, a huge dusty abandoned ballroom, with chandeliers and mirrors.

My hearing was getting confused. Someone said "Do you like to face the direction of travel?"

"What? On a train?"

"In life," said another. And I thought to myself how I had my back to the direction of travel in my life. I looked up to see a complete stranger opening the door and warmly welcoming more people into our suite.

A girl with a glistening patina of sweat was raising her voice, shouting "Trying to leave a mark on the world is a sign of stupidity, you idiot, not leaving any mark – that's what takes talent."

Hours later, anxiety crept like the dawn around the curtains. The girl had fallen asleep cupping a glass of champagne like a pet on her lap. A man who had to catch a flight to Rome in an hour was taken to the door leaning on two friends like a wounded soldier. I tried to find out the time but couldn't read my watch.

Finally the last one left; the door clicked shut and I picked among the wreckage for cigarettes like a scavenger on a battle field. I went to the window; the sky was lightening and I could hear the hush at the end of a long long night. Then my ears tuned into a high pitched whine. I saw the waiter leave the hotel, hurrying home with a friend after finishing their shifts. My mind tightened, and the room seemed to be sweating, beading on my face. I stared at a blanked out doorway to a bedroom, because I thought I saw it move on the wall. I felt suddenly as though my evening had been the opposite of the one in the Adelphi; I had been in a glittering ballroom with mirrors and chandeliers and managed to find a hole through to this airless chamber.

There are probably worse places to feel anxious and sad than a luxe hotel suite, but I don't know them. Things were askew inside me and out; and at that very moment, all over Asia, across India and sweeping towards London with the dawn, computer screens on trading floors and stock exchanges were lit with waterfalls of red as the money fountain sprang its fatal leak.

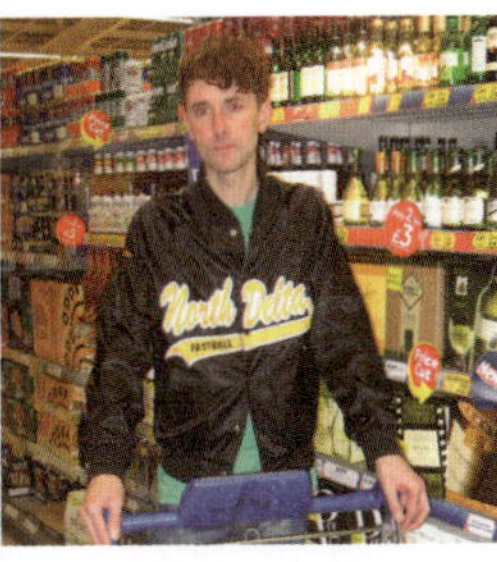 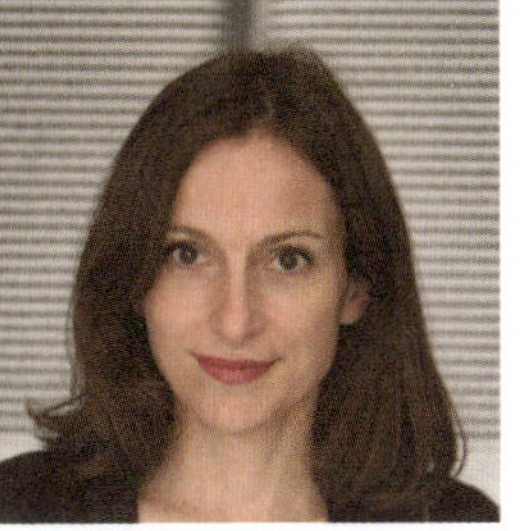

The Pleasures of Being an Artist

A conversation between Peter Davies and Sarah Thornton, in Peter's studio

Peter Davies is a painter represented by The Approach Gallery who also teaches at the Slade School of Fine Art (UCL).

Sarah Thornton is the author of Seven Days in the Art World. She writes about contemporary art for The Economist.

SARAH THORNTON: BEING AN artist is not just a job but an identity. Many people take some time before they feel comfortable declaring themselves an "artist" without apology or qualification. You've just turned 40 and only recently felt at ease with the label "artist."

Peter Davies: A couple of years ago, I was in Edinburgh, talking to my brother-in-law, who was lecturing me, and it dawned on me: Wow, I'm so relieved that I'm not a barrister. When I realised how lucky I was to be an artist, it was easier to be one. I am most happy when I am working in my studio. I love being here. Being an artist requires you to assert your right to exist as one because you are doing something that is non-essential. Artists don't fit into the normal roles of mainstream society but they don't want to.

ST: The mythic identities of the artist swing between the unrecognised ascetic artist slaving away in her garret and the debauched enfant terrible making a spectacle of himself in the limelight. Neither quite captures the real hedonism of being an artist.

THE FUN ONE HUNDRED

1. PABLO PICASSO — he had a lot of the above
2. MARCEL DUCHAMP — what a pisser
3. SALVADOR DALI — liked lots of checks (+ gold)
4. M. KIPPENBERGER — good mood NAZI gas station
5. RICHARD PRINCE — you must be joking
6. RENE MAGRITTE — Ceci n'est pas une blague
7. JEFF KOONS — shagging
8. PAUL McCARTHY — Santa Chocolate Schlop
9. PHILIP GUSTON — very studio(us)
10. CY TWOMBLY — scribble
11. SIGMAR POLKE — magic mushrooms
12. ED RUSCHA — burn Hollywood burn
13. G. MATTACLARK — prime cuts
14. CHRIS BURDEN — shoot to kill
15. BRUCE NAUMAN — fun from rear
16. DAVID SALLE — cavalier of the canvas
17. HENRI MATISSE — original formalist
18. J. POLLOCK — paint spill
19. RICHARD SERRA — weight watcher
20. JOHN BALDESSARI — he's making no more boring art
21. MIKE KELLEY — pant shitter and proud
22. ANDY WARHOL — Ass in hole(s)
23. W. DE KOONING — dutch courage
24. ROBERT SMITHSON — a quake in a lake
25. DUANE HANSON — white trash
26. J-M BASQUIAT — "The FUN'S over"
27. CHARLES RAY — road kill
28. GEORG BASELITZ — thats one way of doing it ....
29. V VAN GOGH — ouch! *@?
30. RAYMOND PETTIBON — goth cartoons
31. JASON RHOADES — total organised chaos
32. CINDY SHERMAN — dressing up
33. JULIAN SCHNABEL — plate rage
34. FRANK STELLA — very protracted
35. NAN GOLDIN — fancy trannies
36. CAROLL DUNHAM — foam filled funk
37. PHILIP TAAFFE — snakes and ladders
38. ROY LICHTENSTEIN — wham
39. STUART DAVIS — jazz bop
40. SOL LE WITT — interior decorator
41. VITO ACCONCI — what a tosser
42. SEAN LANDERS — 'you cannot be serious'
43. FRANCIS BACON — pissed and proud
44. ALEX KATZ — party time
45. F GONZALEZ-TORRES — candy man
46. MATTHEW BARNEY — the man who fell to earth
47. JOSEPH BEUYS — was he for real
48. PIERO MANZONI — shit happens
49. DAMIEN HIRST — silence of the lambs
50. KAREN KILIMNIK — Mrs Peel we're needed
51. DONALD JUDD — boxing clever
52. JOHN CURRIN — Renaissance man
53. CECILY BROWN — orgy-tastic
54. SUE WILLIAMS — fucked up
55. GARY HUME — stadium rock
56. LOUISE BOURGEOIS — hilarious interview style
57. BARRY LE VA — making a mess
58. JENNY SAVILLE — zombie flesh eaters
59. GEORGE CONDO — see number one
60. CHRIS OFILI — shit head
61. CHRISTOPHER WOOL — American graffitti
62. FRANCISCO GOYA — Hannibal the cannibal
63. JESSICA STOCKHOLDER — assembly line
64. GUSTAV KLIMT — oma-MENTAL-as anything
65. ANTHONY CARO — not really funny!
66. GILBERT + GEORGE — smashed
67. CARL ANDRE — nice brickwork
68. CHUCK CLOSE — up close + personal
69. DIETER ROTH — trash the gaff
70. KEN NOLAND — Oin Oin Oin OinOinOin O
71. MARIKO MORI — temple of doom
72. UGO RONDINONE — sooper model wannabes
73. PIET MONDRIAN — celebrity squares
74. LAURA OWENS — feel good art
75. DAN FLAVIN — how many artists does it take to change a lightbulb?
76. TERRY WINTERS — space invader
77. ROBERT GOBER — wall paper
78. ERIC FISCHL — bad boy
79. YVES KLEIN — blue movie style
80. JORG IMMENDORF — bar brawls
81. GLEN SEATOR — checks cashed
82. PIPILOTTI RIST — road rage
83. JAMES ROSENQUIST — stealth bomber
84. JASPER JOHNS — star spangled banner
85. ANDREAS GURSKY — Nike Town
86. DAVID HOCKNEY — pool attendant
87. ELLEN GALLAGHER — funny faces
88. RITA ACKERMANN — get a job
89. RICHARD HAMILTON — The Beatles: The Beatles
90. ASHLEY BICKERTON — beach bum
91. JULIAN OPIE — virtual reality
92. ANDRES SERRANO — pissed christ
93. PETER HALLEY — cell by date
94. TONY OURSLER — ventriloquist dummy
95. ALBERT OEHLEN — portrait of A. Hitler
96. DOUG AITKEN — Electric Earth
97. MARTIN HONERT — tourist trap
98. SARAH LUCAS — toilet humour
99. JACK PIERSON — WHAT THE FUCK
100. VANESSA BEECROFT — hanging out

The Fun One Hundred (The Pink Top Version), 2000 by Peter Davies - Courtesy of The Approach

PD: Artists are basically hedonists with specific interests who indulge them for their job. As an artist, your time is your own and you're answerable to yourself. It's not like doing statistics in some office. You follow your own interests. It's not about being visible, rich, or famous. It's about doing what you want to do. It is a pleasure, but it's also work.

ST: In your painting, The Fun One Hundred, Picasso is ranked number one with the comment "He had a lot of the above." What kind of fun do you think Picasso had?

PD: I think Picasso lived life "large" and indulged his passions. Kind of sex, drugs'n rock'n'roll, but mainly sex. He loved his work. He was a bon viveur. In general, for all the artists in the list, making art is hard work that is fun.

ST: If you take a long historical view, art is related to affluence. It's only after you've covered the necessities in life – like food and shelter - that you get a society with art as we know it. So it's no accident that there are more artists now than ever. Is being an artist a luxury?

PD: In a Neanderthal world, being an artist would be superfluous. But the presence of lots of artists reflects that our world has developed into something sophisticated - a place where we are able to indulge in luxuries, which are the things that make life worth living!

ST: Do you think you have sharper insights when you are having fun? Some research suggests that working too hard - banging your head against the canvas or computer keyboard - is a recipe for artistic block. Do you have any advice for students about the pleasures of art making?

PD: In becoming an artist, a student has to question everything they are told. In other words, to answer back and rebel against prevailing wisdom - that can only be fun - and find a way to celebrate the idiosyncrasies of one's own personality through making art. You can't make exciting work if you're a total square. Curiously the figure seen as the godfather of UCL where I teach, Jeremy Bentham, a radical political thinker, was a legendary proponent of hedonism and that informed his enthusiasm for individual freedoms.

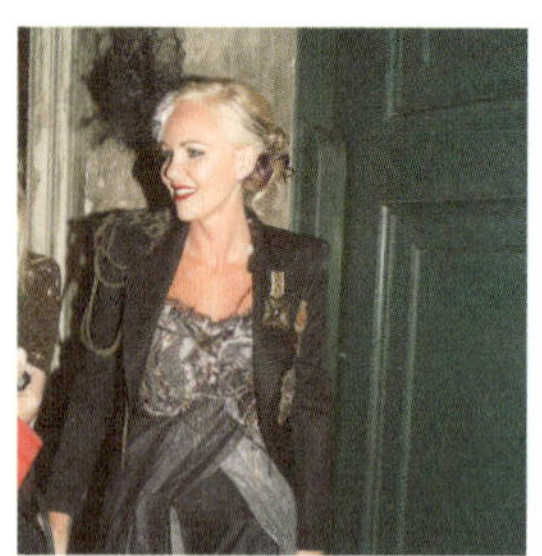

I Welcomed the Art World in, and Life Got More Interesting

By Amanda Eliasch

Amanda Eliasch is the fashion editor of Genlux Magazine, an artist, photographer, writer, and art collector who lives in LA, Paris and London. Her life – dependent on three Blackberry phones - is an international tornado of events. And blogging.

WHAT DOES IT MEAN TO ME? Wild and untamed friends. I like the fact that you can't guarantee what they are going to say, think or do. They are unpredictable in their behaviour, perhaps more so than in their work. I used to claim a million years ago that I hated contemporary art. That was before I met Charles Saatchi, perhaps one of the most interesting men I have ever come across.

I met him in Thailand at the Amanpuri hotel in Christmas 1991. Pregnant and fat, I was laughing with friends and he asked me where I lived. I said Chester Square. He said: "How old is your husband?" I said 28. He said: "I want to meet a man who is able to live in Chester Square at 28". It was the start of an interesting friendship and one in which he apparently called my ex-husband "the cleaner" on account of his ability for tidying up difficult business.

I remember going round to Charles' house in St Leonard's Terrace: contemporary, shiny and new. There was a cartoon baby sculpture by Ron Mueck on the floor, a huge vat containing a sheep by Damien Hirst, and on the wall a stunning pink and green painting by Michael Craig Martin. I had no idea what they were, just that they were unforgettable. Now those artists are familiar friends.

That night I had been invited for dinner - roast chicken - in Kay and Charles's funky kitchen. I liked everything in it except some old boxes of Brillo pads in the corner, and said so out loud in my slow Sloaney drawl. I got a sharp prod on my shins from my husband, and realised I had made a boo-boo, - Warhol's supposedly beautiful work was being criticised by an uneducated fool. I then set myself the task of learning everything I could - eventually ending up photographing and putting together a book for Italian Vogue's Editor Franca Sozzani and Assouline with the title British Artists at Work.

It takes quite a few years to be accepted by this elite group of artists and when Franca first asked me to do a book, I was expecting a fashion commission. Franca is an incredible woman. Slim, vital and a brilliant visionary - there is nobody like her. Anyway, I went down her narrow corridor and entered her office. Piles of books, invitations and billets doux were in front of me: little messages from Galliano, a drawing from Gaultier. It wasn't daunting but an honour to be in such brilliant company. She looked at me and said: "Can you do ten photographs of new artists before March?" (It was February...) Not thinking, I said yes. I left happy and went immediately to find the newest and most interesting creators - Jim Lambie, Martin Maloney, Fiona Rae and Kirsten Glass among them - and showed Franca my work a month later.

She said: "Lets make a book." And this is how I met Tim Noble & Sue Webster, Mat Collishaw and Tracey Emin. I have images of them all - Tim and Sue in front of two humping rats; Mat Collishaw, suave, sophisticated, and quiet; Tracey Emin in her tidy studio with all her patchworks colour co-ordinated and her father watering the plants on her terrace.

Many of them came to stay with me in France, and after ten years I have so many memories of summers together. I love the wonderful presents Tim and Sue have given me, especially the Fairy Liquid bottle they drew all over as we are both 50 this year (Fairy Liquid and me). Then there are the drawings Tracey has sent me, tiny little images of cats and birds, delicately drawn with sweet messages to Mandy Brown (my maiden name). And I treasure the white shirt Mat, Polly Morgan and Tracey drew all over, with helicopters and Princess Diana on it.

The latest present I received was a fantastic video the artists made me for my birthday, ending up with Tim in the nude in a bubble bath. Honestly, get these guys into your life and you will have a lot to be thankful for.

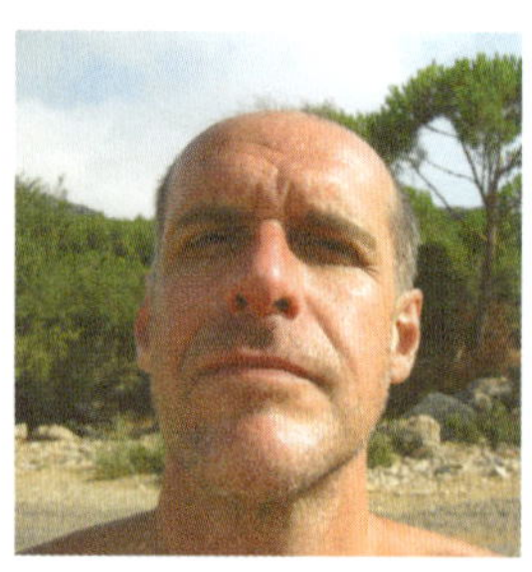

"I Didn't Travel Five Thousand Miles Just to Have Fun" - Leigh Bowery

by Richard Torry

Richard Torry is a fashion designer, DJ and musician. He co-founded the band Minty, with the legendary art figure Leigh Bowery, who was one of the more influential figures in the 80s and early 90s London art scene, and who died in 1994. Richard Torry makes music and designs costumes for, amongst others, the Michael Clark Dance Company.

I MET LEIGH IN 1982 in New York, as part of a series of fashion shows at the The Roxy Roller Rink. He was walking towards me to introduce himself; sweet and eager like a schoolboy but awkward in sub-Westwood fashions.

We visited the bathhouses and became good friends until the middle of the Taboo era when our careers went separate ways. I still saw him a lot, although he was usually in performance mode. Maybe once a year we met socially.

Early Leigh to late Leigh is a straight line. He had clear ambitions and managed to surpass them. In retrospect, his secret HIV diagnosis added more gravitas and maturity to his aims: of freeing inhibitions by exploring behavior, often exploiting the puerile and juvenile; of stimulation of and by interesting people through the heightened awareness created by embarrassment; of a delight in surprises and making space for freedom.

Later as a performer, he became skilled at physical techniques, constantly claiming space, using the sheer bulk of his outfits, moving away and then looming over you, rushing at people, grabbing your hand and dragging you somewhere.

One New Year's Eve, at the artist Andrew Logan's party, I was wearing one of my designs, a sweater covered in woolly loops, talking like the moody cunt I am to Malcolm McLaren, Leigh spotted us and rushed over saying, "Hi Malcolm isn't Richard such a talented designer? Isn't this sweater a work of art?" Leigh hugged me, rubbing his body against me, ensuring the loops of the jumper entangled with the sequins of his outfit, so we were glued together.

Leigh said "Lets all dance!" clearing a big space on the dance floor by bashing into everyone around, making a very funny spectacle I couldn't escape, until the sequins and string were ripped apart.

That jumper had taken ages to make, but it got the party started!

In 1990 I invited Leigh round to re-establish our friendship. I lent him a couple of books, not expecting to get them back. Six months later he came round to return them. We became friends again.

We played lots of 'games' to develop ideas, such as 'Consequences'. Over coffee in Soho, Leigh and I developed a game in which we would point out a passer by and perform a quick quack psychoanalysis of them by asking whether they were a cat or dog person.

Prominent types emerged: 'affirmation seekers reinforcing their self identity' was one but Leigh loved the 'exposers highlighting their own absurdity'.

He would attack me relentlessly with jokes in different styles. Queeniest NY speak, Reeves & Mortimer clowning, and so on, until he had me flipping from the chair, convulsing in laughter on the floor. Then he'd say, "Oh you're so predictable, I just have to turn on that tired old English Monty Python humour and I've got you."

The reason I think Leigh and Minty stood out was because we agreed to show contempt for the club scene. Although we had emerged from that scene it was becoming corporate and skilled at treating people like cattle. The dance genre had become a straitjacket and club land was a conforming force.

We believed there were better ways to move and wanted to encourage people to change, explore and undo their habits and invent NEW dances!

Having said that, we did find something else at the legendary club Fist: a sea of shiny black rubber and leather which Leigh towered over in bright fluorescent pink and green Lycra topped with a tall penis hat; we were inspired by lesbians in the backroom who were fisting gay men. We thought this an incredible cultural change in behavioral patterns and it inspired our hot hit song Useless Man.

Leigh was a modern day court jester or clown - he was really out-there man! And that is rare and undervalued. We both felt comedy to be life affirming

Clowns reflect fears, catalyse thoughts, stir up life, defrost situations. Leigh did all this and teamed it with adroit social critique.

For instance, he would praise and flatter people insightfully, using startling references to other work like "I love the way you've teamed Botticelli with Sarah Lucas, that's revolutionary!" I would think, 'Wow this is something special. I see what he's getting at, this could be the future…' Which made it all the more shocking when, after they left, he would pretend to vomit, and say "What timid wank, where's the poison! Listen to me spout that shit back there! Ughh!" and proceed to give an erudite critique demolishing the work or the outfit in question.

It was his modus operandi: to take two opposing viewpoints to extremes and under-stand them both in depth.

At one point McLaren wanted to manage Minty but we already had management. I think this is telling. Malcolm came from a school of thought where a strong back-story or manifesto was essential to the group he was managing: and so did Minty. Leigh at times tried to deny this manifesto, saying 'Ideas for ideas sake.'

We had a lovely holiday in Greece four months before he died: we enjoyed watching the birds get their breakfast each morning as we awoke after sleeping on the beach. It was during this holiday we decided we wanted to change the way people behaved, and in doing so, change a corner of the world. If his death wasn't so untimely, I believe we would have succeeded.

He was more than the sum of his incredible, memorable looking parts. His influence went further. The 'Bowery-esque' is now an attitude to life.

He was, by all accounts, Australian.

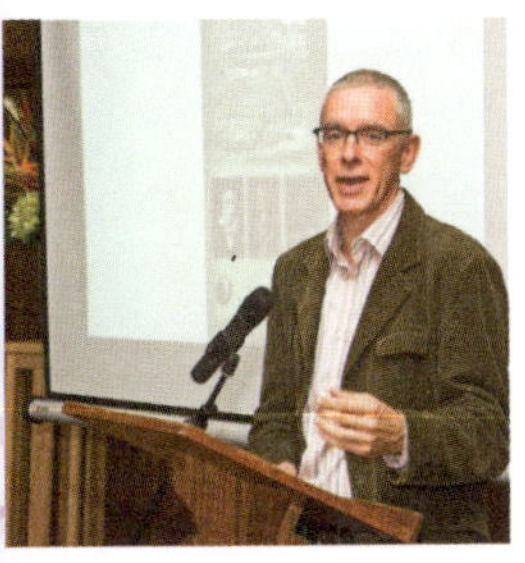

Confessions of a Buddhist Hedonist

by Maitreyabandhu

He attended what became the most talked about conceptual art department in Britain; his contemporaries who were soon to become known as the YBAs, but Maitreyabandhu – then known as Ian Johnson – took a different path and became ordained as a Buddhist. He now leads the uncluttering of minds at the London Buddhist Centre in East London. In 2009 he won both the Keats-Shelley Prize and the Geoffrey Dearmer Prize for poetry.

I WAS ALREADY OUT OF STEP. Damien Hirst was down the corridor nailing books onto pieces of wood, Sarah Lucas was musing on gender, Liam Gillick was saying something I couldn't understand. I was too shy to hob-knob with the tutors at the college bar: I got drunk and pretended to speak fluent French. I was not to become famous.

On the day of my Goldsmith's College interview, I wore white, winklepicker shoes and carried just one small folder of work. My name was Ian Johnson. I'd renounced my job as a staff nurse and gone in search of the Meaning of Life. After a dope-fuelled epiphany in front a Van Gogh landscape, I'd decided that *Art* was the best place to look.

I went to Goldsmith's to have fun and be a success; but I floundered in the highly charged, highly competitive environment. I hadn't read Foucault. 'Fun' kept on evading me. I couldn't plan to *have it* and then reliably *experience* it. And no one talked about 'Meaning' in those days (not with a capital M anyway). It was passé, like an interest in life drawing or watercolours.

I couldn't find anything to base my life upon. I didn't believe in God; I didn't want years of therapy; deconstruction was doing my head in! Someone lent me their copy of *Zen*

Mind, Beginner's Mind. I didn't understand that either, but something fascinated me. So I cycled to the London Buddhist Centre and learnt to meditate. I was 24. As soon as I sat to follow my breath, I knew I was a Buddhist. It was not a profound experience. It was more like hearing someone explain something I'd half-intuited but never been able to put into words. My degree show was a celebration of that: I shrugged off the designer nihilism I'd aspired to and embraced *colour.* One of my tutors said my paintings were almost bad mannered in the context of Goldsmith's College.

I left art school and moved into a Buddhist community; I carried on painting my 'spots and blotches' as a friend called them. I became artist in residence in a boy's Catholic school in Dagenham. The school was on the edge of the largest council estate in Europe. I still wanted fun; but I wanted pleasures that could deepen and enrich, rather than satiate and bloat. But even with my newfound Buddhism, my daily meditation practice, the friends I'd made, I still struggled with the isolation of the studio – the despair and elation of paint, the apparent pointlessness of pictures.

I wanted pleasure *and* meaning. I wanted them hyphenated. And I experienced that from time to time, in the midst of drawing a tree, or in the quiet of meditation. I experienced it looking at a few apples by Cézanne. I'd suddenly have 'the right eyes' as Rainer Maria Rilke put it: a new kind of 'meaning-pleasure' would open up to me. But most of the time I was stuck in a garden shed in Dagenham painting pictures no one wanted. So I became the caretaker at the London Buddhist Centre.

I renounced art and devoted myself to vacuuming. At least it made a difference. I went on my first solitary retreat in Wales – two weeks with no distractions, apart from miserable-looking sheep and the sound of rain. I had to face my mind. It was not a pretty sight. And what surprised me, on that retreat, was not the mad-axe-man fears but the new experience of – what? – faith I suppose, except that sounds too religious. The Buddhist word is *sraddha*; it is the emotional response to the experience of value. My intention for the retreat had been to decide whether to ask for ordination or to apply to do my art MA. It felt like a choice between meaning and pleasure. I chose pleasure.

Or I thought I did. Actually, I asked for ordination. I carried on living in the community and deepening my understanding of Buddhism and meditation. Two years later, in the midst of a four-month retreat in Spain, I was ordained into the Western Buddhist Order now renamed as the Triratna Buddhist Order). I was given my name Maitreyabandhu, which means 'kindly friend'. It was a name to live up to.

I ended up teaching the class I first came along to. I still teach it now, twenty years later. And I've not given up on art. I've written about it, given lectures and led retreats on the relationship between art and spiritual life. I've even carried on making pictures whenever possible, although increasingly the rhythms of poetry have replaced the business of paint. Since my ordination I've wanted to show how art and Buddhism can be part of the same exploration, the same trajectory into whatever lies beyond the banalities of egotism. It is a journey into deeper pleasure and heightened significance. Think of 'pleasure-meaning' as a definition of (old-fashioned word) 'Beauty'. Except beauty is a word meaning *nothing more can be said*.

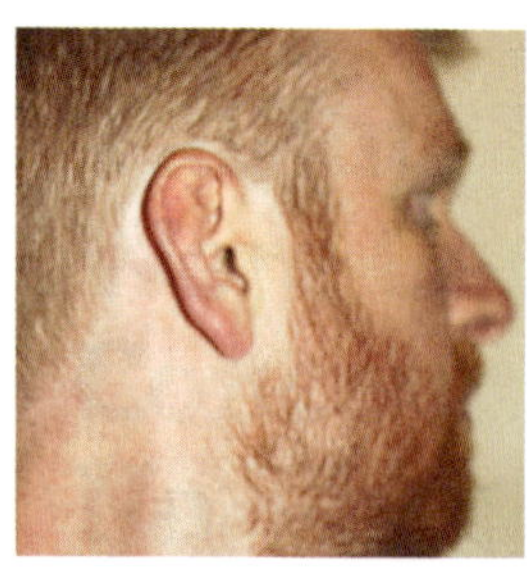

HUG

by Adam James

Adam James is a London based artist and graduate of the Royal College of Art. Working across the disciplines of sculpture, performance and film, his work mixes traditional processes with slapstick and the observations of modern day social tragedies. His practice seeks to exhume the hidden narratives dwelling in the darker recesses of society.

He reached the point of no return recently, when he invited his friends over to a kitten shower for his newly acquired pet. He's not even that embarrassed about it.

H^{EY,}

It's really good to hear from you. Sorry I haven't been in touch in a while, I have had some important news recently and have been trying to piece things together since.

Do you remember I told you that I had never met my dad? Well, my mum and he had a whirlwind romance fuelled by LSD in the 1970s, of which I was the result. Dad had been diagnosed as paranoid schizophrenic, and very soon after I was born became violent, so mum picked me up and left. I have never heard from him since and it had always been something I needed to do, to find him. Well, after years of thinking about it I finally plucked up the courage to go and start looking for him. Me and my girlfriend Boo began looking online to see if I could find him on any of those family tree websites. I searched for his name and the year he was born and very quickly we found him. Staring us in the face was his birth certificate. But there next to the online birth certificate was an option that read 'Click for death certificate'. I was stunned. The search that I had waited thirty years to begin was over in five minutes and a few clicks of the mouse. Click. My dad is dead.

It turns out he died six years ago. The following weeks were an emotional roller coaster. How did he die? Was it really my dad? At that time I didn't know of any family on my father's side, only vague stories of mad aunts and lobotomised grandmas told to me by my mum. Desperate to know the circumstances I contacted the coroner's office in Birmingham, where he died. Frustratingly I was told I would need to wait weeks until his next of kin had been contacted. I was told this was due to the sensitive nature of his case.

A few days later my phone rang. A lady called Shirley with a Brummie accent introduced herself as my step-gran saying she had been contacted by the coroner's office. Turns out dad got married to a lady called Tina, Shirley's daughter. Like my father Tina too suffered from schizophrenia. A letter from the coroner and a long conversation with Shirley broke the news that Dad had hung himself from a tree in a park, near where he lived in Moseley, Birmingham.

I caught the first train to Birmingham to visit his grave and to meet Shirley. She told me about my new family. Two aunts, two uncles, cousins and rumour of two half sisters. My head was spinning.

I visited dad's grave, and left him a letter. Saying goodbye to someone you have never met, isn't easy. Hug, as I found out his family called him, was to me a work of fiction that I had been terrified of, yet as I got older I started to see him in the faces of outsiders and the lives of those forgotten by society. I always took solace in the possibility of finding him.

It was weeks before I told Mum.

1 year later…

'Dead Body' Scare at Art Gallery – Hornsey & Crouch End Journal

… Guards were called to investigate a possible break-in at John Jones Gallery – The Project Space, when an alarm went off in the exhibition room after closing hours.

They found no evidence of a burglary but were spooked when their torches shone on the eerie lone figure in the corner of the room. Rather than investigate further they immediately called the police.

Kate Jones from the gallery said: "We had a call to say a dead body had been found in the project space - shocking news which sent us into a panic too. But we were then called back shortly after, by the police saying that they had been in and discovered the figure was not in fact a real man. At which point it dawned on us that what they had seen was in fact a life size piece of art in our current show."

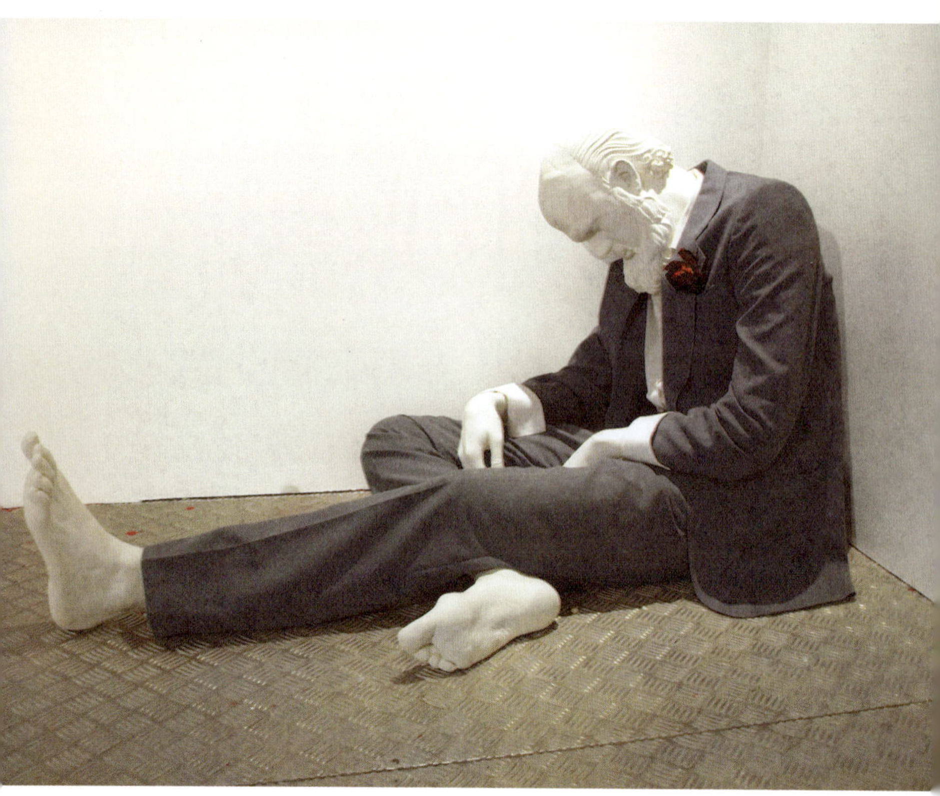

Hug, Adams James

The piece dubbed "Hug" is dressed in wedding tops and tails and modelled on photographs of the artist Adam James's father. A police spokeswoman confirmed they were called to the scene, but then "discovered it was in fact a mannequin".

Him and Me: Possessing the Dispossessed

Finding out about my dad's death caused somewhat of a knee jerk reaction in me. I knew I needed to make work about it, almost unquestionably. I needed to make something that expressed my renewed feeling of closeness to this distant character in my life. It felt wrong to perform as him, but I liked the idea of getting closer through pretending to be him. So I decided to make a statue from a cast of myself dressed as he was in a newly acquired photo of him as the groom at his wedding to Tina. I wanted to make a statue that was asleep, possibly drunk, but resting nevertheless, as I now felt he was. I immersed myself in the process and treated the sculpture of HUG as simply another appropriated character. It wasn't until HUG was assembled and I stood in the

148

gallery with my newly acquainted uncle that I was able to assess how I felt about the experience. Sad, yes. Happy at the thought of what on earth my Dad would think of me making a sculpture of myself dressed as him.

Dealing with the enigma of my father has always been crucial to me and at the heart of my practice. In my life I have always been drawn to figures whom I felt could be him: the outsiders, homeless, drunks or the mentally ill. Those that are displaced and wandering as he very well could have been. The relentless dramas on the street are what keep me engaged: I am attracted to the odd gestures, peculiar voices, laughs and awkward encounters that I am witness to every day. My work is the product of the inevitable osmosis of these observations.

My performances take examples of these momentary gestures and inflate them into the absurd. I take my references from the anonymous man, the local 'weirdo' and the ones on the bus you shouldn't look at but do. I observe them, then copy their every move in order to invent a story about them. They are reconfigured as characters in a performance or in a sculpture where I play on the obvious clichés and stereotypes of the vagabond. In the past I have taken on the mantle of the notorious boxer Paul Sykes, a homeless drunk from Wakefield. I have performed many pieces – as him – including swearing at the public in the Royal Academy, flashing in Tate Britain and hurling cans of lager in the ICA. I will soon be playing the protagonist in Man in Wheelchair (1959-62) by Leon Kossoff – a painting in the Tate's Collection – at Tate Britain.

When I go home to the safety of reflection I meditate on these performances. I have come to the following conclusion: My father was a frightening unknown character, a dark man living in the shadows of the world, ready to come and get me at any time and in any place. I feel the loss but also the presence of my dad woven into these situations, and the tragedy of these characters who miss their children and are shunned by those who love them. These anonymous scoundrels and jesters, drunk and unwieldy on the streets, have become the modern day witches, scapegoats of a brutally capitalist system; laughed at by many, pitied by few. The wasted land of their paths becomes the fabric of my work.

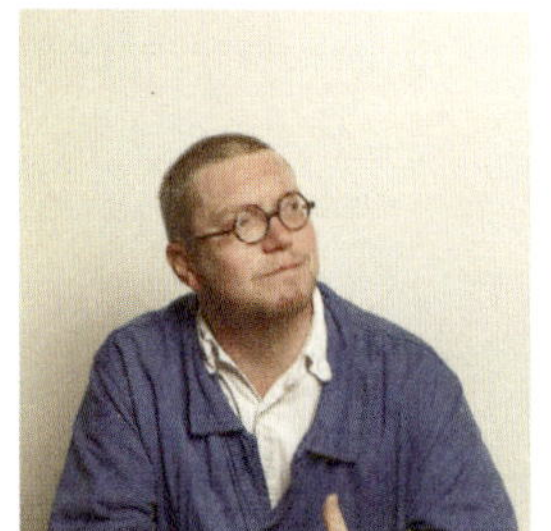

Cooking-Wine Hangover

by Fergus Henderson

Fergus Henderson MBE, a legendary figure in art word circles, is the founder of St John Restaurant – (one of the world's top 50 restaurants according to Restaurant Magazine) - and St John Bread and Wine. He is also the author of Nose To Tail Eating and Don't Try This At Home. This man is responsible for feeding the art world offal.

A HAPPY STORY RECOUNTED to me by Gregor Muir – now director of Hauser and Wirth Gallery London, then director of the Lux Gallery on Hoxton Square - which marks a moment in St John's history and also points out how the YBAs' taste in wine has improved. We go back in time to the dark days when St John (on St John Street, in Clerkenwell) was empty: a bad time.

We were hosting an after-show party of a gallery at the restaurant one night and at this time Sarah Lucas and Angus Fairhurst had a studio down the road from us. So it was back to theirs, including, we discovered the next day, all of our supplies of cooking wine. Those from St John who found their way to the party found it very strange that our cooking wine was the favourite tipple of Angus and Sarah.

All came clear the next morning but as we were cursing the light-fingered artists for helping themselves to our wine, Gregor recounted that the hungover YBAs (particularly bad hangovers are what comes of drinking cooking wine) reached a conclusion (often best made with a hangover) that they liked St John and should not pinch our wine but eat and support St John.

Much appreciated, I might add. I'm glad to report their choice of wine has moved on.

Don't Wake Up Your Daughter's Soldiers

by Zinovy Zinik

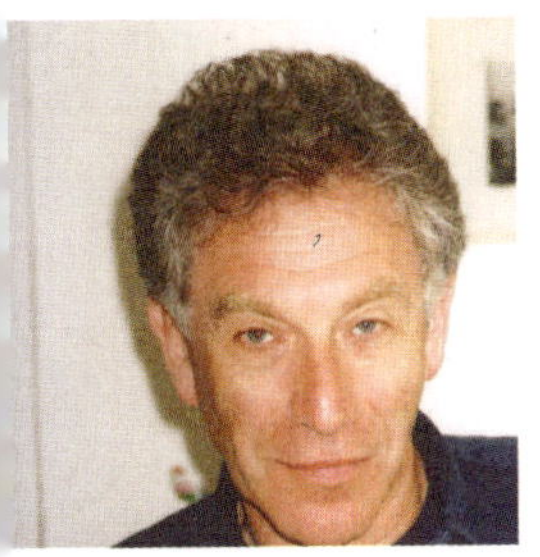

Zinovy Zinik was born again in 1975 outside the Union of Soviet Socialist Republics to become the author of ten books of fiction, translated into English, French, German, Dutch, Hebrew, Polish, Hungarian and Estonian. Having adopted London as his home, he regularly contributes to The Times Literary Supplement and to BBC Radio. His new book of fabricated memoirs History Thieves *will be published by Seagull Books in January 2011.*

THE BOUNDARIES BETWEEN CIVILISATION and barbarity are, as we all know, easily transgressed because they are frequently invisible. Especially when the darkness falls in the slummy and bohemian end of Shoreditch. I happened to be in the area for the opening of Distance and Sensibilities, an exhibition at the Calvert 22 Gallery in which a few British artists, who were not born in this country, tried to make sense of their foreignness by distancing themselves from it.

As a Russian-born novelist and broadcaster, and the author of the seminal essay Emigration as A Literary Device, I was, naturally, invited to share with a worldwide audience my opinion of the show for the BBC World Service. I was a bit apprehensive about it, because my daughter Margarita Gluzberg took part in this event with her enigmatic installation Captive Bird Society.

As the broadcast had to be live, the producer said he would send a studio engineer to the area with some sophisticated phone receiver, equipped with a satellite dish. I would be connected to the whole world as if I was in the BBC studio. I felt humbled. I was told to meet him outside the gallery. Calvert Street was empty, but someone in a white shirt was waving to me from the mound in the centre of Arnold Circle, the cobbled-street roundabout next to a notorious council estate. The flight of steps led to the top, and an old-fashioned bandstand in the middle of thick shrubs and tall trees. Up there, I could discern shadows against the backdrop of the moonless sky. Voices were bragging and swearing loudly. A whiff of marijuana wafted through the air. This somehow didn't worry the sound engineer. Having sorted out the technical side of the event, he was about to go and negotiate a minute's silence with the "local boys". A large black man emerged from the darkness, towering over us.

"Gimme money, man", he said into the microphone. He suspected us of being police officers and of recording their conversation. "If you're not the police, gimme money anyway." The sound engineer kept on telling him that we were not the police, we were the BBC World Service. If we wouldn't give him money, the man said, he and his mates up the hill would create a noise strong enough for the whole world to hear. I watched the two of them disappear into the darkness, arguing, while I was left to speak to the rest of the world. In my earphones, I heard the presenter already introducing me to the listeners, asking my opinion about my daughter's work.

It was not an easy task. Margarita's installation consisted of several old-fashioned record players of the kind I saw in Moscow in my youth. She was meandering between them, and each of them played recorded captive birdsong on old vinyl disks. I would have been totally baffled by these "metaphors for entrapment and desire" (as the exhibition catalogue put it) had I not seen the previous version of the installation, in which Margarita was donning not a stunning outfit, provided by Chanel, but a Soviet Army officer uniform. Here the singing of captive birds was voiced over by the recording of Stalin's Victory Speech of 1945, when he congratulated the Soviet people for bringing about the end of the Second World War. The Soviet people then were captivated. Unlike me, the British audience during Margarita's performance had never heard of the legendary Soviet wartime song in which nightingales are urged "not to wake up our soldiers" before the final battle.

Meanwhile, down below, I saw a police car pull up at the street corner. The corner was well lit by the street lamps and therefore clearly visible also to the noisy company of pot heads in the bandstand. Their paranoid suspicions about the links between the police and us would be confirmed. Would I be able to defend myself, wielding the heavy microphone as my only weapon? Should I interrupt the highbrow discussion about captive birds and cry through the satellite dish for help right now, to the whole world?

Luckily, in my earphones I could hear the voice of the BBC producer congratulating me on the successful performance. At the same time, the sound engineer re-emerged from the bushes. He was unharmed. In fact, he was smiling broadly. The boys, he said, gladly accepted a tenner as a disturbance fee. Or should it be called an honorarium? With CCTV cameras everywhere, these boys and their own birds - the guardians of the place - could have been part of the installation in the nearby gallery.

It was a long night of drinking after the show. Passing by Arnold Circle on my way home, I heard a nightingale sing. I felt I understood my daughter's art more clearly than ever before.

The problem is, the more you like your child's creation, the less she believes you understand it.

Solitude and Sardines

by Keith Coventry

Keith Coventry is an artist who lives in London. The solitude of the studio involves a certain amount of extremism.

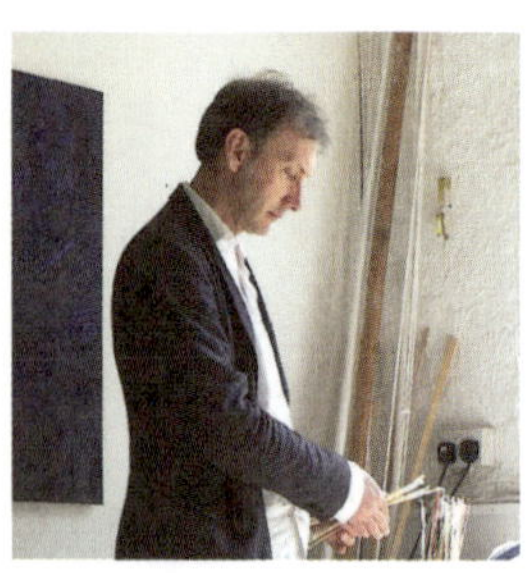

© *Thierry Bal*

MY FIRST COMMERCIAL SHOW was in 1992. It was during the time that the artists who were starting to be called the YBAs were beginning their ascendance. Apparently I was one of them. My involvement with the Karsten Schubert Gallery lasted three years. In 1997 I exhibited at the Royal Academy for the now famous Sensation show. I then showed at the Saatchi Gallery for the BritArt no. 5 show. After that, my career took a nose-dive.

This wasn't supposed to happen.

I spent five years making and selling my own work. From 2000-2001 I showed with the Emily Tsingou Gallery, but I was removed.

From 2001 to 2004, I lived in a "set" at Albany in Piccadilly, a distinguished but (I think secretly licentious) block of apartments that was once home to Byron and three prime ministers, including Gladstone.

Here, I found myself living in a way that ensured the disposal of all my funds. Immediately after Albany, I spent three months living in a hostel for the homeless in Walthamstow: a very productive period as it was necessary to sign in before midnight every night.

The homeless experience enabled me to reflect nostalgically upon what would become the rose-tinted paintings Echoes of Albany - recently shown at the Haunch of Venison Gallery, who I joined in 2009. I also showed there a version of my earlier Estate paintings, but now they were black, depicting only estates where people have been murdered. The homeless days are over and I now find myself in an apartment surrounded by 17th century furniture.

The point of the above potted history is to say that in seventeen years, from 1992 to

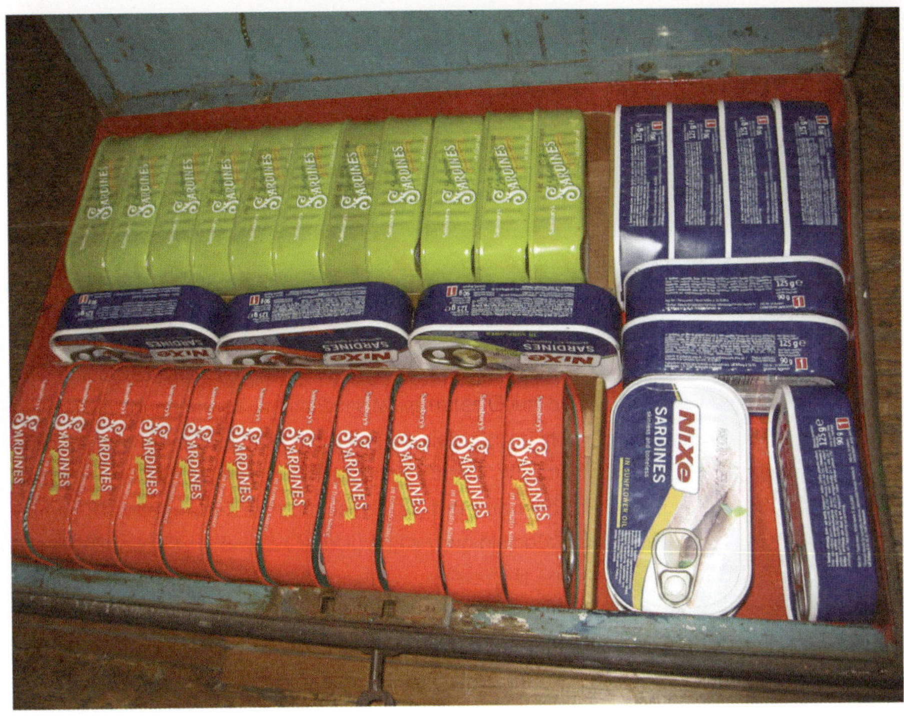

Keith's Sardines

2009, I spent only five of those with a gallery, which meant that the other twelve were spent making, selling and promoting my own work.

This involved going out a lot. I deceived myself trying to believe that I was attending parties to promote myself and my work, only to realise that I was probably just there for the party.

I have successfully managed to avoid any sort of paid employment since 1992.

It was here that I painted the head of Christ 60 times in as many colours. (These were also eventually shown at the Haunch of Venison show too).

To get through this, I decided to eat the same thing every day for weeks on end.

I chose sardines as this meant I didn't have to go out for lunch or take any food breaks. It also meant I was packing myself with Omega 3.

I listened to the same album – Radiohead's 'Hail the Thief' - continuously, yet I still can't remember any of the track titles!

I worked the same hours: 7 till 7, 7 days a week.

This sort of extreme solitude was a welcome break from art parties. It was a discipline, a regime.

If there are no art parties, there is no hangover. No hangover meant no recuperation meant working without hesitation or interruption. Regime meant good form.

The paper thin walls of the studio meant my solitude and my enforced method of working was interrupted by sounds from other studios; it was basically wall to wall Gardener's Question Time. Radio 4 is the staple diet of most artists in their studios.

Maybe I wasn't that alone in the studio? At the end of the project, and completion of the paintings (60), I was surrounded by the many heads of Christ looking down, around and upon me, like a rainbow: I called the set Spectrum Jesus.

Perhaps by regimenting myself in a similar way to Christ himself, I had transported myself to a higher plane.

The solitude of the studio became a religious retreat accompanied only by Christ's multicoloured presence.

I wish I did actually believe in God and Jesus and then those statements would carry more weight.

Mission completed, time to destroy all the good health I had built up, and so, unlike a Christian Scientist, I stepped out from the light and back into the dark.

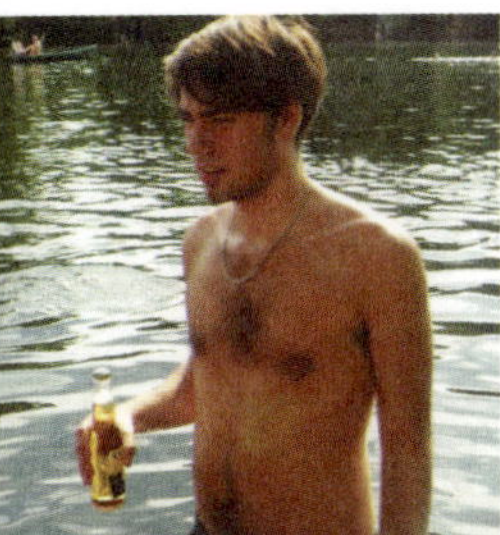

Dad Stop Embarrassing Me

By Alex Collishaw

Alex Collishaw is a 20 year old musician living in Berlin. When he was growing up, his babysitters were the YBAs.

MY FATHER IS AN ARTIST, which I suppose isn't as common as most of the other 'dad' trades. His career began to blossom roughly around the same time as I started to eat solid food, and as a young boy I was always dragged around to all the London openings at which I would position myself underneath the buffet table. Art-party food scraps from the floor made my constitution as robust as it is today.

My life was slightly different compared to that of the majority of kids in my school whose fathers were mostly builders or schoolteachers. My numerous homes were spacious studios always located in the tumbleweed areas of east London. They were vast playgrounds full of paints, colours and textures. Rather than plonk me in front of the TV, my father would project films onto the ceiling directly above my bed or when I was bored he would hand me over the air rifle and challenge me to see who could hit the road sign outside first - (the loser would do the dishes). Home always had interesting stuff laying around, simple bits of scrap wood and metal brought much fun to me and my friends – well, the few friends who weren't weirded out by the pictures on the walls of bullet wounds, pornography or diseased flowers.

Although, the people who seemed to be becoming my real friends were not fellow class mates but rather half of the YBAs. They taught me a lot: a sense of humour, how to play chess, and how to drive (when I was 10 years old and at 3am in a small Irish village). They'd all hang around and educate/entertain me, acting surprisingly spry for grown ups, and exchange funnies and ideas before they would disappear off to this infamous 'Grouchy Club,' as I heard it, which at the time I figured to be some sort of play group. I remember once doing a weird kind of alien voice at one of their parties, my cry for attention being rewarded by one particular artist's fascination. Next day I was dressed as some sort of Orcish gimp in 16th century clothes doing the same voice and being told I was a 'figment of the imagination'. I had somehow ended up becoming a piece of art work.

At school one day we began searching the Internet for all our friends' names to see what pictures would come up. When it came round to my name, a big black and white picture of a zebra humping a blonde woman came up with a biography of my dad and his prior works underneath. I remember my classmates all looking confused until they clocked that my father was the artist. When asked such questions as "Why did your dad do that?," "How is that art?" and my favorite, "Is your dad a perv?" I didn't even attempt to recall the artistic explanations my dad handed on to me, instead I just hung my head and accepted my 'Zebra boy' nickname for two years.

Rather than taking a more traditional route to fatherhood, dad has always done things differently. To combat the laziness and inertia of my late teens, he and his girlfriend wrote, performed and filmed a very drunken and humorous song about my lack of drive, and slipped the DVD underneath my bedroom door. In this respect, he has always treated me as he would have wished to be treated.

Throughout my late teenage years in which most of my peers seemed to distance themselves from their parents and rebel against convention, I did the opposite. The older I became the more respect I held for my father. I was impressed with the courage he must have had to come from a poor background in the Midlands and move to London to pursue art rather than take a more secure route. His hard work and creativity have really inspired me to work hard for the things I really want in life. For this I must thank him. I must also thank him for not being an overly conceptual, pretentious beret-wearing plonker with an easel. Thanks dad.

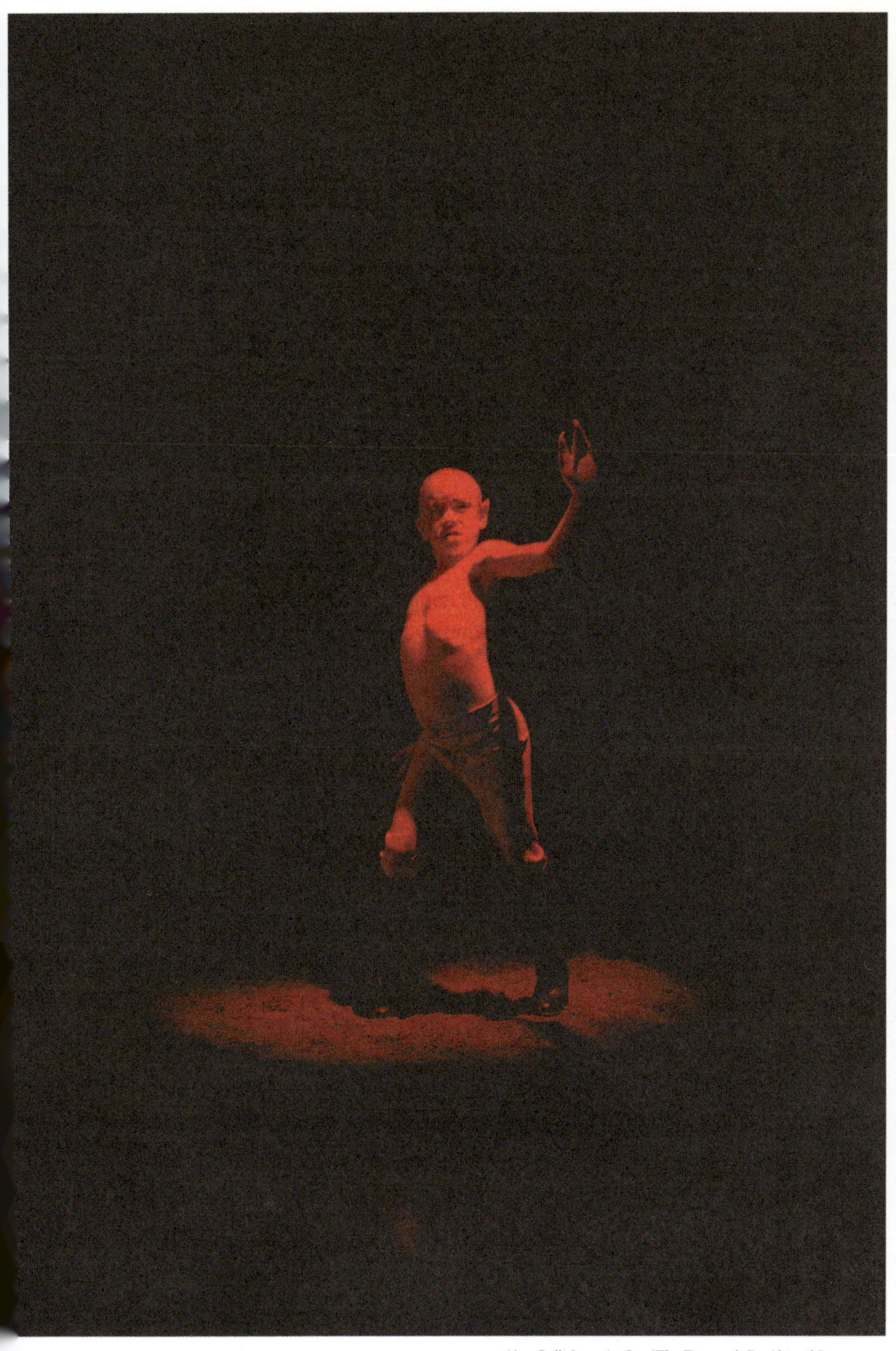

Alex Collishaw As Orc 'The Figment', By Abigail Lane

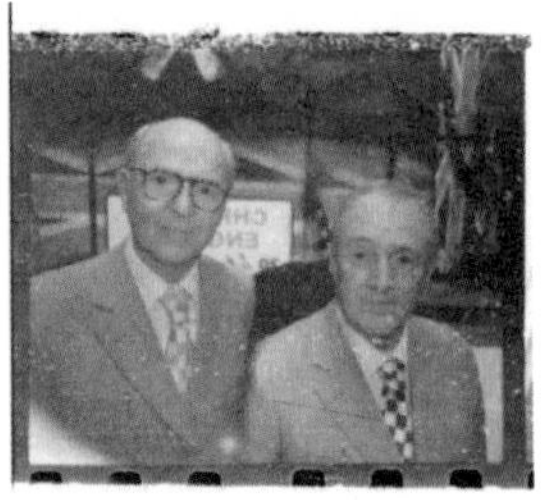

Gilbert and George © Byron Pritchard

Don't Be Fashionable

by Gilbert and George

Gilbert and George are an artist duo who live in a Huguenot house in Spitalfields. Their particular decadence arises in the form of drinking unfashionable drinks, and remaining staunchly suited and Conservative in a world of denim-clad Lefties.

On Bristol Cream

Went up to the bar and ordered•these drinks, lost those
•somewhere ordered a couple more, •found that we had
forgotten the others so we had another •round, found
some and tended •to lose track a shade. (Wonderful
stuff!)

On Politics

"We oppose collectivism," says George. "You're not
allowed to be Conservative in the art world, of course.
Everyone has to be Left. Pop stars and artists are meant
to be so original. How come everyone has the same
opinion?"

On Denim

We are more offended by blue jeans than anything else.:,
says Gilbert. "They are appalling. It's a uniform. It's
the fear of standing out," agrees George. "The fear of
being different."

CHAPTER 3:
BUYERS AND SELLERS –
THE MARKET

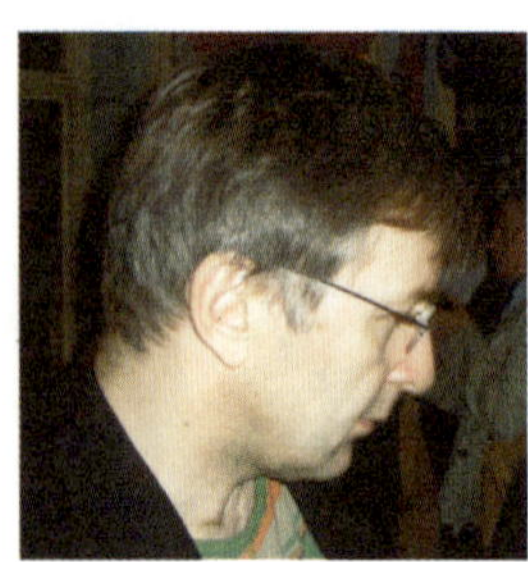

BRIC

by Matthew Bown

Matthew Bown's dealing strategy is to buy what he'd like to live with and sell it if and when he gets the right offer. Sometimes a work sticks around for years and then, miraculously, someone asks for it. Sometimes they don't. He thinks it's not a bad strategy: the more you love a painting, the more money you can ask for it and not care if you are turned down. And living with something really does sort out your feelings about it.

A WISE OLD GALLERY-OWNER once said to me, Scratch a collector and you'll find a dealer. True, up to a point. Charles Saatchi sells work as well as buying it; as does his rival in the Midlands, Frank Cohen (in fact, Cohen sometimes sells to Saatchi). And sometimes the roles are confused to the point of deceit. You get dealers pretending to be collectors, such as Swiss dealer Pierre Huber who acquired top contemporary works at below-market prices on the understanding they'd go to a museum and then, to widespread outrage, sold them in a 2007 Christie's auction. The dealers he bought the work from had to muck in and buy it all back. And you get collectors pretending to be dealers, such as Nasser David Khalil, who used that subterfuge to acquire pieces for his superb Islamic art collection on the cheap.

But usually the interest of collectors in the market for their works is long-term. If they are interested in appreciation, it may be they imagine vaguely that their descendants will benefit from their art purchases. If they keep checking the prices it's really just in order to make sure they aren't being ripped off and perhaps to seek confirmation of their own judgement.

But if the investment value of your collection is your major concern, what's your strategy? A recent auction held by Phillips de Pury in London suggested one. The sale was called BRIC, an acronym borrowed from the world of economics and signifying the emerging economies of Brazil, Russia and India and China. The rationale for the auction was quite simple: "Whenever there is a strong economic upturn in a region or a country it goes hand in hand with a vibrant creative surge in the artistic areas." Yes, I know it sounds like soft porn: I think it's meant to. Go and attend to the vibrant creative surge in your artistic areas, and then read on.

The unspoken point is, a strong economic upturn creates rich people with money to spend on art. Many of them will prefer home-grown art, which pushes up its prices. If you collect that art early on, before the boom, you can benefit.

Such art-booms have taken place in the last twenty years in the countries that threw off the economic shackles of communism *de jure* (Russia) and *de facto* (China). One indicator is the increase in auction turnover. When Joanna Vickery, director of Sotheby's Russian department in London, joined the auction house in 1997 the annual sales turnover for her department was just £1.3 million. By 2003, it had risen tenfold to almost £13 million. The turnover from the summer sales alone in 2010 was £19 million; if you project a similar figure for the autumn sales, you get a total £38 million for the year. That's the market expansion: about 3000% over 13 years. Of course, that means that far more pictures are being bought and sold, not that they have all risen in price by that amount. But the statistics also veil stunning increases in the values of some individual works, particularly those by the most sought-after artists. A hundred thousand pounds judiciously invested in Russian art in the early nineties could have made you a multi-millionaire in 2010. It's the collectors who have benefited from this kind of price-surge, not the dealers, who were always buying and selling. The Sotheby's sales are haunted by anguished figures: downwardly-mobile dealers, priced out of the market, who watch the fantastic prices on the electronic board and weep inwardly at the thought of what they let pass through their hands for a pittance ten years ago.

The Chinese phenomenon is equally well-known and as far as contemporary art is concerned even more egregious than the Russian. In 2008 it became the world's third largest art market. A significant number of Chinese modern artists have become top earners. Not all of them are well-known in the West. Qi Baishi, for example, who died in 1957, had sales of $70 million in 2009, second only to Picasso and Warhol; he is little-known outside China. Some living Chinese artists are also fantastically successful.

You have to add in another factor here: Russia and China are both huge countries, and thus the new wealth is also huge, which pushes the peak prices of the top artists higher. Bulgaria, for example, also emerged from communism, but no-one sings about it as an investors' jamboree. In fact I've got a number of very good paintings bought in Bulgaria circa 1990 which still haven't found their collector.

Of course, the dismantling of communist economics across vast territories is a once-in-a-lifetime event. There are no more Russias or Chinas, and those markets are fairly mature. So where do you look for the next opportunity?

I'm not a financial adviser and this is not financial advice: ask a professional if you want it. But I would think, if you are seeking a country that in the not too distant future could experience "a strong economic upturn" followed by "a vibrant creative surge", then it might be worth looking at Cuba. A liberalisation after Fidel Castro's eventual demise could convert Cuba back into what it once was, the playground of the USA. The big neighbour would take care of the little country caveat (let's hope, without the mafia involvement this time). And there's a load of Cubans sitting in Miami on suitcases full of dollars, just waiting for the moment when they can go home. The result of new economic freedom, which as the Chinese have shown does not necessarily have to be accompanied by political freedom, would be the emergence of some very rich Cubans. Some of them would no doubt set about building collections of Cuban art. Whose work would they buy? That's for you to work out. It's a great place for a holiday in any case.

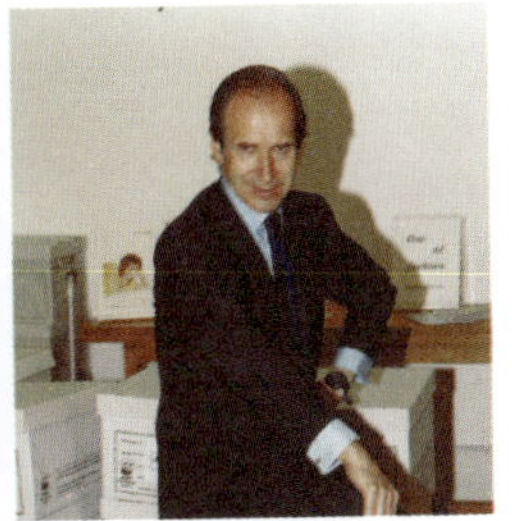

© Roby Rodriguez

Performance Art on the Auction Block

by Simon de Pury

Simon de Pury is Chairman and Chief Auctioneer of Phillips de Pury & Company, one of the principal auction houses in the world. Before that he was Chairman Europe and Chief Auctioneer of Sotheby's and curator of the world renown Thyssen-Bornemisza Collection. He once studied the Japanese painting techniques of 'Sumie' and 'Nihonga' at the Tokyo Academy of Arts. One of the art world's more legendary figures, Swiss-born Simon is renowned for his near-mythical performance on the auction podium.

IT IS MY PASSION for art that made me decide nearly forty years ago to devote my professional life to the art world and in particular the art market. An apprenticeship at Galerie Kornfeld in Bern , still today a leading auction house for prints and drawings, confronted me for the first time with a live auction. Eberhard Kornfeld was sitting for hours at a table on a podium and would coax bids with immense charm and humour from a packed room. Phone bidding was not allowed, which ensured that all the action was in the room. He had a vase with red roses on his table, and whenever he was happy with the price a certain lot had just obtained, he would pick one rose out of the vase and give it to the successful bidder.

My next step was to attend the Sotheby's Works of Art Course in London . It is there that I first witnessed Peter Wilson, the legendary and visionary chairman of Sotheby's, on the podium. He sat on the rounded rostrum that very much resembled a priest's pulpit in a church or cathedral. He was a man with immense distinction and allure. He hardly raised his soft voice and yet commanded the full and undivided attention of his audience. It is Peter Wilson who introduced the black tie evening sales. It is him again who introduced currency converter boards into the sale room. Several of his colleagues were so shocked by this innovation that they threatened to resign, saying that this was too commercial and made the sale room look too much like a bank!

Six weeks into the annual Sotheby's Works of Art course, which was then very much a training scheme for the firm, we were asked who wanted to conduct auctions. I instantly raised my hand and was very surprised to see that there were only three of us to do so amongst the fifty students. We were then asked to go through a mock auction - much to the amusement of our fellow students.

As soon as I joined the ranks of the illustrious firm after the course, I let it be known that I wanted to become an auctioneer. Quite soon after, I was offered my chance to conduct my first real auction in the company's main sale room in New Bond Street . For about a week before, I could hardly sleep and on the day itself I was so tense that I was asking myself why on earth I had insisted so much to inflict this on myself. The sale was a sale of furniture and the first ten to fifteen lots were carpets. The attendees in those days were mostly dealers and the carpet dealers were notoriously undisciplined. Instead of sitting in one place they would walk from one part of the room to another while placing their bids. This was initially quite disconcerting but my nervousness rapidly dissipated and I began to find the whole proceedings most enjoyable. I was hooked then and there.

Since then I have conducted endless auctions all over the globe. I have also conducted innumerable charity auctions and can not count the hundreds of millions of dollars I have raised over the years. I still get incredibly tense before an auction and each time is as if it was my first. I guess however, that as for a pilot, the amount of flight time you have clocked up helps considerably. There is no way you can really prepare yourself for an auction. There is no script to learn in advance and it is all about improvisation and tuning yourself to the audience. Since many attendees are only there to bid on two or three lots, you don't want to bore them; on the contrary you want to make the whole thing an entertaining affair. Every bidder has mentally set himself a maximum limit above which he is not prepared to go. On a good day you can somehow feel when she or he has reached that level, and you try to coax them into just making that one extra bid. If you succeed, you can do the same with another bidder and then even from a third. That can make quite a difference. This is especially so, the higher the price of the lot is, because in some instances one extra increment can make a difference of a million dollars or more.

Early on I learned that you have a better delivery when you stand than when you sit. The rostrum at Sotheby's had to be adapted accordingly and since then I conducted all auctions standing. This practice has spread rapidly and today seems to be the norm.

Conducting auctions must be addictive, since it is very difficult to dissuade a colleague who is not good at it from doing so. At Phillips de Pury & Company we only train people who have the necessary charisma and talent. We don't want to just sell the best upcoming contemporary art but also to field the best auctioneers.

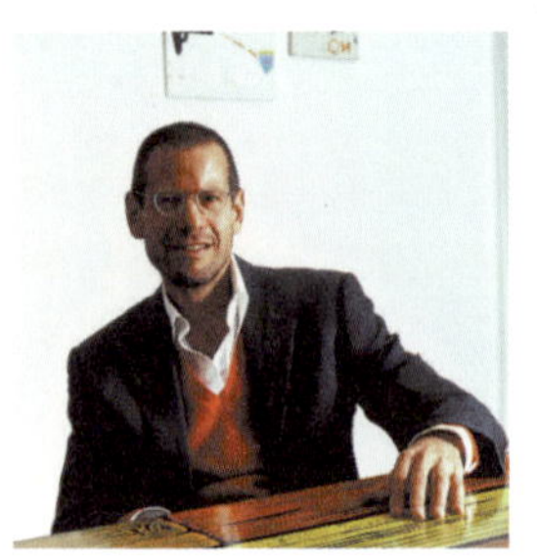

From Long Island to London: A Memoir in Art in 1000 Words (More or Less)

by Kenny Schachter

Kenny Schachter has been collecting and curating art for ever. The recipient of a Rockefeller supported grant, he has also taught and lectured all over the world. He does get around. He received planning for Zaha Hadid's first commercial building in the UK and has exhibited his own work at various galleries including the Sandra Gering Gallery in NYC and International 3 in Manchester. He is now open to suggestions.

I WAS BORN A MIDDLE CLASS fat kid in Long Island, nearly catatonic due to a heavy-handed father and the early death of my mother. Cosseted in the suburbs, there was little in the way of cultural titillation other than reading car and sports magazines and collaging the contents onto my very 1970s, very cork walls.

Procrastinating from a law exam, I hesitantly visited the estate sale of Andy Warhol, which opened my eyes to the commercial side of art; prior to that, and because I had never before stepped into a commercial gallery, I naively thought paintings travelled non-stop from the studio to the museum. When I finally did enter the sterile white walls of a gallery, I was spontaneously smitten (and horrified), took an unsecured loan to acquire a Cy Twombly print, and soon began dealing in works on paper like an *idiot savant*.

Cognisant that there existed a gaping hole in the breadth of my art-historical knowledge, (anyone can become expert in post-war art in six months if they bother

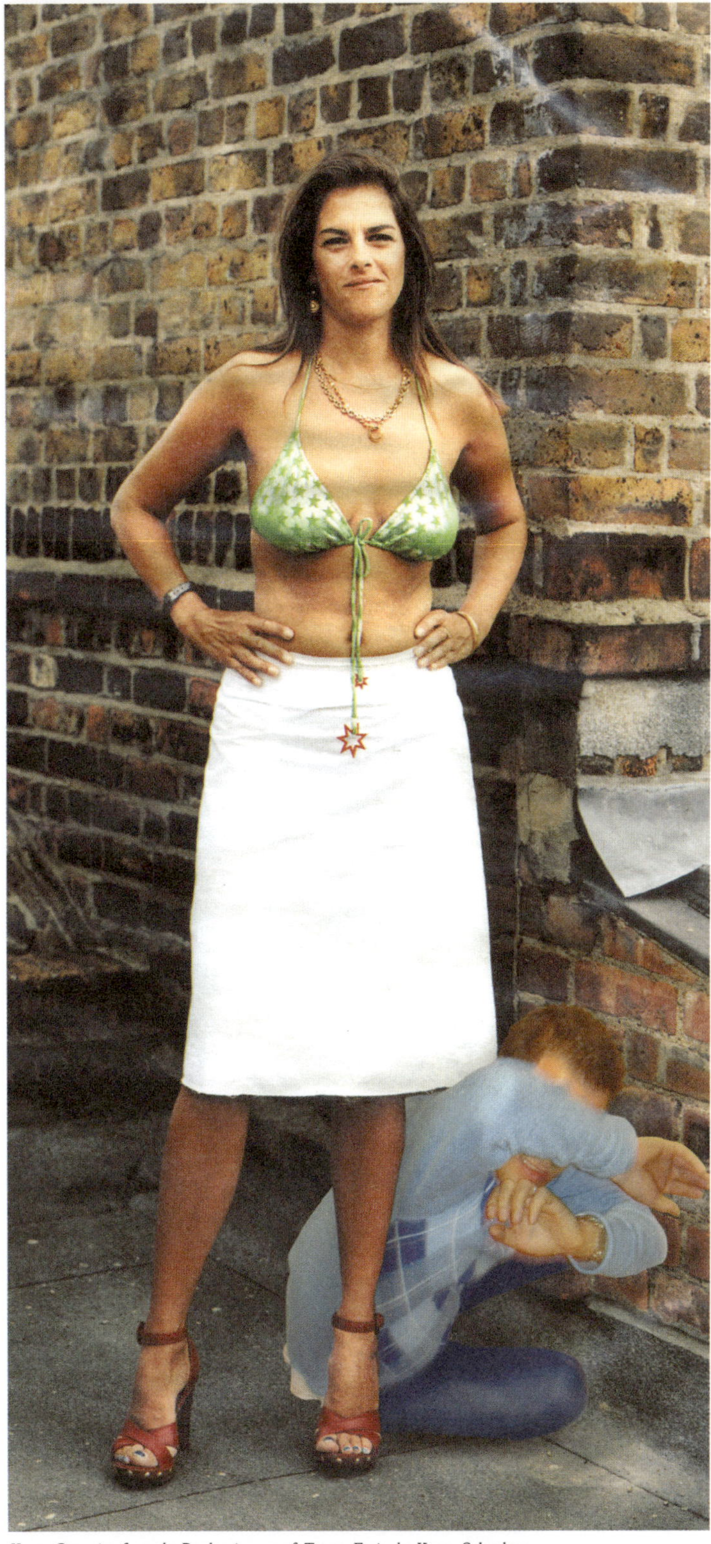

Kenny Cowering from the Predominance of Tracey Emin, by Kenny Schachter

to read), I conned my way into a teaching position at the New School for Social Research rather than suffer another course as a student. After taking an adjunct position on probation, I wormed my way into teaching and lecturing - from New York University, Columbia and Rhode Island School of Design, to the Royal College of Art and Manchester University.

Self-taught about the past, I started curating hit and run exhibits of non-affiliated emerging artists, while also showing my own art and writing. Why not? In effect I had become a middle class, Jewish, outsider artist from Long Island.

Some of the people I exhibited prior to their gallery affiliation were Cecily Brown, Fred Tomaselli, Rachel Harrison, Wade Guyton, Andrea Zittel and Janine Antoni. My calling had become known, albeit as a late bloomer, not having entered a gallery until I was 28. In addition to supporting the work of younger artists, I worked with underappreciated and undervalued artists like Vito Acconci and Paul Thek. It has always struck me as odd that so much energy is spent supporting and writing about artists like Emin, Hirst, and Taylor-Wood who already have a massive network of support. So rather than fret too much, I use them (along with the likes of Jay Jopling and other media figures) as grist for my own send-up art pieces.

Though I swore I'd never open a gallery - I was curating but never much liked the process of selling (not the best mindset for a dealer) - I commissioned conceptualist-turned-designer Acconci to create his first built interior. Though the design was meant to be temporary it was comprised of thousands of pounds of steel, so when I determined to move to the UK, I was faced with a dilemma: store the entire gallery in perpetuity or find a way to flog the contents of the space. In the end, I auctioned the gallery including the front door, desks and walls at a design sale at Phillips. It seems there is always a way round a problem.

Being virtually the only collector of the late artist Paul Thek for years, I recently collaborated on an exhibit of his work at the Reina Sofia Museum in Spain and a 500 page text with MIT Press, the only in English prior to upcoming Whitney and LA County Museum exhibits in 2010-11. The art world is finally taking notice 22 years after his death, so better late than never.

Despite a violent mugging at knifepoint while sitting at an exhibit I'd organized entitled I Hate New York in a temporary space in Shoreditch, I moved to the UK in 2004. The move to London might have been instigated by a midlife crisis, but I prefer to tell myself it was a mix of complacency, boredom with the homogeneity of New York, and some desire for adventure that drove me to jump ship.

I bought a site on Hoxton Square with a view to developing it with Zaha Hadid, prior to her winning the Pritzker Prize. Despite being one of the world's most progressive thinkers and architects, I felt that she was largely ignored in the country she had lived and worked in for 35 years. Since then, I have organised countless exhibits and projects with Zaha from a show at Sonnabend Gallery to commissioning her design of a car. I then achieved planning permission to erect her first building in London to coincide with the 2012 Olympic Swimming Pavilion, although Zaha remains skeptical I can pull it off in this day and age of tightened credit markets. We live in hope.

In today's fungible world, geography is less a factor in our lives then ever before; all we need are our Apples and Blackberries and we are good to go. But there are some subtle differences between London and New York: under the veil of civility, Brits are a fairly violent lot (football matches often being an excuse for a good brawl); the health care system in the UK (largely due to a distinct lack of hygiene) is more than a bit primitive, and the complexity of getting around town is mind boggling. I need a Sat Nav just to get to the newsagents at the end of my street; as for going to a handful of galleries, well that can take days.

But since moving, I have not missed New York for a day, though some things are hard to shake, namely my Long Island accent, which my kids will surely never let me forget.

I have participated in and been thrown out of art fairs due to both my outspokenness and my flouting of the capricious fair rules. I once facilitated an intervention by Vito Acconci in the Basel art fair that was deemed to cut off the circulation down the aisles. They threw me out. I then filled a booth at the Armory Show in New York with secondary market offerings. The Armory specifically precludes such material (or used to anyway). Again, I was thrown out.

As for the Frieze art fair in London, they never invited me to visit, never *mind* to have a stand. I suppose the series of articles I wrote highlighting the pretentiousness of the proprietors didn't help much. The closest I got to joining was when I intercepted a VIP invite that was meant for a former inhabitant of my house, that I happen to know well. But let's move on.

Despite the hiccoughs, I am still at it. By no foresight on my part, art became bigger than the big business that I initially ran away from. I went from dealing in the art of the young unknowns - a lot like selling t-shirts in a market stall – to dealing in Monet, Van Gogh and Picasso. A shift I could never have dreamed of in the beginning. Working with artists, I have nearly been stabbed to death, been shot at with a gun loaded with blanks (at the time I didn't know if the fluid on my lap was blood, urine or Margarita - thankfully it was the latter) - and repeatedly had my life threatened by disgruntled emerging artists. Hence my appreciation of artists no longer breathing: they're much easier to deal with than the ones that still have a detectable pulse.

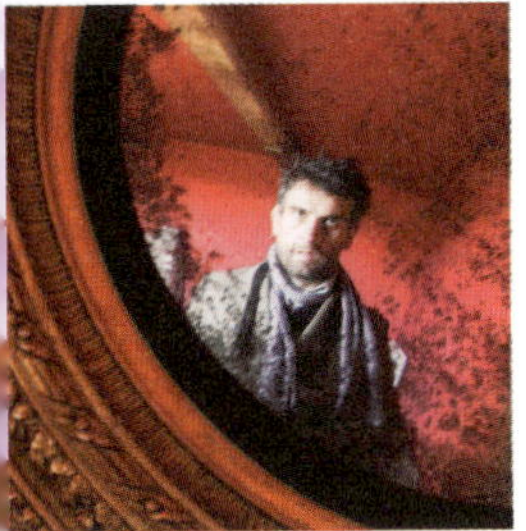

Top Tips for Financial Survival in the Art World

by Paul Fryer

Paul Fryer is an artist living in London and Derbyshire.

WHEN I WAS ASKED to write this, I was recovering from a series of financial trials which had beset me. The following notes are therefore intended as advice for young artists, in the hope that they might avoid the mistakes that I have made. They are points that people in the art dealing business will probably never tell you. Ignorance might be bliss, but it is expensive.

(1) Don't let anyone convince you that you need their involvement, financial or otherwise, to make your work. You can make art anytime, anywhere, with anything.

(2) Never sign a contract if you can avoid it. If you absolutely feel you must sign, then still don't. If you feel obliged then you really need to reassess your position, not sign your life away.

Contracts are rare in the art world, thank goodness. We need to keep it that way - no good can come of them. Anything you can write in a contract can be circumvented, and if it can't, then it's a prison sentence. I'm not talking about agreements, i.e *I promise to do this if you do that* etc, but the kind of contract which demands exclusivity, outlines territories and apportions percentages. I recently made the mistake of signing one which demanded worldwide exclusivity despite the fact that the dealer did not have premises anywhere outside of Fitzrovia. The result? I was unable to work with anyone else without their permission, and, once they had decided that they "had got enough of my inventory for now," this meant that I could not work at all. This contractual ligature, coupled with the withdrawal of support, not only halted my production for a year but also severely undermined my confidence.

You might ask why I signed in the first place. Well, the party in question was preparing to spend a lot of money on my project and I felt they deserved some level of reassurance for their large investment.

Also, I was told that the contract would never be invoked, that it was only there to instill confidence in the investors. Of course, it was wielded with some ferocity within a few months of my signature drying on the page.

The other reason was personal ambition. This level of investment meant I would be able to make works on an unprecedented scale. And so I was blinded to the potential problems by the brilliance of the possibilities. Will I trust an agent again? Certainly. I'll just be more vigilant in future.

A heavy irony here is that this contract was primarily intended to protect the investors. In the event it didn't. They forgot to put in a consignment clause (!), which meant that at the end of the term, no provision was made for the unsold inventory. I walked away with most of the works without a legal shot being fired. In other words, it bit them in the arse too.

The difference is, their attitude appears to be that they will make double sure the next contract they issue is even tighter than the last. Mine is to never sign another.

The main problem with contracts is that as soon as they are signed people are inclined to become complacent and even contemptuous. Demands for works to be completed with entirely unrealistic deadlines emerge; thinly disguised threats are bandied; debts are highlighted and reminders of responsibilities are made with new-found authority. Respect evaporates. But if you still really feel it's worth it make sure it's non exclusive and that it doesn't run for more than a year.

(3) If your production costs are being met, always get your money up front and always pay your own fabricators with it. Don't let anyone interfere with the making of your work or with you developing a relationship with those who assist you.

(4) Always ring-fence production where possible. Avoid agreeing to pay off the fabrication on one work from the proceeds of another. It creates accounting nightmares and is fundamentally unfair. After all, where is the gallery's investment in you if you pay off all your own production?

(5) Don't be greedy, but always question percentages. No one has an automatic entitlement to 50%. Even 49-51% sends out a clear message as to who is the *primum mobile*. That said 100% of nothing is fuck all. Strike a fair deal.

(6) Never give anyone – gallerists, collectors, anyone - free access to your studio. Access is a privilege, not a right.

(7) Don't be bullied. Galleries seldom win in litigation against artists. In fact, they never win. If you're being threatened with legal action it's probably because they're trying to scare you into submission.

(8) Keep advice about your work at arms length. It seems like everyone's an artist, eh? Well, no one is stopping them making their own work. Be discerning about whose advice you take. Some galleries want inordinate amounts of control over artists' output. The net result is normally to corral you into only making saleable bijoux for rich people. But without commitment to ideas which have stretched the imagination and the storage facilities of even the biggest galleries, some of the world's greatest works would never have been realised. Or they might have been very different at least. Pass the Parcel with Christo, Louise Bourgeois making spiders out of pipe cleaners and Walter De Maria on the local football pitch with some coathangers, maybe?

(9) Sales must come second. If it doesn't feel right, don't show it. If you don't like the collector, walk away. If the message isn't getting through, there's always the sledgehammer and the Stanley knife. Destroying your own work can be liberating in more ways than one. But remember this is a last resort, not a reasonable method of negotiation.

(10) Exclusivity is a trap. Cool galleries work with each other; uncool ones rip each other off. Have relationships with as many galleries in as many territories as possible. Why should you be monogamous while they fuck everything that moves?

(11) The argument "well, Picasso accepted these terms", or "Bacon didn't have a problem with it" is not an argument. I haven't had a blue period and I don't have sex with men either, but that doesn't mean I think I'm better than either of them. Your needs are unique - that is what you should base your decisions on.

(12) Watch out for hidden extras. Crating, shipping, storage and insurance should nearly always be paid by the gallery.

(13) Remember that consigning your work to your gallery after a show is a privilege, not a right. Even if they have money invested in the production you have no legal obligation to consign anything to them. But be reasonable, it's good for both of you if the work sells; plus, their (hopefully) safe storage facility should ease your worries about your work going up in smoke. If you do decide to consign work to a gallery, do so for a short period of time particularly if they want exclusivity. Two years is quite long enough. If they can't sell it in a year or so they really ought to get a salesperson or something.

(14) Always chase up your accounts and never take the gallery version as gospel. Get them checked by a trustworthy accountant and better still, have them explained to you. There's no substitute for being on top of the figures however shit you are at maths.

(15) Beware the New Model! The last significant New Model was invented by a gallery in the seventies who shall remain nameless (*cryptic clue: Brokeback Mountain*). This involved doing everything for the artist: putting them up in fancy hotels, ferrying them round in limos, flying them first class, paying their studio rent, throwing countless dinners, and generally making the artists feel good about themselves. In return they would demand 50% of their income. Many artists barricaded the doors of their garrets against this punishing percentage, but enough were curious enough to try it, and the rest is history. A 50% split is now normal, but these days galleries don't push the boat out any further than they need to.

I was recently introduced to another New Model, designed to improve on the messy and archaic practices of the art world. This involves the advancement of large sums of money for production which is then recouped from all sales. The artist thus never gets out of debt, thus:

Dealer: Good news! We sold some work!
Artist: Great! Can I have some money? I'm skint.
Dealer: No, we took the profits to pay off your production on the other works that we haven't sold yet.
Artist: Shit! But I'm broke…
Dealer: Don't worry, we'll lend you some money…

Conclusion: This particular model might have been new once, but not since Victorian times.

(17) Beware large advances. If you end up owing the gallery a lot of money they can force you to give them huge discounts on sales under the pretext of recovering investment.

(18) If possible, fund your own production. Financial independence means you can ask for a better percentage split.

(19) Remember, good galleries are very supportive. If they're not you'll tend to feel it long before you can explain why. Trust your instincts. If something doesn't smell right it's probably gone off.

(20) Don't get too upset when it all goes wrong. Wherever you are, someone has been there before you and survived. Remember how and why you started doing it in the first place. I'll bet you were on your own. And I'll bet it wasn't for the money.

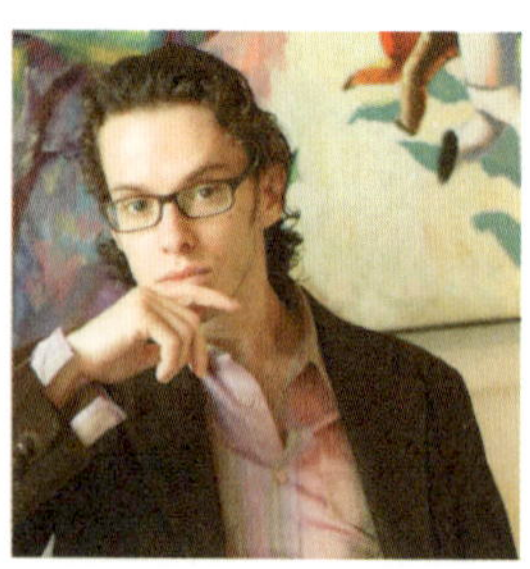

How to Sell to Oligarchs

by Mark Kelner

Since 2001, Mark Kelner has been actively involved in the sourcing and acquisition of Russian post-War art. As a private dealer and curator based in Washington DC, his clients have included major museums and corporate collections in the United States, Europe, and throughout the former Soviet Union. In 2009, he was invited to join the Advisory Board of the Hermitage Museum Foundation. He also happens to be expert in flogging pumpkins and fireworks.

CONSIDER A SEX CHANGE if you're male

It helps to be a girl, or the daughter of another oligarch, or the model-slash-girlfriend of yet another. A supremely fashionable trifecta hybrid of such a species is exemplified in one, Dasha Zhukova, the founder of The Garage in Moscow.

Stay ravenous

Girl or boy, should you have bollocks, be cash-strapped, and thus hungry; know this: the oligarch (and his underachieving brethren, the minigarch) usually have no need for art. It's luxury they desire, which is understandable after obtaining a fortune. Sometimes they want to better understand why art is valuable and perhaps, expensive. Other times, they're verging on the question 'why bother at all?' It usually takes mere seconds for them to decide whether or not they're going to line your pockets.

Know your colours

I got my start in a gallery on the outskirts of Washington DC, where walk-ins would drop by and announce: "Hi. We have a red couch. Do you have anything in red?" And I usually did. It was the blues and greens that always threw me for a curve. Hence, I learned of the decorative nature of the art business here in our nation's capital, where suburban McMansions need landscape paintings too, as long as they are, like, lipstick red. If I called it "Rouge," well, that was an extra five hundred dollars.

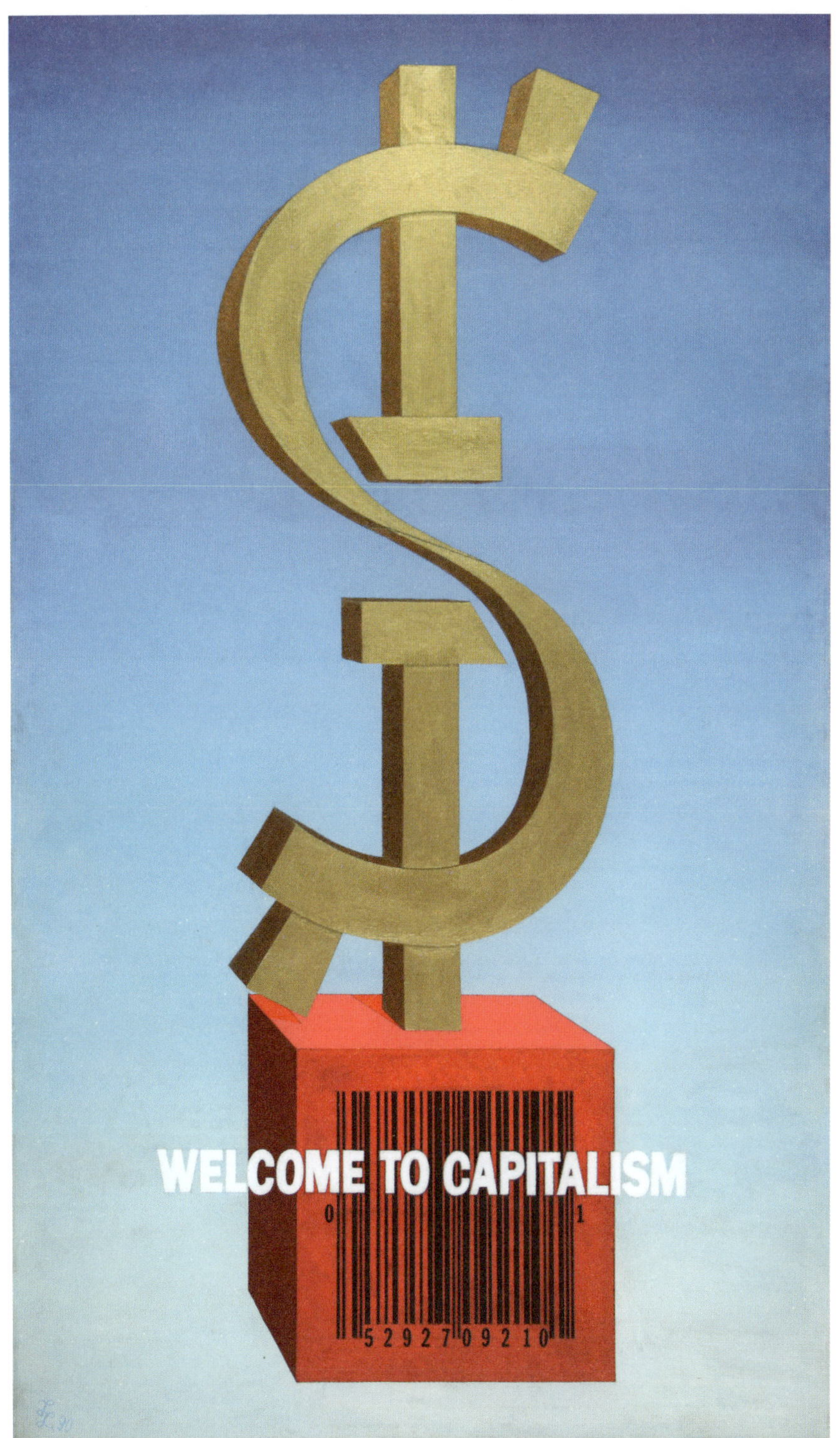

Welcome To Capitalism, Leonid Lamm, 2009

Keep your eye on the clock

As a client, nothing is more fierce in business than the American Soccer Mom with time on her hands. It's the opulence usually denied the oligarch class. The bored housewife can waiver. The oligarch never will. It took years to get a certain meeting with a certain rich someone who changed my life. And given the opportunity, (which I put down to hustling, luck, moderate language skills, and good timing), I knew not to waste anyone else's.

Never arrive empty-handed

Economy and credibility are key, as is showering them with gifts. I made an investment in a series of personalised, hand-signed, hardback-bound, (and most importantly), out-of-print Russian-artist-in-exile monographs, written in English, that no collector in Russia could ever possibly own. I brought a suitcase full of them to Moscow as gifts to anyone willing to take a meeting. Thanks, eBay.

Speak the language. A bit

Broken Russian is a double-edged sword. On the one hand, locals are endeared to you for having studied enough to get a few words out. On the other, you unwillingly become the evening's entertainment. During one memorable dinner at Cipriani's in London, I became the "Borat" of the Russian art world. And while I could speak of provenance and cultural repatriation, when I retold an "anekdot" I had learned, I received a warning: "Mark, if you only knew what filth just came out of your mouth – and were Russian – well, let's just say that I would not be responsible for your security." Truth be told, I knew exactly what I was saying, but felt the need to leave an impression. Poverty being a stable motivator, I had nothing to lose. And then it happened…

Be honest. Kind of

"What qualifies *you* to sell this to *me* for the price you ask?" When it's the owner of a private jet that wants to know, have your answer ready.

Years ago, as a side venture to support the gallery gig, a friend had a business called "Four Seasons," (unfortunately, it had nothing to do with the hotels). It flogged potted plants and flowers in the spring, fireworks in the summer, pumpkins in the fall, and Christmas trees in the winter. I worked them all, along with their spruced up titles. I was in the Seasonal Vegetation Industry for three quarters of the year, interrupted by a summer's expertise in the Explosives Industry. Rest assured, it was more profitable than art at the time.

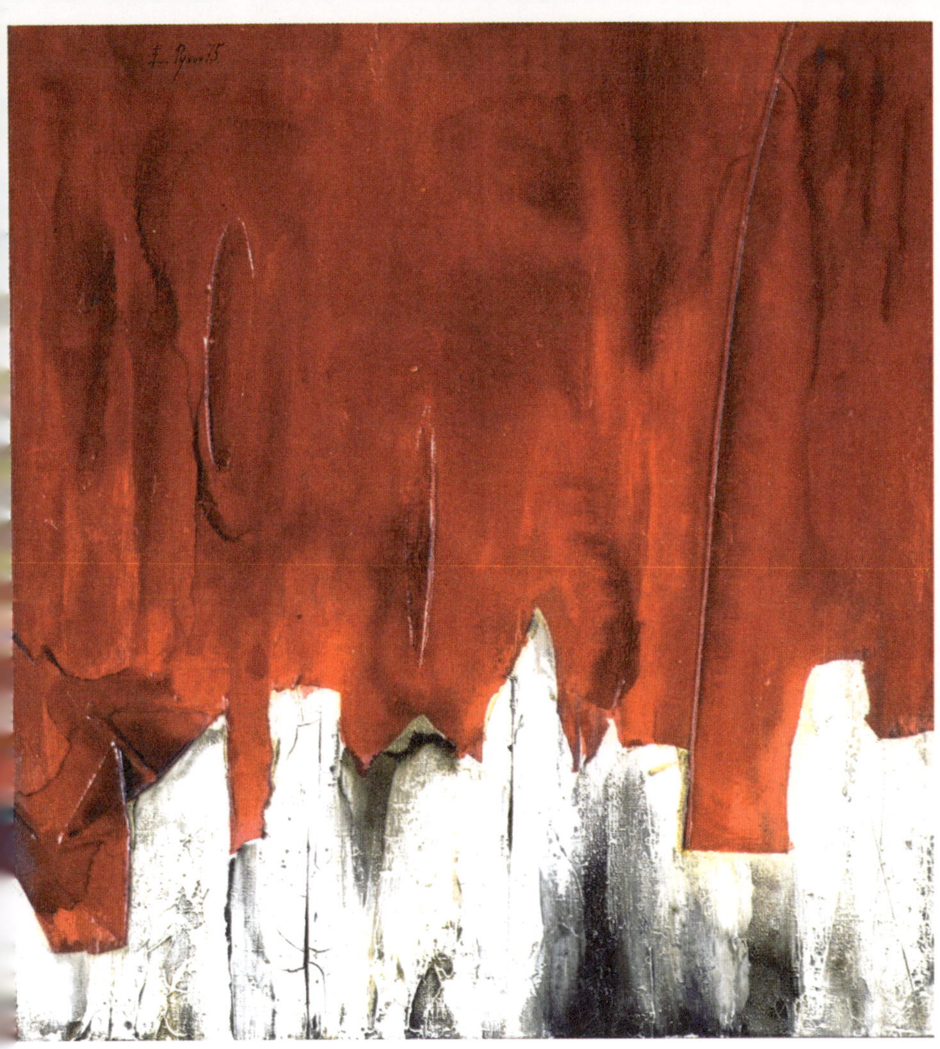

Red, Yevgeny Rukhin, 1975

So that's just how I answered him, dumbfounding everyone else at the table.

"Nu?" he said, which translates as "So?"

"Nu", I replied, "the difference between us is that, in the beginning, (this was getting Biblical), you happened to be selling blue jeans, cars, computers, then oil; you were making the most of the time you had, while you had it. I just happened to be doing it in the United States, and not at the precise moment when state assets were being privatised. Not in historically significant times. But the drive is the same. In truth, we're not that different."

He listened. It was a start.

Give occasional and silent thanks to the modern day security industry

It was a risk to be so frank, to offer no talk of art, but there was no time to really consider what had just transpired. In me, he might have seen a bit of himself. Or more likely, the price of oil was at $150 a barrel at the time – and that might have sealed our first deal as well. Art was a better investment.

A month after our meeting, I learned that my new client had narrowly survived an assassination attempt. It was never publicised. Let's just say, years later, we're still doing business, thanks to armour plating, bulletproof glass, and the occasional 'perfect find' for his budding collection.

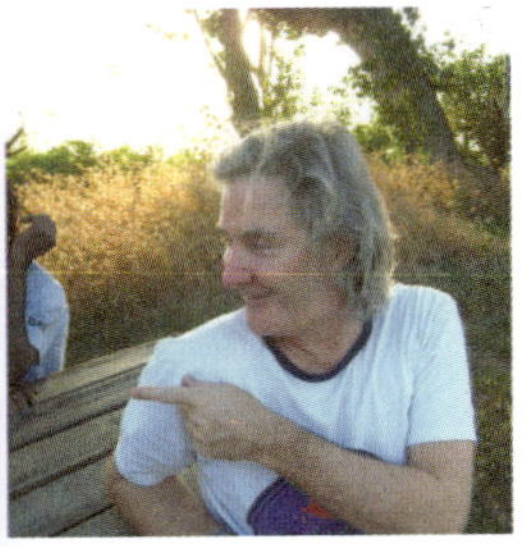

The Collector's Children – How the Rich Ruled the Art World, Until the Artists Got Richer

by Guy Kennaway

An author and journalist who claims to believe unshakably in the last thing he heard, Guy Kennaway stumbled onto the art scene by sharing a house with Jay Jopling in the 1980s. On hearing the news that Jay was to start a gallery he confidently predicted that nothing would come of it, feeling particularly certain that the name White Cube wouldn't work. Retaining an ambivalent view of the world of contemporary art, he yet cannot shake his deep adoration for some of the people who abide in it. Guy's most recent book, Bird Brain, is a story about pheasant shooting, narrated by a pheasant.

YOU HAVE TO HAVE stars at the party; they're social cocaine, and get everyone glancing and talking and moving and grooving and flirting and chatting and all short of breath. That's why the book-world can't throw parties; the stars of publishing are so dim they are barely visible to the naked eye. You see writers in the little photos at the back of OK! magazine gripping a flute of washing wine, but you have to read the caption to see who they are. Even the film business can't throw parties. Actors and actresses have long failed as stars, their dim wattage lost in the light pollution thrown by soap celebrities. Music biz parties used to be able to serve up a genuine old rocker star, but they lost all their fun when their gravy-train was derailed by Napster.

The art world can throw parties because it found stars that could stand at their core radiating energy like a lump of plutonium on six Es. Not the artists. The artists were just the entertainment, the artists were like the caterers. Necessary, but hardly likely to get the party going. The stars of the art parties were The Rich. Just a couple of them could get a whole room abuzz. A billion dollars in a pair of shoes. They didn't even need to be recognisable, and could retreat from the cameras like real stars, like Garbo and Hemingway.

In a world of celebrities hungry for recognition The Rich were the new famous. Everyone wanted them close but they had the cachet of needing no-one, and never trod any red carpet nor submitted themselves to interrogation from a bank of cameras. It was in the 90s that The Rich found contemporary art, and it was love at first sight. With The Rich on board, every other scene in town suddenly looked cheap. The spangle and lopsided glamour of a red carpet film premier seemed like a supermarket opening. With a judicious sprinkling of The Rich, like fairy dust over Sleeping Beauty, art parties woke up and rocked every other gig in town.

It's easy to see what the rich people were getting out of it. If you live in a world of sycophants and yes-men, the art world, with its combination of cheeky, clever, rude and charming artists, and its diplomatic, discreet and courtly dealers, offered a new level of sophistication when it came to being flattered. Those of an artistic disposition could endlessly discuss work, and pick up all that exciting new terminology from the people who actually made the stuff, and those with an eye for profit could indulge in speculation with the dealers. The Rich were referred to by the artists as prey, but with their power to buy or to ignore, it was the artists who lived in fear of them and not the other way round.

There developed a relationship between The Rich and the artists that was more than patronage; the artists were like the clever and talented children The Rich didn't possess. Artists who liked nothing more than to be childish thrived in the arrangement, and adored their new doting, loving and indulgent parents who showered them with attention and money. They hung out together, they met and partied at Basel and Miami, and cavorted in the sumptuous rooms and on the well-rolled lawns of their new parents' houses.

But inevitably cracks began to appear, as the intentions of the players could not be disguised forever. For instance, there are few scenes more risible in the farce of life than when the artist plays with the collectors' *actual* children.

A real example: As The Collector watched the Painter being attentive to his son, (who was a sorry disappointment compared to the Collector's mercurial and brilliant adoptees), showing him a trick with pencils and paper, The Collector's wife hurriedly searched for her camera, saying breathlessly "I've got to get this, I've got to get this." While the Artist worked hard on the Collector's son, the Collector worried that the Artist was thinking to himself – *good idea to make friends with this one too, because he'll inherit*, and then felt depressed to have had such a thought. The Artist's own child, a girl of about ten, looked on with a frightening coldness. We must feel sorry for this girl, watching her father lavish attention on this doltish, spoilt boy, and beginning to detect her own personal terror of not inheriting her father's talent, which she could already feel grown-ups searching for in her.

As time wore on, so all the children grew up. The Artist's progress went unchecked. The first shock The Collector got was when suddenly The Artist started turning up in the same restaurant that The Rich ate in – paying for himself and even sitting at a better table. Appallingly humiliating scenes followed: an artist giving advice on property deals, artists helping The Rich get an invite to a party; it had all got turned round the wrong way. Worse followed: the Artist made new friends, who were richer than The Collector was. A few artists even got richer than The Rich. That was horrible. Now, the Artist was so in demand that he started taking days to return texts from The Collector, when in the old happy days it had been mere seconds before the phone throbbed with his witty little one liners. Artists turned down dinner invitations, and even vacation invitations – things that would have been unthinkable five years before. But there were tender moments still to be had when they would see each other across a crowded gallery and get together and remember the old times, before The Artist saw someone more important and excused himself and left.

For The Collector the future was grim, no longer able to afford the new work of his protégés, and invited only to the drinks and not the dinner at the openings, all he had to console himself with was the unassailable fact of his ownership of the important early pieces. In dark moments he toyed with the idea of selling them and finding a new, younger generation of artists as fine and bright as his first family of adoptees. But he knew there were none out there, and you couldn't sell any work, unless you had a bloody good excuse. The dealers combed the market looking for collectors who were selling. Those who did were closed down, cut out and left in the cold. Forget dinner at the opening, forget drinks, forget the *opening*. You made a sale, you were off that list. Anyway, rich people don't sell. If you sold, other rich people noticed. And that really was the end.

So we must leave our Collector at home, in his sitting-room, staring at the very first work he bought. It is a little dirty from age now, because the Collector had a programme of lending art to museums around the world, to please the artist and the dealer, and for the thrill of seeing people leaning in to the little caption card on the museum wall with The Collector's and the Artist's name together on it, which was proof of how far back they went. That card was the marriage certificate of a painfully brief union. The piece had been round the globe a few times. It looked exhausted by the experience of being crated up and freighted and loaded and inspected and hung and then re-hung and repacked for the rest of its world tour. It was back at home, resting and re-configuring its dignity, staring at an empty room, glanced at every now and then by the Collector's cleaner and the cable guy.

To the Collector the work was the first child of his failed marriage to its creator. The Collector remembered the euphoria he had felt when he had bought it home all those years ago, in those sweet, heady times. Its power endured, but the party, for this collector, was over.

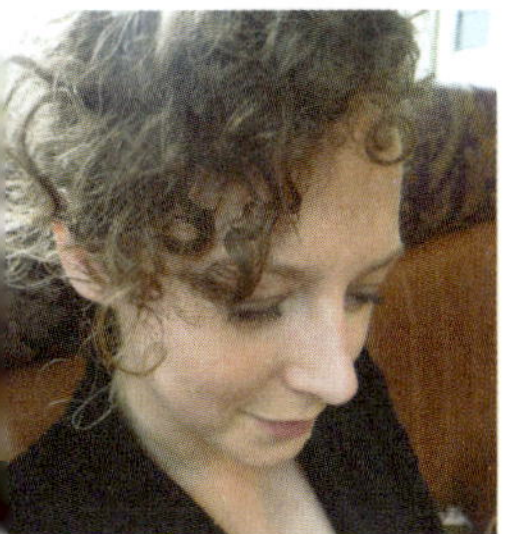

Forging Ahead – The Barefaced Cheek of the World's Art Forgers

by Nancy Durrant

Having "no artistic ability to speak of", Nancy Durrant is an arts editor at The Times. By opining rather than doing, she has been rewarded with invitations to judge several prizes, including the Zoo Art Fair prize, the Sunny Dupree Family Award at the Royal Academy Summer Exhibition and the first Cass Prize for Sculpture. She couldn't spot a fake if it bit her on the nose but knows a good story when she sees it.

IT'S A TOUGH LIFE as an artist, more often than not. For every Rothko or Warhol there are hundreds of hungry hopefuls shivering in dingy flats, surrounded by a wealth of artworks but no actual riches. Even Van Gogh had to wait until he was dead to make any cash. So when paintings are going for millions at auction and Damien Hirst is raking in silly money for his daubings, you can see the attraction for a competent copyist of sneaking a slice of the pie. For as long as people have been buying art, people have been faking it. Even Michelangelo dabbled in his early days, falsely ageing a small cupid sculpture and selling it as an antique to one Cardinal Riario (Riario was so impressed when the lie came to light that he became a loyal patron of the artist). But what does it take to be a great forger of art?

Learn from the experts

No faker can expect to get it right first time. In 1998, Australian painter William Blundell admitted to having spent 10 years churning out what he called 'innuendos' of works by Australian artists such as Sidney Nolan, Brett Whiteley, Russell Drysdale and Charles Blackman (not to mention the odd Picasso, Pollock or Monet) for French gallerist Germaine Curvers, who then sold them on as originals. In the early days though, Blundell and his twin brother John would visit the Art Gallery of New South Wales to see the head curator of Australian art Barry Pearce, ostensibly to find out whether works they'd picked up were genuine. It was only after a number of visits, during which Pearce had helpfully pointed out their various errors that he finally twigged – "After a while one of our curators said, 'You'd better button up; you're telling them how to improve their copies," he later said. Though various experts have since poured scorn on Blundell's forged efforts, there are still hundreds unaccounted for. One was once sold at auction by Christie's as 'another version' of a genuine painting called *Sydney Harbour* by Australian Impressionist Arthur Streeton, despite the fact that Blundell had painted media tycoon Kerry Packer's face into the rock.

Keep up with the paperwork

It's all very well having a perfect forgery, but without provenance, it's going to be an uphill struggle. With a good paper trail, however, it's amazing what you can slip past the experts. John Drewe, a master manipulator and fantasist whose own girlfriend and the mother of his two children repeatedly refused to marry him on the grounds that there was just "something wrong", was the mastermind behind what the police at the time called "the biggest contemporary art fraud the 20th century has seen". When police raided his house in 1996 they found hundreds of documents from institutions such as the Tate and the Victoria & Albert Museum's National Art Library, as well as faked certificates from the estates of artists like Giacometti and Dubuffet, rubber authentication stamps and receipts for paintings which had never existed until they were made in the rural cottage studio of Drewe's accomplice John Myatt, who for a decade had been cranking out paintings 'by' the likes of Chagall, Le Corbusier, Ben Nicholson and Braque using easily identified household emulsion given a bit of texture with a squirt of K-Y Jelly.

Drewe's genius, once he'd ensnared the rather suggestible Myatt, was to establish brilliant bogus histories for the paintings by infiltrating the archives of important institutions armed with a scalpel, and inserting false records. Even now, nearly a decade after his release from prison, the full consequences of Drewe's scheme is still unknown – his alterations to the archives constitute an alteration to art history, but he was so successful it's almost impossible to tell whether they have all been detected. The prosecution service called him "a menace to Britain's cultural patrimony".

Give them what their hearts desire

The art world is essentially driven by covetousness, and it's a sad truth that if people really want to believe you have something they want, it's very easy to convince them.

Shaun Greenhalgh and his parents, Olive and George (George was dubbed 'the artful codger' by the delighted newspapers) sold a headless alabaster statue of one of the daughters of the Egyptian pharaoh Akhenaten and his queen Nefertiti (and thus probably a sister of the boy-king Tutankhamun) to the Bolton Museum in 2003 for the very tidy sum of £439,000. Works in the unique 'Amarna' style dating from this period are extremely desirable due to their rarity and are something of a pet challenge for forgers. The Greenhalgh's voluptuous princess was, it turned out, knocked up in Shaun's shed, along with a terracotta goose bought for £3,000 by the Henry Moore Institute as a work by Barbara Hepworth and a bust of Thomas Jefferson allegedly by Horatio Greenough, which went for £48,000 at Sotheby's. The 'antiques rogue show' was finally ended in 2007 when George flogged the British Museum one of three Assyrian reliefs – the two remaining went to Bonham's auction house where one was found to have a spelling mistake in the cuneiform, modern harnesses on the horses and to be carved in stone which originated in Wiltshire.

Fight the power

Just because you get caught, doesn't mean you're doing it wrong. Some forgers sail close to the wind in the hope that, eventually, someone will spot what they're up to. British master forger Tom Keating was one such art world anarchist. Enraged by the lukewarm critical reception to his own original paintings, the art restorer and house painter rejected the gallery system as 'rotten', claiming that it was driven by "avant-garde fashion, with critics and dealers often conniving to line their own pockets at the expense both of naïve collectors and impoverished artists".

His solution was to attempt to destroy the system from within, by creating elaborate and accomplished forgeries to fool experts and prove that they were motivated by greed. To ensure that this would happen, Keating planted 'time bombs' in his paintings, so that if anyone cared to make a proper, detailed analysis of them at a later date, they would be exposed as forgeries. A layer of glycerine under the oil paint would dissolve if the painting were cleaned, destroying the picture. He'd even write a rude message onto the canvas in lead white before he began painting, so that should a diligent expert x-ray the work, the message would be clearly visible. He estimated that around 2,000 of his forgeries remained in circulation when he was at last arrested in 1977. True to self-publicising form, he published his autobiography in the same year, going on to present TV programmes on the painting techniques of old masters. Keating's known forgeries are still sought after.

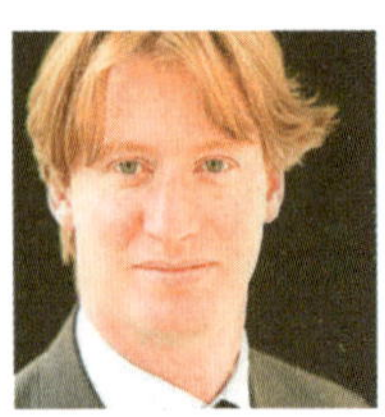

The Accidental Gallerist

by Mark Inglefield

Mark Inglefield was a journalist, working variously for the Times *(as a political correspondent) and the* Sunday Telegraph *where he edited the Mandrake column. Since then he has been involved with property, principally in Berlin, and now works, in various capacities, for Haunch of Venison Gallery.*

IT WAS PITCH BLACK and water was falling heavily from the roof. "Don't worry," said Horsley, "that only happens when it rains. The exhibition's in July. There'll be no rain then." Then the earth shook. I pointed the torch to the ceiling.

"What's that?"
"A train," he said.

Of course it was. We were underneath the arches in Borough, below the rail track that leads to London Bridge. This was where Horsley – Sebastian, the self-styled Dandy of the Underworld, God rest his soul - wanted me to show his paintings. It was unsuitable in every respect bar one, the address, which was Crucifix Lane. Horsley had been crucified the year before in a private ceremony in the Philippines and the work he wanted to show – paintings of crucifixes - was inspired by that experience. Why had he done this? I didn't ask, but as Sarah Lucas, his then girlfriend, had filmed the spectacle, and Dennis Morris, the famed chronicler of The Sex Pistols, had caught it on camera, it seemed like a sure-fire winner.

But back to Crucifix Lane. It was essentially a cave. The floor was mud broken up by the odd puddle, the brickwork when touched was as fragile as a Digestive biscuit just lifted from a mug of tea, and there was no natural light – no light at all, in fact. To rent this palace, I had to link up with someone Horsley had met at the Colony Room Club. This bloke knew the owner. "Reliable, is he?" I asked. "Of course not, darling. He's a mess."

After a number of missed appointments (on his part), myself and the Mess finally got together at Soho House. I found him in the Circle bar puffing on a fag. He was about thirty-five and had on a smartish blue suit with grubby double cuffs flowering from the sleeves, *sans* cufflinks. His face had not seen a razor in days and his eyes were on stalks: he was wired, an advert for Class A + unreliability - far worse than I expected.

I had coffee – it was 11am – and he had vodka, certainly not his first. A few drinks later – and some prolonged absences in the lavatory, from which he returned more goggle-eyed than when he left – he told me I was the sort of person he could do business with and that he would fix up a meeting with the owner. As we left the club he put his hand on my shoulder and asked for fifty quid to 'cover his out-of-pocket expenses'. When I agreed he looked astonished, like he'd pulled three bells on a fruit machine. But he was good to his word. He called me back the next day – even though it was four in the morning. Sensing trouble, I let it go to answer machine and did the same with half a dozen other calls he made. When I did return his call a girl answered and asked if I was Wayne. I said not.

"Why've you got his phone, then?"
"I haven't."
"Then you're f—-king Wayne. Don't piss us about. How long are you gonna be? We're dying here."

A different voice came on the line.
"Wayne, it's" – the Mess said his name – "what the f—-k are you playing at ..?"
"It's Mark, not Wayne."
"Who the f--k's Mark?"

This sounded like it was addressed to the room, not me. The phone went dead.

A week passed - and then: "Right, it's fixed. Come to – [he gave me an address in Chelsea, a good one] – and we'll go and see the owner."

I was just getting in a cab when the Mess called again, asking me to bring five hundred pounds (his cut on the deal) – "Because this is when the deal gets done and we part company, my friend". I did as asked. The person who answered the door at the apartment was another Mess, a female Mess, wearing only a pair of knickers and sleeveless t-shirt. She led me through to a bedroom. The male Mess was lying face down on the bed. An acrid, chemical smell hung in the air. The cause of that sat on a table - an Evian bottle half-filled with water with Bacofoil™ wrapped around its neck secured by a rubber band with a Bic™ biro sticking out the side. Eventually he got up and faced me.

"Oh, it's you. Fancy a smoke?"

I did meet the owner that day, a normal sort called Tim, and secured Crucifix Lane for Horsley. I never saw The Mess again. He didn't even come to the show. In that he wasn't alone. It was a disaster. Didn't sell a thing. And it rained most of July, too.

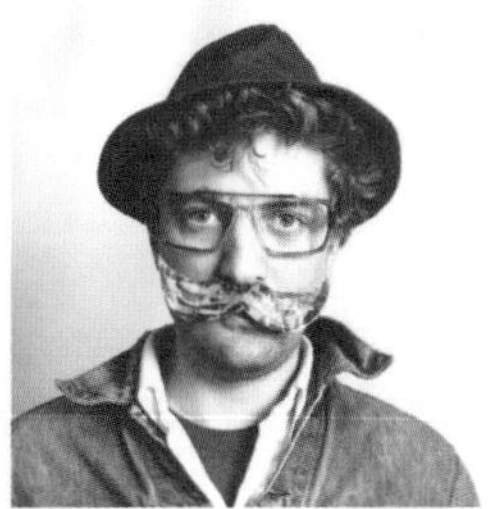

Pretty Things – The Erotic Dialectic in High Art

by Walter Robinson

Walter Robinson is founding editor of Artnet Magazine, which launched in 1996. He has also written for Art in America and is author of Instant Art History (Ballantine). He is a painter who has shown his work at Metro Pictures in New York.

SPENDING MONEY CAN MAKE you feel better. This we all know, but I remember really feeling it almost 30 years ago, when I was lonely and poor and living on the Lower East Side. My $150-a-month apartment was rigged with heavy drapes over the windows like a drug den, three layers of old linoleum on the floor, and it hit me like a bolt from the blue, this terrific idea that I should go downstairs and do some shopping. I can't honestly say what it was that I bought, but I can feel even now the sensation of relief washing over me, once I had a goal, a purpose, a plan, something that I could actually accomplish.

Last month I had a kind of inverse experience in which I looked at something that was supposed to encompass all kinds of feeling but instead was about money, a vast amount of it. I was standing in a darkened, relatively small gallery at Sotheby's New York in front of a giant red and orange painting by Mark Rothko from 1961. I looked at this 8 x 9 ft. picture of emptiness, looming above me, and I could sense Capital with all its invisible force, glowing, throbbing, "expressing" the essence of *its* being in this pretty abstract thing. Valued at as much as $25 million, the untitled painting eventually sold for more than $31 million, with the auctioneer's percentage added in.

That particular Rothko comes with a funny story, or one that seems funny to those of us who take a dim view of art-market high jinks. A collector, a big art patron who had promised her collection (including the Rothko) to the Dallas Art Museum, agreed to sell the painting as long as the dealer buying it promised to keep the deal on the down-low. Sure, sure, no problem, said the dealer, who promptly turned around and put the picture in a very public New York auction. The lady collector is suing, but she still hasn't let on how much the dealer skimmed her for.

The art market makes you stupid, the art critic Jerry Saltz said back in 2007, as the auction frenzy reached impossible heights. Sure, but what kind of stupid? It's an important question. You can be dumb in a really useless kind of blockhead way, or stupid like a stoner, like a flower child, like the drunk who leans out of the telephone booth to look for a street sign and says, "I'm at the corner of telephone and telephone."

That's how I feel at art fairs, at least if I'm not working (writing stuff down, taking pictures, getting prices out of dealers). Pleasure domes, that's what they are, filled with free-floating libidinal energy, aisles aglow with the blush of youth, whether it's the stuff on the walls or the pretty young things on the floors. Art fairs are a utopia of plenty, a chance to stroll and chat, look and explore, the kind of erotically charged shopping aesthetic that so turned on Baudelaire and Walter Benjamin. Be open, be friendly, spend some money, it's hot.

Art is basically about showing and looking, which are themselves about loving, as Pablo Picasso emphatically demonstrates throughout his career with art – art that is essentially avant-garde versions of the kinds of paintings that serve as covers for Harlequin Romances. The most expensive painting to sell at auction, Picasso's *Nude, Green Leaves and Bust* (1932), shows -- needless to say -- his nude young blonde lover all blessed out.

The persistence of this erotic dialectic in high art is a testimony to the life force, whether Sigmund Freud's or God's, a compulsion to go forth and multiply in a world that sometimes just seems to want you to wither and die. Emblem of all this is the omnipresent pin-up, which even finds its way into the art market, though with its ordinariness just a little bit bent.

Having a little fun in its own uncanny way, the art market has given a special high value to photographs of young women, models usually, who went on to become First Ladies, art collector's wives, and other such contemporary icons. It's a pin-up version of the Horatio Alger story.

At the top of the heap is Richard Avedon's 1992 photograph of a then-freshly punked-out Stephanie Seymour, lifting the hem of a body-hugging, see-through black gauze dress to show her escutcheon. It has sold several times, most recently for an impressive $262,400. Another master of fashion photography, Irving Penn, took a photograph in 1999 of the supermodel Gisele that shows the slim, big-busted young woman bending over as if awaiting approach from behind. In 2008, it brought $193,000 at Christie's; two years later she married the football star Tom Brady.

Best of all is the nude photo from 1993 by Michel Conte of a willowy Carla Bruni, who stands stark naked and knock-kneed -- a submissive, immature pose -- but brazenly gazes at the viewer, her hands covering her sex like a Venus who is neither chaste nor shy. The picture sold for $91,000, no doubt in honor of her exceptionally contemporary metamorphosis in 2008, from a pretty young thing into the First Lady of France.

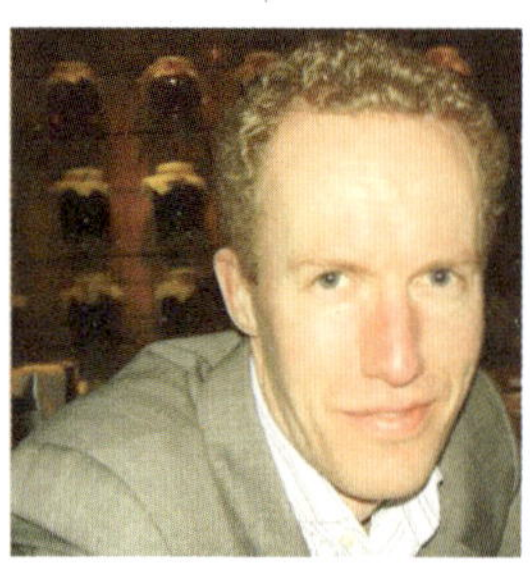

What is it with the Ugly Girl?
A Utilitarian Approach to Art

by Henrik Riis

Henrik Riis is founder of Artica.com, an eGallery of Young Contemporary Art, and co-founder of the creative management company Dutch Uncle, a leading illustration agency. Henrik believes that any act in life should be based on complete rational behaviour – except when being irrational has a higher utility.

" **I** DON'T FEEL COMFORTABLE in being commissioned by Pepsi to work on a nationwide campaign in the US. All my life I have been drinking Coca Cola."

This (wants-to-remain-anonymous) artist's quote more or less sums up the new environment I found myself immersed in when I took my first steps into the creative world of art. I was on a steep learning curve. Considering the budget in play, most people from my background would have replied "Pepsi? Great!, What do I need to do? Where do I sign? – and can I keep my clothes on?". But this was different. I had to take a deep breath, count to ten slowly and employ a modicum of 'artistic integrity' - the myriad nuanced meanings of which I was just beginning to learn.

Perhaps I shouldn't be thinking about the art-world equivalents of Pepsi *or* Coca-Cola, I told myself.

I didn't study art at a top tier university – I studied law and economics. I wasn't taken through how one -ism developed into the next -ism and why. I can engage in a complex discussion on behavioural incentives within socialism and capitalism, but ask me about analytic and synthetic cubism and my eyes will glaze over.

My love of art has developed from the heart, but with a utilitarian perspective attached to it. I started collecting it some fifteen years ago, beginning, as most do, with the number one gallery cliché in mind: 'Collect the art you like'. I fell in love with the Dutch/Danish/Belgian collective CoBrA in my late teenage years and I can still be moved by the way they portrayed the world. So I bought CoBrA artists – which wasn't a bad start in retrospect. Obviously I went off to buy more art that I shouldn't have bought, and that I now can't sell, swap, or even give away.

If you want to be a successful collector keep one thing in mind. Buying and collecting art is no different from any other luxury item and luxury's main function is a social one. We define ourselves by the luxury items we buy, and even though we all like to consider ourselves as rational consumers – we aren't. Regardless of how intelligent we are – or consider ourselves to be – we never seem to get it exactly right. So over the years I have developed a few guidelines for myself whenever I consider any work of art for my collection - these are the same guidelines I'd advise anyone to use.

Art as an investment: Only buy art from artists who have sold artworks at auction within the past year, and use the latest auction price as a guideline. I don't care if the artist can walk on water – or what the gallerist, promoter, friend or any other may tell me about him. The chance you have of spotting the next Warhol is tiny and you are more likely to win the lottery – in which case I will congratulate you.

Art as a way to enhance your hip-factor: To be honest, this is the art you get into your collection for no other purpose than to brag about it – you don't even necessarily want to hang it in your living room. (It being the equivalent of the custom-built Köenig sports car idling away in the garage). It's the art you "happen" to mention in a casual conversation and which the "right" listener will not let go unnoticed. Here is a little tip. Should you have been unfortunate enough to get carried away at an auction and pay way too much for that particular Lichtenstein, guess what, the piece of art can be "moved" unnoticed from the "art as investment" category straight over to the " hip-factor" category. No one need notice.

There are many people (even well established folk in the art world) who will be impressed when you confess to them that you know £75,000 was a bit over the top for that limited edition print, but hey, you liked it and what is the point of money these days anyway?

Art for your home: Nothing is more depressing than your home resembling the white-wall decor of a hospital. Your walls are the projection of your artistic soul. Depending on what kind of establishment you run and how often you entertain guests in your home, you may have to compromise and "dress" accordingly. Your mother-in-law may not appreciate very naked women above her daughter's (and your) sofa, even if signed "With love" by Sally Mann.

Art for pleasure: If you find art that fits into all of the categories above, your future within art is bright. You have great taste, a large disposable income and a fantastic home. From a utilitarian's perspective, there may be art which doesn't fit the above categories, but will give you great pleasure and enhance your quality of life. But this is tricky – and a new collector may not be able to accurately assess future utility.

Collecting art for any other reason: Don't – unless there is a significant positive externality (I will leave this to your own imagination). "Any other reason" is simply what economists will a call a losing strategy. You will always end up with the short stick.

One last thing: I always advise honesty. I can still get intimidated when, on walking into a gallery or a posh art fair, I get the rolling of the eyes by the person in charge. Never try to pretend you are an expert. This will only get you into trouble and may lead to arrogance whereby you will say something like I once did - with the artist present - "What is it with the ugly girl in the painting?"

The girl in the painting is always the artist's girlfriend.

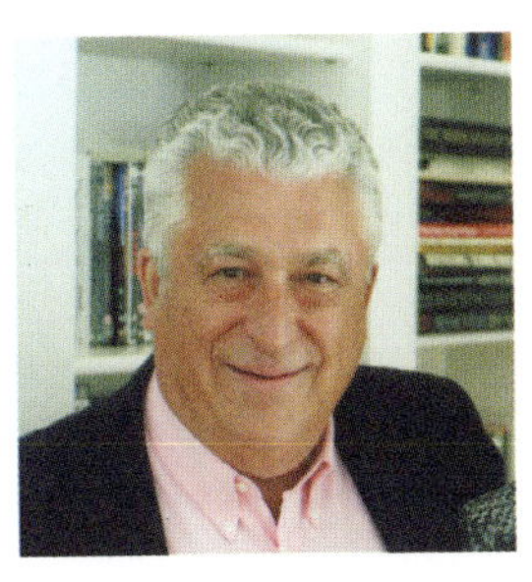

How to Become an Art Dealer

by Alex Wengraf

Alex Wengraf qualified in Dentistry and Maxillo-Facial surgery, and then used these skills to become an art dealer: first by inheritance, then by negotiation to be Managing Director of Colnaghi on Old Bond Street. Then he went independent again. He has retired now but still acts as éminence grise to certain of his clients. He feels he was always more grise than eminent.

THERE ARE ROUGHLY FIVE ways to enter, but none of these is necessarily an easier option.

1. To **inherit** sounds easy - but you can't very well arrange it and many children of dealers want to do ANYTHING except follow their parents. Some drift into the trade, and the more serious ones go to the Courtauld Institute to learn Art History from whence they either become penniless academics, or leave with a PhD to become a porter at Christeby's. Some seamlessly join their parents and squabble till they set up alone.

2. **Marriage** is an excellent way of becoming a dealer. Most commonly a husband/wife team works with one buying and the other selling. This set up works for both sexes: the secretary bird becoming the proprietess after marrying her art dealer husband.

Or, the accountant with the safe job chucks it in and joins his dealer wife, first just to help with the VAT and occasional shop-sitting and then....he is lost to art for ever. She had fondly imagined that she was marrying a man with a safe job so that she could continue her funny little penchant for art.

Alternatively a dealer dies relatively young leaving a distraught and penniless widow with three small kids and a rotten stock of unsold pictures. On selling said stock, she is offered some items from a collection that her husband sold ten years ago. She feels safe to buy them since she still has the old records, so she sells at a whopping profit, gets bitten by the bug, sends the kids to public school and the Courtauld (as in 1. above) - saying "I'm just keeping the business going for young Henry".

But she never does let go of the reins, and young Henry, at thirty five, is an aesthetic gay with an overpowering mother. He is anyway more interested in string quartets than money, which she has made far more of than her late husband ever did.

3. Many **collectors** end up as dealers. Like an actor who becomes disenchanted playing Dick Whittington at the Watford Palace Theatre when he had left drama school with the intention of playing Hamlet or Pozzo at Stratford, he uses the 'panto' money to buy his opening stock. Ditto ex-bankers, doctors, ambassadors, lawyers and even, so help them, politicians who lost their elections.

4. And then there are the real **bootstrap** people. Let us say he comes from a family of the true working class or, a middle class family of total philistines. He leaves school at fifteen having traded in buttons and stamps, coins and cigarette cards by the age of six, and bartered his bootlaces by year twelve. He goes on to buy trays of stuff for a fiver at local auctions, and sells the contents individually on a market stall on the other side of the road the next day. He combs the regional fairs, puts things in to Bonhams that he has bought at Gorringes, graduates to vintage cars and works his way up to the Chelsea and Barbican fairs and/or a shop-let near Portobello Road.

But he also goes to museums and slowly learns about real art. The late Lillian Browse was a ballet dancer from South Africa who hurt a leg, took a job as a secretary in an art gallery and became a most respected dealer in Cork Street. But it took work and effort – see her memoir, The Duchess of Cork Street. The dealer Robert Noortman came up that way too.

I know a housewife, who, in order to hide an extra-marital affair, needed an excuse to come to London every week. So she started frequenting the auctions and buying paintings and prints each week, but this got expensive so she tried to sell some of them too. Slowly the affair faded, the lover proving no match for the lure of the art trade. Nowadays the husband is permitted to help load and unload the van before and after a fair, the lover's flat is used as a central warehouse, and she is far too busy and successful to worry about, let alone have time for, making love.

5. **High Finance**: You have made a lot of money and you want to become an art dealer for fun? A good hobby for a rich man. Start slowly, collect and learn about the art and get the experience. If you just hire a young man marketing himself as a 'consultant' you will quickly discover that though you have indeed acquired some experience, he has acquired your money. Better to find yourself a glamorous marketing PR/manager and someone genuinely long in the tooth, who'll provide you with sound advice for a flat fee and a couple of holidays every year. Maybe a yacht helps. But learn about the art yourself – which is after all the point.

Contrariwise, if you happen to work in an auction house and are sacked, take the client list before you go, and get one of those clients to put up a few million pounds as backer. You have the experience and he has the money – an ideal partnership. After a couple of years, you have the money and he has the experience. Time to move on.

What unifies these people in 1 - 5? A love of the objects of course, a curiosity about what it is, or where it came from, and where it can be made to go to. A certain driving ambition also helps - most dealers work rather longer hours than most of their friends.

You want to be a dealer? Learn, work hard and don't cheat. Don't cheat your colleagues, but more importantly don't cheat yourself into believing the objects you have are other than they really are. Find out - because if your stock is no good, there may yet be a market for it, but if you don't even know it is junk, you are…well, sunk.

Polonius said something similar.

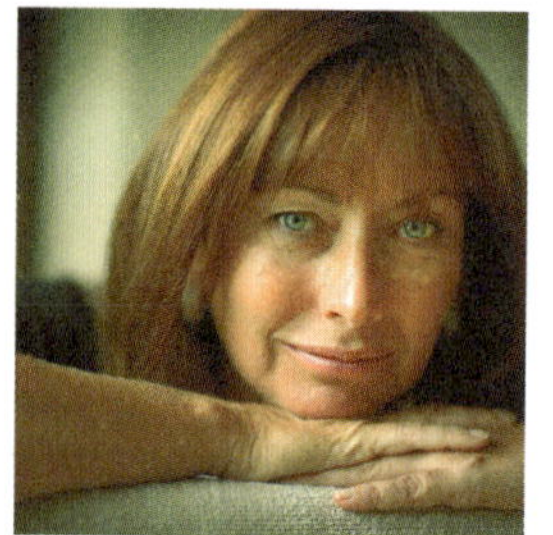

A Day in the Life of an Art Collector

by Anita Zabludowicz

Anita Zabludowicz and her husband Poju founded the Zabludowicz Collection in the early 1990s to collect international contemporary art and support their ongoing philanthropic endeavours. They opened their London exhibition space in a former Methodist Chapel at 176 Prince of Wales Road in 2007 with the aim of exhibiting the collection and facilitating projects with artists and curators both in the UK and overseas.

I WAS ASKED TO write 'A Day in the Life of an Art Collector' but what if that day is boring? I hope it's not. Ever since I can remember, one of my main goals in life has been to never waste one single day. I often feel like a kid in a sweet shop, maybe you can call this an innocent hedonism! I am lucky enough to be able to see and be involved in so many interesting happenings with inspirational people almost every day. Three years ago I decided to document this and started to blog my 'Art Diary'. This task turned out to be great fun, the worst injury to date on my adventures was when Lucian Freud threw a bread roll at my friend Stefan! I sometimes get very embarrassed when I take photos and deep down I guess I must be quite voyeuristic. So here goes with my 'Day in the Life!'

After a lazy morning in the gym and making myself presentable I joined artist Jim Hodges for a lunch given by Jenni Lomax and Camden Arts Centre, where I am a Trustee. I had not seen Jim since 1992, two years before I started collecting in earnest. It was incredibly nostalgic to be bumping into him again; my life has changed so much since those days. His show at Camden Arts Centre was beautiful; Stephen Friedman, Maureen Paley and Jenni Lomax were walking around like proud family members, Maureen being the first ever to show his work in the UK. I had my tail between my legs thinking how I had missed the whole essence of his artworks at the very beginning when I met him in the basement of art philanthropist and collector Mrs Danhauser's art space in Downtown, New York. This was in fact the first ever art space I ever visited. Back then I could not understand what he was doing with his flowers and serviettes from the cafe down the road.

I then found myself at the Tate Britain, where I am also a Trustee of the Tate Foundation, for the opening of Rude Britannia; there were some lovely works such as David Shrigley's dead cat and Barry Reigate's lamps. I love Brit humour; if I ever find it difficult to define what it is to be British, I return to our humour. It is part of our psychology and it reminds us of who we really are.

Later that day it was off to the Barbican with Elizabeth Neilson - who heads our collection and all our art projects - to see John Bock's wacky performance and his spidery pods. We recently made a serious commitment to John's work by buying a spectacular video and sculpture installation. That night he was in great company with artists Tim Noble & Sue Webster, Anne Hardy and Neil Hamon all joining in to watch his performance. All these artist works we have in the collection. Tim and Sue's work was in our first show at 176 Prince of Wales Road called An Archaeology. Neil Hamon's work I discovered by chance when I was eating with my posh girl friends in Cipriani and a City friend spotted me through the window. He dragged me out of my lunch and across the road to a pop-up show - he thought Hamon's work was hilarious and to his surprise I thought his work was brilliant and was so impressed I bought the lot! My friend was totally shocked and stumped!

Dipping out of the packed Bock performance, Elizabeth and I spent a little time viewing the Barbican's Surreal House exhibition which was like a dream. There, amongst such masters as Magritte and Dali, were the future greats Rachael Kneebone as well as Tim & Sue.

I know I am meant to be sticking to one day, but talking about surrealism, the very next day I visited the works of Nancy Fouts, a wonderful artist in her 50s, whose work is an homage to surrealism in her own distinct absurdist style. Her home;

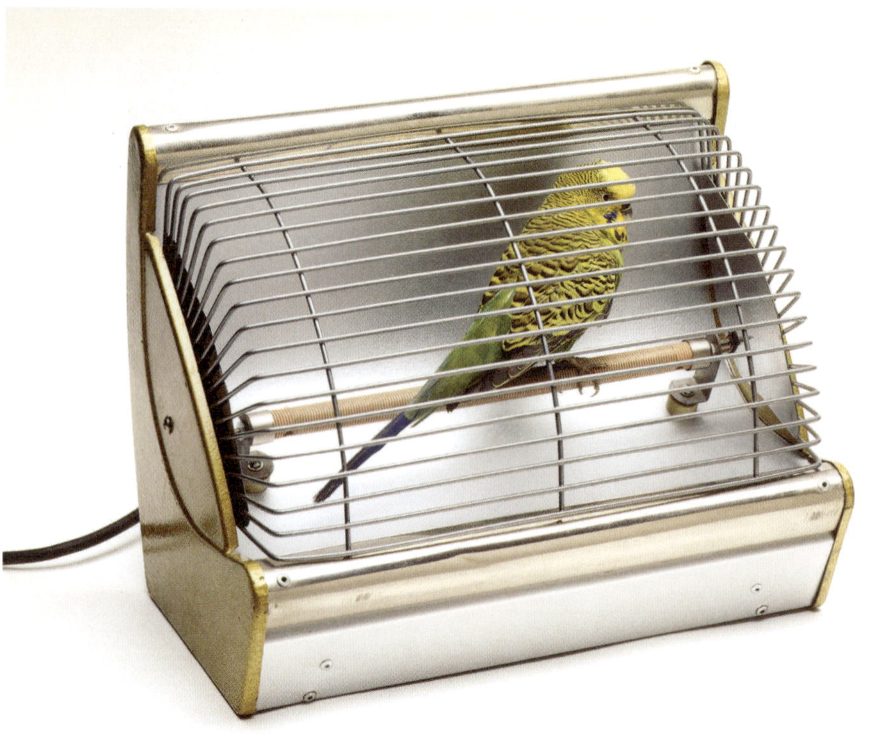

Bird On Heater, 2008, Found Heater, Taxidermy Budgie, Nancy Fouts

an old vicarage with the most wonderful keepsakes, with her art works integrated throughout the house. Like Neil's work, I indulged my impulse to purchase. One of the works was a razor blade embedded into a bar of Pear's soap, another was a taxidermy budgie inside a heater.

Back to my day - from the Barbican we dashed to the Whitechapel Gallery and were most astonished by Act One of Dimitris Daskolopoulos's Collection exhibition Keeping it Real, which defined for me the essence of the early 90s. The heat of the 1980s was over, recession had hit hard, countries were broke, the stock market had crashed, AIDS was at a climax and the streets were not safe to walk in. Now it was time to strip the glitz and actually see what was underneath.

As I was standing in front of these great works of art, including pieces by Jim Hodges, Robert Gober and David Hammons, I was suddenly transported for the second time that day back to Mrs Danhauser's collection where I had very early on seen the most wonderful Matthew Barneys, Gobers and Bruce Naumans and I recalled how sensitive and vulnerable their work appeared to be. How odd it was to be looking back at these artists, and to think of where they are now – international art superstars but still honest to themselves.

I arrived into the collecting scene in 1994. It was after four years of intense research and further education that my husband and I made the decision to collect Modern British Art. But no one took me seriously, so it was a very difficult journey. But thanks to the help of Thomas Dane, Edward Lee, Nicholas Serota, Faye Ballard (daughter of JG) and Vanessa Branson (sister of Richard) we became contemporary art collectors. Do not think for one moment this was an easy ride, there were barriers almost everywhere. Not being a pushy person, and perhaps because I am a woman, things were very hard. We were seen as insignificant by great galleries, who put us on 'The Waiting List' for works by Gursky and Doig which we then never received. It was only thanks to the serious help of such gallerists as Maureen Paley, Shaun Regen, Max Hetzler, Marc Foxx and Nicholas Logsdail that we started to get taken a little more seriously.

Our collection is now quite substantial and for the past three years has been housed in a philanthropic art space in north London (we all call it '176' for ease's sake). This year we have also initiated a residency program in Finland. I am very lucky to be surrounded by 'future greats' in the art world, and lucky that our work has become part of art history -sealed in posterity through the ten books we have published to date.

Back to Dimitri's magnificent dinner for Keeping it Real. It was held in the former residence of the Astor family, which overlooks the Thames. The dinner guests were the crème de la crème of the art world who are indeed intent on 'keeping it real'; Achim Borchardt-Hume, Iwona Blazwick, Nicholas Serota, Dakis Joannou, Iwan Wirth, Gregor Muir, Dimitris Paleocrassas, Brian Boylan and many more.

After such a magnificent day I was swept home able to sleep content with the direction our collection is moving in, thanks to all the wonderful people around me.

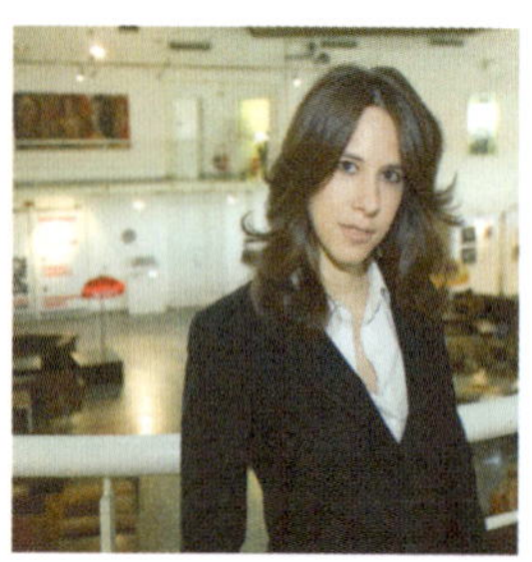

Ten Commandments for the Aspiring Contemporary Art Collector

by Tammy Smulders

Tammy Smulders is the Managing Director of SCB Partners, a marketing insights consultancy based in London.

THE ART WORLD IS a complicated place. Follow these ten commandments, and you too can be joshing with Larry and Jay. Success guaranteed.

THOU SHALT SUFFER THE WINNER'S CURSE:

Over-bid with record setting prices for a series of artists - emerging, mid-career and established - in evening sales at Christie's, Sotheby's and Phillips. Have your assistant accidentally leak details to Bear Facts newsletter helmsman Josh Bear and Bloomberg reporter Scott Raeburn. Smugly offer no comment and watch the invitations to dinner with dealers roll in.

THOUGH SHALT GO SHOPPING WITH ARM CANDY ART ADVISOR:

Carefully select your art advisor based on a) looks; b) access to key art world events and dinners and c) the chance to rub shoulders with his/her other clients, with whom you want to socialise. Upgrade as appropriate – "it's not you, it's me."

THOU SHALT INDULGE YOUR INNER MEDICI:

Take an 'interest' in a young artist from one of the leading galleries in London or New York (select one of the following: Gagosian, Marian Goodman, David Zwirner, Pace, Hauser & Wirth, White Cube, Lisson, Barbara Gladstone). Become his NBF and host dinners in his honour to broadcast your association.

THOU SHALT BUY A PAIR OF BRIGHLY COLOURED TROUSERS AND DORK GLASSES:
Look creative and unconventional to set yourself apart from the bankers. Show off your eccentric side with trousers in hues such as orange, lime green or matte red. Available from Hentschman or Hackett or the like. Compliment with dork glasses to gain extra kudos from the curators.

THOU SHALT GIVE GENEROUSLY (BUT GET YOUR MONEY'S WORTH):
Make donations of £10K+ to all major art institutions, including MoMA, Tate, Whitney, LACMA, Serpentine, the Met, etc. Increase donations until invitation is extended to be on one of the acquisition committees.

THOU SHALT THROW SHAPES ON THE DANCEFLOOR:
Celebrate the day's purchases by 'letting loose' on the floors of Le Baron (Miami), Kunsthalle (Basel) and the Bauer (Venice). Make a fool of oneself by inducing wardrobe malfunction with a gallerina from one the top galleries (see commandment # for list of accepted galleries). Make it up to her the next day with an apologetic purchase from her gallery.

THOU SHALT BECOME A STAPLE OF ARTFORUM.COM'S SCENE & HERD COLUMN OR ARTNET MAGAZINE'S 'LONDON DISPATCH':
In additional to the art calendar staples (i.e. Venice, Documenta, Manifesta, Armory), attend a critical mass of private views in order to maximise potential for exposure in the above columns. Feign indifference for the camera while positioning yourself nonchalantly talking to key artists.

THOU SHALT INVITE THE ENTIRE ART WORLD TO YOUR REHANG PARTY:
In order to showcase your recent purchases, open up your home to fellow collectors and art world insiders. Give personal tours of the collection, chortling as you drop anecdotes on each work. Commission a site-specific participatory food project by Jennifer Rubell to set tongues wagging.

THOUGH SHALT LOAN WORKS TO MAJOR MUSEUM SHOWS:
Cement your position by ensuring that your collection includes significant works by artists with forthcoming major shows and retrospectives. Tell everyone. Drop it into conversations, even when irrelevant. Derive self-importance from the fact that your name features on the museum's wall – you've now made it.

THOU SHALT AVOID THE DETECTION OF YOUR EGOTISTICAL AMBITIONS: Hide thy true nature. Steer clear of cathedralofshit.com - even though it's the funniest blog to come out of the art world in years - and hire a hacker if you appear on the site.

Good luck.

Buy The Art You Hate

by Ben Lewis

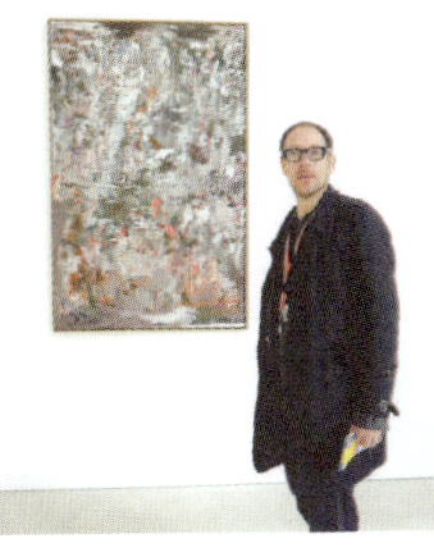

Ben Lewis is an award-winning documentary film-maker, author and art critic, best known for Art Safari, his series of programmes about contemporary artists. He is currently raising finance for a third series. Author of a monthly column on art for Prospect magazine, his writing is also frequently published in major national newspapers. He has been banned from various art world locations, probably because his opinions on contemporary art don't fit the prevailing mould. This hasn't stopped him yet.

THE ART WORLD LIKES to tell you how diverse and varied it is, using wherever possible in its description of itself, the word 'complexity'. But there is one thing in the art world that is the same wherever you go - from the tiny galleries of Hoxton to the art fair of Dubai, from the contemporary art auctions of Sotheby's and Christie's to the white cubes of New York's Chelsea district - the abysmal rule-of-thumb advice ladled out to collectors: 'Buy What You Like.'

Buy What You Like? Oh no. No no no no. Please never do that. Ever. That is the worst thing you can do. Buy What You Like if you want to get bored of it in two weeks. Buy What You Like if you want your friends to sneer at you behind your back. Buy What You Like if you want to own something that you can't give away in five years time.

'Buy What You Like' is the art world's most dishonest sales pitch. No one smart buys what they like. If anything, they buy what someone richer than them likes, and has bought a ton of. Or they buy what the curators of big public museums are planning to put on a show of. Or they buy what their art advisor tells them they'll like, that is currently available for a good price.

But if you don't want to do that then you still mustn't Buy What You Like. Please. Simply because you will like it *too much*. You will end up with a collection that has a bit of everything in it, and is the same as everyone else's. Remember all those billionaires' homes you've visited recently, and how they had a Richard Prince Nurse painting in the hall, some Cindy Sherman photos in the corridor, a Damien over the sofa and a Giacometti next to it. You don't want your collection to look just like theirs, do you?

Another classic problem of buying what you like rears its head at the art fair. If you are anything like me, for the first ten minutes of an art fair, everything looks wonderful. You are blown away by the diversity of the human imagination. You walk excitedly from booth to booth, stunned by how many good artists there are from Wigan, Belgrade and Shanghai, imagining you are instantly discovering the twenty-first century's Picasso, Goya and Vermeer. Twenty minutes later it's all changed. You are oxygen deprived. The white light hurts your eyes, everything has taken on the look of the section of Camden Lock were they sell tie-dye sarongs and Fimo earrings. You hate everything. This is the reason not to buy what you *instantly* like.

Even before you get to this point other dangers arise during the euphoric 'like' phase. It's to be expected that you'll gravitate towards what it technically known as *Something By Some Unknown Artist That Looks A Bit Like Something Else By Someone Really Famous.* Beware of all those ultra-crisp large format photographs of banal panoramas of globalisation that look a bit like Gursky…but aren't. Avoid those shiny cartoons à la Murakami that ironically celebrate Asian consumer culture. Don't go for those rough-and-ready collages of newspaper clippings, industrial junk and screen prints – they are just fourth division *scuola di* Rauschenberg.

The ubiquitous formulae of contemporary art offer other temptations, but please avoid them: pass on catchy slogans written in neon, collections of objects arranged in a grid, anything with a simple minimalist geometry and paintings with lots of dripping brushstrokes. And for pity's sake, don't buy anything with skulls and hand grenades, the lowest common denominators of street art.

There are three basic rules to follow if you are starting an art collection. Firstly, find out what ideas are behind the work of art you like. They should hold your interest and tell us about the times in which we are living. Secondly, find out what else the artist has done. An artist, whose reputation survives will always have produced a body of work, that develops over time. Thirdly - specialise. Decide what your focus is going to be – Modernist collage? European mixed-media sculpture? African contemporary? Middle Eastern photography? A focused collection will make you look more intelligent and be easier to sell, if you need the money one day. Followed those three rules? Okay, ask them for a twenty per cent discount, and their IBAN number. Oh, one last check: take a look at the gallery owner who is selling you the work. Millions of dollars and pounds have been wasted on bad art by collectors who confuse liking the art with liking the slinky 5 foot 10" Italian-American gallerina. What I'm saying is, make sure the gallerist is ugly.

That may be too many rules for you to remember, while you're contemplating great art and being transported to a higher plane, so I will give you just one that will sear itself in to your brain. Its basis was spoken to me a few years ago, when I was making a film about the American-Thai artist Rirkrit Tiravanija. Tiravajina cooks food in art galleries as works of art, exhibits facsimiles of his empty apartment for visitors to lounge around in, and makes sculptures out of crates of empty beer bottles that he and his arty friends have drunk. I remember asking his laconic New York gallerist Gavin Brown why he'd given Tiravanija his first exhibition. "Because I found it kind of irritating," was his reply.

If that line doesn't impart the best advice anyone can give you about collecting great art, I don't know what does. Even if you are an über cool gallerist, the art of tomorrow is something you're not supposed to understand. It shouldn't fit in; it should assault all the values you hold dear. So do yourself a favour: buy the art you hate.

CHAPTER 4:
THE ART ITSELF

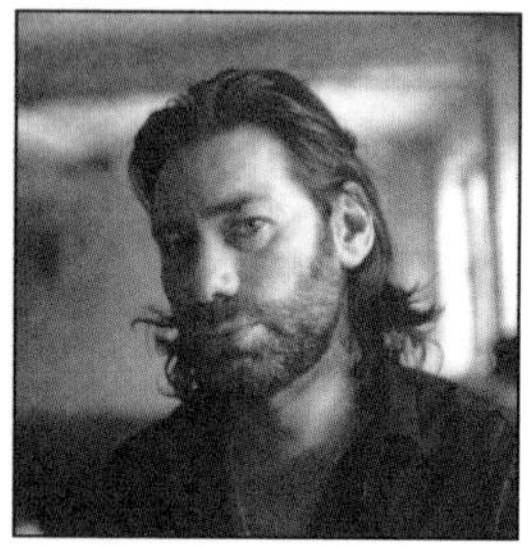

Light Me Up

by Mat Collishaw

Mat Collishaw is an artist.

When I asked Mat Collishaw to do me an original piece for the book, he gave me this wonderful thing. His new way of sparking up his fags. It looks like an antidote to the Liam and Patsy Vanity Fair cover to me. Finally.

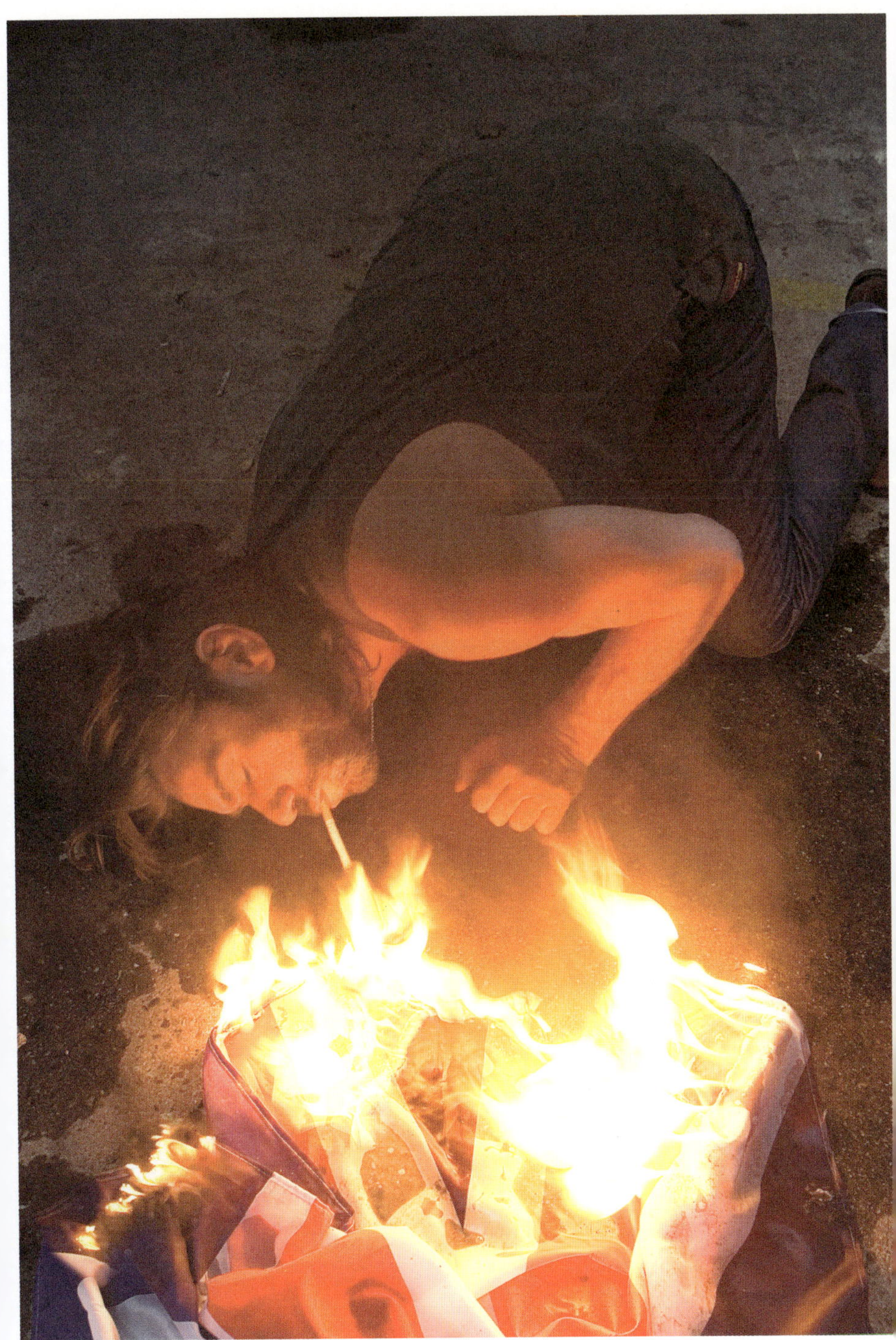

Light Me Up, 2010, by Mat Collishaw

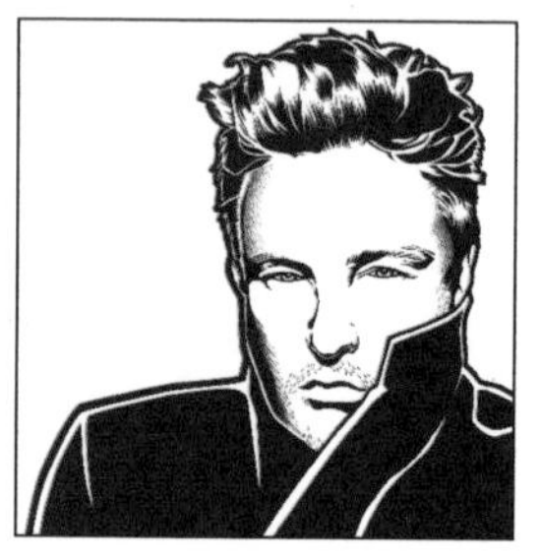

If Only My Cock Was As Big As My Head

by Rankin

Iconic photographer, publisher and film director Rankin has gained a reputation as one of the world's leading photographers. He lives in London with his wife, Tuuli, and his son, Lyle. When asked to contribute something to the book, he came up with this quite amazingly unfettered contribution.

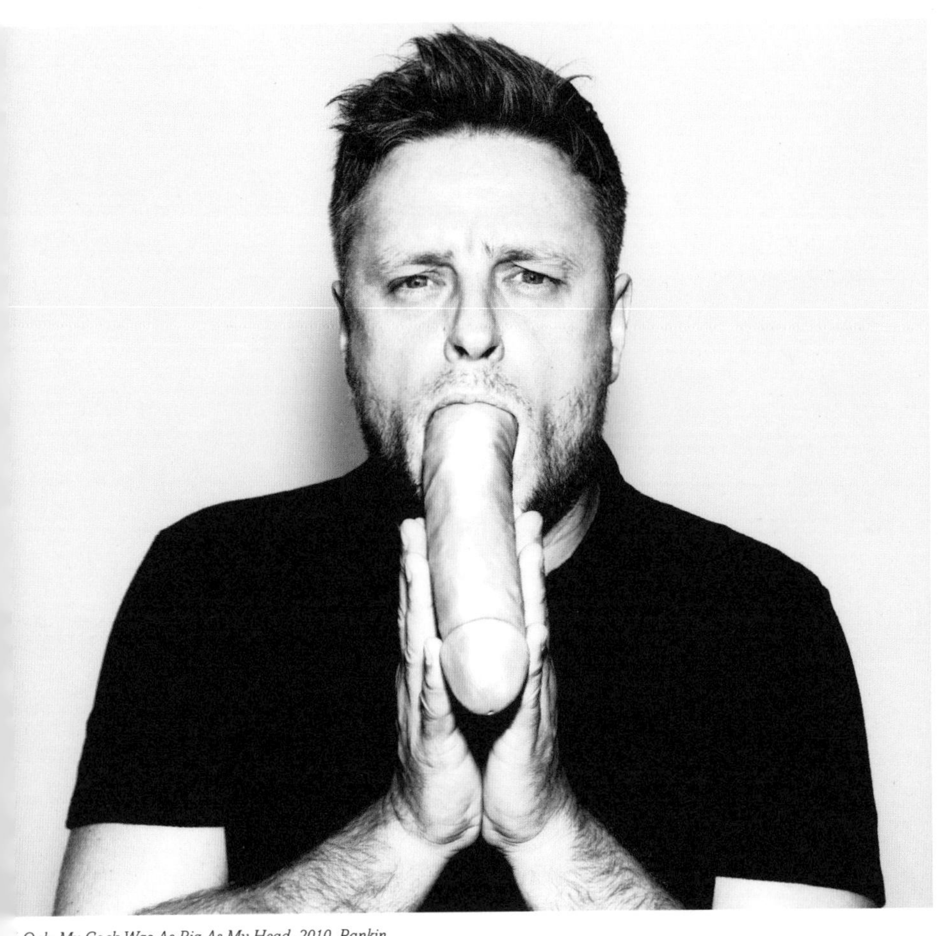

Only My Cock Was As Big As My Head, 2010, Rankin

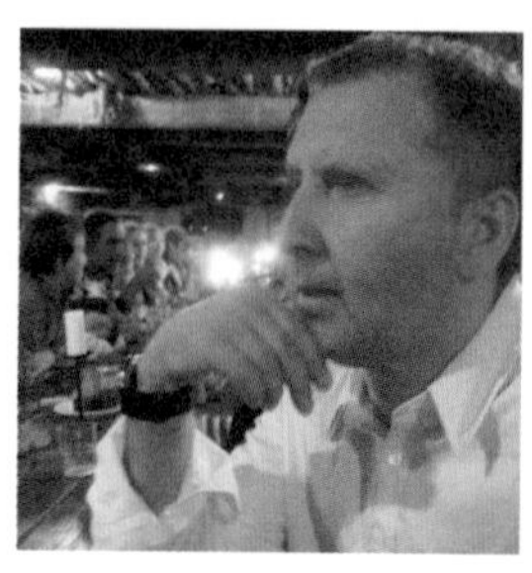

Untitled

by Hugh Allan

Hugh Allan is the director of Other Criteria, a company that he started with Damien Hirst, to commission and sell artists' editions and multiples.

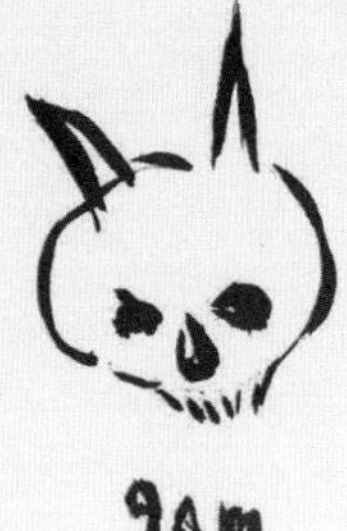

9am

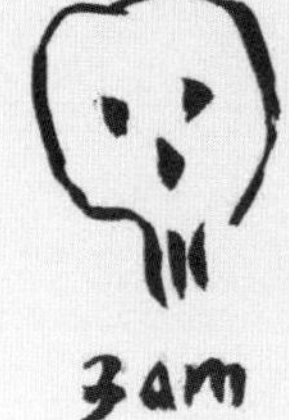

3am

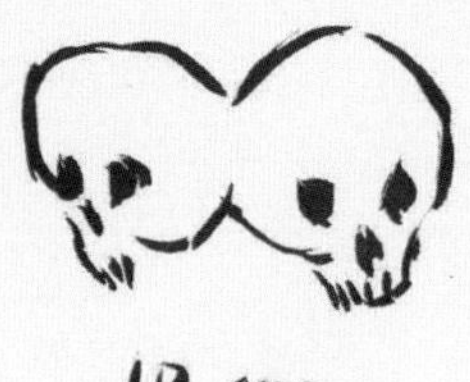

10 am

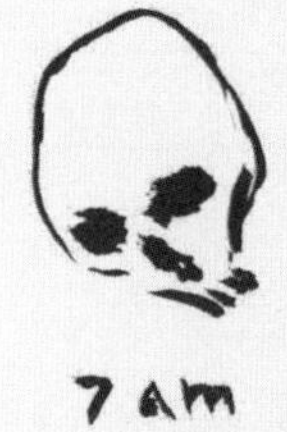

7am

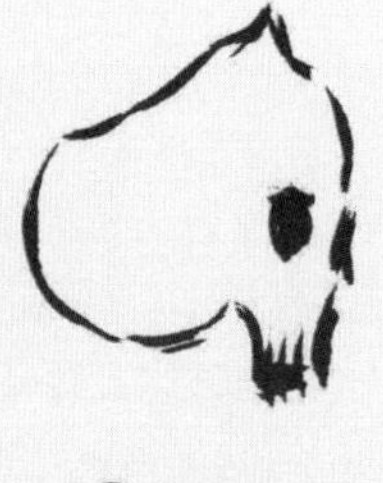

5am

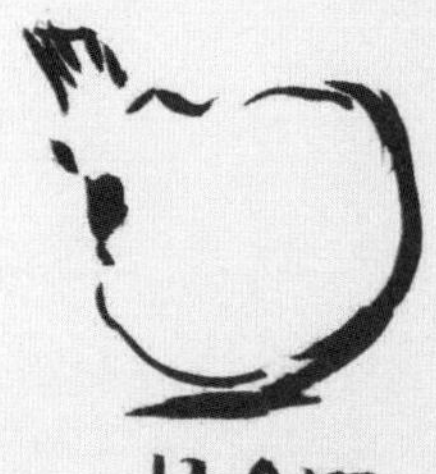

12 am

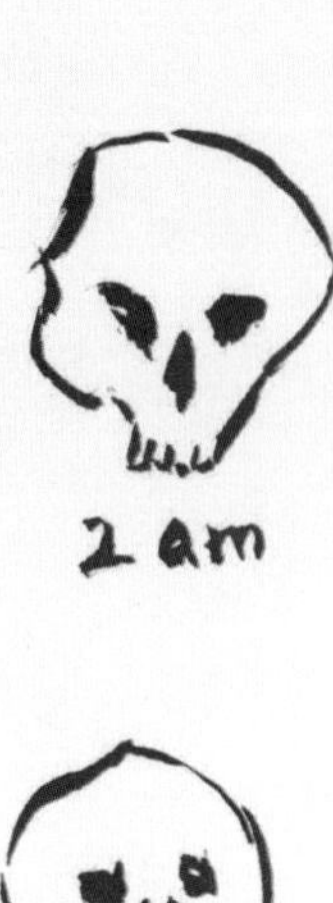

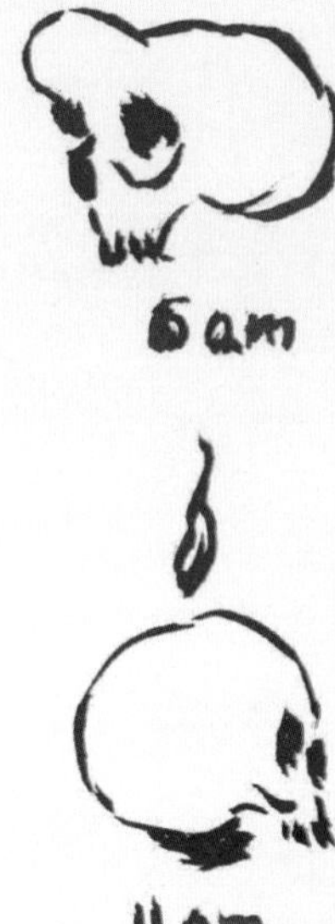

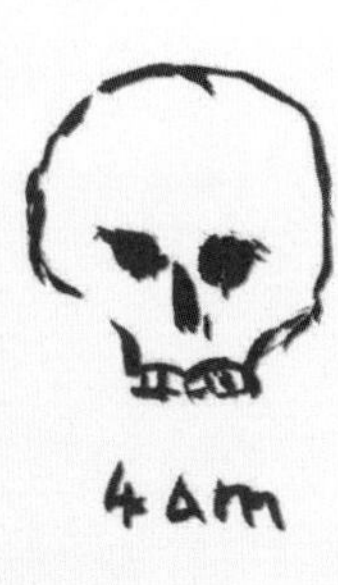

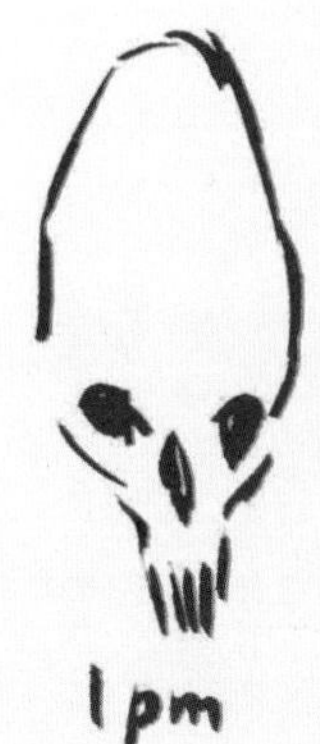

Untitled, Hugh Allan

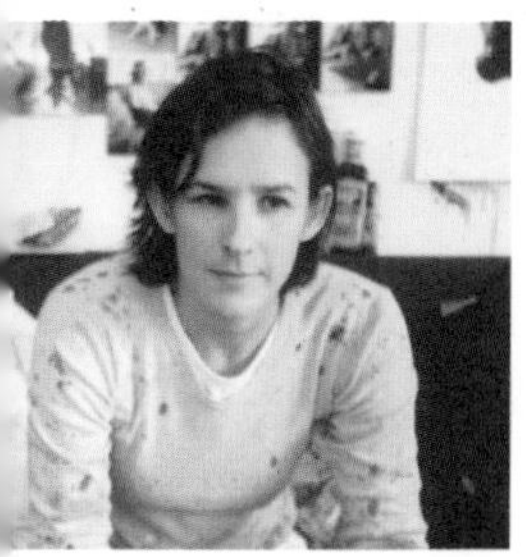

Two Works (Especially for the Book)

By Rachel Howard

Rachel Howard is a painter.

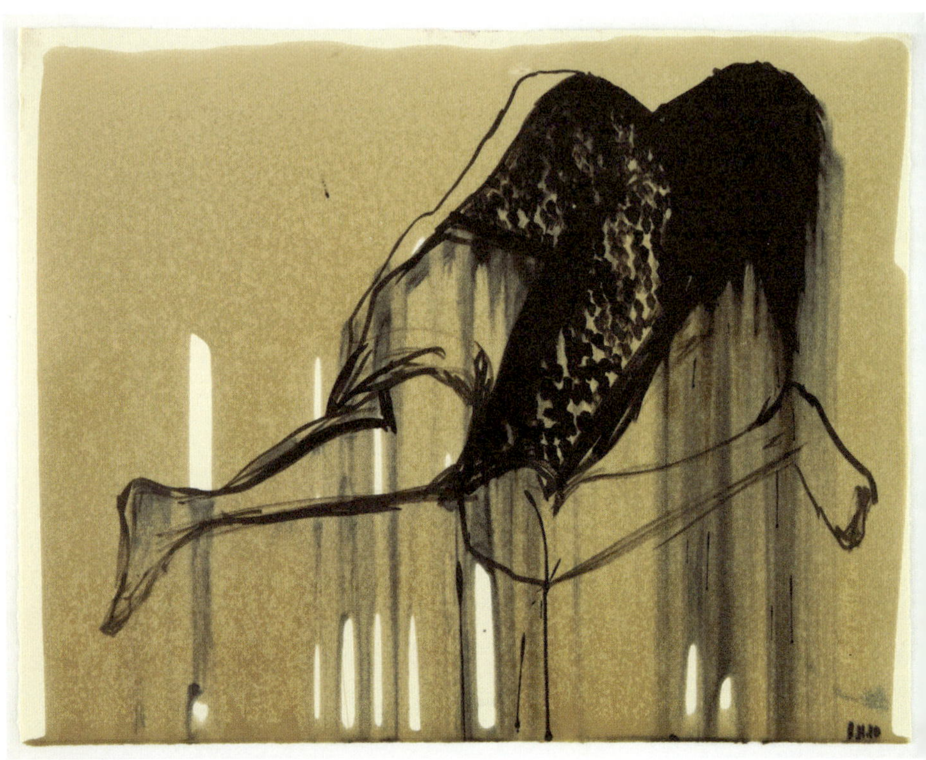

Big Night Out 2010 Oil and Varnish On Paper. Rachel Howard

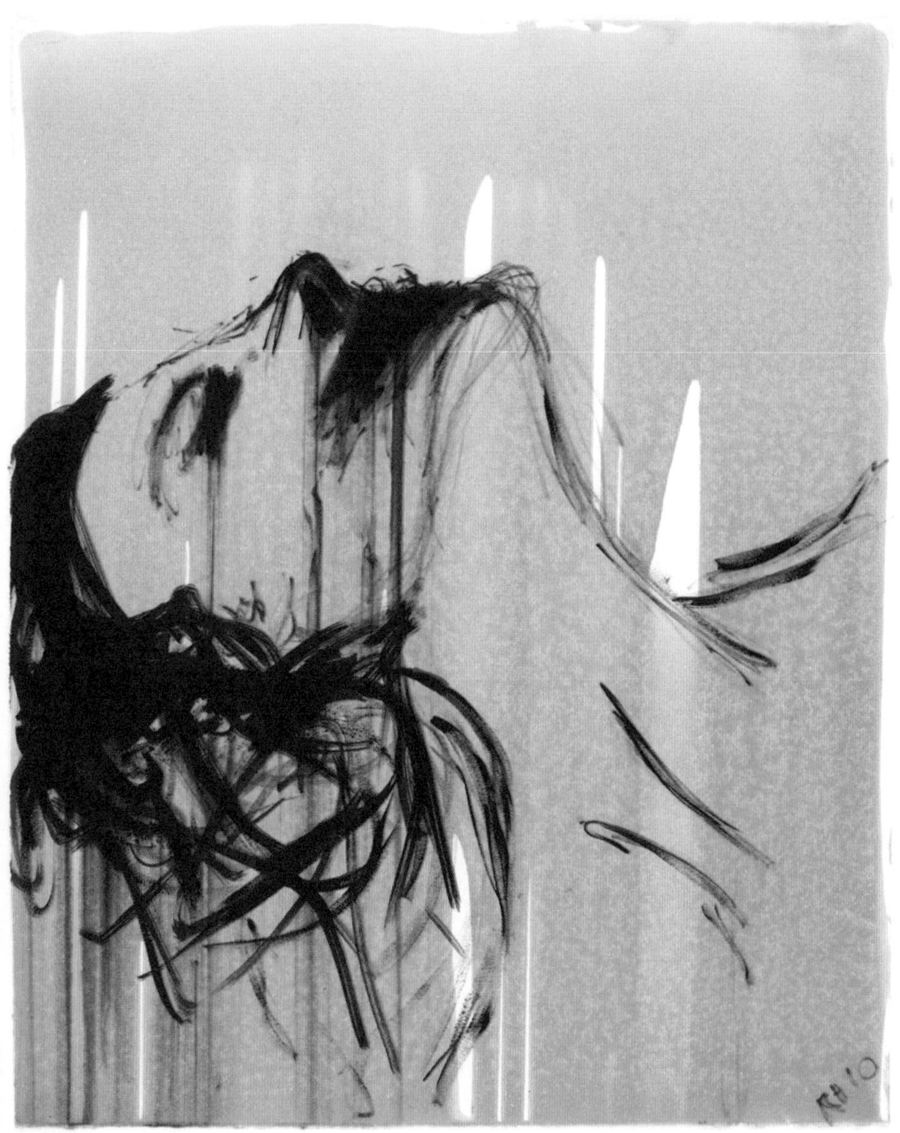

Friend 2010 Oil and Varnish On Paper. Rachel Howard

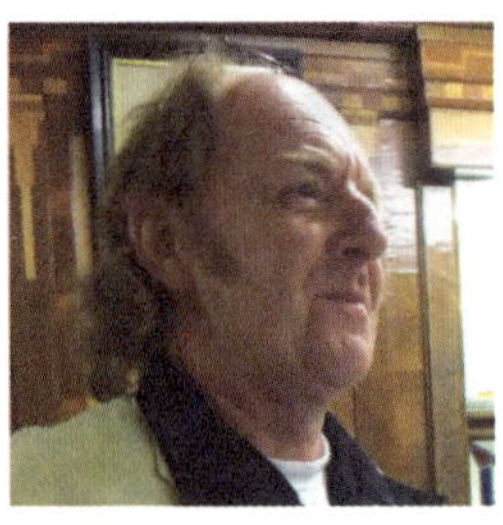

Red Hot

by Richard Wilson

Richard Wilson is a Turner-Prize nominated artist who lives in London. He's best known for his audacious site-specific installations, not least the iconic room full of sump oil, 20:50, now on permanent display at the Saatchi Gallery. His fascination with architectural and perceived space has resulted in a 30-year body of work where our accepted comprehension of space is questioned and subverted. "These interventions are characterised by concerns with size and structural daring and the fact that I'm not cheap but I'm slow," says Richard.

HE RECENTLY CREATED A steel cube sculpture for the Matthew Bown Gallery in Berlin, which was heated to such an extreme temperature, that it teetered on the edge of becoming a liquid.

At the centre of the gallery space positioned on a specially designed plinth made from high refractive brick, stands an almost molten hot eight inch cube of steel. Surrounding this cube is a rippling heat haze, filling the space with an almost unbearable heat. On the wall is fastened a digital display that reads the cubes temperature. The room is bathed in a low light level.

We experience, first through light, then through heat - an object; neither solid nor liquid, balanced at the edges of its own being

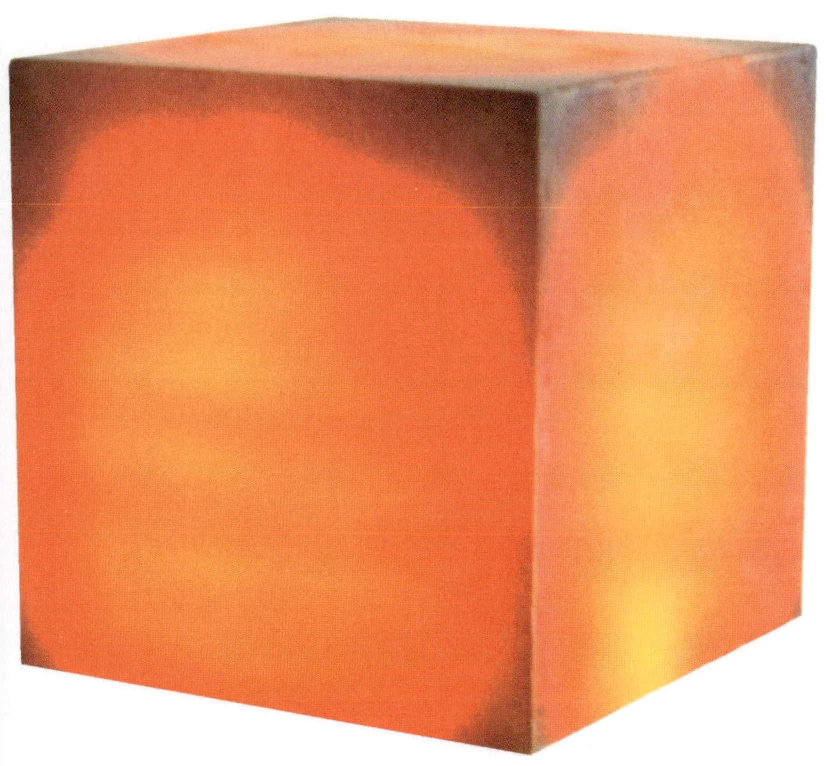

Red Hot, 2010. Richard Wilson

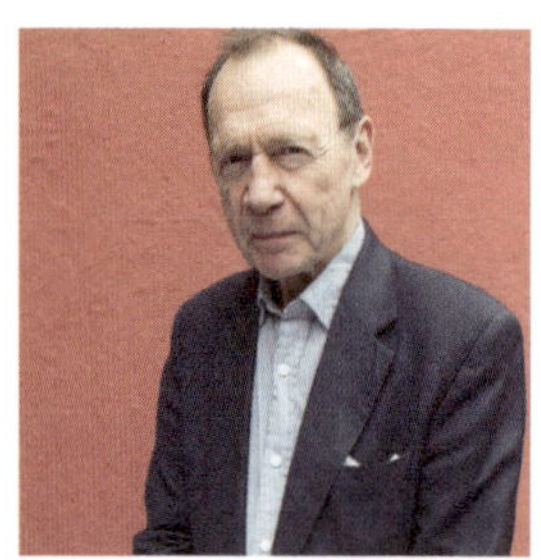

The Secret History of Modern Art

by Anthony Haden-Guest

Anthony Haden-Guest is a writer, reporter and cartoonist. He lives in London and New York.

CHAPTER/ I: THE PLOT is Hatched.

Our story begins with Gustave Courbet
Who was a Communard by the way
He knew just which painterly button to push
A slap in the face with a fat girl's bush
And it's goodbye, Boldini, Bougereau,
Winterhalter, James Tissot
The Last of the Masters have had their day
And the War Against Beauty was underway

It's a muddy road to Paul Cezanne
If you like awkward, Paul's your man
Inedible apples, unbeddable nudes
Nature in one of her nastier moods
If a carpenter made a table like that
He'd be out of a job in ten seconds flat
Your school friend, Zola, thought you'd gone mad*
But you made it okay to paint real bad
And that was your part in the anti-art plan

So let's catch up with Vincent Van Gogh's
Provencal idyll with Paul Gauguin
Then that field of corn, those terrible crows
In the sullen glare of a clouded sun
Take that yellow chair and lend me an ear
Madness has entered the picture here
And Modernism has truly begun

George Seurat's stuff looks placid at first
But he's painting a world just about to burst
Ahead lie Bridget Riley and Op
And the spots epidemic of Damien Hirst
To say nothing of Stephen Sondheim's slop
They applaud Seurat as a Pointilliste
Did you know he was also an anarchist
Like his bomb-maker pal, Felix Feneon?
Top hats in the park, high time they were gone!
Those particle clusters were only the start
Of a negative force-field too strong to resist
That would tear apart beauty and art

Pablo Picasso, a giant among men,
Said he painted like Raphael when he was ten
Came La Vie en Rose, then his whole world blued
Did someone say kitsch? That's really quite rude!
Witchdoctors to the rescue! Picasso plunged on
To *Les Demoiselles d'Avignon*
Catch a whiff of the girls' Barcelona pong!
He shut it away. Sadly, not for long
Then he and Braque sliced and diced and glued
Some called it "Cubism" which sounded crude**
So as -isms go it was quite a good fit
But can you explain it? Wish somebody would!

Matisse couldn't make heads or tails of it***
Luxe, calme et volupte
That was Henri's way and Henri would say
That a businessman after a long hard day
Should treat his work like an easy chair
Picasso ripped through styles like a man possessed
And as if in some eerie way he guessed
The needs, and the greed, the hungers he'd feed
Of collectors to come, a predator breed
It was Picasso wheeled out the shopping cart
And created the Supermarket of Art

Picasso, Modernism's first deity,

Kissed the girls and made them cry

As is the right of celebrity

But when Gary Cooper and Chaplin dropped by

His English embarrassed him, and that's

Why he pulled silly faces and wore silly hats

It was David Douglas Duncan's pix

In *Life* that cured his celebrity fix****

When Picasso grew old, this giant amongst men,

Didn't paint like Raphael but a child of ten

Raymond and Jacques really painted quite well

Better by miles than their brother Marcel

But it's Marcel who's the toast of the crème de la crème.

While Raymond and Jacques have dropped out of the frame

They're goner than gone, buster than bust

While Picasso is eating Duchamp's dust

Do you want to know the reason for this?

Forget Francis Naumann's analysis

Those painful puns, LHOOQ,

Make people feel cool, like nobody's fool

He saw the importance of taking the piss!

Cocteau said the trick to being a star

Is knowing just how far to go too far

Now the Picassoid garden has long gone to seed

While Duchamp Inc. makes much of product we need

So anyone can be a belle at the art world ball

With one half-smart idea, a huge helping of gall

And no visible art-making talent at all

(To be continued with Chapter II, The Plot Sickens)

*   Clear from reading Zola's The Masterpiece
**   Louis Vauxcelles, who came up with the phrase "Les Fauves" in 1905 and   used the word "cubism"
about a Braque in 1908. He meant it kindly in neither case.
***   As he said to Michel Georges-Michel, quoted in From Renoir to Picasso.
****   Told to me by John Richardson

Work No. 1029 3 Stills: 1 Down, 1 Up and 1 in the Middle

by Martin Creed

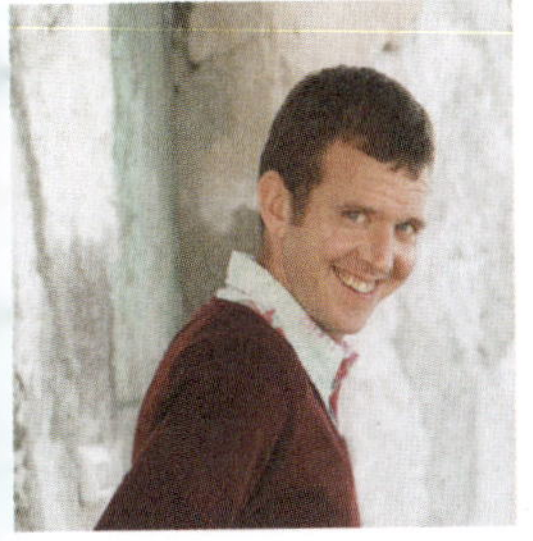

Martin Creed is an artist who lives in London and Alicudi.

When Martin was asked to provide something for the book, he gave this three stage - shall we say - salute.

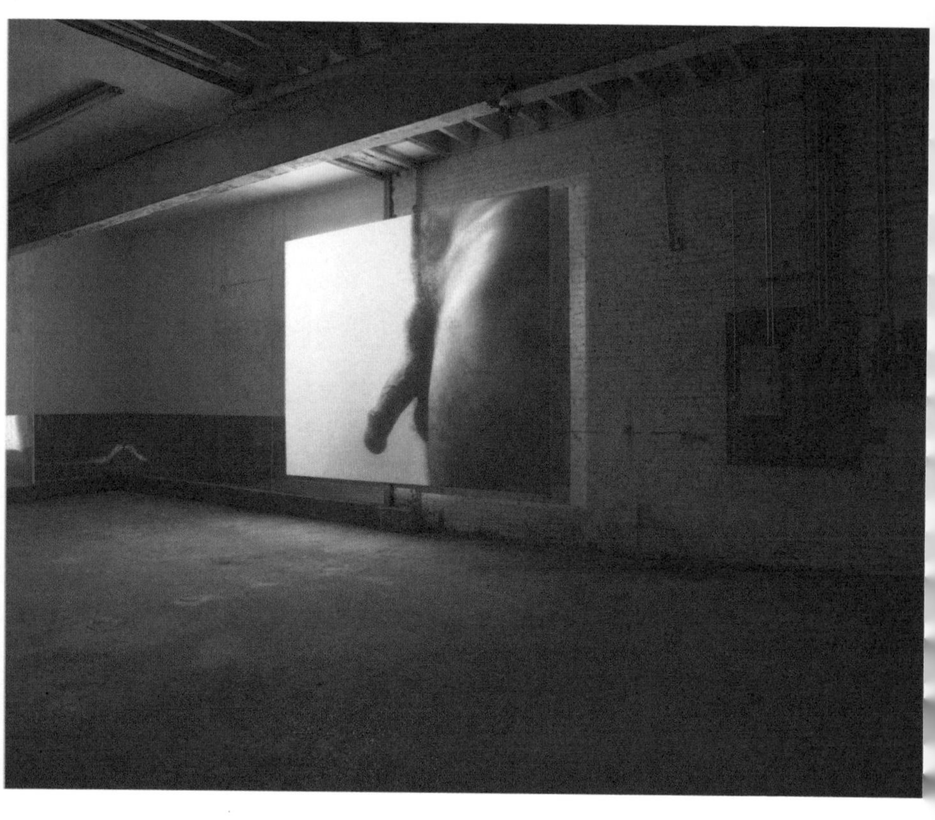

Martin Creed Work No. 1029 Detail A - 35mm film; b/w, silent Courtesy the Artist and Gavin Brown's Enterprise, New York

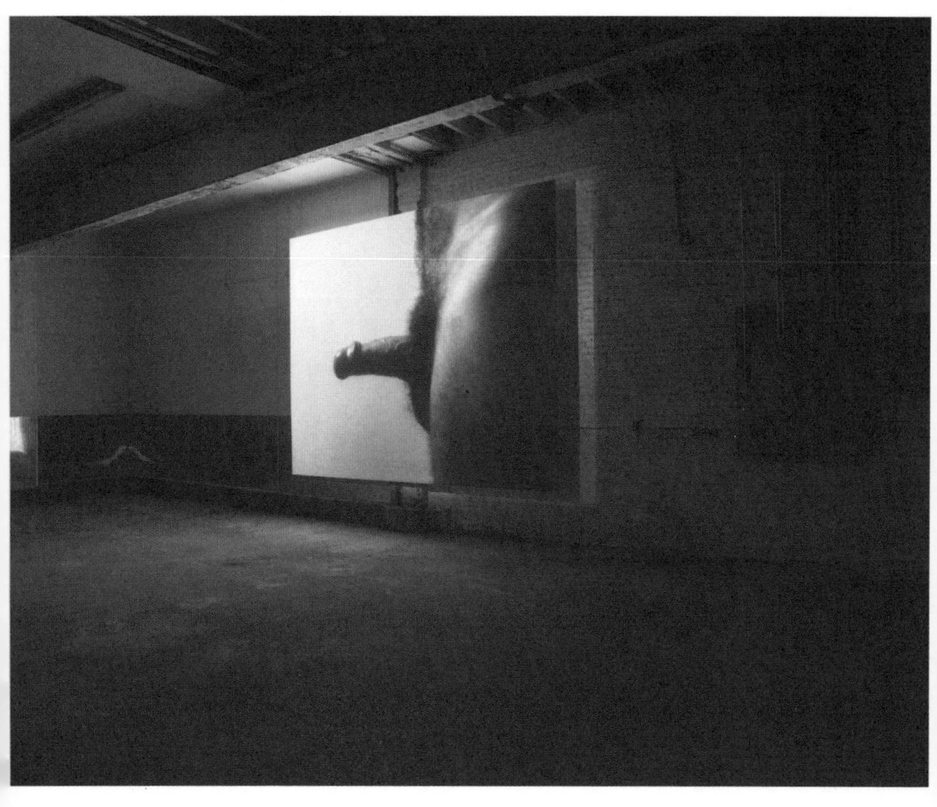

Martin Creed Work No. 1029 Detail B - 35mm film; b/w, silent Courtesy the Artist and Gavin Brown's Enterprise, New York

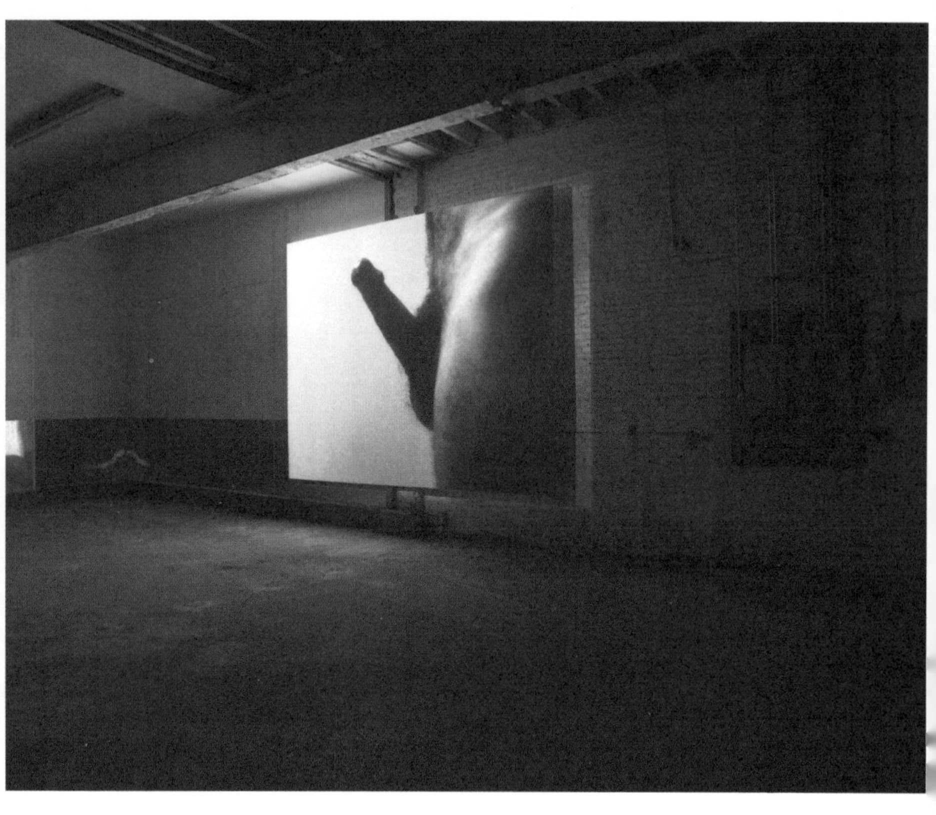

Martin Creed Work No. 1029 Detail C - 35mm film; b/w, silent Courtesy the Artist and Gavin Brown's Enterprise, New York

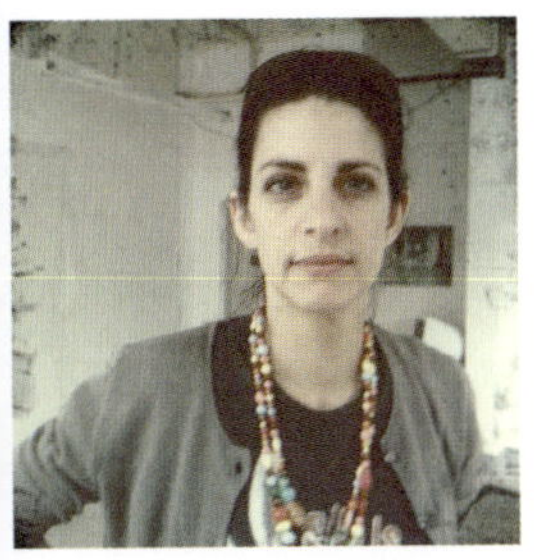

Royal Academy

by Carla Borel

Carla Borel is an Anglo/Gallic photographer, born in Paris, resident in London. Her first job was picking up feathers at the Moulin Rouge. Sticking with the dark-in-the-daytime job location theme, she was then a croupier, and after that a bartender at the French House, that art world staple of watering-holes in Soho. She moonlights as a gallerina for the Timothy Taylor Gallery and likes taking pictures of the fast and louche. Swedish crime novels and smoking roll ups also get a look-in. [Let's keep this representative of understated glamour in London (Ed.)]

ON THE NEXT PAGE is one of my all-time favourite pictures taken of the art world. Curator and art dealer James Birch, artist Tim Noble and book dealer Aaron Budnik at the first GSK opening at the Royal Academy, 2008. Hungover, tired, bored, and about to be thrown out for smoking.

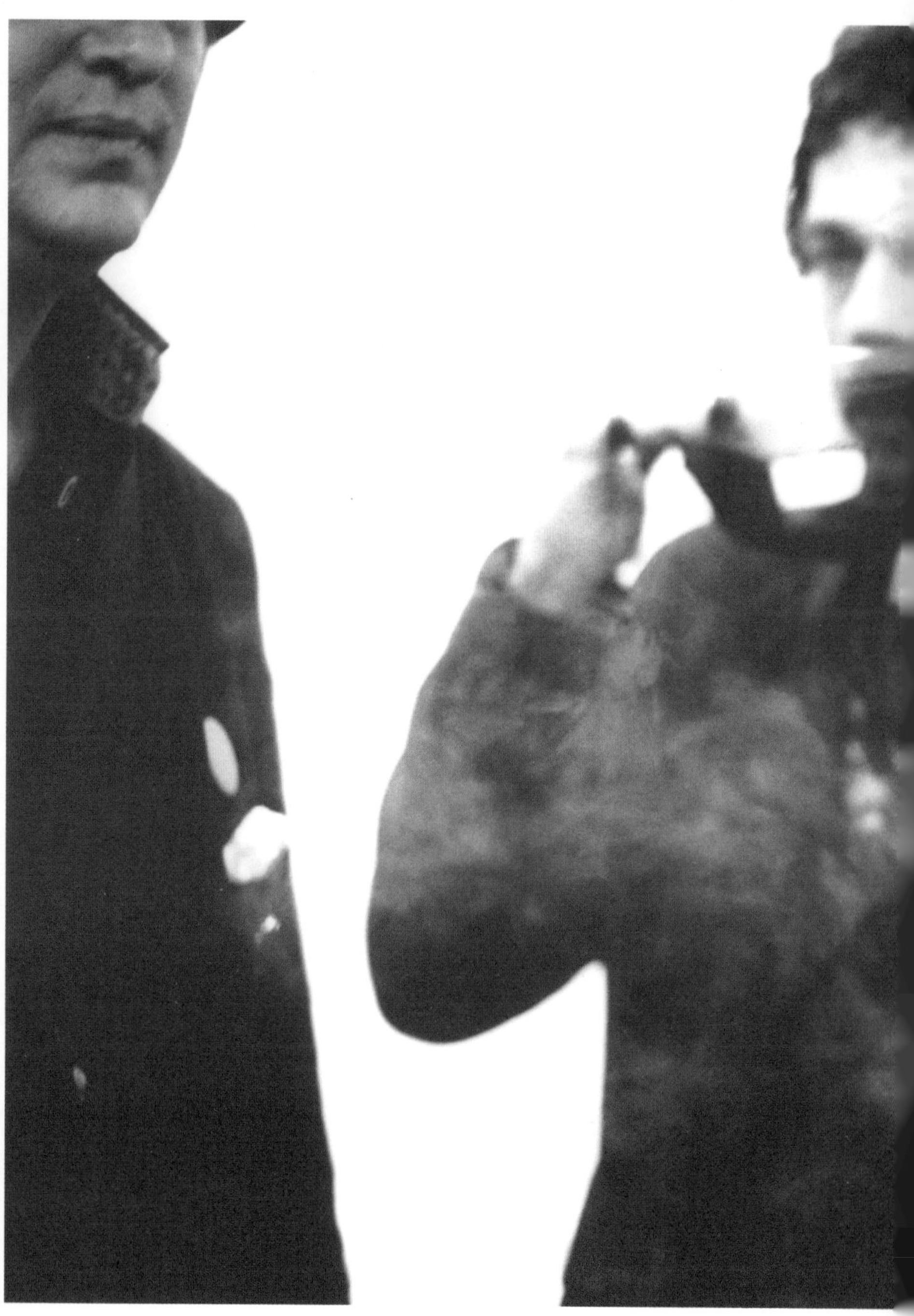

Royal Academy, Carla Borel

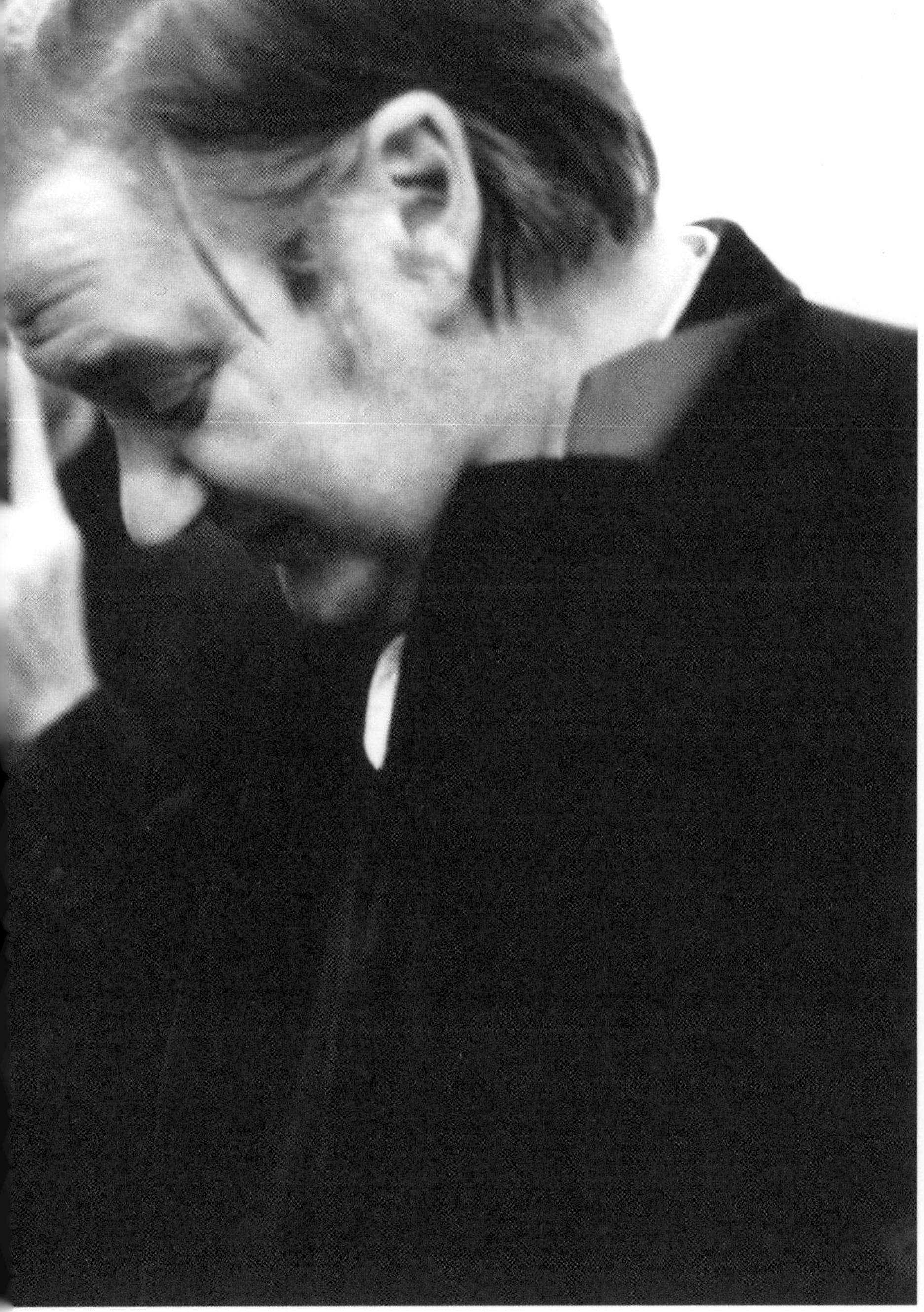

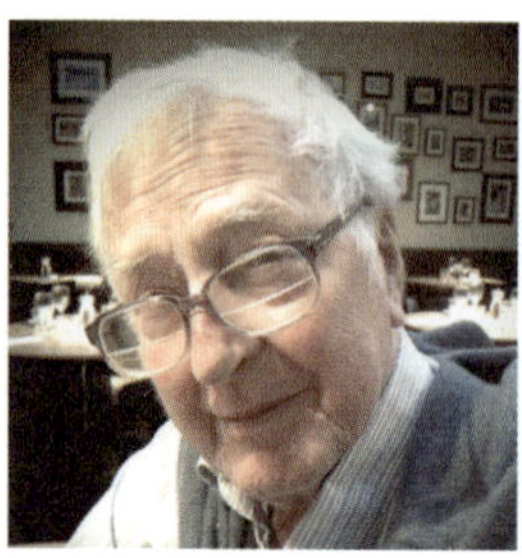

Still-Life

by Clive Cullerne Bown

Clive Cullerne Bown is a retired civil servant and poet. He
lived with a Kovalevskaya painting for three years – this is
his homage to it.

The Russian artist Kovalevskaya loved red:
Sumptuous reds of merchants' cloaks
In the bazaars of Samarkand, crimson
Of girls' lips and cheeks on feast days,
Blush of bare arms shadowed rose and green
Reaching among the spicy vines at the tomato harvest.

One day, eighty or so years ago
In some house in Uzbekistan
She came across an array of poppies in a jug
And watched one or two petals fall
To settle in scarlet splashes upon a white tablecloth.

In her painting, the silky corollas,
Enclosing deep purple capsules in their black depths,
Incline as it were tenderly
Over a rabble of hairy stalks and fronds,
Dominating their surroundings by force of beauty
As a beautiful person may dominate a crowded room.

From a wild looking garden beyond a verandah
Green tones tinge the afternoon light.

That some little throng of friends or kin
Have recently gone out of the room is suggested
By chairs pushed back anyhow from the table.
A half open door and a litter
Of cups, mugs and a golden porcelain beaker
Left among the fallen petals on the tablecloth.

This homely interior seems to summon echoes
Of their talk, of tones intimate, soft and pliable,
Of laughter, hope and regret.
I should have liked to be of that company
In the friendly house, sitting around
The tender bowed heads of the poppies.

Was this house hers or her lover's?
One dewy morning did they gather
These flowers of the field together
Their hands sometimes colliding in the wet grass?

I wander the house of my own life
Opening or closing doors at random
Or according to a logic hidden from me,
Remembering sweet imperatives of old,
Regretting not so much acts as omissions,
The word unspoken, the hand not grasped.

Truncated,dying, stuck in a jug, nevertheless
These scarlet blossoms like living flames
Blaze against the white nap of the tablecloth.
How ardent still! Passionate as an embrace.
I suppose they might have kept their freshness
A day or two longer, frail emblems of desire
Painted some eighty summers ago
By the artist Zinaida Kovalevskaya
Working not in the great cities but
In her Arcadia somewhere in Asia Minor.

(2003 – 2010)

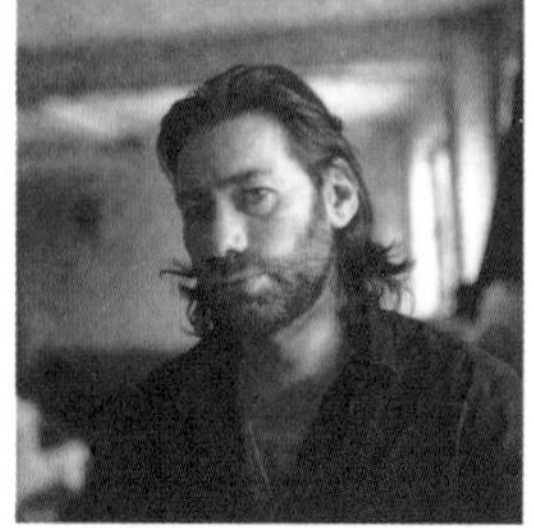

© Alex Hoedt

Dogsknob

by Mat Collishaw

Mat Collishaw is an artist who is represented by the Haunch of Venison Gallery.

[An image of a man who has had his crown jewels removed by a dog bite. God alive. (Ed.)]

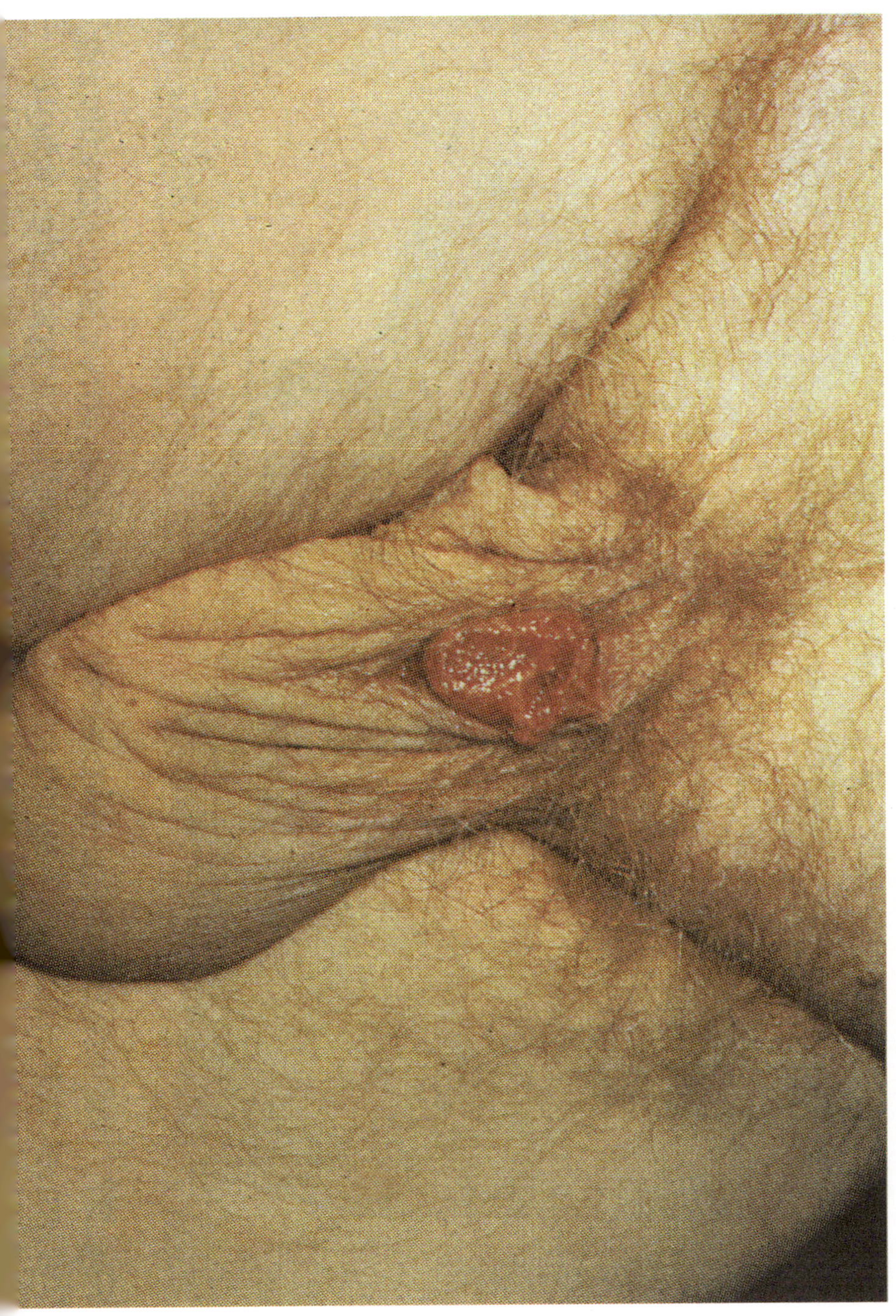

Dogsknob, 2010, by Mat Collishaw

Talking to Artists: Were Cartoons the First Conceptual Art? No That Was the Pyramids, Dummy

by Anthony Haden-Guest

Anthony Haden-Guest was born in Paris, grew up in London and now lives in London and New York. He won a New York Emmy for writing and narrating a programme about the coming of Eurotrash to Manhattan. Amongst his books are True Colours: The Real Life of the Art World (Grove Atlantic); The Last Party: Studio 54, Disco and the Culture of the Night (Morrow) and The Chronicles of Now, a book of cartoons (Allworth).

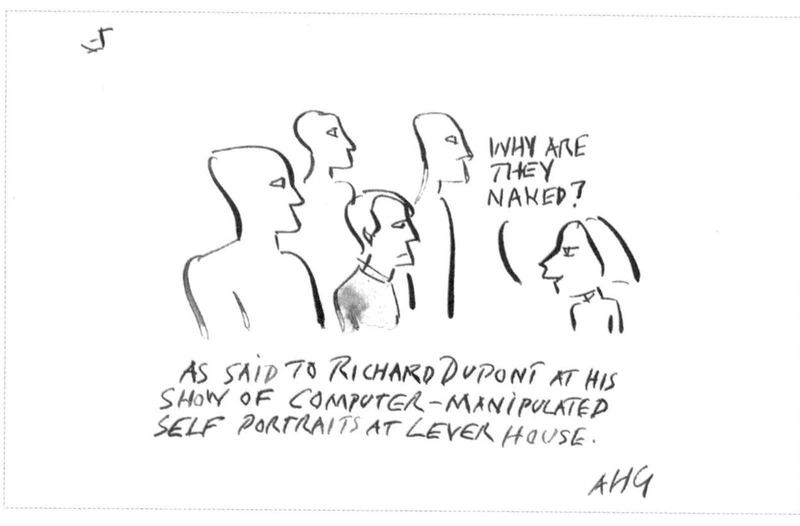

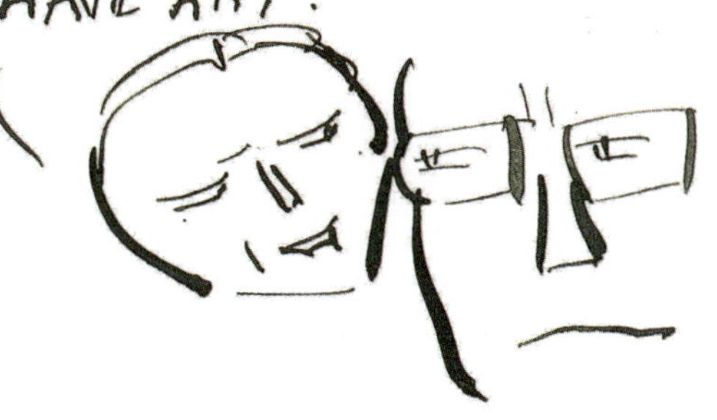

I LOVE YOUR EARLY WORK, DO YOU STILL HAVE ANY?
(AS SAID TO DAMIEN HIRST)
AHG

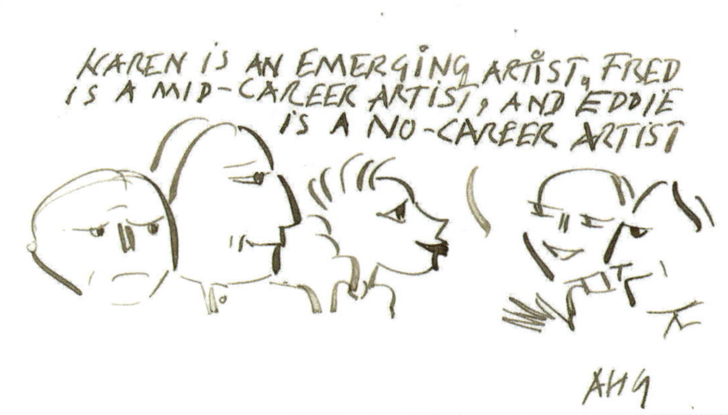

KAREN IS AN EMERGING ARTIST, FRED IS A MID-CAREER ARTIST, AND EDDIE IS A NO-CAREER ARTIST
AHG

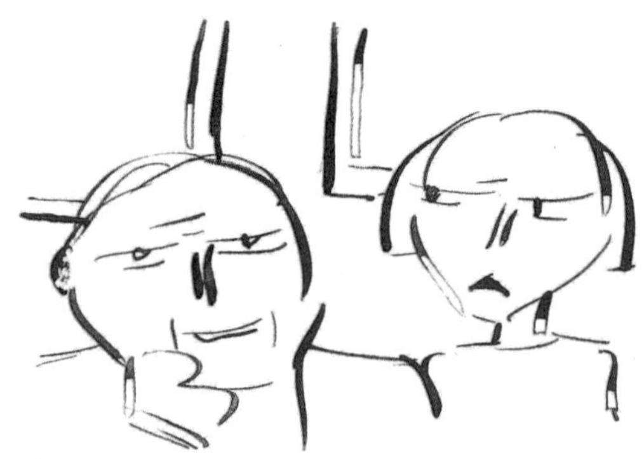

I HAVE THIS FEELING I'VE SEEN YOUR WORK BEFORE. EITHER THAT OR SOMETHING TREMENDOUSLY SIMILAR.
AHG

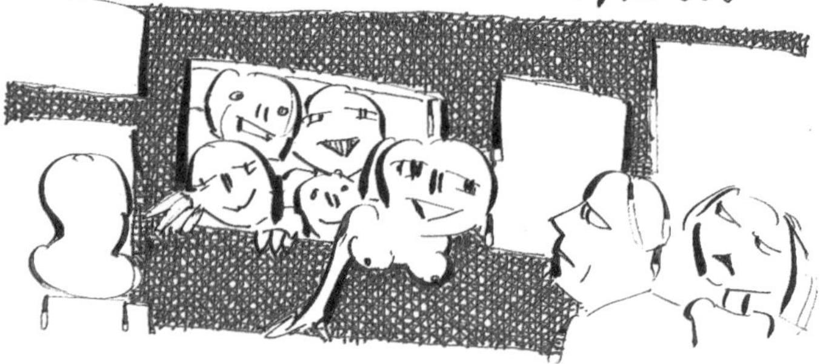

THE GREGSONS WERE TRYING TO BUILD A DECENT CONTEMPORARY COLLECTION. BUT OUTSIDER ARTISTS KEPT BREAKING IN ...
AHG

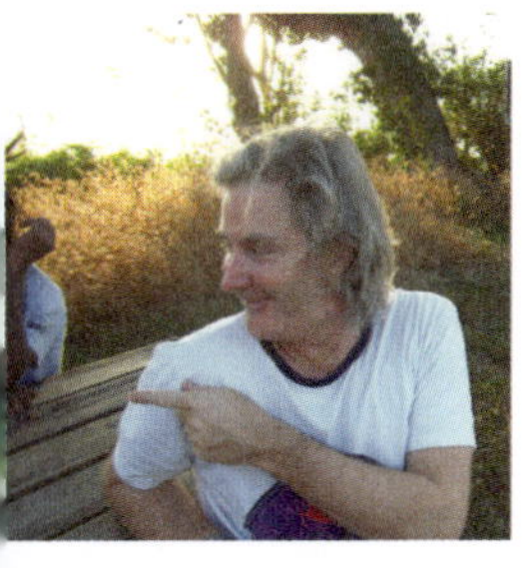

'Twas the Night Before Lehmans

by Guy Kennaway

Guy Kennaway is a writer whose pastiche poem came from a thought he had while reading Dr. Seuss' The Cat In The Hat to his children, when he noticed the striking similarities between the characters of The Cat and the youthful Damien Hirst: "I can hold you two books/ I can hold up the fish/ And a little toy ship/ And some milk in a dish…He should not be here!/ He should not be about/When your mother is out…" etc. Early one morning after a long, long night celebrating Hirst's 2009 auction at Sotheby's, which made either £200 or £50 million depending on who you spoke to, Kennaway realised it wasn't only The Cat who the great artist reminded him of.

'Twas the night before Lehmans, when all through the house
Not a creature was stirring, not even a mouse.
The stockings were hung at Sotheby's with care,
In hopes that old Hirsty soon would be there.

The moon on the roof of the new-opened show
Gave the lustre of mid-day to objects below.
When, what to my wondering eyes should appear,
But a miniature sleigh, and eight tiny reindeer.

With a little bold driver, so lively and tan,
I knew in a moment it must be the man.
More rapid than eagles his installers they came,
And he whistled, and shouted, and called them by name!

As dry leaves that before the wild hurricane fly,
When they meet with an obstacle, mount to the sky.
So up to the auction house the fabricators flew,
With the sleigh full of art, and Damien too.

He was dressed all in fur, from his head to his foot,
And his clothes were all tarnished with ashes and soot.
A bundle of art he had flung on his back,
And he looked like a peddler, just opening his pack.

His eyes-how they twinkled! his dimples how merry!
His cheeks were like roses, his nose like a cherry!
His droll little mouth was drawn up like a bow,
And the stubble on his chin was as white as the snow.

The stump of a fag he held tight in his teeth,
And the smoke it encircled his head like a wreath.
He had a broad face and a little round belly,
That shook when he laughed, like a bowlful of jelly!

He was chubby and plump, a right jolly old elf,
And I laughed when I saw him, in spite of myself!
A wink of his eye and a twist of his head,
Soon gave me to know we had plenty to dread.

He spoke not a word, but went straight to his work,
And filled all the stockings, then turned with a jerk.
And laying his finger aside of his nose,
And giving a nod, down Bond Street he rose!

And I heard him exclaim, 'ere he drove out of sight,
"Happy Credit Crunch to all, and to all a good-night!"

CHAPTER 5:
INNER WORKINGS

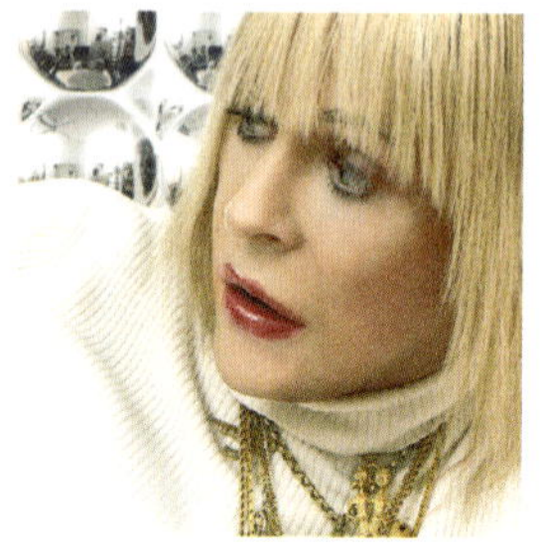

© *PEROU*

Tagged for Life, Or How I Learned to Leave England and Love the Tate Without Really Trying…

by Genesis Breyer P-Orridge

Genesis Breyer P-Orridge was born in Manchester in 1950. A friend of Derek Jarman, William S Burroughs and Dr Timothy Leary, he co-founded COUM Transmissions, and the bands Throbbing Gristle and Psychic TV. In 2003, Genesis and his wife Lady Jaye became two halves of one artist Breyer P-Orridge and dedicated all their projects to Pandrogeny, the creation of a hermaphroditic Third Being. Lady Jaye dropped her body in 2007 but Breyer P-Orridge continue to create in all media. The Tate Britain acquired their life's archives in 2009. P-Orridge and COUM's now infamous 1976 Prostitution show at the ICA caused intense debate in Parliament and the British press, and led P-Orridge and his collaborators to be vilified as "wreckers of civilisation". He later moved to New York.

IN 1991 I WAS VISITING Samye Ling Tibetan Monastery in Scotland, and was recounting to Lama Yeshe my ever increasing disenchantment with British culture in general and the art 'world' in particular. "Go to Kathmandu, Genesis," he said to me and then turned back to watching children's cartoons on a giant old television set. I decided to do exactly what he proposed and from then on my hedonistic search for enlightenment turned into a most intensely vivid cartoon.

But to backtrack, in early 1976 the 'Establishment', as we shall call them, had prosecuted me for sending "indecent mail" through the postal system. At that time I was deeply active in the UK Fluxus movement, and this had led to my making 'Mail Art'. I would spend hours every day collaging, typing, and rubber-stamping hand-made correspondence to a network of similarly engaged artists all over the world. As years went by one of my recurring themes was taking souvenir tourist postcards of Queen Elizabeth II and meticulously collaging 'soft-core' porn from various sources to create pretty seamless new tableaux. After a very unfriendly visit and interview from Royal Mail detectives whilst I was wearing a rather obviously semen-soiled Victorian nightie, I eventually found myself in Highbury Magistrates Court being sentenced to a year in prison, and receiving the maximum fine possible per offending postcard. This, despite having Richard Cork (art critic then of the Times), William S. Burroughs (you know!), Bridget Riley (Op Artist extraordinaire!), Sir Norman Reid (then Director of the Tate Britain), Gerald Forty (British Council) and a veritable host of artists behind me.

An appeal to the court gave me a chance to avoid prison if I could pay the fines in thirty days! Fortunately a combination of all these amazing people AND the timely intervention of artist John Armleder, who published an Ecart Gallery book of documentation of the trial called G.P.O. versus G. P-O, enough funds were raised.

As we left the court two detectives took me aside and pulled several more Queen cards from a brown envelope. "We can put you inside with these whenever we want to Genesis", they happily chirped. And they could. It transpired that concealing the cards in envelopes so they were not "displayed" (which counts as 'publication') would have exempted me from these charges and endowed me artistic immunity! By being naked and on display through the lack of appropriate dress in the form of a brown envelope - with all its associations (in those days) with illicit material and perverted pleasure - we had been caught with our pants down!

(n.b. At this juncture it should be pointed out to readers in many countries, in particular in the U.S.A., that England does NOT have a "Bill of Rights". Over and over when we explain this in America, people are speechless. Somehow the (Dis)United Kingdom has a world-wide reputation as the "Home of Democracy"! Yes…go figure? With no Bill of Rights the artist is incredibly vulnerable.)

I was naively unaware that once you have been tagged by British monoliths of authority, you are tagged for life!

As the seventies progressed in the United Kingdom, an ever-accelerating dissatisfaction was growing. A hedonistic virus of discontent. COUM Transmissions mutated further and further away from happenings-based improvised street actions/performances into darker and more volatile investigations.

As Britain became more austere, working itself up to a frenzy of self-loathing and hypocrisy, so my actions within COUM became more ferocious. I was brutal to my flesh, in a venomous rage at all the symptoms of deluded social stability surrounding me. I had reached a point in my art actions where 'slash and burn' was literally and metaphorically just not 'doing it' for me anymore. I had no more inhibitions to smash. I had masturbated on a satin cushion while dressed as an English schoolgirl at the R.C.A., drunk bottles of whisky, pints of milk, syringes of blood and puked, licking up the vomit afterwards. I had used roses (yes with thorns) more syringes, long rusty nails, dildos, chains and clips and mortified my flesh and bones in every way possible using every orifice, but it was not working or waking anymore. Creating my SELF as sacrifice in a vain hope that my distress would shame humanity into nurturing and preserving itself in a Messianic discharge, had only one finale - my death in an action. Pointless!

Ted Little, then Director of the I.C.A. was curating amazing, prophetic exhibitions and events. In COUM's PROSTITUTION retrospective, various vitrines contained left over props from our more intense, sexually explicit era of performances – as example, a walking stick with a spiral of used tampons that were meant to represent DNA. I had created four-foot boxes, in a somewhat Fluxus moment, called Tampax Romana. They were silly, funny and destined to attempt the "Wrecking of Civilization". Little did I know these "innocent" jokes were to become the fuse that lit a thermobaric media conflagration! Law Lords were sent by Buckingham Palace to request we close the exhibition as it was taking place near the Queen in a building she owned. I told them if they tried to close us down we would occupy the ICA and paint it pink.

I suddenly felt vulnerable that moral outrage would turn to violence, as had happened to Johnny Rotten. A pattern was emerging. It seemed that the Queen and I were clashing over my rights as an artist to have freedom to create whatever I wanted.

Later, in our Thee Temple Ov Psychick Youth organization, we noticed that our mail was being opened and resealed. A T.O.P.Y. sympathizer in the local Brighton Post Office warned us that we were being investigated and that we were considered "Satanists".

T.O.P.Y. had several communal houses in Brighton. We tried to evolve loving, compassionate, alternative ways of living that included magick, Shamanism and creativity in various ratios. It was communally agreed that whatever sexual explorations took place were never taken outside. No jealousy, no sexual preconceptions, no gossip nor recriminations. Surprisingly it worked. Sometimes people would tell the household of their most secret, hedonistic, sexual fantasy or fetish. The rest of the household would then collaborate to try and make the desire actually take place.

As always there were people who threatened us and slandered us. Having been the primary founder of this network of autonomous social experiments, I was the central scapegoat, the media icon that was victimised. So much so that I decided to walk away.

As I drove away from Lama Yeshe I decided that, yes, I would go to Nepal and take my daughters Caresse and Genesse. We collected a crate of good quality baby clothes from T.O.P.Y. individuals and flew to Kathmandu in the late summer of 1991. If the media could see the evil "Satanists" funding an altruistic "soup kitchen" for the most needy in a country where the average yearly wage was $140.

It was such an amazing and cleansing experience that when, eventually we were due to fly back home, we chose to stay until our funds ran out. Our hedonism had led us to altruism...I felt pure. But wait...

The very next day a fax arrived in the hotel office. "Please call home immediately, serious trouble". I walked back to the only international phone and called. "Scotland Yard just raided your house at 6am and took a truck load of your art archives and belongings. Three tons of your things!" Yes, Her Majesty's finest had received an anonymous phone call saying we were...wait for it...SATANISTS!! I spoke to my lawyer who said "Don't come back, I spoke to the police and they cannot guarantee your physical safety if you return." To this day the irony of these accusations coming exactly when we were using own savings to feed and clothe refugees, lepers and beggar children astonishes me. There were more insane inflammatory newspaper headlines. Claims of forensic proof on videos and even a one hour TV documentary called "Dispatches". I was told to go into hiding. This was a time when even one phone call by a jealous lover or angry relative, even a stranger, was considered damning enough to take your children into foster care. Now, thank GOD, all that is totally invalidated to the point of farce. We hope. Back then though, it was no joke and I was not going to risk my children's psychological health for the sake of engaging in a media biased fight with the authorities that controlled every aspect of the law. For those who do not remember the past...Oscar Wilde, Aleister Crowley, Quentin Crisp all failed to get justice in a British court of law, and in the British Court of the Public.

I have NEVER imposed any of my ideas upon anyone but I have however paid a price. Overnight my children had no belongings, no photos of their childhood - they could never see their friends and relatives again, they had no home. I had owned a beautiful house in Brighton, a record label, a car, a nice quality of life. Gone overnight.

I went to see my Buddhist teacher Dzongsar Khyentse Rinpoche and asked, "I am a refugee now too, where shall I go?" To my surprise he replied, "America". It was February 1992…he was right.

(p.s. I was NEVER charged with anything, yet was unable to return for seven years. I am still not officially allowed in…and nothing they took was ever returned despite their actions being an illegal seizure.)

Surviving Frieze

by Laura K Jones

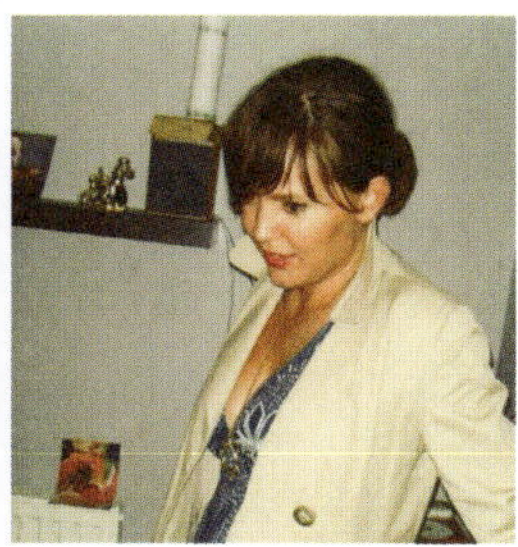

Laura K Jones is a writer. She has lived in New York, New Orleans, Austin, Greece and India and now — with a little bit of resistance and a lot of whining - has decided to settle in London. It hosts the Frieze art fair, don't forget.

WHAT DO YOU DO with yourself when Frieze week is over? Well, you usually just sit there dribbling, rocking gently from side to side and waiting for the after-shocks to subside. Then you'll probably find yourself looking around this grey world, a sigh catching in your throat, as you bemoan the flatness of a life that is reverting back to *just* the *usual,* prosaic rounds of openings, dinners and parties. They're just not going to cut it.

It's true, the mini-world-in-a-tent in Regent's Park, and its myriad ancillary events that make up what is actually Frieze fortnight – (if you count everything leading up to it, and leading down from it too) - can make the real world afterwards appear truly stale, flat and unprofitable. It's a veritable whirlwind when it's happening, and it invokes moments where you have trouble actually keeping yourself upright. Here are some tips for surviving it.

Get some fresh air

The David Thorp-selected Sculpture Park outside the main marquee is a mini world in itself - last year's assortment included Louise Bourgeois's silver entwined The Couple hanging from a tree like a caterpillar in a cocoon, and heaps of other world-class sculptures glinting and nestling in the grass. Many were covered in real life ladybirds last year. A different sort of creative source entirely.

Talk to some dealers

Even if you're not a journalist or a collector, and so don't strictly need to do this, you'll always be astounded by their stories. A member of the public will have inevitably knocked over a priceless sculpture or smeared chocolate on a million dollar painting, the day before.

You could even pretend to be a collector, and find out how much things cost. Little jolts within their answers can always be counted on to wake you up, if and when you're flagging.

Iwan Wirth of the Hauser & Wirth Gallery told me he'd sold the above-mentioned sculpture The Couple to a European collection for $3.5 million, last year. *And* we were supposed to be in a recession.

Make a beeline for Frame

Twenty-nine new galleries under six years old made up the new, lively Frame section last year, the single-artist booths introduced to "freshen up" proceedings. It's more like a nightclub in this section, and people are more willing to have a rambling conversation. In fact there *was* a nightclub in Frame last year, Club Nutz – a fully operational re-creation of the world's smallest comedy club of the same name, located in Milwaukee, Wisconsin. It was kept ship-shape by the glamorously mad-looking Scott Reeder and the NY artist Spencer Sweeney. In a tiny darkened room, you could get a beer for £4, (free if you told a joke), or watch a screening of Gillian Wearing's Dancing in Peckham.

Keep drinking

Might as well. There are so many parties and events to go to, that if you were to stop, you'd get a really unhelpful hangover and have to lie down for days. You may even get the shakes or at worst, a low level panic attack: either way, you'd miss out on the fun, so keep slurping the free champagne. Pay for it via premature ageing and patchy but frequent depressive episodes at a later date.

Go to odd, out of the way events

I can't imagine a more funny, melancholic way to end Frieze fortnight 2009 than going to see Turner Prize winning Martin Creed's first ever ballet, Work no. 1020, commissioned by Frieze Music and performed at the Sadlers Wells Theatre for three nights only.

Rules set by Creed beforehand meant the professional dancers were only allowed to do ballet's five basic positions, moving forward, backwards and sideways, but never diagonally. Only in the art world.

The point of this description is to encourage you to get across town. Get emotional, throw your back into it. Whip back and forth to specially curated shows at the Freud Museum, at the Trolley Gallery, at pop up exhibitions and restaurants across London. Don't forget the Zoo art fair too, that runs concurrently with Frieze. (Venues vary from year to year). Stick to a frenzied schedule. Do *anything* to get to where you want to be. You can rest when you're dead. Or in November.

Laugh along with the doling out of lists and prizes

The Frieze Best Stand Prize awards £10,000 to the best gallery stand each year. There's always a mini party at the successful stand, when this is announced. Keep your ear to the ground. Get thee to the winning booth. You can make new friends if you're feeling lonely. Or maybe that's a nonsense of an idea. Do what comes naturally.

Hans Ulrich Obrist, the über-curator based at the Serpentine Gallery, was named head of Art Review's Power 100 list on the first full day of Frieze 09. When the Art Newspaper asked him how he felt about this, he gave them this short and, er, punchy reply. "When I hear about lists, I always think about Oulipo and Raymond Queneau and Georges Perec. Oulipo is a literary group which functions like a permanent research laboratory for innovation and the invention of new rules of the game to produce literature which played with arithmetical ideas. Francois Le Lionnais, an Oulipo protagonist, emphasises the importance of the term potentiality, which he prefers to experimental, potentiality meaning the attempt to find something which has not yet been done and which could be realised."

It was worth printing this out verbatim, because you see, lists and prizes are funny and make people ramble on incessantly. You'll need these little lifts as the late nights take their toll.

Eat

At Mark Hix's restaurant in the Frieze marquee itself. Spend a little bit too much money there, on oysters, beetroot and crab. Throw caution to the wind. Brain food – you'll need it.

Go to ALL of the specially curated Frieze Talks

However geeky you may feel, they are nearly always fascinating and pull in names like John Baldessari and Agnes Varda. (Book in advance if you can). The Frieze Talks also give you some time each day to hide away from the glaring bright lights of the fair. Reconfigure your reasons for continuing to live, in the gentle low lights.

Wear sunglasses inside

Who cares. The fair is swarming with NY collectors wearing shades anyway. Who's going to notice? They make you feel invisible too, and allow you to avoid encounters you don't feel up to. If they can't see your eyes, you can't see their eyes, right?

Read the special-to-Frieze daily Art Newspaper, free from various stands around the fair

Unbelievable, blanket, exhaustive coverage of all aspects of the fair, and frequently hilarious, especially the diary section. The newspapers are collectors' items in themselves. Keep them for ever.

Join in with the Frieze Projects

Joining in with these commissioned-for-the fair-projects can remind you of mucking in at Brownies or Cubs. But with a conceptual tinge. I once walked around the fair for 45 minutes with a theoretical physicist who taught me about the fundamentals of String Theory. He told me that our universe is in fact ten dimensional, not four-dimensional as most people think, and that we may well be living on a "kind of sheet of paper."

The conversation was recorded – as was that of the other 150 people who took part - and played out in Regent's Park the next morning by two actors sitting on a blanket, and on, for the duration of the fair.

There are usually about six different artist's projects going on each year, most of them seem to involve interacting with the fair's visitors in a sideways, interesting way. It's worth looking into most of them.

Buy some cheap art, if you can't afford the real thing

Copystand is a booth that was copying pieces of work from around the fair last year, using cheap materials like sticky tape, polystyrene and clay. I loved the reproduction of Richard Artschwager's Pianofart (2008), the original of which was at Sprüth Magers' stand for many thousands of pounds. I could hardly tell the difference. The artist Stephanie Syjuco was selling her works for under £500 although she had an 'Everything Must Go' sale on Sunday. That bootleg Artschwager went for a song at £150. A snip. Copystand must surely come back another year? A travesty if not.

Worm your way into the VIP bar

There are points in the day when this is easier than others. There's no pattern. Just be brazen.

Get your arse photographed

I got my (clothed) derrière photographed by artist Tomomi Sayuda inside the Resonance 104.4 FM booth a few years ago. She'd made the seat of a rather comfy chair into a photocopier. Tomomi kept telling me, as I was sitting on her photocopier, "This is to make embarrassment." Yes, indeed. You must keep embarrassing yourself. No point being shy in the art world. Especially at Frieze. It's where we shine.

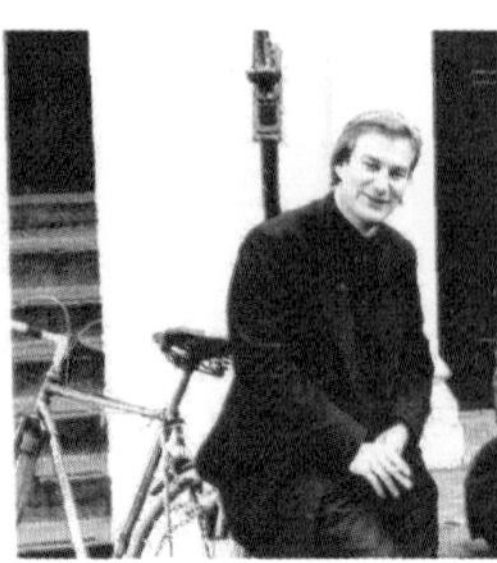

Taking British Art Where It's Not Strictly Welcomed

by James Birch

James Birch is a curator who takes artists to very, very unexpected places. In 1988, he organised the seminal Francis Bacon show Francis Bacon in Moscow, and the Gilbert and George show One World two years after. In 1993, thanks to James, Gilbert and George were the first major western artists to show in China, in both Beijing and Shanghai. From one brave decision springs another…

ON DECEMBER 22ND 1988 Francis Bacon opened a retrospective at the Central House of Artists in Moscow. This was the first time a living western artist of such status had exhibited in the USSR. I was instrumental in the convoluted process of securing this show. It was an interesting enterprise because of the light it shed on Soviet attitudes to art and to the west.

In December 1985 I met my friend Bob Chenciner at a party. He asked me what I was doing and I said I wanted to take ten young artists that were with my gallery on the King's Road, to New York. He said forget New York, take them to Moscow. The next day he told me to go to Paris, to the Soviet department at UNESCO, and to ask for a Mr Klokov.

I duly arrived in Paris, went to UNESCO and met the said Mr. Klokov, a man who was influential in the ruling circles of Soviet cultural life. One must remember that this was December 1985 - in March of that same year Gorbachev had got into power and was beginning to instigate his changes to the Soviet operation; first with Glasnost and then Perestroika - but it was all still very closed.

Over lunch in Paris I showed Mr Klokov slides of the artist's work and he expressed doubts over the possibility of a show in Moscow, but told me whom I should write to at the Union of Artists in Russia, a very powerful body. This was a major breakthrough as many people had written before to the USSR and the letters had ended up on empty desks or in the bin.

Nothing happened for six months, and despite me thinking things may be loosening up in Moscow – there had after all been a Sotheby's contemporary art sale in Russia earlier that year - I almost forgot about the proposal. In those days all western artists were considered decadent monsters by many Russians. But then in July 1986 I received a telegram inviting me to come to Moscow immediately.

I realised after one day in Moscow that the show of the ten young artists – who included Grayson Perry - would be a hard thing to pull off. Largely because I didn't know who was going to pay for it.

Abandoning the initial idea, I asked Klokov which major western artist he would like to see exhibiting in Moscow and the reply was "Francis Bacon, to break the ice for Andy Warhol…" Amazing.

I gathered, mainly from what I'd learned at various artists' studios I'd been taken to, that admiration for Francis Bacon was clear. Reproductions of his work would also have been seen in art magazines and supplements that the handful of tourists left behind in hotels.

Klokov suggested that we should have lunch with his uncle who was Vice President of the Union of Artists. Over lunch at Klokov's parents' dacha - located in a highly guarded military zone (complete with rockets) just outside Moscow, and awarded by Stalin to Klokov's grandparents for their 'heroism' - the uncle said he thought Bacon would be an excellent artist to show and that the queues would be longer than those for Lenin's tomb.

I had known Francis Bacon through my parents, off and on since I was a child. Over dinner, I asked him if he would be interested in having a show in Moscow. He was delighted, having recently had an exhibition in America with poor reviews. I then booked a call to Klokov in Moscow. In those days it could take up to five hours to go through.

The exhibition was to be a small retrospective comprising of 30 or 40 paintings including diptychs and triptychs. Obviously certain things had to be ironed out. The pictures had to be hung five or six feet from the floor as Francis said this made maximum impact. There was also the question of alcohol at the private view, which Gorbachev was trying to ban at the time. Also food - there seemed to be a lot of indescribable meat (I became vegetarian for a while after Moscow) and a boiled egg for breakfast took 20 minutes to arrive…

Francis was very excited about the exhibition and wanted to come but someone, incredibly, had put some poison in his ear and he decided against it, but meanwhile he had bought a Russian language course on cassette. The morning we flew out for the opening, I went to pick up Francis' boyfriend George Edwards from Bacon's studio. Francis entertained us with fried eggs and bacon before we took the taxi.

The opening was the following night and the Russians had put me up in the large Empire State Building-esque hotel called The Ukraine. There I was asked many times in the lift if I would sell anything western, if I happened to have things like spare socks, underpants, toothbrush, toothpaste for sale.

The Central House of the Artist was reminiscent of the Hayward Gallery - stark and concrete. The ceremony was opened by Lord Gowrie, the then chairman of Sotheby's, and thousands of people arrived, including many artists I had met over the countless trips I had made to organise the exhibition.

A few bottles of champagne had been especially laid on. Everyone was very excited.

The next day I went back to the exhibition space and noticed that the viewers wouldn't look at a Bacon painting for just five minutes as they would in the west, but would spend many hours, even half a day, absorbing these works…something I found really astonishing. It completely changed my outlook on life, to think that art could bring some light to a culture that has been suppressed by its own government.

Striking while the iron was hot, I proposed an exhibition of Gilbert and George to the Russians, which was realised two years later.

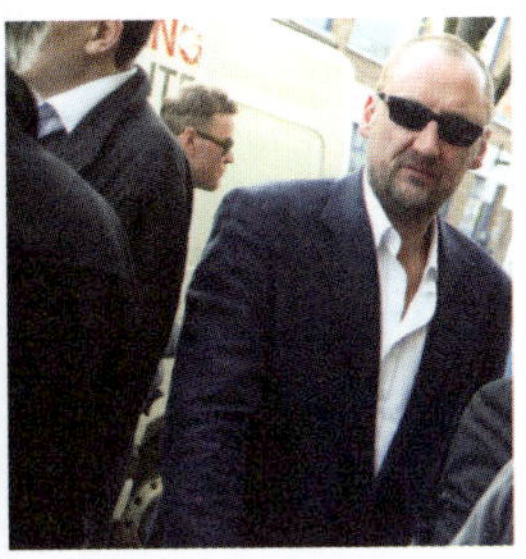

The Story of Neon

by Kerry Ryan

*Kerry Ryan is the founder of Neon and Signmakers London.
Who made all those iconic neon pieces of art – for Tracey
Emin, Franco B, Anselm Kiefer etc? He did.*

1982

My mum called all kinds of print firms in London trying to find me a job: I'd been kicked out of school for constant fucking about.

My dad had me working for him running a groceries shop on the Isle of Dogs. This was before Asda arrived & fucked all small grocery stores.

I then started an apprenticeship as a silk screen technician for a company called Sign & Display Industries on the corner of Osborn Street, Brick Lane. I attended college - The LCP in Elephant & Castle - for 2 years 8 months and left there with a credit. Commercial screen print was a fucking messy job. I left Brick Lane and went to Well Signs in Hackney where I was introduced to neon. Bending glass & West End installs. I went from 11 quid a week to 50 quid a day. Fuck the printing...neon, ladders, tools & a van was for me.

I worked 18 hours a day for 2 years & set up my own shop (Island Signs) opposite Pellici's on Bethnal Green Road. I was still only 18.

Pellici's by the way is still the best café in London.

1988

Spitalfields Fruit Market moved to Leyton and I took a unit on the corner of Brushfield Street in the freed up space. Neon & Signmakers was born while the art scene was just kicking off.

Gilbert & George lived almost next door and were always in the café opposite the Ten Bells pub. Here you could have a roast dinner at 4 in the morning followed by a pint in Sandra's (the Golden Heart).

The fruit had gone but all the surrounding businesses continued to cater for these weird hours.

Our basement kept flooding, driving me fucking mad, so I decided to chase a groove out of the floor. We started drilling and cutting on a Friday afternoon. By the middle of the night the water had dropped, sp we had a pint and patted each other on the back. A good job done... or so we thought.

I got a call early Saturday morning. 'Get to the shop,' shouted Malcolm the Market Manager. When I arrived, without a word of a lie, there must have been 300 rats fucking running all over the shop. People were crowded around the windows. It was a fucking rat circus. I've got goose-pimples thinking about it. The shop next door was the Organic Pie Shop... they wasn't happy. The rats soon packed up, left the sign shop & headed next door for pies.

We didn't know at the time but we had hit the main sewer. We filled the holes & denied everything.

Luckily enough, and because of the floors, Spitalfields offered me a smaller shop on the corner of Lamb Street & Commercial Street. The whole block was empty so, again, we cut a hole in the wooden floor, blocked up all the doorways & ended up with a 2000 sq ft basement. We stayed there for 15 years.

1995
A young artist called Tracey Emin asked for a neon to be made...for 'The Tracey Emin Museum'.
I thought she was a bit strange.
I took a deposit and after words & negotiations we got the neon made and installed at a little shop in Waterloo. When we got there to install, all that was in the lock up was a tent with hundreds of names sewn inside and a chair with the same. Anyway, after a few beers & a bit of bullshit about electrics (I wasn't really an electrician) we got the neon up and everyone was happy.
This was my first introduction to the art world.
Not long after this I was asked by Mat Collishaw if I wanted to be in a photoshoot: I had to dress like a Nazi SS and pose like I was dead in the Clerkenwell Jail.
2 days before the photoshoot we were installing a job in Bishopsgate. I was inside talking to the client when we heard screaming. I looked through the window and saw my fitter's feet tap dancing on the ladder. We ran out to the screams, the power had come on. It was on a timer and Dal, the fitter, was in fucking trouble. He had a power cable in one hand and a metal ladder in the other. All I could think to do was kick the ladder away & try to catch him. He hit me like a bag of rocks. We both woke up in hospital... him with

third degree burns and me with a broken cheek bone. Needless to say when we turned up for the photoshoot. Mat thought it was the best makeup he had ever seen. Another happy customer. We are still good friends to this day.

Tracey and I became friends too and I carried on making neons for her. Our shop in Spitalfields bacame a visiting point. Always something new to see.

I was introduced to Gregor Muir (a gallerist), Max Wigram (another gallerist) & Mustafa Hulusi, artist. Tracey suggested we used the basement as a gallery. It went well, Sarah Lucas and Angus Fairhurst, Mat Collishaw, Gavin Turk, Rebecca Warren & Fiona Banner all put work in. I liked the art business and I think it liked me. Unfortunately, late night drinks and the police got involved and in 1998 I got 18 months for handling stolen goods. My good friend Jimmy Munro (Monty) who is sadly no longer with us, and my dad, ran the business whilst I was away.

I studied art in prison, and got my head down. 12 months later I was back. Tracey was going from strength to strength and I was still doing the neon drawings I'd started in Pentonville.

Once I was home and back to work, we turned the basement into a neon gallery. Now I began to collect art works for payment. Something I still do today.

We had a few casino night openings, a blend of Cockney mates & the art world. Good Nights... I remember Cerith Wyn Evans laying in the Sarah Lucas neon coffin with Tracey's 'my cunt is wet with fear' piece in the background. How he never got electro-cuted I will never know. He did break it..

Since then I have worked with Anselm Kiefer who I met whilst working in Lorcan O'Neill's gallery in Rome. He invited me to his home in Barjac and the install was a mass of neon words on big concrete towers balanced on lead books in the Pirelli building in Milan. A crane would not reach the top of the tower so I climbed out of the boom and up the side of the tower where I wired the two top words ready for the tower to be pushed over. The tower went over, the neons were still alight. The dust settled, it was fucking brilliant. Anselm was as happy as a pig in shit.

I was shaking.

Joseph Kosuth has been a good customer and I had helped him out with a neon job in Leathermarket Street in south London. His piece, There Are Dark Shadows, is still up & working today. We had three weeks to meet, make & install the piece after another company had let him down.

Jospeh & Anselm have both given me their works.

I have now worked for a mass of artists in England, Asia, America & Europe. I have also done works for Douglas Gordon in Russia working on the Chocolate Factory in Moscow. Fucking mad house. I ended up getting drugged & mugged out there on the de-install. Another drama. But I like dramas.

About five years ago I had a run-in in Bethnal Green over a parking situation. I got stabbed in the eye. It put me back for a while.
Darrel Edwards who came to work with me as a work experience with Monty's boy 16 years ago, now runs my Neon and Signmakers shop in Cambridge Heath Road in Bethnal Green. We got out-priced in Spitalfields, high rent, congestion charge etc,- just got too much especially with only the one eye. So we moved.

Yana, one of my four daughters, is now working with Darrel.
These days I stick to working from my studio in Bow. I think they are both happy anyway when I stay away from the shop. I can't blame them.

Neons & art shows... that's the way forward for me.
I will still drive anywhere, anytime - if it can be done, I will do it.
Thanks to everyone I have worked with.
Kerry Ryan.

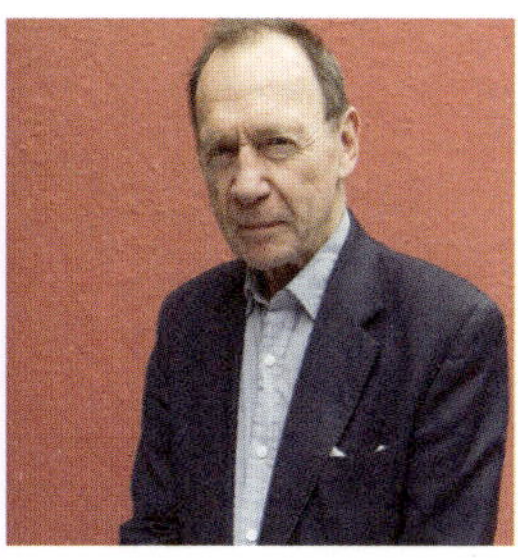

Neo-Banquet Years

by Anthony Haden-Guest

Anthony Haden-Guest is the author of the gruesomely readable
True Colours: The Real Life of the Art World. He is also a
pugilist, and frequently performs his written verses, most recently
at Art Basel Miami and the New York Armory.

"*THE FINE ARTS ARE five in number, namely: painting, sculpture, poetry, music, and architecture, the principal branch of the latter being pastry,*" observed Marie-Antoine Carême.

Carême was a pastrycook and the world's first nomadic Celebrity Chef – he worked for Talleyrand until the fall of Napoleon, was then *chef de cuisine* for the Prince Regent in London, then the Tsar in St Petersburg, then Baron Rothschild– and he was perhaps joking. But he was also making a point. Yes, cooking and eating – and, okay, drinking – can be a legit Fine Art. And as over-the-top as any other Fine Art.

That banquets have played a necessary bonding role in the art world since the earliest days of Modernism is explicit in the title of Roger Shattuck's great book, *The Banquet Years: The Origins of the Avant-Garde in France, 1885 to World War I*. It was Shattuck, I think, who recorded that Toulouse-Lautrec could make a cocktail that tasted like "a peacock's tail in the mouth." Henry Van De Velde, the master of Belgian Art Nouveau, gave elaborate meals where everything was the same colour.

In more recent times, invitations to a meal at Andy Warhol's various Factories, were hot tickets and pleasantly low-key. And maybe I am being naïf but I don't recall accounts of them being spoon-fed to the columnists. The most delightfully old-fashioned – in being completely personal - of artist dinners in Manhattan, though, have been the dinners given by Christo and his late wife, Jeanne-Claude. It was at these that I first met writers like David Bourdon and artists like Roy Lichtenstein.

Art dinners flourished during the boom, coasted through the Bust – I think it was more or less mid-Bust that Jay Jopling threw a zinger for Raquib Shaw, and I remember a couple of excellent dos at Bernard Jacobson's - and now, well, now the Art Dinner flourishes in ways that might even surprise Toulouse-Lautrec. Herewith my paper napkin notes on just three of them.

The first was in Manhattan and the host was Raphael Castoriano of Kreemart. It was called The Social Violence Dinner and it was produced by Keil Borrman, a performance artist, who had recently done a birthday dinner for Marina Abramovich. The food was inventive – the menu noted that it included *poached Black Cod with American Sturgeon caviar (for the workers)* – and the programme more so. Keil, a young man of mild demeanour, began by quoting Walter Benjamin on violence and moved on during the first course – *Falafel from Oasis in Williamsburg*, according to the printed menu – to a peroration on the Gaza Strip, which references Nietzsche.

The reading/performance channelled a luminously revolutionary past, including such elements as a poem by Brecht that might have made any of the Good Liberals at the table a bit uneasy - *We shall put you in front of a good wall and shoot you? With a good bullet from a good gun and bury you/ With a good shovel in the good earth* - if they hadn't been getting stuck into the kimchi and shrimp. And just before the foie gras there was a familiarly lurid description of what is inflicted upon the actual birds during the preparation of that (to me repulsive in its fatness) delicacy.

Keil's reading concluded, mordantly. *Their plumage becomes encrusted with filth, as they are deprived of water and are unable to clean themselves … Production is concentrated in France, which produces and consumes roughly 75 % of the world's foie gras, though the example before you was produced in upstate New York.* But had Tom Wolfe been present I don't think he would have found much to sink his teeth into. Neo-Radical Chic, this wasn't. This was performance art.

My second Art Dinner was at Gigi Giannuzzi and Hannah Watson's Trolley Gallery on Redchurch Street in east London. It was part of the Trolley's Manifesten series, nine art events at Shoreditch Church, each being followed by a dinner in the gallery. "The whole inspiration was Marinetti's Futurist Cookbook," Gigi said of the dinner. "You had flying asparagus and floating bed. And you were flying around the table like a bird."

Okay, I have to say that I am under the instructions of my editor – who was present at the fête – to be utterly candid here. My perceptual apparatus lasted long enough for me to purchase a drawn-upon (and highly explicit) limited edition napkin by the young London painter Henry Hudson but it began to fizzle shortly after I clambered up to my chair, the seat of which was six feet off the floor. (The table was designed so all the top of our heads were brushing the ceiling). There were a dozen guests, who seemed increasingly glittering as the evening progressed, there were hanging foodstuffs, there were wait-staff popping up through holes in the table, then disappearing, as if in a cyber-*Alice.*

And there was me hitting the floor three times. "The third time we thought you might have hurt yourself," my editor said, airily. She did not say anybody had leaned down to take a look. But she added. "Your head appeared at my knee; your right finger and thumb were gently pinching the cloth of my trousers. You said: "Darling, can you help me? I think I'm entering into some kind of trance." I am told I did get back up on to the eight-foot high table and ate my meringue which was hanging down from an invisible string.

Well, that was an Art Dinner, Old School. But Art Dinner number three was New School and perhaps even more extraordinary. It was for the wedding of Simon de Pury (the chairman of Phillips de Pury auction house) and Michaela Neumeister. It had taken place almost exactly six months before and it was at the Saatchi Gallery, just off the Kings Road, and such faces were floating around as Irving and Jackie Blum, Benedikt Taschen , Anita Zabludowicz and … well, you can guess the cast-list.

We had been asked to be there at 7PM promptly, which seemed a bit severe. When at the Saatchi you realised why. De Pury and Neumeister were being prepared for the carrying-ons in separate glass-fronted cubicles. It was only when de Pury was properly coiffed that he smashed the glass and claimed his bride.

There had already been hanging sausages and a welter of foodstuffs before anybody focused on their place cards, to work out in which of the galleries they were to be seated. There was a prodigal array of foodstuffs – crayfish, whole hams – and I had already eaten more oysters than I have ever managed in one go. "They were harvested this morning," said Jennifer Rubell, who created the event.

Rubell is an artist who works with food. And, heaven knows, she has the right genes. Her parents are Don and Mera Rubell, heavy-duty collectors, who run a private museum in Florida, and her late uncle was Steve Rubell, one of the progenitors of Studio 54 and hence the entire Disco era. We finally sat down to dinner on one of the 68 multiple-use beds with fluffy cushions, spread over four galleries. There was a kinetic performance by the New-York-based jazz/rock pianist, Eric Lewis aka Elew, and then DJing duties were assumed by the multiple-hatted De Pury himself. One for the books.

Art Fiascos

by Laura K Jones

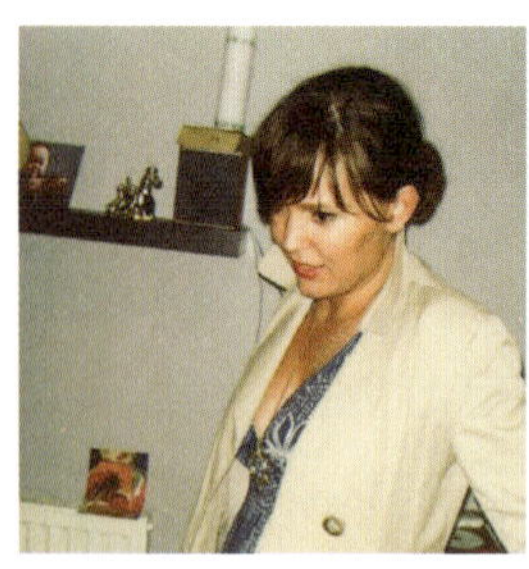

Laura K Jones is a severely ornithophobic writer and editor who lives in Bethnal Green. She sometimes paints fowl, and members of the Xenartha super-order of animals. She is also in the process of writing her early-mid-life memoirs, Strange Encounters With Old Men. It's probably a bit morbid listing the art world's catastrophes, but we can't all be jolly, all the time. And there's a certain hedonism in melancholia, is there not?

DOH! LAS VEGAS CASINO magnate, multi-billionaire Steve Wynn poked an elbow through his prized $139 million Picasso - 'Le Reve' (1932) - in 2001. Wynn said "I can't believe I just did that. Oh, shit. Oh, man."

German artist Gustav Metzger's bin-bag installation at the Tate Britain in 2004 was said to demonstrate the "finite existence" of art. Just so for the Tate cleaner who threw it into the crusher one night.

Intense paint drooler Jackson Pollock, frustrated by the cropping of his mural in order to fit on Peggy Guggenheim's apartment wall, took a slash in his patron's fireplace. Well, he was known as 'Jack the Dripper'.

More of a tragedy than a fiasco; a steel rigger was squashed and killed while dismantling a mammoth sculpture by Richard Serra in 1971.

More Serra-related bad luck: In 1988, while dismantling a 16-tonne Serra sculpture at the Leo Castelli Gallery in New York, a worker lost his leg when the artwork collapsed.

American artist Paul McCarthy's 'Painter' (1995) installation got pulverized in transit to the Sydney Biennale. The installation arrived in toothpick-sized pieces.

RIP YBAs. On the evening of 24 May 2004, fire broke out in the Momart storage warehouse in East London, the biggest storage unit for art in Britain. The blaze destroyed

£50m of Britart, including Tracey Emin's embroidered tent Everyone I Have Ever Slept With 1963-1995, and the Chapman Brothers' Hell sculpture. Lesson: check your art storage fire sprinklers.

Popinjay and painter, the dear departed Sebastian Horsley, crucified himself in the Philippines in 2000. He asked his then girlfriend, the artist Sarah Lucas, to film the whole grisly episode. She puked and fainted. Horsley's footrest broke off and he nearly died as he fell from the cross. Sadly he then died for real this year, 2010, from an accidental heroin overdose.

You'd think the Munch Museum in Oslo would have put some serious security measures in place to protect their world-famous painting, Edvard Munch's The Scream. But no. In broad daylight in August 2004, two gunmen walked in and strolled back out with it, observed by 70 witnesses.

Not necessarily a fiasco, but Tracey Emin turned up drunk and disorderly at a live Channel 4 TV debate following the Turner Prize awards in 1997. After many expletives and much pointing (one of her favourite things - pointing), she walked out. Ms Emin later claimed to not even remember being there.

Less of a catastrophe, more of a genius bit of thinking. Mexico 2006: 28 Damien Hirst works were flown over along with the set of tools required to install them for an exhibition at the Hilario Galguera Gallery. The tools were considered too dangerous for entry by Mexico City airport officials. So Hirst's Cheltenham studio built a glass vitrine, arranged the returned tools inside, and flew the whole thing back disguised as a piece of art called 'Immaculate Conception.'

2007, Avignon Museum of Contemporary Art: French woman Rindy Sam was so overcome with passion for an immaculate white painting by Cy Twombly, that she planted a smacker on it. Her red lipstick irreversibly stained the $2.8 million work.

For two weeks in October 1991, Christo, the artist who wraps mammoth bridges and buildings, unfurled nearly 2000 large yellow umbrellas in a valley about 70 miles north of Los Angeles. He simultaneously unfurled 1,340 blue umbrellas in a valley in Japan. Each parapluie was 6 metres high and 8.66 metres across, so the size of a small house. A Californian woman died when she was crushed by one of them. A worker, operating a crane for the project in Japan, then died when his arm touched a live power cable. Before the days of elf and safety, no doubt. Still, too sad.

Things went more awry than even the violent, short-lived Austrian art movement the Vienna Actionists had perhaps hoped for, when, in June 1969, Rudolf Schwarzkogler, the most conceptual of the artists but also the most vulnerable of the group, fell out of a window – possibly during one of the group's infamous orgies - and died.

Complaining that Tracey Emin's Turner Prize-nominated installation 'My Bed' (1999) was "not interesting enough", two Chinese 'satirists' repeatedly jumped up and down on it and drank from the installation's vodka bottles. Tate Britain employees wrestled them to the floor.

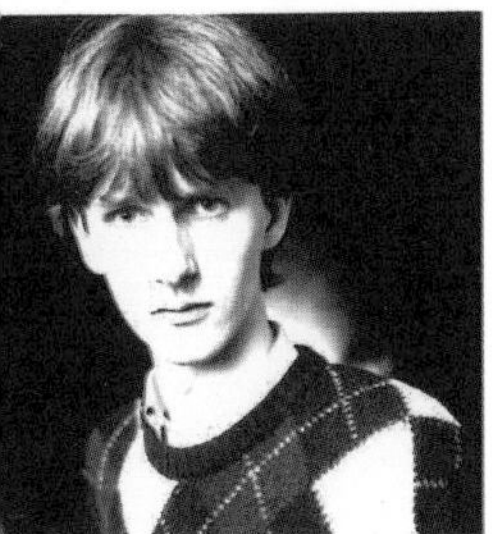

The Fireplace

by Tobias Meyer

Tobias Meyer is Sotheby's Principal Auctioneer and Worldwide Head of Sotheby's Contemporary Art Department.

WHEN I WAS 18, my father, (who always made sure that I would engage in commercial ventures more than just art historical ones), had the brilliant idea of getting me into the Christie's course. He had heard about it from a colleague of his who was a cousin of the Head of the Christie's office in Vienna. Normally there would have been a lengthy process of admission tests and all kinds of essays to be written, but in this case my father just managed to get me in. All I had to do was to present myself to Vincent Windisch-Graetz, the head of the office at the time. I was summoned into a huge apartment on the Esteplatz in the third district of Vienna, where I - mildly intimidated - looked at him and his collection of Maiolica. He asked me some polite questions, I answered them, and so I was admitted on to September's course. Through a family friend, I found a small flat in St. James, under the roof of a house in Duke Street, with running water but no heating. This was a choice that I came to regret deeply in December of that year as I learned to warm up my bed with a blow dryer before bedtime. It was that cold.

A whole new world opened up for me. Suddenly people asked me questions about things that I had wanted to study all my life. I could tell my tutors that a certain piece of furniture was actually made in Dresden when all they wanted to know is whether it was German. I could tell them that the bronzes were stamped with the *C-couronnée* sign when all they wanted to know was whether they were 18th century or not. I had suddenly found a world where people actually wanted to talk to me and I wanted to learn what they had to say. Previously I had thought that my interest in art was something to be enjoyed in complete isolation or in the company of very few.

So here I was on the course in the winter of 1981. A couple of my classmates decided to go to Paris – one of them was my friend, Olivia, who for some reason always seemed to have impeccable connections. I never really found out why she was so well connected - she just was. We stayed, the five of us, in a house belonging to her uncle. It was a Louis XIII palais on the Left Bank with a very beautiful, quiet courtyard and the living rooms filled with paintings by Tanguy. Upon reflection, it was also furnished with Jean Michel Frank furniture, although at the time I could not identify it.

One day while we were looking at the Hotel de Soubise and studying its Rococo architecture, I was told that we had been summoned that afternoon for tea at the house of the famous American art historian, James Lord. I had no idea who James Lord was. I did not go with my friends but joined them later at James' flat in the Rue des Beaux Arts. I pressed the code at the front door and went up in the elevator. It was raining that day and as I pressed the bell of the apartment, Lord, a very handsome man of around sixty, opened the door and said to me 'Oh, it's raining outside', and then he brushed the water off the navy blue blazer that I had worn for the occasion. He looked me in the eye and then I went into the apartment.

The apartment was on the top floor of the building, all white, and I saw on the walls paintings with dedications such as 'To James de Diego' or to 'Lord from Pablo.' Against the walls and next to the white sofas were furniture and tables made out of bronze with animals climbing up the legs – these of course I subsequently realised were by Giacometti. My friends were already in the living room where I sat down on a white sofa. Behind me were two big Aztec gold masks in a vitrine and through the window on my right I could see a roof garden with a very beautiful Roman marble horse head that was illuminated.

It was about 5 o'clock in the afternoon, it was already dark, we were in December, and across from me was a pink marble fireplace and above it a pink cubist painting. It didn't look like a Picasso, it was another cubist artist that I didn't know. The painting itself was pink. We were all making polite conversation and suddenly I looked at Mr. Lord and said "Mr Lord did you choose the pink marble fireplace to go with that painting?" Everybody else started to laugh at this rather strange question and James Lord took one look at me, and smiled. "Of course Tobias, I did choose the marble to go with the painting - you are a very perceptive young man". He looked at me again and I turned the colour of the fireplace. I realised that he realised that I was gay and he was the first man to ever actually find out that I was.

I left the apartment and didn't see Mr Lord again for fifteen years. When I did see him again it was in a house of a friend of mine in London. He had come over there for a drink and I told him the story which of course he did not remember at all because these were my memories, not his. He didn't know what he had done; he had opened my eyes in more than one way.

Art Loves Miami

by Jake Miller

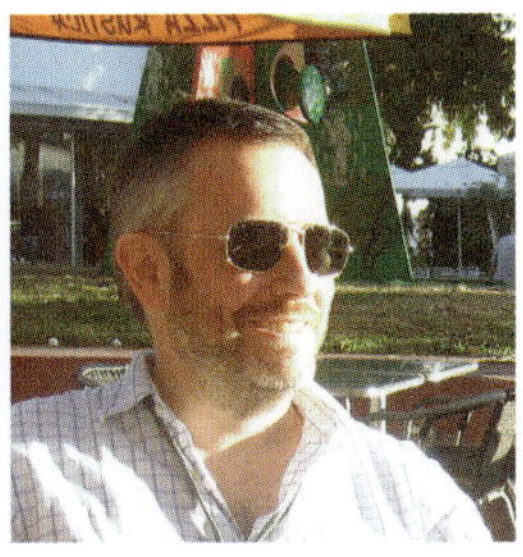

Jake Miller is the owner of The Approach Gallery in East London. He and his gallery exhibit at all the international art fairs: Basel, New York, Frieze - but memories of Miami Basel are the ones that never fail to make him sigh.

MIAMI BASEL OPENED ITS doors in 2002 following a postponed start in 2001 due to Al-Qaeda-funded party poopers a couple of months earlier. December was the chosen month as - the thinking went - the winter sun in Miami would draw in the shivering art collectors from the drizzly northern climes.

Unlike its serious Swiss counterpart, Miami Basel's raison d'être is to firmly place the buying of contemporary art into a lifestyle of sun, sea and excess. This seemed a little more appropriate post-recession and during the years the Approach participated between 2003 and 2008.

The evenings of my first years there were mostly spent at the back of the Raleigh Hotel were I found the bar to be more pleasant than the surrounding South Beach hotels. The ornate pool, palm trees and hanging lanterns gave it a relaxed old money charm that was soon shattered as the smallish back bar became over run by rowdy Brits, Germans and Americans in the process of "unwinding".

The overcrowding led to the discovery that the sandy garden went on so much further than the pool. On one night of the week, the impresario and one time gallery owner Jeffrey Deitch – now director of MOCA - would organise performances there by the likes of Chicks On Speed, The Voluptuous Horror of Karen Black, Gossip, and Devendra Banhart (a gig I found myself actually having to climb over a fence... to escape from).

The noise of the Raleigh concerts clash with larger concerts on the beach, which fall under the slightly irritating title of 'Art Loves Music'. Stage strutters there have included Iggy Pop, The New York Dolls and Peaches. The latter once finished her set by encouraging the fairly indifferent audience to follow her (disrobed) into the sea to the sounds of 'Fuck The Pain Away'. She threw herself into the waves declaring "I do this in honour of the naked swimmer who livened up a boring party last night by jumping in the pool," and she was gone. I hope the jellyfish didn't get her.

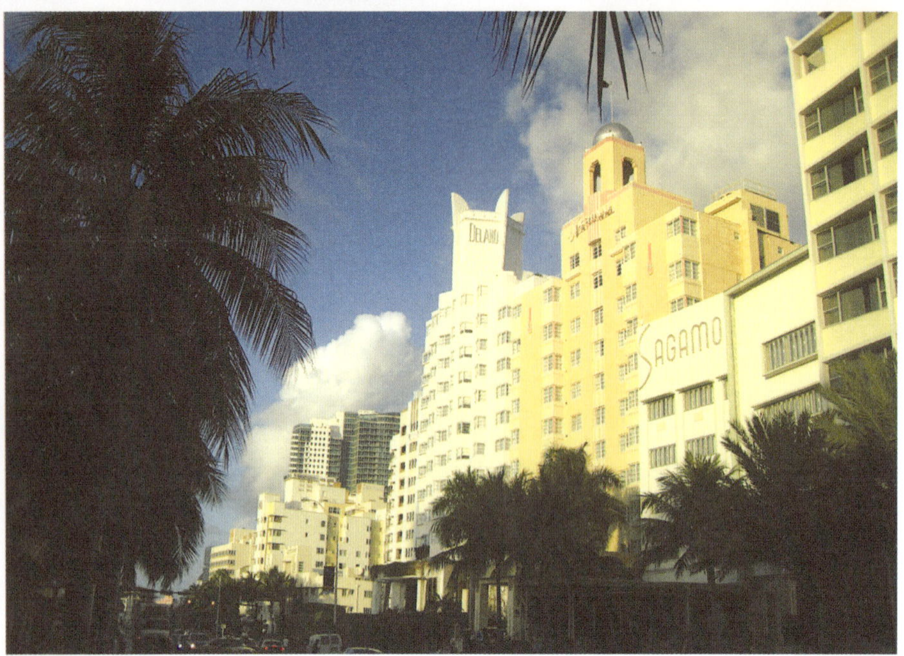

Miami. Jake Miller

I was also at the party she mentioned, one of many held on rooftops or by pools where free drinks flow in plastic beakers and the only corporate branding that seems appropriate is 'Art Loves To Get Hammered'.

These first years were far less crowded and the revelry seemed to be more authentically funny somehow. The first year was also when a major local collector family held a very generous party at their new home. After a great night that resulted in some busted artworks, the hosts wisely decided to stick to the more civilised 'collectors brunch,' a common feature of any art fair week.

Even in these early years, people were talking of the last days of the Roman Empire and of how the whole overblown net jet scene - where everyone is a VIP - was on its last bloated legs.

But still it all continued.

Friends of mine that are not so familiar with the art fair life look at me as though I'm mad when I complain that it's "Miami time again", but the constant dull boom boom boom thud from each poolside bar just gets to you after a while, and however perfect the blowing white muslin might be, one soon starts to crave a bit of grime. Not that grime doesn't exist in Miami – you just sometimes have to create it.

The Studio Karaoke Bar was the basement venue for a great birthday party for Modern Institute Gallery director Toby Webster; it also had something to do with the Brit-born New York gallerist Gavin Brown (a man that seems to have more art fair parties than even he seems to be aware of). The atmosphere was such a wonderful antithesis to the plastic world above that somehow the dark, sweaty, noisy dump seemed so beautiful. Another bit of dirty escapism is the infamous neon lit dive Club Deuce, located a late night stagger away from the main drag of Collins Avenue.

But, to the reason we all find ourselves in this unlikely place - the fair. Located at the Miami Beach Convention Centre, you may as well be in any other convention centre from Chicago to Stuttgart. The only giveaway is the amount of deformed plastic faces, big synthetic hair and luminous colours crawling around. And that's just the men. Sometimes a strange cross-over of worlds takes place. I remember a fragrant, bling-laden Beyoncé coming up against a violently hung-over Darren Flook – director of east London's Hotel Gallery. She disturbed him from his sorry state to ask about some work on his stand. Only in the art world.

I have spotted Karl Lagerfeld entering darkened exhibits with his sunglasses still on, a lady bouncing up and down on a Franz West sculpture shouting to her partner, "Look baby, you can sit on it AND it goes outside!" The disheartened looking gallerist Christian Nagel could only look on. I also loved the news that a staff member of a friend's gallery was found to be dealing drugs from the booth. She then asked the boss if he would like a line, and was later that evening found having it off in a hotel's ice cupboard (lying to security by telling them that she was Mari Spirito, the director of New York's 303 Gallery, aswell). She was fired the next day.

Ahh... memories. Writing this has started to make me miss the place a little – something I never thought I'd say. The gallery decided to not participate in 2009 but I have found myself being gently persuaded to apply again this year. For all its soul-destroying tackiness, Miami Beach is still a significant part of the art world calendar and the all-important Basel branding does have clout.

Maybe the party was over for a while and the very hungover art world hadn't come round to the thought of ever drinking again, but now, over the last few months, at least they seem to be warming to the idea.

Basel Miami 2010? Maybe all is forgiven.

Renoir's Phantom

by Allan Scott

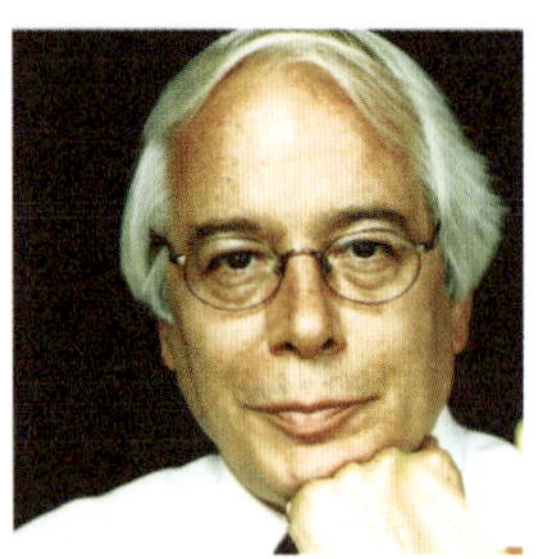

Allan Scott is a film writer and producer. He was executive producer of Shallow Grave. He is also the originator, co-writer and producer of Priscilla - The Musical which opens on Broadway in early 2011. He collaborated with director Nicolas Roeg as co-writer on the seminal film Don't Look Now. Surely that alone qualifies him to tell us a ghost story from the art world.

I LAST SAW NANA before the turn of the new millennium. It was summer and her remarkable home at the top of Haut de Cagnes was, as always, filled with light, shade, flowers and paintings. The paintings were mostly her own, but included a random number being stored for her pal the actress and singer Suzy Solidor whose small art shop - which rarely had enough space for her inventory - was in the square below.

Nana, who was by then well over eighty, had lived in this rambling chateau-apartment since the outbreak of war. Two English women, who owned the place, asked her to look after it for them while they returned to England to await the outcome of the war. They never made contact with her again and despite her making every effort in the after-war years to re-establish contact, the two women had simply disappeared. It was assumed that they had been killed, unremarked, in a bombing raid on London, and Nana went through the legal procedures that eventually resulted in the apartment being declared her property.

As a child, Nana's family had been friends of the Renoir family and had more than once been painted by Pierre-Auguste. Nana's daughter Denise had, in later years, married the painter's grandson, the film director Claude Renoir.

All this is background to the fact that in more recent years, age and life's expenditures finally drove Nana - serene, artistic and always a pragmatic French woman - to seek to sell the most valuable item in her collection, a small but very distinctive pastoral scene painted by and fondly given to her decades earlier by Renoir himself. The painting had been executed before his hands became crippled with arthritis. It was fluent, vivid and sun-filled. Along with a large, bronze portrait medallion of Renoir's grandson, also a gift to Nana which she had disposed of previously, its authenticity was certain and its provenance immaculate. It was also worth a fortune and she knew it.

She asked her English friend, Randoll, to monitor the shipment of the painting to London and to ensure its serene path through the auction house they had chosen. Randoll and Nana had been friends before the war and when he was dropped behind enemy lines in 1944 with orders to make contact with the local resistance in the South of France, it was inevitable that Nana would provide him a fine range of contacts and shelter in her (then) borrowed home in Haut de Cagnes. Perhaps they had been lovers. Certainly they remained friends, having gone their separate ways, more than forty years after the war ended. Randoll could be trusted with more than mere artworks.

Randoll took his daughter, an art student, to the preview at the auction gallery in London and together they inspected the painting carefully. It might have looked different so completely out of its context above Nana's smokeless fireplace. But it was without doubt the painting Nana wished to sell and that evening Randoll phoned to tell her of the excitement in the showroom at such a rare and perfect little Renoir coming up for sale.

Two days later, the auction was held and with brisk bidding from all corners of the planet, the painting went for a record – and stress-relieving - sum to an undisclosed bidder. When the auction ended, Randoll went up to the painting for one last look.

Only this time, something was different. It was the painting, certainly. It was in the right frame, the signature marginally smudged, the dappled sunlight so elegantly strewn across the cornfield. But surely.....surely there was something missing.

Unwilling to trust his memory, Randoll dashed for a telephone and called his daughter.

"When you looked at the painting day before yesterday, was there a figure in the cornfield or not?" he asked her.

"Of course, there was. You remember we joked that it might have been Nana when she was a little girl. Just a dot in the distance, but a girl looking out."

Randoll went back to the painting for a final time. There was no child in the cornfield, no dot in the distance. Just the rural scene. The auctioneers and experts all confirmed that if there had been a figure in the picture, it would certainly have been recorded.

Randoll and his daughter had seen a ghost girl who never reappeared. And now that Nana is dead, perhaps it never will.

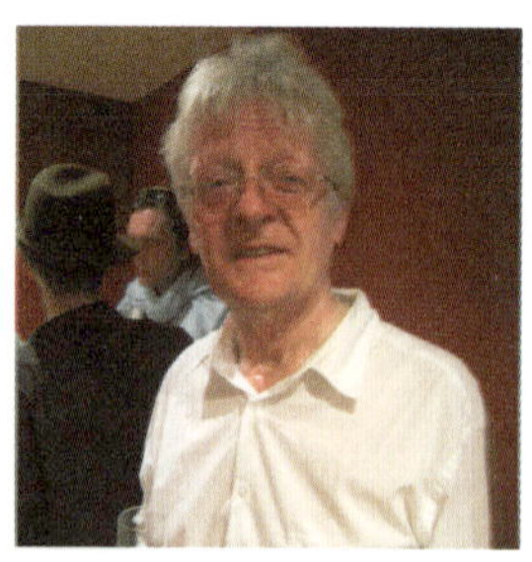

A Cabbage for Andy

by Barry Miles

Barry Miles co-founded Indica Books and Gallery in 1965 then went on to set up International Times, the first European underground newspaper, in 1966. As if he wasn't busy enough, he then became label chief of the Beatles' spoken word Zapple experimental label where he recorded albums by Allen Ginsberg, Richard Brautigan, Charles Bukowski and others. He now writes voraciously on art and artists.

IT WAS 1981 AND I was in New York, helping Nigel Finch and Anthony Wall with their BBC Arena television documentary on the Hotel Chelsea (or the Chelsea Hotel). I was involved with the segment concerning William Burroughs and Andy Warhol: Burroughs had lived at the Chelsea for a few months in 1964 and Andy, of course, filmed *Chelsea Girls* there, as well as some of his *Screen Tests*.

My friend Victor Bockris had the job of persuading Andy to take part; Andy had not visited the hotel ever since Valerie Solanas, who lived there, shot him in June 1968. My role was to cook a meal for Bill and Andy so that Arena could film their dinner conversation. There were about eight of us dining. I decided to cook *lapin au moutard* and the Area camera crew had fun taking horror shots of the rabbit pieces as I cut them up. It was very crowded in the room: in addition to Nigel, Anthony and Arena chief Alan Yentob there was a full BBC crew, plus a film crew belonging to Howard Brookner, who was making a documentary about Burroughs and wanted to film Bill being filmed. There was so little room that Brookner's soundman had to sit in the built-in wardrobe where he was forgotten and only after the shooting could he be heard calling "Are you ready to record yet, Howard?"

The filming went well and a couple of days later, at Victor's instigation, we decided to take Andy a present to thank him for taking part in the show. We went to a florist, but Victor lived in Greenwich Village and all the flowers were fantastically expensive. We didn't want to take Andy a single bloom; it had to be something substantial. The

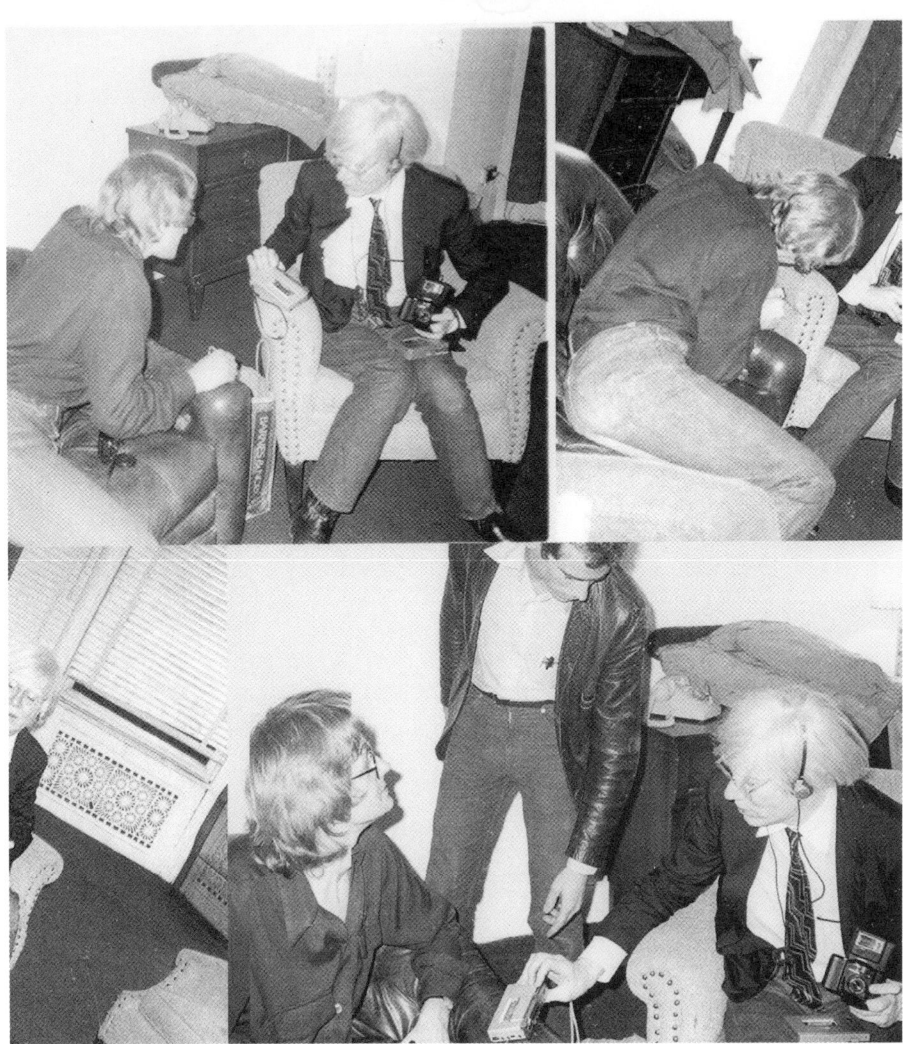

Barry Miles with Andy Warhol

cheapest large offering was an ornamental cabbage. It was a Brassica, with a large pink heart and light green frilly outer leaves with steely blue edges. I wasn't at all sure. It did look beautiful, and it was only $15, but it was still a cabbage. I questioned whether Andy would be pleased to receive a vegetable. I knew that the French had cultivated them for centuries as decoration but would Andy understand? Victor assured me that he would.

He said "Andy's very sophisticated. He'll know all about that. He'll know its not just any old cabbage. He won't be insulted. He'll be pleased." We bought the cabbage and walked over to Union Square, to 860 Broadway where Andy had his Factory on the third floor of an office block. Victor wrote for the Warhol-founded *Interview* magazine so we were welcomed and spent ten minutes looking through a rack of Andy's silkscreen portraits all done in candy colour acrylic. Then Andy appeared from one of the back rooms wearing his white fright wig. He was pleased to see us. We gave him the bouquet. Andy tore off the thin florist's paper and stared at the flower. There was an embarrassed silence. Andy didn't even say "Great!" like he usually did.

"But it's a cabbage!" he said.

He didn't thank us, just put it on a work surface next to a pile of Polaroid portraits, and stared at it with a sort of frozen, horrified fascination. Victor launched into an elaborate explanation of how cabbages and kales were used as flowers and how unspeakably cool flowering cabbages were and how you could only get them in Greenwich Village. In the middle of all this Andy turned to me, so that Victor could not see, and gave me a big wink.

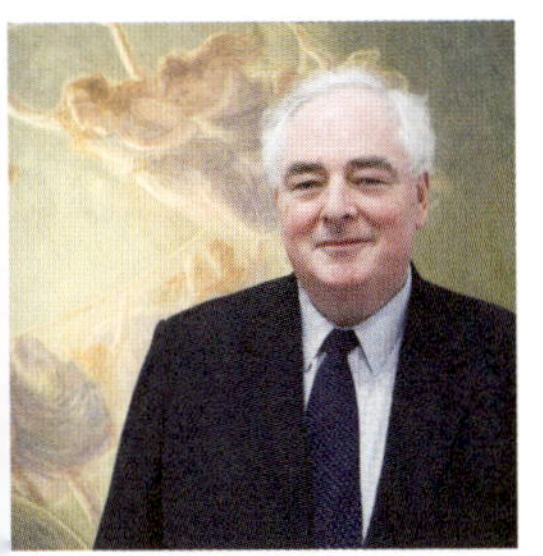

Guggenheim 24/7

by Nic Iljine

Nic Iljine has worked in Development at the Guggenheim Foundation for 12 years and is now VP International Development at Global Cultural Asset Management. He has initiated many exhibitions worldwide, linked to Russian art. Is his life an international whirl of cultural events? Is the Pope Catholic?

IF THERE IS ONE THING that my long service at the Guggenheim Museum has taught me, it is that art is always personal. You never have to look far for a connection from life to art, or for a connection back from art to life. Oh – and the food and drink is never far away.

An unusual form of sponsorship

During the opening days of the Venice Biennale of Architecture a few years ago, the Peggy Guggenheim Collection gave its traditional dinner party for VIPs, architects, trustees, curators et al. in the elegant setting of its rooftop terrace.

One of the guests at my table was somewhat exhausted by the heat of the day and the many drinks imbibed. After refusing to shake hands with the host Tom Krens, then director of the Guggenheim Foundation New York, who was doing his welcome round at the tables, the sozzled guest whom I shall call simply Sergey insisted on showing everyone how great his art collection was. He did this by clicking on postage stamp-size images of Chagalls, Renoirs, and Légers on his mobile phone. Later he asked how much Guggenheim Trustees contributed to the Guggenheim Foundation endowment. I explained that for instance, a Russian oligarch who is on the board had supported the Museum with xx millions over the years.

Sergey laughed; this was a mere pittance, he snorted. His boasting, enhanced by the good Prosecco, reached unprecedented levels. He claimed that he was surely the richest person sitting on the terrace at that exact moment. He suggested we bet on it, to the tune of one million dollars. This money the Guggenheim would receive if he lost - if I lost, I would have to give a lecture at Moscow University about the Western reception of Russian contemporary art.

Our table looked on excitedly as Sergey and I shook hands to seal the bet. It was only then that I told him to turn around and look at who was sitting at the adjoining table – just His Highness the Sheikh Sultan of Abu Dhabi.

Sergey turned pale and humbly accepted his defeat.

The astonishing part is that his million dollars arrived in the Guggenheim account five days later. The annoying part was, a year later, Sergey said. "Nic, you were stupid and should have bet ten million instead of one: I would have paid up without blinking an eye."

Putin and the Kalashnikov

Before the formal black tie opening ceremony of the 2005 RUSSIA! exhibition at the Guggenheim in New York, President Vladimir Putin and his entourage (Foreign Minister Lavrov, Culture Minister Shwydkoi, Vladimir Potanin etc.) were shown around the exhibition.

This was followed by a "tea party" for the President - (his favorite is Ronnefeldt "Morning Dew" green tea with a hint of mango and citrus, if you want to know) - and a dozen dignitaries in Tom Krens' large office. Tom was entertaining with small talk, showing photos of his son's christening in a derelict Russian church in Brooklyn with Joseph Brodsky as godfather etc. He turned to the President and said, "You know, Vladimir, we even have Russian tourists visiting the Guggenheim museums and some of them even give us souvenirs; here is an example," while pulling out a large military green wooden case with the word Kalashnikov printed on the side.

The case contained a life size AK47 machine gun made out of glass, filled with 'Kalashnikov' vodka. Mr Putin, holding the glass machine gun with a broad grin, explained that in 1894 the great Russian physicist Dmitri Mendeleyev introduced new official legal standards for producing the drink at 40 per cent alcohol. He then put the thing back into its wooden case and handed it to one of his bodyguards who proceeded to exit the office at lightning speed with our vodka-gun tucked neatly under his arm. I was about to scream 'Stop!' but thought better of it, and kept schtum.

Later Putin's spokesperson said to me "Nic, we know your photographer was shooting photos all the time but we do not want to see a single picture anywhere with the President holding that gun."

Early breakfast on Lafayette Street

After closing down New York's B Bar, curators Matthew Drutt & Tim Hunt, PR guru Ben Hartley and I walked south down the Bowery and swerved east onto Lafayette Street where on the pavement outside number 292 we found several pages of a Franz Kafka novel just lying there forlornly. Finally we realised that it was Douglas Gordon who had thrown them out of his window presumably just to watch them float down the street. It was around 3.30am, we were hungry and so decided to look up Douglas in his apartment. But it would have been uncouth to just drop in without food, so we made a beeline for an all-night Ukrainian deli where we bought industrial quantities of garlic, eggs, eggplant, onions, buckwheat, tomatoes, parsley and sardines and arrived, ready to cook breakfast at 4am. Gordon was happy to be distracted from his nocturnal creative process and put Taking Heads, Tom Waits, and Bowie on the stereo as we cooked up a storm. We settled down to a breakfast that lasted until 11am.

At that time I promised Douglas an exhibition in Moscow and must shamefully admit that I have not delivered as yet but there is light at the end of the tunnel.

Sandunovsky Bathhouse

In autumn 1988, after persuading Tom Krens to honour the budding Perestroika, Tom, Michael Govan (now LACMA Director), Joe Thomson (now director of MASSMOCA) Christoph Vitali (then, director of the Shirn Kunsthalle in Frankfurt) and myself travelled to Moscow to secure the major works of the Russian avant-garde for the forthcoming exhibition The Great Utopia.

We struggled with Soviet bureaucracy for a whole week and tried to relax with our Russian artist friends in an Armenian restaurant Tchakhadzor on Lesnaya Street (later closed down for arms smuggling). As a revitalisation procedure, I persuaded our group to visit the legendary Sandunovsky Bathhouse, created in the early 19th century. After a difficult waking up process at the Hotel Ukraine we finally arrived in our gentlemen's suite at the bathhouse; canapés, white linen, and suits were ironed while we enjoyed the steam baths, massages and saunas replete with beatings.

I can explain.

First, you lie on hot stones and get rubbed down with frothy liquid soap and wood shavings to cleanse your skin, then you get a tough massage by a Sumo-esque Georgian. After, you enter the sauna and get a full body beat-down with fresh birch branches so the leaves can dissipate their chlorophyll. Finally, after your siesta in the suite, you leave as fresh as a newborn baby.

The problem was, that whereas a naked Tom with his fogged glasses, at 6 foot 6 merely looked like an alien zombie, skinny Dr Vitali could not handle the pummeling massage. The 300-pound Georgian was a little overzealous with the featherweight 120 pounder, who let out a piercing scream when, as it later became clear, two of his ribs were cleanly snapped in half.

The Great Utopia went on to become the best exhibition of early 20th century Soviet Art ever shown, and ran in Frankfurt, Amsterdam, New York and Moscow, but its early beginnings were a little violent.

No Pain – No Art, as the saying goes.

Hedonism is Hard Work

by Dafydd Jones

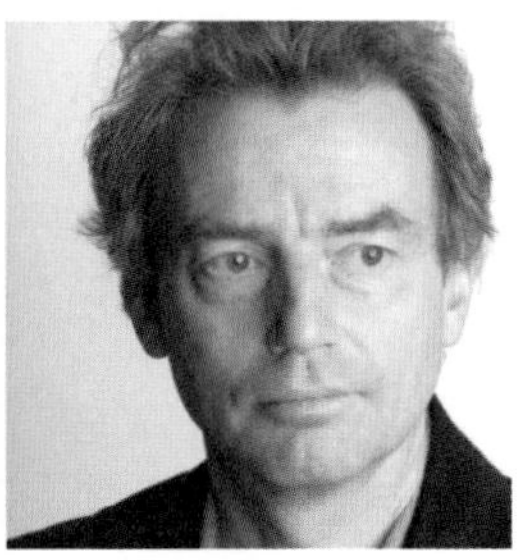

Dafydd Jones is a celebrated art world photographer. He toiled under Graydon Carter at Vanity Fair in New York for many moons then hightailed it back to England where he takes pictures for all the national newspapers. Wherever artists go, Dafydd Jones and his Leica are not far behind.

I WENT TO WINCHESTER School of Art in the seventies. The Fine Art department was run by a cabal of Glaswegian abstract painters and the head of department, if cornered, would admit that he didn't believe art could be taught. The result was that we were left to our own devices. The mood was nihilistic and we argued over ideas circulating about the inconsequence of having a tangible skill in art. A visiting tutor John Hoyland told us that having work exhibited and sold depended on knowing the Cork Street gallerist Leslie Waddington. Nobody expected to be able to survive as an artist.

On leaving, my plan was to do black & white Hollywood style photographic portraits on commission. In reality though, I survived by doing part-time cleaning. In 1980 I was shortlisted for a Sunday Times competition for photojournalists. The subject was 'The Return of the Bright Young Things'. First of all I had to find out who these bright young things were, and how it was I could get into their world. I asked questions incessantly, learning the most from an old school friend who'd got mixed up with a posh group that alternated between Chelsea and Oxford. With striking good looks and impeccable connections, he had become their drug dealer, providing the fashionable drug of the time - heroin. During the course of a long evening, and in between his bouts of heating up bitter-smelling junk, he explained who was who in smart English upper-class circles. He gave me an insiders view and also provided phone numbers.

My detective work was paying off and once I got into one decadent fancy dress party I was invited to another. It was the first time I'd photographed parties. Pointing a camera at someone and getting something that isn't banal is difficult. I wanted to take photographs that recorded the memorable moments and described what was actually happening. Clicking the shutter at that deliciously inopportune moment became the most rewarding part. Suddenly I was doing reportage photography but with a paparazzi edge.

These shots, when published, caused a small sensation and led to a job offer from the young, ambitious editor Tina Brown, to photograph high society for Tatler magazine.

It was a fantastic opportunity - I was really covering the old style establishment and ended up spending ten years doing these rounds.

Tatler also wanted to cover art world parties and dinners but none of the public galleries would allow social photographers. Funny to think of that now. However, in 1986 I successfully infiltrated an opening at the Tate. It was an exhibition of the Cubism collection of Douglas Cooper. He was delighted that I was there and encouraged me to take more pictures of his mainly handsome young male friends. I could see the then director of the Tate Alan Bowness narrowing his eyes at me, but he didn't dare stop me. However when I turned up for the next opening at the Tate a month later, Bowness had his revenge, getting his security to throw me out before I had a chance to take one picture. I didn't go back to the Tate until the Turner Prize started to invite photographers, when museums and galleries were finally becoming aware of the usefulness of PR. Nowadays the Tate actually *hire* me to cover their openings and dinners. You can't help but smile.

Artists at the parties in the early and mid-eighties were a rare sight and the art world itself was very small. Lucian Freud came to a book party for Lord Lambton and literally jumped in fright when I photographed him. Andy Warhol's opening at the D'Offay Gallery was a disappointment. Warhol's sidekick Fred Hughes was very funny and interesting but all Warhol did was sit down and sign books.

In the late eighties and on into the nineties, behind the scenes Anthony Fawcett – aka Tony Tap - helped revitalise the struggling London art scene. He had the brilliant idea of persuading Becks to provide free beer for openings and then somehow made a living for himself as a kind of art sponsorship consultant. Suddenly there was free booze for openings and small struggling galleries seemed to be popping up everywhere.

Frustratingly each year I was invited to parties and openings at the Miami Basel art fair, but magazines would balk at the cost of an air ticket and hotel. Finally In 2008 I was transported there courtesy of an Italian fashion company. The luxury brands companies

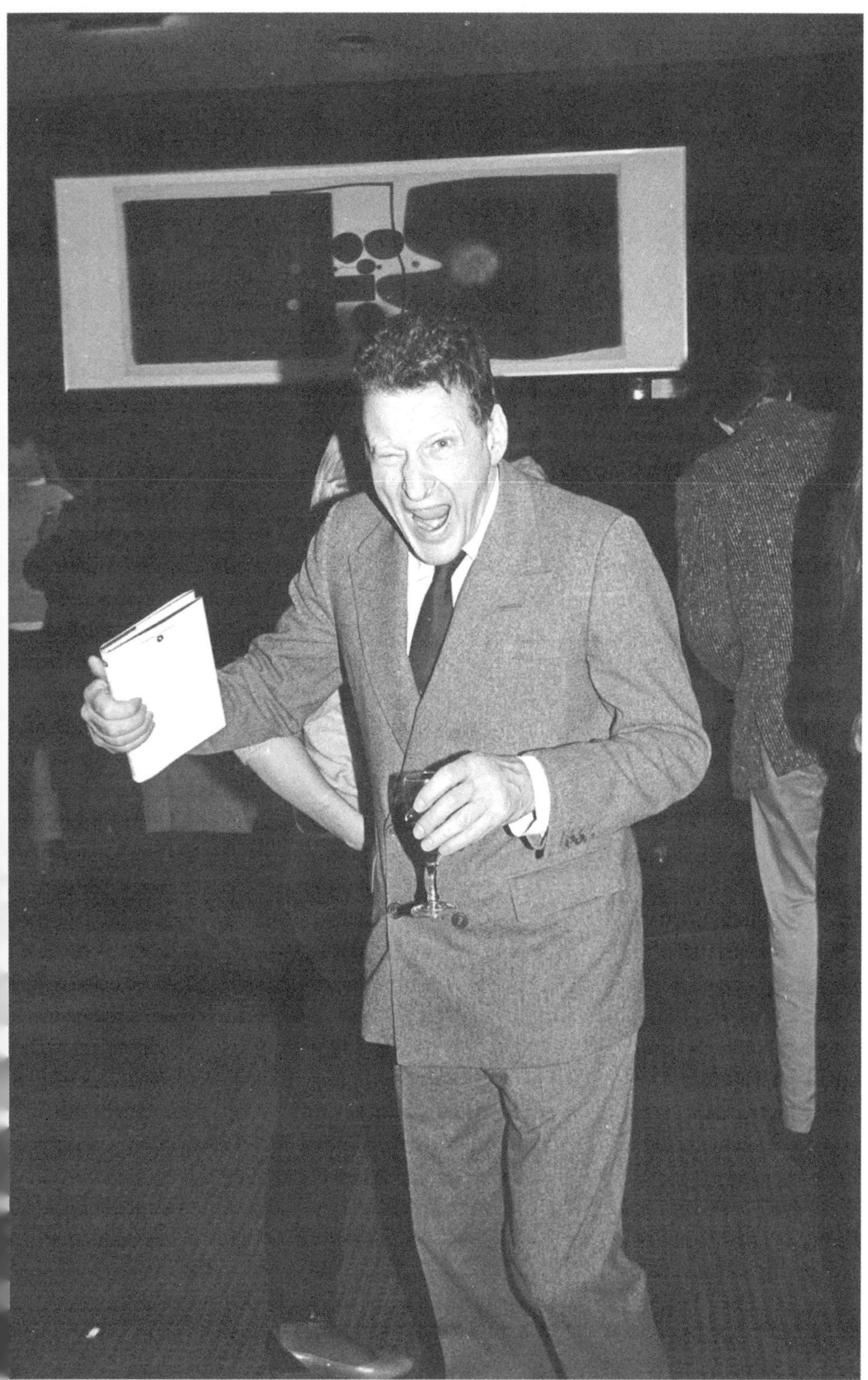

Lucain Freud genuinely shocked at Lord Anthony Lambton's book party, 1983 © Dafydd Jones

had invaded en masse yet in my hotel room the recession was spilling out of every TV network. America seemed right on the edge but the parties carried on regardless.

Twenty years ago companies such as Hermès and Cartier were sponsoring polo games: for the last three years the Halcyon Gallery has sponsored a polo match at Cirencester. Halcyon actually exhibits and sells work right off the polo match marquee's walls - this year there was even a Degas for sale and the gallery's clients were introduced to HRH Prince William.

But the benefit of sponsorship has been that for the last ten years or so it's been possible for artists living on the breadline to go out every night, look at work, and - let's be honest - eat and drink for free. We still all live off the canapés and the after show dinners, even if we don't need to. And the canapés are now good canapés, no more mushroom vol-au-vents or cheese & pineapple on sticks, and they're often made by the rash of really good art world restaurateurs like Mark Hix or Margot Henderson.

In the early nineties Vanity Fair magazine hosted a fundraiser at the Serpentine with the Princess of Wales as the guest of honour. Rubbing shoulders with the aristocrats, actors, writers and pop stars was a small group of artists including Damien Hirst, Jane and Louise Wilson and Jay Jopling snogging with Annabel Neilson. Their table seemed to be having the most fun. Unlike most of the room they were not fazed by the presence of the Princess. That's because the art world (particularly the British one) knows how to party and is essentially democratic. People from all backgrounds hold equal status in the art world, as long as they are making interesting work.

The mixture of suits, Russian collectors, socialites, starving artists, newly rich artists, the hangers on, the models, like-minded journalists and some unknowns makes for the best art parties. That formula has worked for the last 15 years now, but often magazine or newspaper editors seem to be fixated on the wrong things. They only want to know which celebrities buy art work and which celebrities go to the openings, and most are not confident enough to send photographers out to find new subjects. That's why I remain freelance. If editors want to wait until there's a loud crescendo of noise, so be it, but I don't have the time.

After seeing Damien Hirst arriving by helicopter to the bi-annual country house art party at Sudeley castle in Gloucestershire I now think that the new establishment is so entrenched it really has turned into the old one.

I've begun to wonder whether it's really necessary for artists to spend their time going to parties at up-market luxury goods stores. The recent Louis Vuitton party had more artists present than at any art exhibition I've been to. Are promotional parties like this a distraction? Does it make them money and bring in commissions? How does everyone keep up?

Hedonism if you have too much of it is hard work. Tracey Emin was defensive recently when I greeted her with a comment that she'd been at every party I'd been to that week. She told me that I only saw one side of her and that she would be working all of the next week in her studio in the south of France.

I began doing panoramic stitched-together pictures for magazines a few years ago to try and cram in more of the madness and variety going on. Artists seemed to be under more and more pressure to produce. Back-room, cordoned off areas started to appear at art parties, where no photographers were allowed. I wonder if the pressure to make work went hand in hand with a ratcheting up of cocaine casualties. So many of the bigger artists are now off the drugs, some are even off the booze.

At one party at Tramp, the Hauser and 'Wirth a Lot'- (someone joked) Gallery forgot to remind a member of staff to put a limit on the bar bill, and everyone stayed and drank…and drank until the bill came in at over £60,000. At the close of the Serpentine Summer Party a few years back, the Champagne company's French PR found it almost impossible to accept the amount of champagne actually drunk. "But did they actually drink that much? Its more than two and a half bottles a head.." she said, white as a sheet.

Perhaps she'd never heard about London's noble and feisty group of art-party gate-crashers who enjoy nothing more than slipping in and helping themselves to the bubbly. They warrant a whole story on their own.

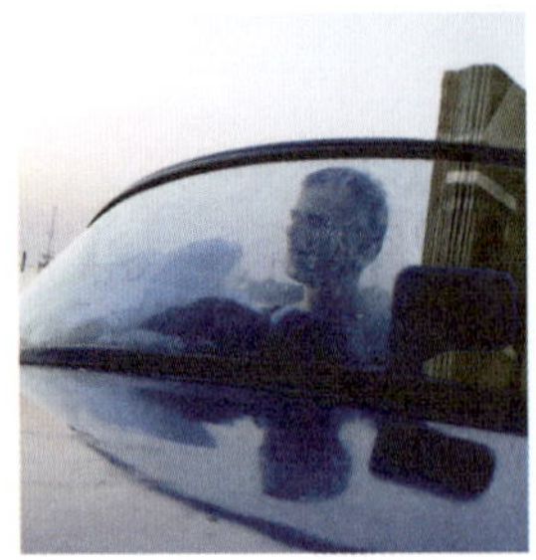

The Former Fantastical Far East

by Gigi Giannuzzi

Gigi Giannuzzi is the founder and co-director of Trolley Books and Trolley Gallery. A book like this just wouldn't really be complete without him.

IT WAS THE BEGINNING of the new millennium and little did I know, after a few years spent in Venice, how I would make my decision to come back to London - where I had first landed in 1986 - and where this would actually take me.

Money as usual was an issue, it was difficult to imagine how to face such an important relocation, moving a publishing company and over 100 boxes of books, amongst the rest of the typical human detritus, from Venice to London. But nothing could have stopped me and Ruby, my assistant of the time, from reaching what we felt was a vital move. We had to get out of the lagoon and come back to London Town.

I knew London quite well by then, having mainly lived in the Ladbroke Grove area until 1992, but since 1997 I had started spending more and more time in the Eastend, and I totally melted into the great artistic community active in the area.

Although showing mild signs of the end of an era, the atmosphere was still ebullient, the sense of community tangible, life in the street real compared to the rarefied air of the West. And most important of all, a community of artists could still find in these destitute lands proper spaces at very good rates. Large warehouses would be available for the brave, given under fair conditions, and they would be transformed into magic environments for living, working and partying. Volcanic egos would take over immense spaces and transform them into artworks in their own right.

One of these magic spaces had been created in Hackney Wick by AL and PF, at the crossroads of two canals running through post-apocalyptic landscapes of burnt down houses, abandoned industrial complexes and the constant noise of the scrap metal being worked.

PF, as an insatiable little devil, would run across the perfectly ordered 10,000 square feet, popping out from the "music studio" and running into the courtyard to service one of the beloved mutoid vehicles of his "historic" collection. A regal toilette built by his hands would take a good proportion of the total surface, radiating the necessary peace and harmony that such an important place should carry.

White Post Lane became rapidly synonymous with the promise of a new "Far East" of London, a land of fascination and conquest of which PF was the undisputable prince, a multi-faceted artist with the enthusiasm of a kid with his favourite games, totally immersed in his art/music/physics researches and using all the elements he had to hand in the Wild East.

I cannot forget the trip on his boat for half a day up the canals, departing from his "base camp" to visit an electric power station, getting as close as we could to the grids to better hear and feel the noise of the electric power.

Another environment that became very important and a real point of reference in those first years of my new life in London was a more urban warehouse called Universal House, at the bottom of Brick Lane.

A group of artists had established themselves on the large top floor and had embraced me as part of the family. Among them Philippe Bradshaw, a dear friend and talented artist, who I would also like to remember in these lines, considering that in this year, on the 25th of August, falls the fifth anniversary of his death.

Entering the "boys" part of the sixth floor of Universal House was like entering a magical and sexy tropical forest where Philippe would hang from the ceiling his lianas - his colourful metal tapestries, the anodized aluminium curtains that he would constantly create, projecting onto the walls all sort of images (mostly porn), with the cement of the ceiling reduced to Gruyère cheese and the space surrounded by an all-encompassing glitter and glow.

Philippe was the portrait of excess, and mainly in a good way. He was hyper active, hyper reactive, hyper sensitive, hyper loving, hyper creative, hyper caring, hyper every-thing. His "mad" way eventually brought him in a collision route with somebody, but those who knew him could not avoid loving him to the bone.

Against all odds the publishing company would be established in the UK on the 21 September 2001, ten days after 9/11, and moved to a narrow office shared with our saint designers, M&W, in a classic Hackney warehouse in Long Street. It faced the sunset and an old railway line that would become an enormous suspended garden, exploding every spring in front of our eyes.

Later in 2003 we moved to a gallery space in Shoreditch, that had recently vacated by Modern Art (Staurt Shave's Gallery). I arrived to speak to the landlord with the invitation to our first show already printed, and I could finally begin with my partner Hannah to start contributing something to this community, trying to give back what had been given to me in the first place, inevitably working hard and playing hard.

After eight years of life in the Eastend as contributors, we are still waiting to see where that decision will take us, but possibly out of an Eastend which has been gentrified and deprived of the character that made its history so rich and intense. Not even a quote by Joe Strummer stuck on the top of our door for so many years has managed to defuse a predictable destiny:

"Greed, it ain't going anywhere".

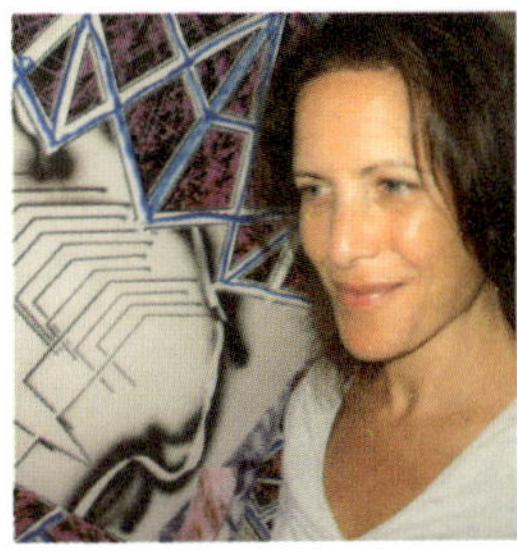

Round the Clock PR

by Theresa Simon

Theresa Simon has been running her own PR agency for art, architecture and design clients since the dawn of the 21st century.

CRACK OF DAWN. (VENICE Biennale, June 2009). Speed walking the for-once deserted streets to get to La Maddalena. I'm just in time for the sombre call of the conch shell. The Haka performers have got there before me. They do dawn on a regular basis, to catch the first rays and turn them into the stuff of blessings. Here comes the German TV crew and that slightly obscure Belgian freelancer – can't believe they've actually shown up - and the performers launch into their confusingly war-like prayer for the success of the New Zealand pavilion. Shutters around us are thrown open as locals get the Maori wake-up call. I see an old lady holding a telephone receiver out the window in Italian: "No, honest, listen. Yes, it's outside the church. They're all virtually naked." Then they're off, this hefty troupe of tattooed dancers, jogging in formation towards Piazza San Marco. And I'm trying to get ahead of them to line up the BBC cameraman and chat up Rai Tre – can we get it on Rai Uno too?

10am. (Hampstead, London, January 2008). Frozen in Phillip King's studio. He's showing us work for his imminent new exhibition at Bernard Jacobson Gallery. There's a huge bit of metal outside, a kind of blue doorway with a sunny yellow edge to it, a cone and a rhomboid leaning up inside it. That rhomboid is black and a bit formidable. It's sort of edging its way into the foreground, overshadowing the cone, literally casting shadow on it. "I think you might just have made that too big to get into the gallery, Phillip", we laugh, nervously. Inside there is more geometry, hewn into blocks of plaster, some coloured-in, flat and bold. "And then, to go with all of this furniture I've been making, I need some things to complete the 'room set' I'm constructing", he says. "There'll be a lamp and a clock. I haven't really started on the clock yet, but it will be a bit like this …" and he tugs a scrap of thick paper that's lying wedged under some paint tins and starts to rough out the clock in pencil. And I am standing there thinking: 'This is it. I'm watching one of the great sculptors of our time conceptualise and draw a work.' Wonder. Gratitude. Will he get it finished on time?

2pm. (Bloomsbury, London, February, 2010). Only twelve minutes on my bike, weaving through Goodge Street traffic on this eye piercingly sky-blue day, to the back entrance of the British Museum. There's a polite librarian in classic library brown who asks us to sign the ledger and then we're through, into the hushed space of the Prints and Drawings study room. Barrel vault ceiling and wall-to-wall mahogany shelving and plan chests; this is one of the most important print collections in the world. It's staggering. Antony Griffiths, the Keeper of the collection for the last 34 years, comes to meet us. We're here to wrangle a story out of him for the London Original Print Fair. But we don't need to wrangle in the end; the story is Antony himself. He is captivating. I am evangelical about him and prints. I'm going to get him onto Front Row and Night Waves to talk about this rabbit, for instance, a 16th century drawing, its trembling body caught so delicately on this parchment that you can feel its whiskers quivering. And you'd never guess it's the equivalent of a dartboard, an early target practice.

Warm summer's evening. (Frankfurt, 2007). Standing in a (small) throng of expectant fans at the launch party for the Frankfurt Fine Art Fair. A bohemian club, all velvet drapes and 80s metal banisters. Waiters in white tux with trays of little tiny things to eat and drink. But we're not interested in those. We're all craning our necks upwards to a dimly lit balcony, waiting for the spotlights to go on. Waiting for Grace Jones to appear. Could it be that the journalists I dragged along on this press trip have really come for her, and not so much for the reinvigorated Fair, with its theme of the sculptural form? Grace ends up singing a capella, because her backing track doesn't work, or doesn't arrive. But it really doesn't matter. In fact, it's better. She is transcendentally great. That deep voice resonates out from the balcony, confident, mellow and rich. The (small, VIP) crowd go wild.

7.30pm. (London, October 2009). Frieze time. Cold night. Client's exhibition opening, just down the road from the auspicious tent entrance. Crush of people trying to get to the cocktails. Then, from nowhere, burly men break up the throng: "Clear the room please, ladies and gents. Gas leak! Just take your glasses with you and leave the building as quickly and calmly as you can." Look of horror on client's face as, not only does his private view comes to a crashing halt, but he loses all his deposit on the hired glasses. Now Marylebone is full of disenchanted private view-goers and not a cab in sight. Until, that is, one draws up to deposit someone at the now non-event. My friend runs for it and beckons me to join her – "We're on." And it's only Tracey Emin in the back of the cab. "What am I going to do now?", she whines. "It's only quarter to eight and I'm not due at Jay's [Jopling] 'til 9 and I haven't got any cash on me and nowhere to go …" "Come with us!" I say, nervously. "We'll go to another private view and, if it's not very nice, we can all have a lovely drink at Claridge's." This seems to work. And the accolades I get for bringing Tracey to the gallery run and run.

10pm. Back home. Wishing there was an email from that journalist I've been chasing, as politely as possible, for months now. Nope. But there is an invitation to a dawn Haka at the British Museum to bless the new Oceania exhibits case ….

An East End Guide to Art

by Laura K Jones

Laura K Jones is a writer who happens to live in the East End of London but sometimes goes out in the West End of London. She is also, er, me.

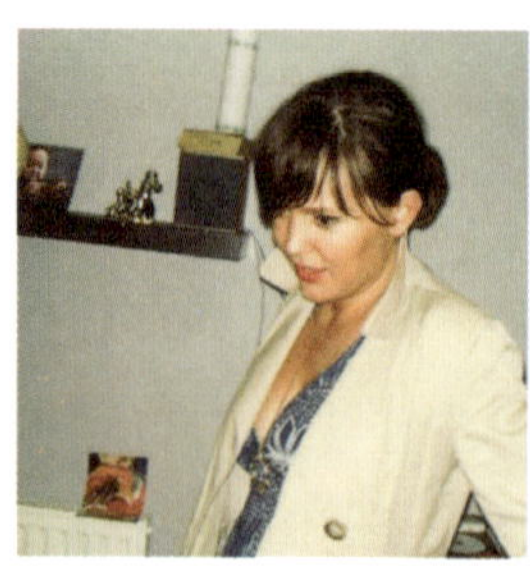

THE WEST END HAS the Groucho, but one can easily tire of that playpen, and the days of Damien Hirst and Keith Allen's wild parties under the snooker tables are long gone anyway. The artists' alternative second living-room, the Colony Room, has checked out too, no longer able to support itself. To hammer this point home perhaps, Michael Wojas - its much loved chess-playing proprietor – just popped his clogs aswell, his corpse taking a last sardonic journey to its burning place at the Kensal Green Cemetery, not only inside a fish and chip van, but also inside a cardboard coffin made for him by YBA Sarah Lucas. Gawd rest his soul.

Galleries 'up West' have been flourishing of late. Eastcastle Street north of Oxford Street is picking up somewhat, especially with the injection of heavyweights like Stuart Shave's Modern Art. But the greater part of your true art rough and tumble still lies east.

So, having decided to fill your horrible little East End boots with modern art and all that is ensnared in its orbit, should you go to the place where it all began? – well, where it all began in Hoxton, at least. Some might say avoid Jay Jopling's White Cube Gallery – they'll point out that it's all too über, too damn glitzy. But you can still catch a good show there if you're lucky. Its presence has certainly generated interest and money. Now Hoxton Square alone plays host to Kenny Schachter's Rove Gallery, and the 20 Hoxton Square Projects lot too. The always interesting Seventeen Gallery, Carl Freedman's Counter Editions, and a rash of other distinctive galleries nearby - provide a welcome antidote to the mercantile leanings of their mighty Hoxton Square foil.

Don't forget the cobbled East End charm of Vyner Street, a bit further east though. There's a dozen galleries on that short street. From the black spaceship that is Wilkinson

Gallery, a heavy-hitter that has bouncers on the door - (really, it does) - to the more low-key Ibid Projects, you can't really go wrong. Do not forget to swoop round the corner to the Approach Gallery (in The Approach pub on Approach Road), for a great stable of painters, or to the Hotel Gallery on Greenfield Road, and to Maureen Paley Interim Arts and Herald St. Gallery both on Herald Street.

You might even spot Keanu Reeves, Mario Testino or Spiderman, (well, Toby Maguire anyway), flâneuring about. They are often to be seen weighing up a possible new purchase, especially around Frieze time in October.

When your mid-morning growls of hunger can be heard back in Hoxton Square, pick your way across the cobblestones towards Wadeson Street and the Bistrotheque restaurant. You'll always find a piano player, a band of lip-synchers, a cabaret, some famous artists or a good brunch there. You could actually find all of the above, at one sitting - it has been known. Bistrotheque feels more like a venue in grainy but glamorous early 90s New York, than any other place in London. If the Bistrotheque's too fly for your tastes, take aim at the Rochelle School Canteen on Arnold Circus. Margot Henderson's menu never fails to impress. She is also the only person in the art world over 25 - except for your author, Dear Reader - that can still do the splits. Well, you have to have a party piece, or things get boring.

Margot's husband, the legendary chef Fergus Henderson, will feed you posh offal at the original St John restaurant in Clerkenwell, or at his other gaff, St John Bread and Wine in Spitalfields. While you're there you may as well pop in to Tracey Emin's local The Golden Heart on Commerical Street, if only for the eccentric conversation you are guaranteed to have with the incomparable landlady Sandra Esqulant.

Back down to Old Street, the discerning flâneur can secure a short back and sides at the art world's favourite barbershop, Murdock.

The very antithesis of Blockbusters – The Film Shop on Broadway Market in London Fields - is a place where you can chew the fat with other artists and rent out any arthouse film on earth.

Seize the opportunity then for an early dinner up the road at the favourite eatery of Sarah Lucas and pals. Huong Viet's summer rolls will make you weep with gratitude; the building on Englefield Road is also the old community centre for the Vietnamese boat people that came to London in the seventies.

To sustain the historical angle, you'd be silly not to drop in on William Blake's grave in the graceful and verdant cemetery that is Bunhill Fields, just south of Old Street round-about. Spookier at night of course.

All of Hoxton bohemia (including, sometimes, the winsome, willowy Wolfgang Tillmans) will then be found at the decidedly theatrical George and Dragon pub, or its neighbour, the quite extraordinarily seedy Joiner's Arms. Here, you can find the occasional piece of ultra-strange performance art by underground performers e.g. Racky La Rue.

If you have hollow legs, a desire to look at more art luminaries, and a friend who's a member, you might as well then advance with gay abandon down the High Street to the private members' club Shoreditch House for a martini and a swim in its sixth-floor rooftop pool.

Beware heartburn and too much soft soap.

How to finish? A nightcap at the Bethnal Green Working Men's Club? A salt beef Bagel from Brick Lane? Maybe, yes. It *is* probably time to wend your way home anyway, to get some shut-eye and plan your next night of openings. Actually, scrap that - don't plan a thing: it will all fall into place somehow. Trust your barrow boy instincts. It is the East End after all.

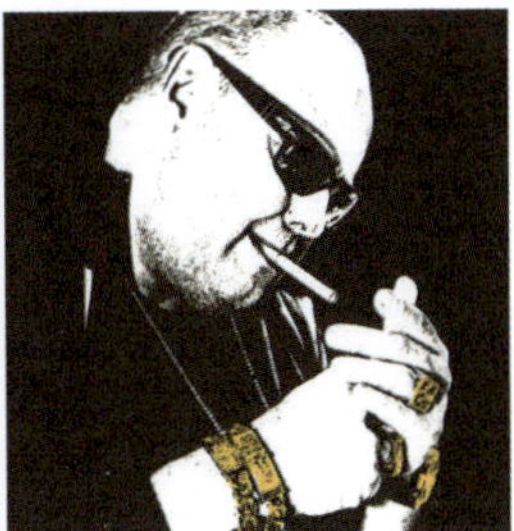
© John Jarasa

It's Because You're Dying

by Patrick Painter

Patrick Painter is an art dealer who runs Patrick Painter Inc. and Patrick Painter Editions. Patrick Painter Inc. was opened in 1997 with the backing and support of Mike Kelley and Paul McCarthy. Patrick lives and works in Los Angeles, California.

(Felix Gonzales-Torres was selected as the United State's official representative at the Venice Biennale in 2007, ten years after his death.)

THIS STORY IS ABOUT the late Felix Gonzalez-Torres, who is someone I have been missing quite a bit lately. When I first got to know Felix he told me that, no matter what job he had, he made sure to have health insurance. As it turned out, boy did he ever need it.

When I began to get to know him, my first impression was, "Man, this guy has got some kind of bullshit going on." It wasn't until about the third time that we spoke that I realised, "Man, this dude is real." He is the only guy I have known from my entire adult life that could make you feel like a boy in the schoolyard with no problems, no wars, no taxes – just nice goofy conversation.

When we worked together on an edition, he sent me his drawn instructions by fax. The instructions said the piece was to have two 16" silver rings touch at a single point. The touching rings were intended to act as a metaphor for two people in a relationship.

I said to him, "So you want me to make two silver rings?"

And he said, "Yeah, it's the only permanent sculpture I've ever made. They can stop making the paper from my stacks, the light bulbs from my lights, or the batteries for my clocks, but these will always remain."

I asked, "Can you clean the rings, or do you want them to be untouched?" because I knew they would tarnish over time, and he said, "Sure."

I then asked, "Can you clean just one ring, and not the other?"

And he replied, "Man, that would be horrible."

It took some time before they started to sell, but once they did I would make regular calls to give him reports on sales. At the time, it was getting towards the end of his life, and I would sometimes have to talk to him over his answering machine for ten minutes before he could pick up the phone. But when he did answer, you would hear his sickly yet brave voice on the other end.

I would ask him, "Should I be calling you about this business shit? I feel bad about making these calls."

He would assure me, "Man, are you kidding me, it's the only thing keeping me going."

One time he asked me, "Why are these things starting to sell?"

I responded, "Do you really want to know, bro?"

And he said, "Yeah, I really do."

I told him, "It's because people say you're dying."

I heard him start to laugh in that schoolyard boy way that I came to love so much. It was this jovial spirit that would get me to call him whenever I felt overly business-ed out, and felt like I needed to get real again. Once his laughter died down a bit, he said, "Well, in that case, maybe we should make some Happy Face Urns."

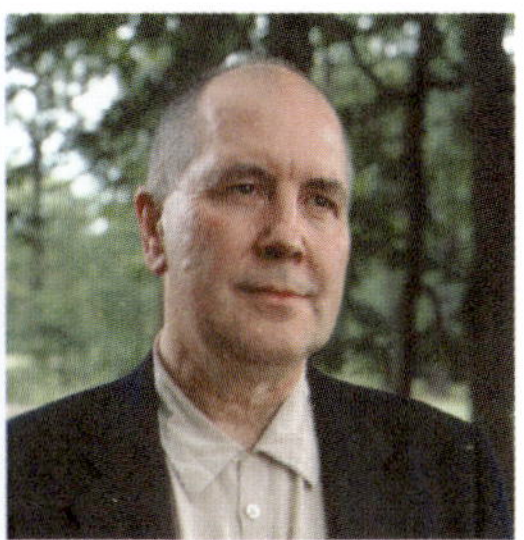

© Thomas Florschuetz

Trading in the Sauce for the Sausage

by Mark Gisbourne

Former President of the British Association of Arts Critics (AICA), and an International Vice President, Mark Gisbourne co-organised the World Congress of Art Critics at Tate Modern in 2000. A post-graduate lecturer at the Slade School of Fine Art, and at Sotheby's Institute, he chose to leave London for Berlin in 2003, where he writes and curates international art exhibitions. His next is the second part of a diptych entitled ROHKUNSTBAU XVII Atlantis: Hidden Histories - Imagined Identities. Mr Gisbourne originally qualified as an art historian at the Courtauld Institute, after earlier lives as a copper, civil servant, carpetbagger, and monk.

MAKING A COMPARISON BETWEEN two of Europe's leading contemporary art cities is a bit like choosing between different fruits in a fruit basket. It all depends on what you're after – or feel you need – at the time of choosing. In the last thirty years I have lived and worked as a teacher, art critic and writer, both in London and Berlin, moving to the latter seven years ago. Why I have come to prefer living in Berlin is tied to what London has become, and yet more importantly what I feel Berlin is becoming. In a certain sense it is to do with choosing economies, and by that I do not mean economics in a directly commercial sense. I mean rather the daily economies of life, be they social, cultural and/or libidinal.

Certainly in terms of material economics (Berlin is technically bankrupt – the city's Mayor Klaus Wowereit once even delighted in calling his city "poor but sexy") - the two cities bear no wealth comparison. But Berlin presents a precious commodity that has become all but lacking in London; namely the time needed to develop ideas, make mistakes, and avoid the disastrous way contemporary culture has become voraciously consumed. In this way the free availability of time and space has become an increasingly valuable asset to both myself and many artists.

As for contemporary art, while London and Berlin share obvious international affinities, reactions and engagements are not so lifestyle mediated in Berlin. There are less of the 'false frenetic' twitterings of pop stars and hangers-on, who approximate themselves to the art world in London. There is still a sense that art has some expression or message built into its production and presentation, and it is not buried in media and marketing to anything like the same extent as the London scene.

While there is always an aspect of hype – the ubiquitous canker of the current age – it does not travel far or penetrate very deeply here in Berlin. Also, thankfully, bouncers do not guard the doors to pseudo-trendy openings, as has become the case in London. Indeed, in the recent Damien Hirst/Michael Joo exhibition in Berlin people stood around in amazement wondering at the purpose of the grey-suited 'blokes' standing guard at the entrances.

In terms of practice, and given the fact that so many international artists either live in or keep studios in Berlin, there are obvious shared platforms and coalescences of direction. However, as always in Berlin there is always an inclination towards the political, and less towards those issues of personal confessions and the marketing of the personal ego that seemed to have beset British art of the last twenty years.

Fortunately, perhaps, there is no tradition of 'panto' in Berlin, something that many yBa ideas of transgression have to my mind always tended to depend upon. The theatrically naughty 'bad boy' or 'girl' has little leverage here. This said, Berlin lacks the rich ethnic plurality, such as is found in London, and this is a particular weakness in the city. But in shows that deal with 'heimat' (homeland), as in the Neue Heimat exhibition a couple of years ago, sixty per cent were international artists, and of the remaining dozen or so Germans ten of them came from other parts of the country. Berlin is in the midst of a process, (remember that it has 4.3 million less inhabitants), and this energising process creates a feeling of a city passing through self-reflecting stages of re-making. Certain edgy uncertainties between the East and West of the city still persist just under the surface.

Much is made of that fact that it is cheaper to live in Berlin for artists, but that has become a self fulfilling cliché that no longer has any legs. There are other cities in Europe where it would be cheaper to live than in Berlin. The ability to have space and time is foremost; allied to that, young artists live, work, and have studios almost everywhere in the city, and they have not been pushed to the periphery as is the case in London. Arguments pertain as to a lack of collectors in Berlin, though that is changing.

Given the status of the highly successful recent "Gallery Weekends", and of the Berlin Biennial, the city is continually in a state of visitation.

The U-Bahn and S Bahn transport system (twenty-four hours a day at the weekend), means that there is rapid access to all parts of the city. I remember well in London the failed attempts to see South London events and East End openings in the same evening. This feeds directly into what is the social fabric, and that in turn leads to an open cultural facilitation in the city.

To speak of consumer economies is also to speak of human desire, and at the level of our heterosexual and homosexual natures, even these coteries of special tastes are framed and organised in more practically evaluated ways. One notices immediately that libidinal mores in Berlin are extended and inclusive, with clubs for 'mares' and 'stallions', dark rooms, and a general domestication of what some might call elsewhere deviance. Indeed, paradoxically, notions of perversion are quite polite and well organised in Berlin, with informal beginner, intermediate, and advanced classes in S & M, and the development of sexual role play. But while this might eventually sap the libidinal frisson, it has none of the Anglo-Saxon sense of superiority and moral humbug familiarly attached to it. But speaking personally, more, perhaps, than anything else, it is the release from a pervading residual sense of Dickensian moralising, that I have been most pleased to leave behind.

Transports of Delight: A Guide to the Highs and Lows of Art Shipping

by Matthew Bown

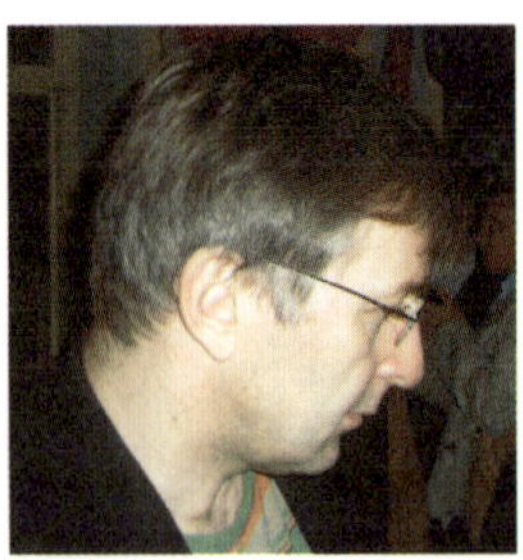

Matthew Bown lives in London and runs what he refers to as a "Skype Gallery" in Berlin. Occasionally he makes it over there on Easyjet and re-introduces himself to his staff. During what Londoners used to term the "kipper season", i.e. the month of August, he likes to hang out on street corners in Moscow with a camera and wearing a pair of running shoes. In fact he has a whole concordance of books about Russian art to his name, (which used to be Matthew Cullerne Bown) all out of print and now for some reason so expensive he can't afford to buy them.

SOMEWHERE OUT IN WEST LONDON there's a kind of graveyard, it's the place where all the art packing-cases go to when they're no longer wanted. If you're looking for a cheap but sturdy, large and unbelievably heavy plywood box, for whatever purpose, that's your first port of call. Don't forget to take four strong men with you to load it into the back of the transit.

They do come in handy. Once upon a time my business involved shipping large quantities of Soviet Socialist Realism from various points in the USSR to London, usually by truck. That was before Russia threw off the Communist shackles and woke up to its own heritage, at which point the same art began to be shipped back again for ten times the price. My paintings were packed into haphazard crates – let's call them "lash-ups" – that would be the laughing stock of the professional art-shippers you might use today. But crates they were, and thank God for that. One day I received the kind of phone call that I imagine all art dealers dread: "Hello, Mr Bown. I'm sorry to inform you that the van carrying your paintings caught fire just as it was entering our depot. We've put the fire out, but the boxes are looking pretty black. And wet." There was of course no such thing as insurance for moving art from Moscow to London by SovTransAvto in 1988. The boxes were indeed black, and sodden, but the paintings inside were, without exception, intact and salvageable with only minor restoration work. I was as pleased as… as… well, as the

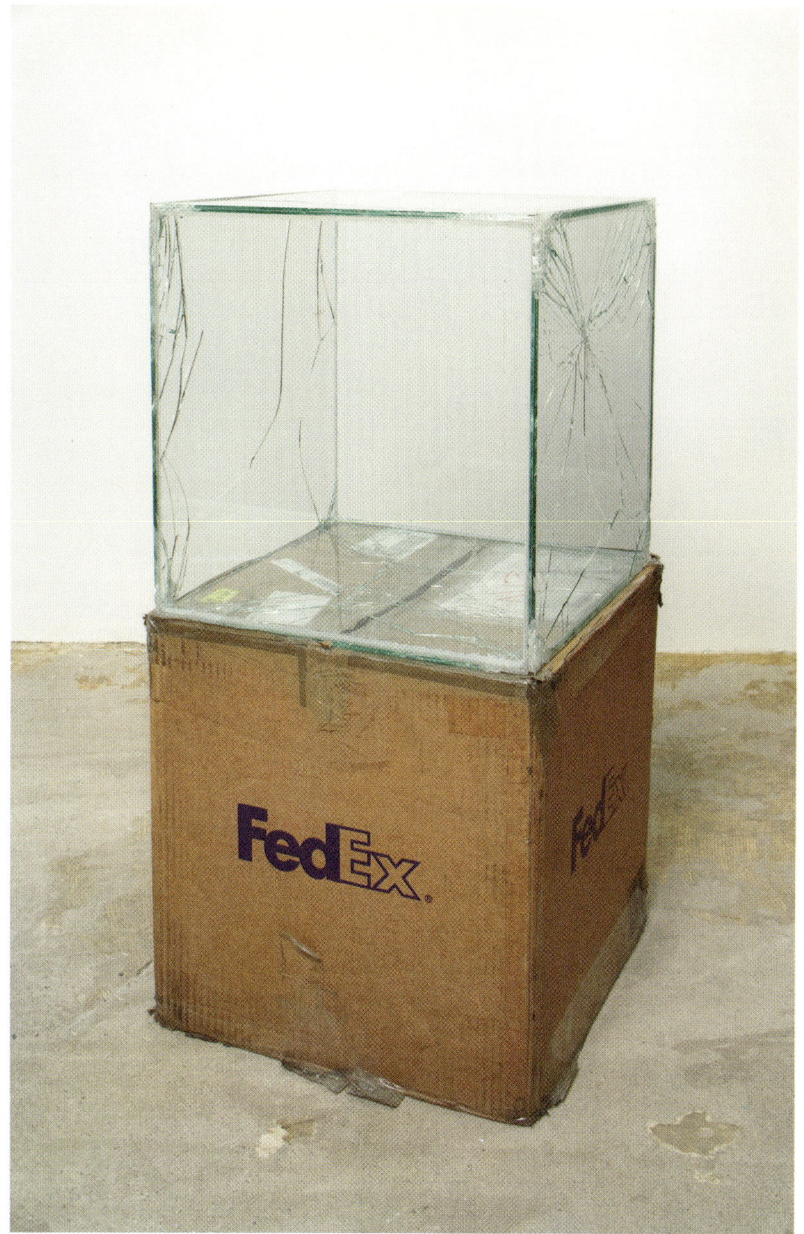

Walead Beshty
FedEx® Kraft Box ©2005 FEDEX 330504, Priority Overnight, Los Angeles-Miami trk#865344981314 October 29-30, 2008, Priority Overnight, Miami-Los Angeles trk#861049125089 November 17-18, 2008, Priority Overnight, Los Angeles-Miami trk#860147611241, December 1-2, 2008, Priority Overnight, Miami-Los Angeles trk#867525901310, December 8-9, 2008, Priority Overnight, Los Angeles-Ann Arbor trk#867525901228, March 9-10, 2009, Standard Overnight, Ann Arbor-Los Angeles trk#868274625705, June 9-10, 2009,
Laminated glass, silicone, metal, FedEx shipping box, packing tape, and accrued FedEx tracking labels
16 x 16 x 16 inches
2008-
Copyright of Walead Beshty, courtesy of the Thomas Dane Gallery, London

monks of Palermo after the painting they commissioned from Raphael was lost at sea but then miraculously floated into port, in its crate, undamaged. At least, that's what the first art historian, Giorgio Vasari, tells us.

Talking of the professional shippers of today, you wonder how to put it to your clients that you are using a firm called Hedley's Humpers. They have an excuse: the firm started out, back in the seventies, by carting equipment around for rock bands: I guess humping was the order of the day. And night.

But of course the most basic form of transport is under your arm. Through customs, onto the plane; then you cajole the stewardesses into stowing your priceless canvas in the safety of their own coat cupboard, a convenient tall narrow slot near the entrance hatch that could have been custom-made for it (don't forget it when you exit the aircraft). Or around town: the secondary art market runs on its runners: these self-employed dealers ferry works to potential clients often with no more packaging than a Waitrose carrier-bag. Items worth, literally, millions of pounds are taken all over the place in black cabs and, I can assure you, they are not insured. Not only are they not insured, they're probably borrowed without any paperwork, on trust. If there's a potential collector in town and he has twenty minutes to see you, there's no time for niceties.

An alternative to under your arm, as I learned when I had a gallery on a first floor walk-up in Savile Row and whiled away the afternoons looking down into the street through the French windows, is in the passenger seat of your open-topped sports car. Just check the barometer before you leave the house.

The under-the-arm method gets a bit hairy sometimes. In 2006 I was transporting a show by the satirical, sarcastical duo Blue Noses from Moscow to London when a Russian customs officer decided to inspect the works. He got a little agitated at what he saw and referred to his superior officers. Eventually, in a scene reminiscent of a spy thriller, I was removed from the plane by men in plain clothes just as it was about to take off, and subsequently questioned for several hours in a small room plastered with posters warning of the evils of bribe-taking. It is still unclear what exactly it was that disturbed the customs men. Was it the image of Putin, Bush and Bin Laden lounging lasciviously on a sofa in their underwear? Was it the suicide bomber with an explosives belt and a mini-skirt which had wafted up Marilyn-style to reveal her black knickers and lacy stocking-tops? Was it religious imagery in the form of a cross parodied in bread and sausage? I don't know, but I was suddenly inundated with calls from people around the world who had read the story as it broke on the New York Times website; it led to brief notoriety for this shrinking violet, who found himself demonised on Russian TV as one of the chief threats to Russian culture.

Artists, of course, are responsive to everything, including the act of transport. Walead Beshty makes cuboids from safety glass that he ships to exhibitions in standard corrugated-card FedEx packing boxes; they arrive with the glass cracked but still intact. The resulting works are objects of great beauty that literally register the movement of the artwork across the globe. The act of transport, if I may call it that, is indeed one of those moments that impress on you the fragility of works of art. In this fragility is something essential: it is an aspect of their being in some sense alive, vital, and so a reflection of ourselves.

So, what should you do if you need to transport a work of art from A to B? The short answer is to employ someone who knows what they're doing. There are ways of stacking paintings in the back of a van, and ways of not stacking them. But it's not always convenient or economical to employ a third party. When I'm moving something myself, I'm a great believer in foamboard: it's very light, rigid, easily cut to size: the perfect stuff to quickly and easily cover the front and back of a picture with. To wrap up, I avoid bubble-wrap unless it's really heavy-duty (that flimsy stuff you get at the Post Office offers just an illusion of protection) and go for good polythene: if you use really thick stuff, the corners will tend to stick out a bit, providing an extra cushion just where it's needed. Prop it up against the partition in a black-cab and enjoy the disconcerting realisation that alone and unarmed you're carrying something worth more than the contents of that Securicor van idling in the traffic jam ahead of you.

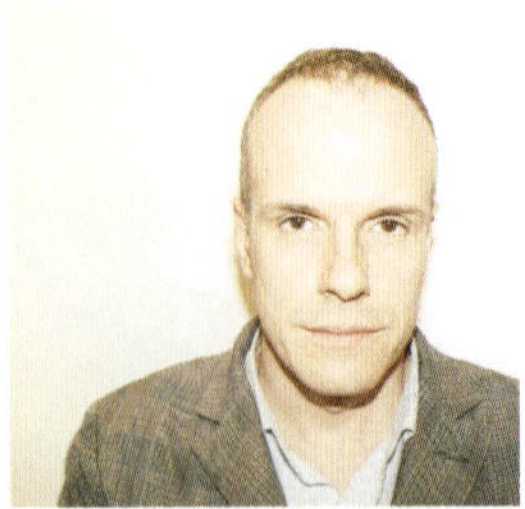

The Mother of All Lists- An Incomplete A-Z of the Internet

by Hans Ulrich Obrist

Hans Ulrich Obrist became Co-director of Exhibitions and Programmes and Director of International Projects at the Serpentine Gallery in 2006. Since 1991, he has curated and co-curated over 200 international exhibitions and biennales. In 2009 he topped Art Review's Power 100 List. Being a great fan of Oulipian lists, this amused him.

A IS FOR AND And
The Internet made me think more BOTH AND instead of EITHER OR instead of NOR NOR

B is for Beginnings

C is for Curating the World
The Internet made me think towards a more expanded notion of curating. Stemming from the Latin word 'curare', the word 'curating' originally meant 'to take care of objects in museums'. Curation has long since evolved. Just as art is no longer limited to traditional genres, curating is no longer confined to the gallery or museum but has expanded across all boundaries. The rather obscure and very specialised notion of curating has become much more publicly used since you hear people talking about curating of websites, and this marks a very good moment to rediscover the pioneering history of art curating as a toolbox for 21st century society at large.

D is for Delinking
In the years before being online, I remember that there were many interruptions by phone and fax day and night. The reality of being permanently linked to the phone triggered my increasing awareness of the importance of moments of concentration – moments without interruption that require me to be completely unreachable. I no longer answer the phone at home and I only answer my mobile phone in the case of fixed telephone appointments. To link is beautiful. To delink is sublime. (Paul Chan)
D is for Disrupted narrative continuity

Forms of film montage, as the disruption of narrative and the disruption of spatial and temporal continuity, have been a staple tactic of the avant-garde from Cubism and Eisenstein, through Brecht to Kluge or Godard. For avant-gardism as a whole, it was essential that these tactics were recognized (experienced) as a disruption. The Internet has made disruption and montage the operative bases of everyday experience. Today, these forms of disruption can be harnessed and poeticised. They can foster new connections, new relationships, new productions of reality: reality as life-montage / life as reality-disruption? Not one story but many stories.........

D is for Doubt

A certain unreliability of technical and material information on the Internet brings us to the notion of doubt. I feel that doubt has become more pervasive. The artist Carsten Höller has invented the Laboratory of Doubt, which is opposed to mere representation. As he has told me, "Doubt and perplexity ... are unsightly states of mind we'd rather keep under lock and key because we associate them with uneasiness, with a failure of values." Höller's credo is not to do; not to intervene. To exist is to do and not to do is a way of doing. "Doubt is alive; it paralyses certainty," says Carsten.

E is for Evolutive exhibitions

The Internet makes me think more about non-final exhibitions and exhibitions in a state of becoming. When conceiving exhibitions, I sometimes like to think of randomised algorithms, access, transmission, mutation, infiltration and circulation (the list goes on). The Internet makes me think less of exhibitions as top down master-plans but bottom up processes of self organisation like Do It or Cities on the Move.

F is for Forgetting

The ever growing, ever pervasive records that the Internet produces make me think sometimes about the virtues of forgetting. Is a limited life space of certain information and data becoming more urgent?

H is for Handwriting (and Drawing ever Drawing)

The Internet has made me aware of the importance of handwriting and drawing. Personally, I typed all my early texts, but the more the Internet has become all-encompassing, the more I have felt that something went missing. Hence the idea to reintroduce handwriting. I do more and more of my correspondence as handwritten letters scanned and sent by email. On a professional note, I observe, as a curator, the importance of drawing in current art production. One can also see it in art schools: a moment when drawing is an incredibly fertile zone.

I is for Identity
"Identity is shifty, identity is a choice." (Etel Adnan)

I is for Inactual considerations
The future is always built out of fragments of the past. The Internet has brought thinking more into the present tense, raising questions of what it means to be contemporary. Recently, Giorgio Agamben revisited Nietzsche's Inactual Considerations, arguing that the one who belongs to his or her own time is the one who does not coincide perfectly with it. It is because of this shift, this anachronism, that he or she is more apt than others to perceive and to catch his or her time. Agamben follows this observation with his second definition of contemporaneity: the contemporary is the one who is able to perceive obscurity, who is not blinded by the lights of his or her time or century. This leads us, interestingly enough, to the importance of astrophysics in explaining the relevance of obscurity for contemporaneity. The seeming obscurity in the sky is the light that travels to us at full speed but which can't reach us because the galaxies from which it originates are ceaselessly moving away from us at a speed superior to that of light. The Internet and a certain resistance to its present tense have made me increasingly aware that there is an urgent call to be contemporary. To be contemporary means to perpetually come back to a present where we have never yet been. To be contemporary means to resist the homogenisation of time, through ruptures and discontinuities.

I is for Internet
In terms of my curatorial thinking, my 'Eureka moments' occurred pre-Internet, when I met visionary Swiss artists Fischli/Weiss in 1985. These conversations freed me up – freed my thoughts as to what curating could be and how curating can produce reality.

The arrival of the Internet was a trigger for me to think more in the form of Oulipian lists – practical-poetical, evolutive and often nonlinear, lists. This A to Z is an incomplete list. …. Umberto Eco calls the World Wide Web the 'mother of all lists': infinite by definition and in constant evolution.

M is for Maps
The Internet increased the presence of maps in my thinking. It's become easier to make maps, to change them, and also to work on them collaboratively and collectively and share them (e.g. Google Maps and Google Earth). After the focus on social networks of the last couple of years, I have come to see the focus on location as a key dimension.
N is for New geographies

The Internet has fuelled (and been fuelled by) a relentless economic and cultural globalisation, with all its positive and negative aspects. On the one hand, there is the danger of homogenising forces, which is also at stake in the world of the arts. On the other hand, there are unprecedented possibilities for difference enhancing global dialogues. In the long view there have been seismic shifts, like that in the 16th century when the paradigm shifted from the Mediterranean to the Atlantic. We are living through a period in which the centre of gravity is transferring to new centres. The early 21st century is seeing the growth of a polyphony of art centres in the East and West in the North and South.

N is for Non-mediated experiences   N is for the New Live
I feel an increased desire for non-mediated experiences. Depending on one's point of view, the virtual may be a new and liberating prosthesis of the body or it may threaten the body. Many visual artists today negotiate and mediate between these two staging encounters of non-mediated intersubjectivity. In the music fields, the crisis of the record industry goes hand in hand with an increased importance of live concerts.

P is for Parallel realities
The Internet creates and fosters new constituencies; new micro-communities. As a system that infinitely breeds new realities, it is predisposed to reproduce itself in a proliferating series of ever more functionally differentiated subsystems. As such, it makes my thinking go towards the production of parallel realities, bearing witness to the multiverse, as the physicist David Deutsch might say, and for better or worse, the Internet allows that which is already latent in the fabric of reality to unravel itself and expand in all directions.

P is for Protest against forgetting
Over the last few years I feel an increasing urgency to more and more interviews, to make an effort to preserve traces of intelligence from the last decades. One particularly urgent part of this is the testimonies of the 20th century pioneers who are in their 80s or 90s or older and whom I regularly interview, testimonies of a century from those who are not online and who very often fall into oblivion. This protest might, as Rem Koolhaas has told me, act as "a hedge against the systematic forgetting that hides at the core of the information age and which may in fact be its secret agenda."

S is for Salon of the 21st century
The Internet has made me think more about whom I would like to introduce to whom; to cyber-introduce people as a daily practice or to introduce people in person through actual salons for the 21st century (see the Brutally Early Club).

Never Mind the Art Bollocks – A Sort of Glossary Masquerading as an Article

by The Editor

Laura K Jones is signing off now, with a brief meander through the obscure corners of Artspeak; that language of willed obscurantism spoken by every other art press release in the land.

IF THE ART WORLD can be seen as having its own, often obscure code of conduct then one of the most infuriating and perplexing aspects of this code must be the vernacular, the lingo, the artspeak, or as it has been technically termed – the 'art bollocks'.

First introduced to serious art-critical writing by Brian Ashbee in his 1999 article for Art Review, A Beginners Guide to Art Bollocks and How to be a Critic, art bollocks is now rife, with no sign of abating. It has become an impenetrable form of pseudo communication. Often found lurking in galleries in the seemingly benign form of the photocopied press release, to many gallery visitors it remains an indecipherable ritualistic lingo of abstract verbal constructions, obscure or enigmatic lexicon and meanings far more impenetrable than the art it is trying to describe.

Art bollocks' very intention is to obfuscate, it wants to create a smokescreen in which the struggling, uncertain mind can veil itself behind a multitude of linguistic sins. There really is no better word than 'bollocks' to sum this up either: it is both very British – a country from whence a great deal of this art bollocks spouts forth - and at the same time almost universally recognised: an all encompassing word that needs no further explanation.

The formula of the press-release composed in art bollocks is simple: it starts deceptively simply, a warm and welcoming opening gambit saying the gallery is pleased/proud/ delighted - (quick research reveals White Cube and Gagosian are generally pleased, Lisson is proud and Victoria Miro delighted, while public institutions Whitechapel, Tate and Serpentine are none of the above) - to be showing Exhibition X before launching in to three or four paragraphs of increasingly mind-bending commentary.

David Thompson's Art Bollocks Revisited in 2005, six years after Ashbee first defined the term, found that things had in fact got worse, not better. "Art bollocks has become institutionalised, normalised, and is now practically the default way of writing about art and culture for seasoned journalists and A-level students alike," he says. "Like Orwell's Newspeak, art bollocks is variously used in a knowing way, as an in-joke, a private language, a posture, or maybe out of fear – to maintain some questionable status among equally questionable peers."

The words 'iconography', 'banal' and 'fetishisation' are bandied around. A simple word like 'gaze' becomes anything but a good old fashioned stare. Oh, and 'gaze' leads (whoops, art bollocks...) to 'scopophilia', which means delight in seeing

You may also have noticed how many art exhibitions are said to be doing one vague, fuzzy thing and – simultaneously – its equally vague, abstracted opposite.

The modern art theories that are couched in this obscurantist blather, produce a "facsimile of thinking" (says the Guardian's Jonathan Jones), between critics and curators, and are all generated by feelings of inadequacy and insecurity. "Art today likes to think of itself as very, very clever…You can learn all these big words – 'narrativisa- tion' is a good one - and feel you know something," he says.

I would like to offer the simple word 'space,' as one that is pimped out by artspeak.

Art folk tend to say, "that's a great space," when *surely* they just mean "that's a great studio" or "that's a great gallery". The verbs 'to critique, 'to contextualise' and 'to interrogate' get thrown about a lot too, along with talk of 'strategies', 'projection', 'commodification' 'assimilation', 'appropriation' and 'the other' and epithets such as 'semiotic', 'symbiotic' and 'dialogic'. Issues are endlessly 'raised' while the artist's conclusion is never clarified. Sculptures 'hover' between something and something else, while 'examining' issues of immense social significance (again, no conclusions from the examination are made public).

But, in order to ram the point home, perhaps it's best I leave you - slack jawed and horrified - with two extracts from the worst of the worst.

Your head hanging heavy in you hands, take anything you like from this essay by the academic Carolyn Guertin - Wanderlust: The Kinesthetic Browser in Cyberfeminist Space:

"The shuffling and unfolding of the information of her body in sensory space is enacted across a gap or trajectory of subjecthood that is multiple and present. Subjectivity is the lens and connector through which the spatio-temporal dislocation gets focused and bridged. The gap is outside vision – felt not seen – and always existing on the threshold in between nodes. Like the monster's subjectivities, all knots in the matrix are linked."

Or perhaps you may notice your eyes beginning to bleed as you read the following from an article called Bacterial Sex by Luciana Parisi, a professor of 'cybernetic culture' at the University of East London:

"This practice of intensifying bodily potentials to act and become is an affirmation of desire without lack which signals the nonclimactic, aimless circulation of bodies in a symbiotic assemblage.'

Elsewhere in the same issue:

'To be mediatised literally means to lose one's rights. Hence, what happens to the idea of government by the people and for the people if the "false" is produced as a third relation which is not the synthetic union of two ideas in the conscious mind of the citizen or the general intellect of the organic community, but is a statistical coming together of variables?"

No, this is not an attempt at satire. This is deadly serious. And it's enough to make a grown man cry.

THANKS TO THE GOLDEN half pint of milk, Miss Polly Morgan, for always being a pillar of strength and common sense, and for frequently bringing round her sweet little boy-dog Trotsky for company. It was his stout little frame I leant on and it was his biscuit-y smelling fur I silently screamed into, in the depths of madness.

Thank you to David C. West who helped me greatly by acting as conduit between myself and Gilbert and George. They quite sensibly shun the world of email. For Mr West's troubles, I must mention his art book sales website www.drugaddict.co.uk. It's only fair.

Thanks to Mr Matthew Bown for all of his solid advice and calming words.

Mr Mat Collishaw gets a significant mention for being a general brick, as do his folks Joy and Maurice.

To my lovely mum and dad, Jeanie and Cliff, who are the best mum and dad in the world. A cliché, but true. And to my ridiculously helpful and kind brother Stephen, and his girl Clare Harrison, for all their help with the book and for putting up with a lifetime of my rambling.

To Henrik at Artica for great insight and oversight, to Isabella at Artica for incredible administrative support, to the ex-hedonist Charlotte Tiley who, as project director, acted impeccably, kindly and calmly throughout, and to all at Hg2 – Tremayne of course, Nick Clarke and the wonderful Nick Randall for his excellent design, and endless patience.

To the contributors, who offered me the most shocking, unusual and unique pieces of writing and art. It was you, of course, who made this book.

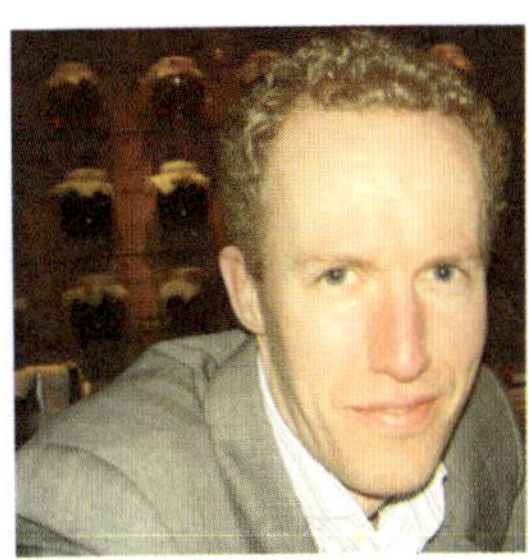

Artica: Art in Progress

*Artica Worldwide Ltd is an eGallery of Young Contemporary
Art founded by Henrik Riis and based in London.
Artica has financially supported this book.*

IT WASN'T IN A metropolis like New York, London or Paris, it was in a small town in Denmark. It wasn't one of the great masters who intrigued me and got me asking questions – it was a painting quietly hanging in a museum off the beaten track entitled The Troll and the Birds by the CoBrA artist Asger Jorn.

There it was – saturated with colour, brim-full with trees and birds. Hundreds and hundreds of birds. I sat down and started counting them – a seemingly Sisyphean task; the deeper you were dragged into this forest, the more birds began to appear from the canvas. From that moment on I was fascinated with the CoBrA artists and their way of seeing things, and my love affair with art had begun.

My work over the years since has allowed me to travel around the world and stand face to face with the greats - Picasso at the Prado, Botticelli and Da Vinci at the Uffizi and Rembrandt at the Hermitage - but it was that canvas of birds that affected me the most.

Although I started collecting in my early twenties, it would take about fifteen more years before I started working with artists. One of the reasons for founding Artica was to make art by young contemporaries accessible, while at the same time providing a quality service in an exciting environment. Since the early days, both friends and strangers have asked me all kinds of questions about artists and collecting art. I have found much pleasure in advising them, helping them get started, and finding art that is right for them.

The vision for Artica is to present a range of work that inspires me. Much of the art shown on Artica.com has stopped me in my tracks and made me think, if only for a moment.

To me, this is what art should be about.

For many people, the art world can be intimidating. When I started visiting galleries and art fairs I felt I didn't really fit in, but as I started to get to know people, I was fascinated with the marvellous and strange anecdotes they relayed, and with the advice they generously offered. It was and is a fascinating world.

The initial purpose of this book was to get some of those tales and stories down and collected into an anthology that would be an inspiration to collectors – be they long in the tooth, brand new to the game, or as yet just a little bit curious.

Henrik Riis
Director

For more information about Artica Worldwide Ltd.
www.artica.com
info@artica.com

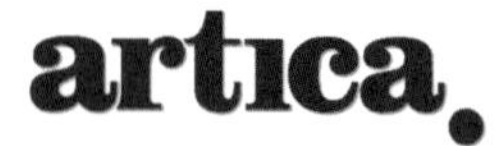